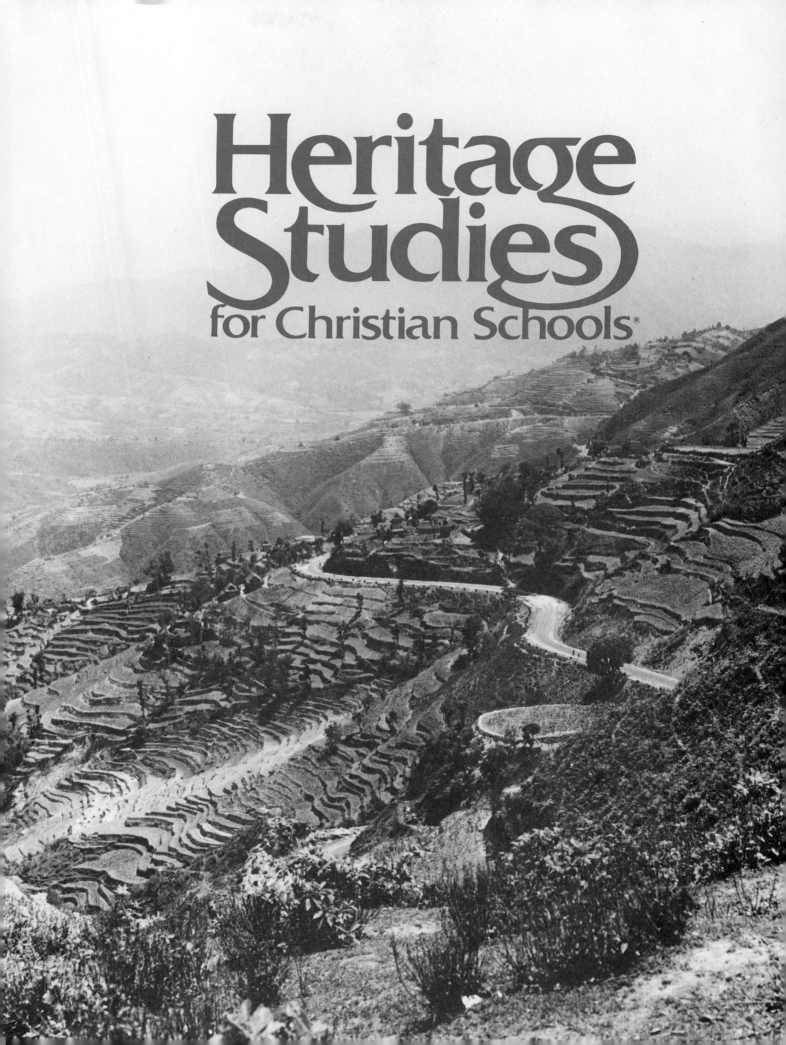

Heritage Studies
for Christian Schools®

Advisory Committee

Edward M. Panosian, B.A., M.A., Ph.D.
Timothy Watson, B.A., M.A., Ph.D.
Linda Hayner, B.A., M.A., Ph.D.
Charlene Killian, B.A.
Susan M. Bunker, B.A., M.A.

NOTE:
The fact that materials produced by other publishers are referred to in this volume does not constitute an endorsement by Bob Jones University Press of the content or theological position of these materials produced by such publishers. The position of the Bob Jones University Press, and the University itself, is well known. Any references and ancillary materials are listed as an aid to the student or the teacher and in an attempt to maintain accepted academic standards of the publishing industry.

Pam Berkstresser Creason

Heritage Studies for Christian Schools®: Book 6

Produced in cooperation with the Bob Jones University Department of History of the College of Arts and Science, the School of Education, and Bob Jones Elementary School.

ISBN 0-89084-104-7

Contents

INTRODUCTION

The earth is the Lord's, and the fulness thereof; the world, and they that dwell therein. For he hath founded it upon the seas, and established it upon the floods. (Psalm 24:1-2)

God created our world and all that it contains. He designed its landscapes, formed its oceans and seas, and established its seasons. He made plants and animals of all kinds to live in the sea and on the land. The earth displays the many wonders of God's creation that add beauty, variety, and useful resources to our lives.

You probably are familiar with the area of the earth that is near where you live.

You know its hills, plains, mountains, rivers, or seashore. You know what its climate is like and which plants and animals live there. You know about the people that live there—what they wear, what they eat, where they live, and where they work. The earth, however, is much larger than your home area.

Perhaps you have traveled in the United States so that you recognize the scenery and way of life in its different regions. Maybe you have studied the lands of Canada and Latin America and learned about their heritage. Even so, there is still much more to this world. Beyond the oceans lie the continents and oceans of another hemisphere—the Eastern Hemisphere. Its lands await our exploration.

Our discoveries in Heritage Studies this year will remind us that "the earth is full of the goodness of the Lord" (Psalm 33:5b), and they will awaken us to the needs of the people of the Eastern Hemisphere.

On the next few pages you will find an atlas full of helpful maps. As you learn about such countries as Luxembourg, Bhutan, Fiji, and Rwanda . . . about high mountains, barren deserts, useful plants, and exotic animals . . . about the people of faraway lands and their ways of life, these maps will help you locate the places you study and analyze the information you gather about the earth.

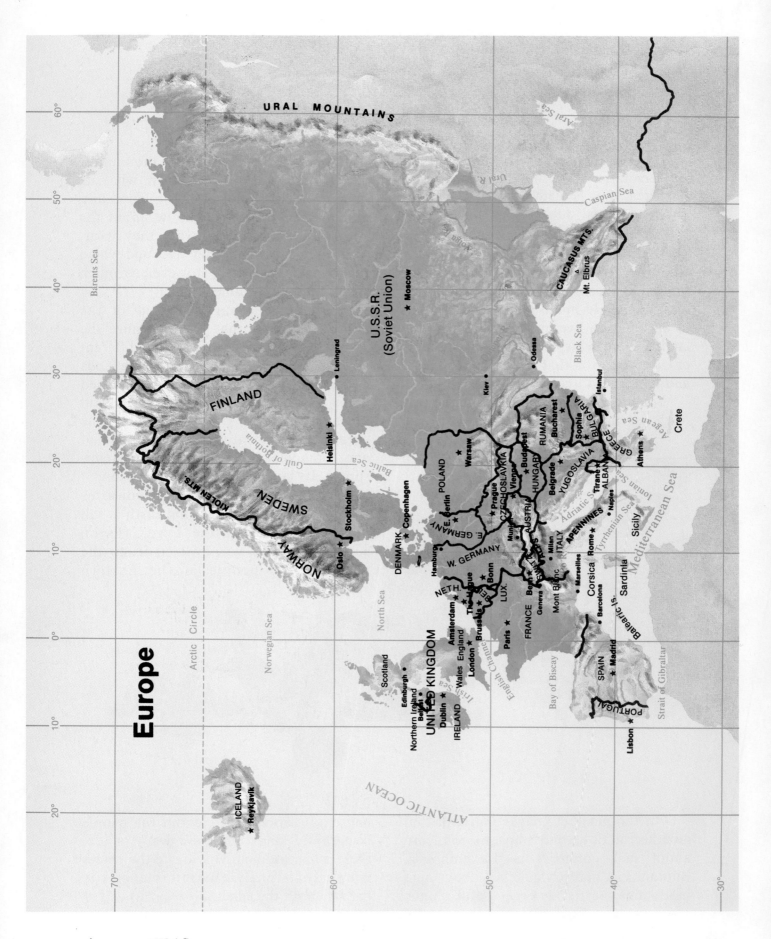

Europe

URAL MOUNTAINS

Barents Sea

Caspian Sea

CAUCASUS MTS.

Aral Sea

Mt. Elbrus

U.S.S.R.
(Soviet Union)

★ Moscow

• Leningrad

Volga R.

Ural R.

FINLAND

Helsinki •

Gulf of Bothnia

Baltic Sea

Kiev •

• Odessa

Istanbul •

Black Sea

KJOLEN MTS.

SWEDEN

Stockholm ★

POLAND

Warsaw ★

RUMANIA

Bucharest ★

Sophie ★

BULGARIA

GREECE

Aegean Sea

Crete

NORWAY

Oslo ★

DENMARK

Copenhagen ★

E. Berlin

Prague ★

CZECHOSLAVIA

Vienna

HUNGARY

Budapest ★

YUGOSLAVIA

Belgrade ★

Tirane ★

ALBANIA

Athens ★

Ionian Sea

Adriatic Sea

Hamburg •

W. GERMANY

Munich •

AUSTRIA

SWITZ.

Milan •

ITALY

APENNINES

Naples •

Tyrrhenian Sea

Sicily

Mediterranean Sea

E. GERMANY

North Sea

Norwegian Sea

Arctic Circle

NETH.

Amsterdam •

The Hague •

BEL.

Brussels ★

LUX.

Bonn •

Bern ★

Geneva •

Mont Blanc

FRANCE

Marseilles •

Corsica

Rome ★

Sardinia

Balearic Is.

Paris ★

Scotland

Edinburgh •

UNITED KINGDOM

Northern Ireland

Belfast •

Dublin ★

IRELAND

Wales

England

London ★

English Channel

Irish Sea

Bay of Biscay

SPAIN

Madrid ★

Barcelona •

Strait of Gibraltar

PORTUGAL

Lisbon ★

ICELAND

★ Reykjavik

ATLANTIC OCEAN

60°

50°

40°

30°

20°

10°

0°

10°

20°

70°

60°

50°

40°

30°

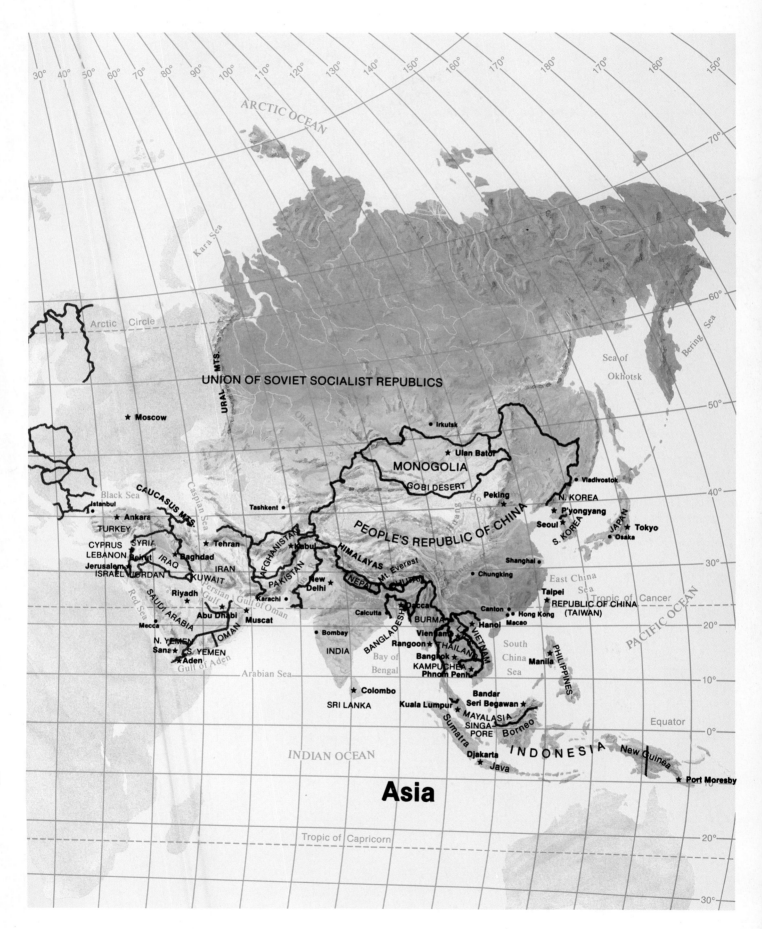

Asia

ARCTIC OCEAN

Kara Sea

Arctic Circle

Bering Sea

Sea of Okhotsk

UNION OF SOVIET SOCIALIST REPUBLICS

URAL MTS.

Ob R.

★ Moscow

• Irkutsk

★ Ulan Bator

MONOGOLIA

GOBI DESERT

• Vladivostok

CAUCASUS MTS.

Black Sea

Caspian Sea

Tashkent •

Peking
★

N. KOREA

★ P'yongyang

Istanbul
●

★ Ankara

TURKEY

PEOPLE'S REPUBLIC OF CHINA

Seoul ★ S. KOREA

JAPAN ★ Tokyo
• Osaka

CYPRUS
SYRIA
LEBANON Beirut
Jerusalem
ISRAEL JORDAN

★ Tehran

IRAQ
★ Baghdad

IRAN

AFGHANISTAN

★ Kabul

HIMALAYAS

Shanghai ●

KUWAIT

PAKISTAN

NEPAL

Mt. Everest

New Delhi

• Chungking

Taipei
★

Tropic of Cancer

REPUBLIC OF CHINA
(TAIWAN)

SAUDI ARABIA

Riyadh
★

Karachi

Calcutta

Dacca

BANGLADESH

BURMA

Canton
●

Hanoi

• Hong Kong
Macao

PACIFIC OCEAN

Red Sea

Abu Dhabi
★

Muscat

OMAN

• Bombay

INDIA

Vientiane

Rangoon

THAILAND

VIETNAM

Persian Gulf

Gulf of Oman

South China Sea

Manila

PHILIPPINES

Mecca
●

N. YEMEN

Sana
★ S. YEMEN

★ Aden

Gulf of Aden

Arabian Sea

Bay of Bengal

Bangkok
★

KAMPUCHEA

Phnom Penh

★ Colombo

SRI LANKA

Kuala Lumpur

Bandar
Seri Begawan ★

INDIAN OCEAN

MAYALASIA

SINGA-
PORE

Borneo

Sumatra

Djakarta
★ Java

INDONESIA

New Guinea

Equator

★ Port Moresby

Tropic of Capricorn

GREENLAND

(DENMARK)

Arctic Ocean

Arctic Circle

Longitude

Latitude

CANADA

Pacific

UNITED STATES

Atlantic

Ocean

Ocean

Tropic of Cancer

Gulf of Mexico

MEXICO

CUBA

HAITI

DOMINICAN REPUBLIC

BELIZE

JAMAICA

GUATEMALA

Caribbean Sea

EL SALVADOR

HONDURAS

GUYANA

NICARAGUA

VENEZUELA

SURINAM

COSTA RICA

PANAMA

COLOMBIA

Equator

ECUADOR

PERU

BRAZIL

BOLIVIA

15°

PARAGUAY

Tropic of Capricorn

CHILE

30°

URUGUAY

NEW

ARGENTINA

ZEALAND

45°

Antarctic Circle

60°

ICELAND

NETHERLANDS
UNITED KINGDOM
IRELAND
BELGIUM
WEST GERMANY
FRANCE
SWITZERLAND

PORTUGAL   SPAIN

DENMARK
EAST GERMANY
POLAND
CZECHOSLOVAKIA
AUSTRIA
HUNGARY
ROMANIA
YUGO-
SLAVIA
BULGARIA
ALBANIA
ITALY
GREECE

NORWAY
SWEDEN
FINLAND

Arctic Circle

U.   S.   S.   R.

(Soviet Union)

Latitude

Longitude

MONGOLIA

PEOPLE'S REPUBLIC OF
CHINA

NORTH
KOREA

SOUTH
KOREA

JAPAN

Mediterranean Sea

TUNISIA

MOROCCO

ALGERIA

LIBYA

EGYPT

TURKEY

SYRIA
LEBANON
ISRAEL
JORDAN

IRAQ

IRAN

KUWAIT
QATAR

SAUDI
ARABIA

AFGHANISTAN

PAKISTAN

NEPAL

BHUTAN

BURMA

Tropic of Cancer

REPUBLIC OF CHINA
(TAIWAN)

PHILIPPINES

SENEGAL
GAMBIA
GUINEA—
BISSAU
GUINEA
SIERRA LEONE
LIBERIA
UPPER VOLTA
(NOW BURKINA FASO)
IVORY COAST
GHANA
TOGO
CAMEROON
EQUATORIAL GUINEA
CENTRAL AFRICAN REPUBLIC
GABON

MAURITANIA

MALI

NIGER

CHAD

SUDAN

NIGERIA

BENIN

CONGO

ZAIRE

ETHIOPIA

OMAN

UNITED ARAB
EMIRATES
SOUTH YEMEN
NORTH YEMEN
DJIBOUTI

SOMALIA

KENYA

UGANDA
RWANDA
BURUNDI
TANZANIA
MALAWI
ZIMBABWE

INDIA

BANGLADESH
THAILAND
KAMPUCHEA
(CAMBODIA)
SRI LANKA

LAOS

VIETNAM

MALAYSIA

INDONESIA

PAPUA
NEW GUINEA

Equator

Indian

Ocean

ANGOLA

ZAMBIA

NAMIBIA

BOTSWANA

SOUTH
AFRICA

MADAGASCAR

MOZAMBIQUE
SWAZILAND
LESOTHO

Tropic of Capricorn

AUSTRALIA

Prime Meridian

Prime Meridian

Antarctic Circle

ANTARCTICA

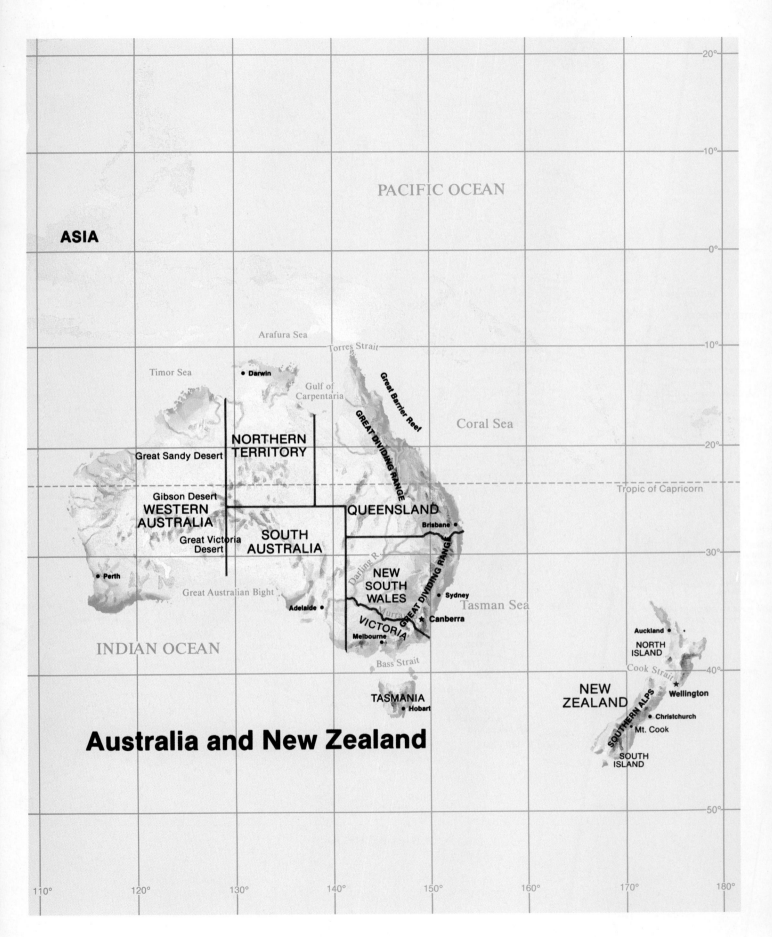

PACIFIC OCEAN

ASIA

Arafura Sea

Torres Strait

Timor Sea

• Darwin

Gulf of
Carpentaria

Great Barrier Reef

Coral Sea

**NORTHERN
TERRITORY**

GREAT DIVIDING RANGE

Great Sandy Desert

20°

Tropic of Capricorn

Gibson Desert

**WESTERN
AUSTRALIA**

QUEENSLAND

Great Victoria
Desert

**SOUTH
AUSTRALIA**

Brisbane •

• Perth

Darling R.

**NEW
SOUTH
WALES**

GREAT DIVIDING RANGE

Great Australian Bight

• Sydney

Adelaide •

Murray

Tasman Sea

★ Canberra

VICTORIA

INDIAN OCEAN

Melbourne
•

Auckland •

**NORTH
ISLAND**

Bass Strait

Cook Strait

TASMANIA

**NEW
ZEALAND**

★ Wellington

• Hobart

Australia and New Zealand

SOUTHERN ALPS

• Christchurch

Mt. Cook

**SOUTH
ISLAND**

20°

10°

0°

10°

20°

30°

40°

50°

110°   120°   130°   140°   150°   160°   170°   180°

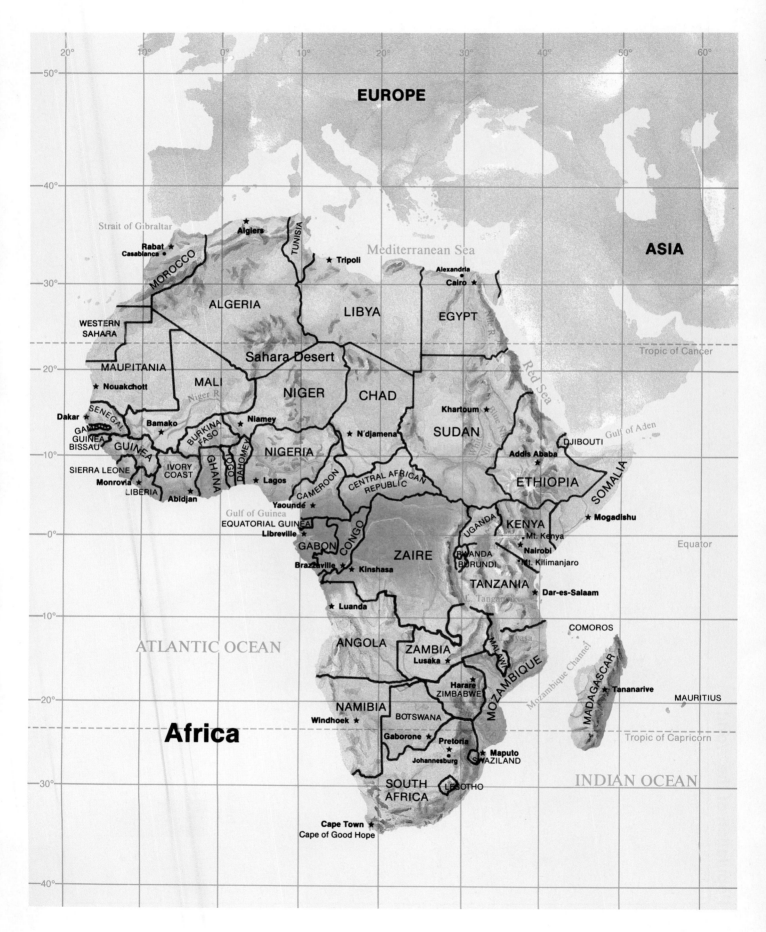

EUROPE

ASIA

Strait of Gibraltar

Mediterranean Sea

★ Algiers

Rabat ★
Casablanca •

MOROCCO

TUNISIA

★ Tripoli

Alexandria •
Cairo •

WESTERN
SAHARA

ALGERIA

LIBYA

EGYPT

Tropic of Cancer

Sahara Desert

MAUPITANIA

★ Nouakchott

MALI

Niger R.

NIGER

CHAD

Khartoum ★

Dakar ★

SENEGAL

GAMBIA
GUINEA
BISSAU

Bamako ★

BURKINA
FASO

Niamey ★

★ N'djamena

SUDAN

Blue Nile

Red Sea

DJIBOUTI

Gulf of Aden

GUINEA

SIERRA LEONE

Monrovia ★
LIBERIA

IVORY
COAST

GHANA

TOGO

DAHOMEY

NIGERIA

★ Lagos

CAMEROON

Addis Ababa
★

ETHIOPIA

SOMALIA

White Nile

Abidjan ★

Yaoundé ★

Gulf of Guinea

EQUATORIAL GUINEA

Libreville ★

CENTRAL AFRICAN
REPUBLIC

UGANDA

KENYA

Mt. Kenya

★ Mogadishu

GABON

CONGO

ZAIRE

RWANDA

Nairobi ★

BURUNDI

Mt. Kilimanjaro

Equator

Brazzaville ★

★ Kinshasa

TANZANIA

Dar-es-Salaam ★

★ Luanda

L. Tanganyika

ATLANTIC OCEAN

ANGOLA

ZAMBIA

Lusaka ★

L. Nyasa

COMOROS

Mozambique Channel

MADAGASCAR

MALAWI

MOZAMBIQUE

Harare ★
ZIMBABWE

Tananarive ★

NAMIBIA

Windhoek ★

BOTSWANA

MAURITIUS

Tropic of Capricorn

Africa

Gaborone ★

Pretoria ★

★ Maputo

Johannesburg ★

SWAZILAND

INDIAN OCEAN

SOUTH
AFRICA

LESOTHO

Cape Town ★
Cape of Good Hope

Population of the World

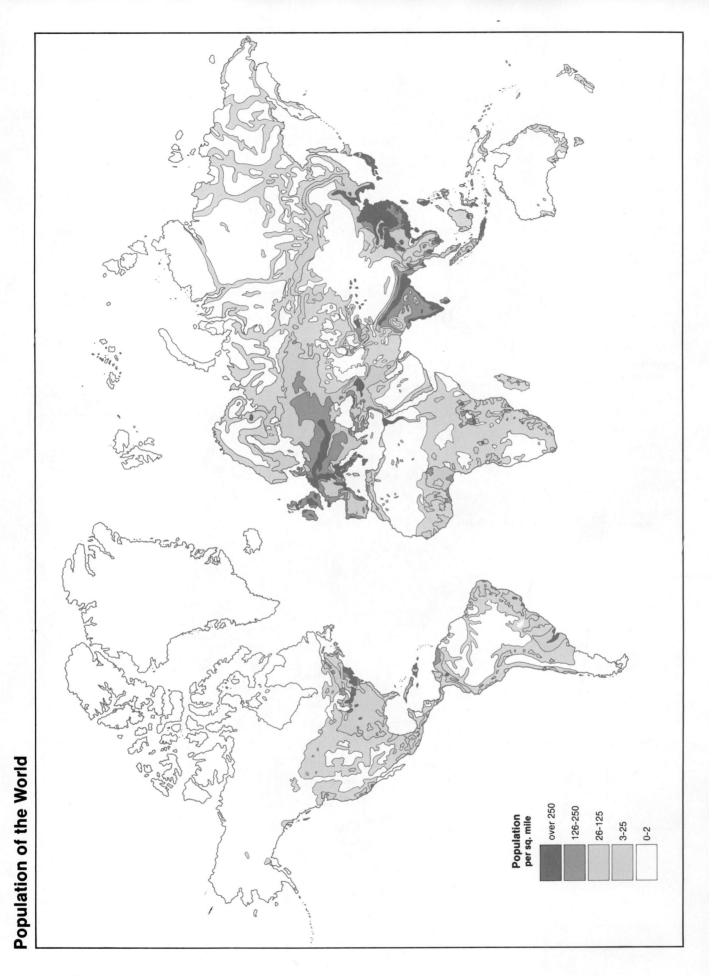

Population
per sq. mile

over 250

126-250

26-125

3-25

0-2

Time Zones of the World

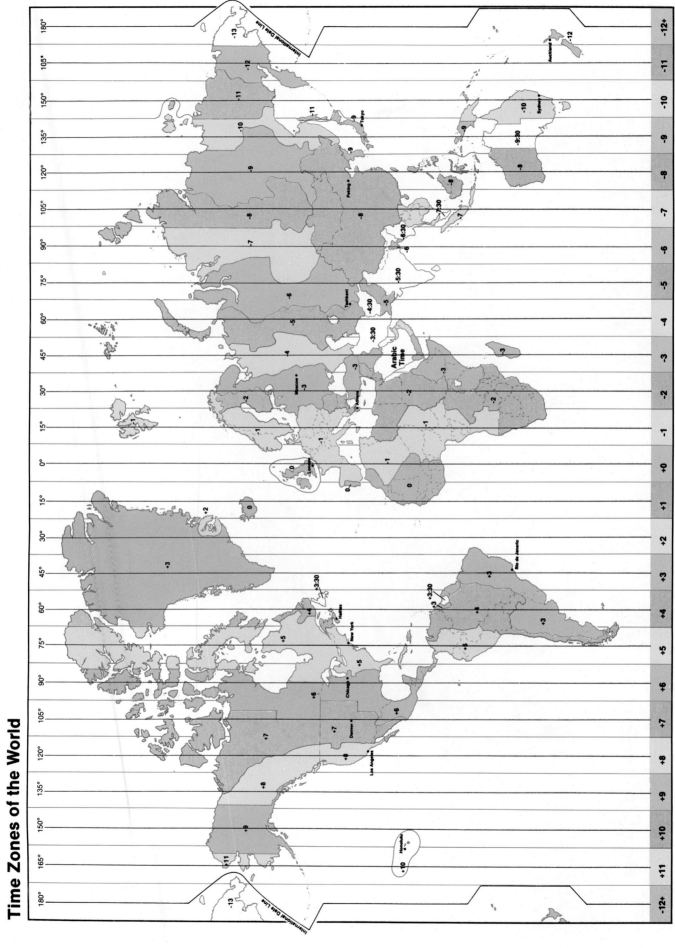

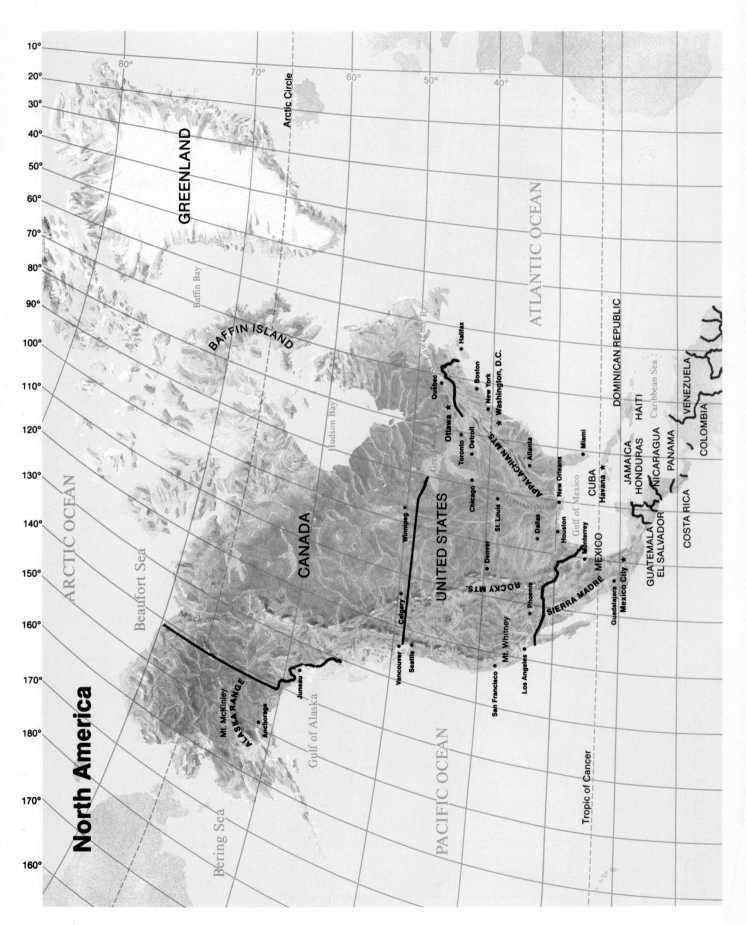

North America

GREENLAND

ARCTIC OCEAN

Beaufort Sea

Baffin Bay

BAFFIN ISLAND

Hudson Bay

Bering Sea

Mackenzie

ALASKA RANGE

Mt. McKinley

Anchorage

Juneau

Gulf of Alaska

CANADA

St. Lawrence R.

Halifax

Québec

Ottawa

Boston

New York

Washington, D.C.

Toronto

Detroit

Great Lakes

Winnipeg

Calgary

Vancouver

Seattle

San Francisco

Los Angeles

Mt. Whitney

ROCKY MTS.

Denver

Phoenix

UNITED STATES

Chicago

St. Louis

Mississippi

Dallas

Houston

New Orleans

Atlanta

APPALACHIAN MTS.

Miami

Gulf of Mexico

Monterrey

SIERRA MADRE

MEXICO

Guadalajara

Mexico City

PACIFIC OCEAN

ATLANTIC OCEAN

CUBA

Havana

JAMAICA

HAITI

DOMINICAN REPUBLIC

Caribbean Sea

HONDURAS

GUATEMALA

EL SALVADOR

NICARAGUA

COSTA RICA

PANAMA

COLOMBIA

VENEZUELA

Arctic Circle

Tropic of Cancer

10°
20°
30°
40°
50°
60°
70°
80°
90°
100°
110°
120°
130°
140°
150°
160°
170°
180°
170°
160°

80°
70°
60°
50°
40°

South America

Caribbean Sea

LESSER ANTILLES

★ Caracas

L. Maracaibo

VENEZUELA

Georgetown ★
GUYANA
SURINAM
★ Paramaribo
FRENCH GUIANA
★ Cayenne

Guiana Highlands

Bogotá ★

COLOMBIA

Quito ★
ECUADOR
Guayaquil ●

• Belém

• Manaus

Amazon Basin

PERU

BRAZIL

• Recife

Lima ★

Cuzco ●

BOLIVIA

L. Titicaca

★ La Paz

★ Brasilia

★ Sucre

Brazilian Highlands

Paraguay R.

ATACAMA DESERT

PARAGUAY

• Concepción

São Paulo ●

● Rio de Janeiro

Gran Chaco

Paraná R.

★ Asunción

PACIFIC OCEAN

ARGENTINA

Mt. Aconcagua

URUGUAY

Santiago ★

Buenos Aires ★

★ ● Montevideo

Río de la Plata

CHILE

Pampas

ATLANTIC OCEAN

Patagonia

FALKLAND ISLANDS
★ Stanley

Strait of Magellan

Tierra del Fuego

10°
0°
10°
20°
30°
40°
50°

90°   80°   60°   50°   40°   30°

REGIONS OF THE

Europe

The continent of Europe was the homeland of most of the settlers and immigrants that came to the United States and Canada. Europe, a land of many small countries, contains snow-capped mountains, fertile plains, and many bustling cities. Its people speak many languages, and many Europeans still cling to the customs of their region. The nations of Western Europe have maintained basic freedoms, but the people of Eastern Europe are held under the power of Communist governments. While most Europeans acknowledge some form of Christianity, few truly know the Saviour.

Africa

Largely unexplored until the last 150 years, the great continent of Africa contains wide grasslands, scorched deserts, and shadowy rain forests. Though their lands are rich in resources, most Africans live with few material possessions. Many of their countries suffer from political turmoil and conflicts. Unless the gospel reaches their hearts, most of Africa's people face their problems with only superstitious beliefs or an Islamic faith that can never meet their needs.

EASTERN HEMISPHERE

Asia

The largest continent, Asia, is the home of over half of the world's population. Most Asians are followers of Islam, Hinduism, Buddhism, or other false religions that leave them in the darkness of sin. Though their continent contains a wealth of resources, most of the people are very poor, and many suffer under communism.

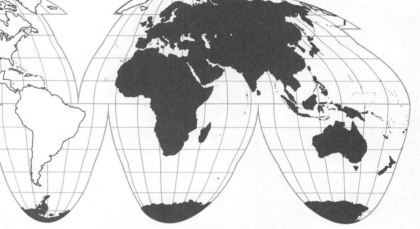

Oceania

At the edge of the Pacific Ocean lie two small continents, Australia and Antarctica. Australia is dry and warm, and nearly all of its small population live near the coasts; Antarctica, on the other hand, is a cold, icy continent, and uninhabited. These two continents along with thousands of islands in the wide Pacific form a region of the world called Oceania.

Geography

ONE

CHAPTER 1

THE EARTH GOD MADE

This year we will be learning of distant lands and peoples. We will explore regions of the earth that are very different from the places where we live. We will meet people whose culture or way of life is unlike ours. Before we begin, however, we need to know some important information about the way God made our earth.

And, Thou, Lord, in the beginning hast laid the foundation of the earth; and the heavens are the works of thine hands. (Hebrews 1:10)

God created our world. He designed every part of the universe with His limitless wisdom. He placed the earth, the sun, the moon, and the stars in space with great care. He made the earth to be a good home for mankind.

The Earth and Its Motions

The Earth Is a Sphere

A globe is a small model of our earth. A globe is round like a ball, and so is our earth. We call its shape a sphere. If we could cut the globe into halves, each half would be a **hemisphere** (HEM ih SFEER).

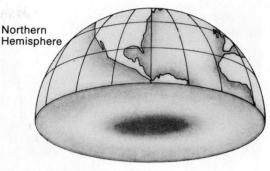

Northern Hemisphere

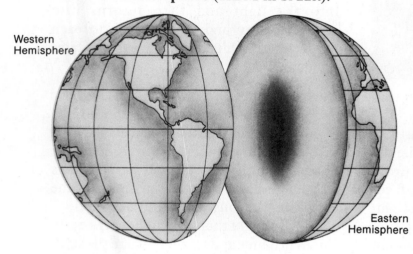

Western Hemisphere

Eastern Hemisphere

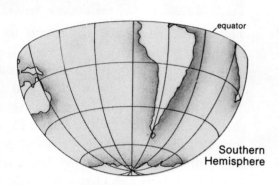

equator

Southern Hemisphere

At the top of the globe is the **North Pole.** At the bottom of the globe is the **South Pole.** Find the two poles on your classroom globe. Halfway between the North and the South Poles is a line that is drawn all the way around the globe. This imaginary line is an equal distance from the two poles, and we call it the **equator.** Find the equator on your globe.

The equator divides the earth into two hemispheres. We call the half above the equator the Northern Hemisphere. The half below the equator is the Southern Hemisphere. Find your country on the globe. Is it in the Northern or the Southern Hemisphere?

We may divide a globe in other ways to make it easier to study. We can divide it in half by drawing a line from the North Pole through the Atlantic Ocean to the South Pole and then back through the Pacific Ocean to the North Pole. This divides the globe into the Eastern and the Western Hemispheres.

The Earth Has Two Motions

The day is thine, the night also is thine: thou hast prepared the light and the sun. Thou hast set all the borders of the earth: thou hast made summer and winter. (Psalm 74:16-17)

Our earth does not sit still in space. It rotates on its **axis** while it revolves around the sun. These two motions have some important effects on the earth.

Rotation on Its Axis

The earth rotates or spins on its axis. It spins as if there were a gigantic rod passing through the center of the earth from the North Pole to the South Pole. Perhaps your classroom globe rotates in the same way that the earth does. The earth makes one complete rotation every twenty-four hours. Find the place where you live on the globe. Now turn the globe around one time from west to east until the place where you live is in front of you again.

The whole earth rotates much like that in one day.

The rotating motion of the earth is what causes us to have days and nights. You know that we receive our light from the sun. The side of the earth that faces the sun receives the bright rays of sunlight. The side of the earth away from the sun, however, is in the shadows. The sun cannot shine on both sides of the earth at one time just as you cannot shine the light from one flashlight on two opposite sides of a ball at the same time.

Half of the earth is always in sunlight and half is always in darkness. The rotation of the earth allows the regions of the earth to spin from the dark side to the light side and back again. If you shine a light on one side of your globe and turn the globe at the same time, you will see how each part of the earth spins into the light and then returns into darkness. Day and night comes to each part of the earth because the earth rotates on its axis.

Revolution around the Sun

The earth has a second motion. It revolves around the sun once every year. While the earth spins on its axis, it moves in a path all the way around the sun. This movement helps to give many parts of the earth four seasons. Let's find out why.

The sunlight that gives light to the earth shines brighter and warmer where the sun's rays shine straight on the earth. Near the equator the sun's rays shine directly on the earth's surface. Away from the equator, the rays of the sun are slanted as they touch

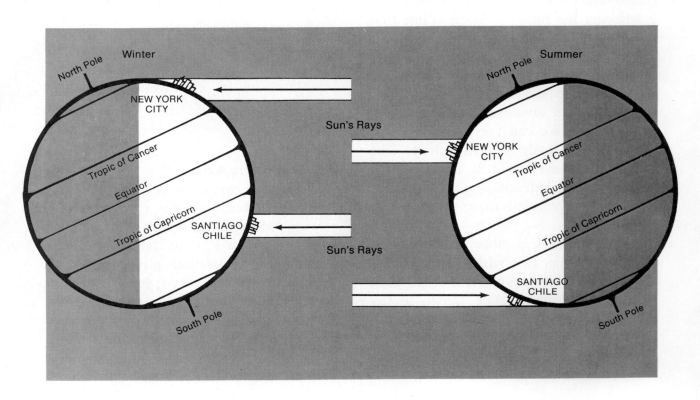

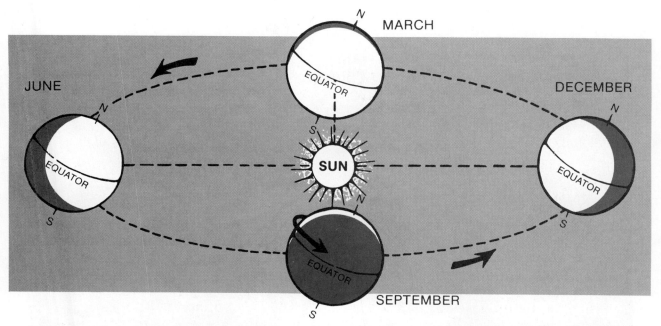

MARCH

JUNE

DECEMBER

SUN

SEPTEMBER

the surface of the earth. The slanted rays do not give as much light and warmth as the more direct rays near the equator.

If the earth were positioned with the North Pole straight up and the South Pole straight down as the earth rotated on its axis, the sun's most direct rays would always shine on the equator. The earth, however, is slightly tilted. It remains in the same tilted position as it travels in its path around the sun. When the earth is on one side of the sun, the North Pole is tilted toward the sun. When the earth is on the opposite side of the sun, the North Pole leans away from the sun.

You can see from the picture that when the North Pole is tilted toward the sun, the direct rays of sunlight shine north of the equator. When the North Pole is tilted away from the sun, the direct rays shine south of the equator. As the earth revolves in its orbit around the sun, the direct rays of sunlight shine as far north as an imaginary line called the **Tropic of Cancer.** Then, as the earth continues around the sun, the direct rays fall farther south. In three months they shine directly on the equator. And, three months after that, they shine as far south as the imaginary line called the **Tropic of Capricorn.**

When the direct rays of the sun are shining north of the equator, the Northern

Hemisphere receives more heat and light. The sunshine warms the lands of the Northern Hemisphere, and those lands have their seasons of spring and summer. The Southern Hemisphere receives less sunlight, and so the lands there have their fall and winter. Thus, the seasons in the Southern Hemisphere are the opposite of the seasons in the Northern Hemisphere. When the sun's direct rays are shining below the equator, the Northern Hemisphere receives less heat and light. The Northern Hemisphere has its seasons of fall and winter while the Southern Hemisphere enjoys the warmer sunlight of spring and summer.

The days, nights, and seasons of the year are part of God's wonderful design for our world. We should remember to thank Him for the beauty and the variety that these changes bring to our lives.

Section Review
1. What is one half of the earth called?
2. What imaginary line is found halfway between the North and South Poles?
3. What are the earth's two motions?
4. What imaginary line marks the northernmost area that can receive the direct rays of the sun?
5. What line marks the southernmost area that can receive the direct rays of the sun?

Climate

God has made provision for every need that man has. Because everyone has sinned, every person needs to be saved from sin's penalty. God has provided salvation through Jesus Christ. People also need food, shelter, and clothing. God has provided the resources to meet these needs as well.

The food people eat, the houses they build, and the clothes they wear differ from region to region around the world. People generally eat the plants and the animals that are raised nearby. They use available materials to make the shelter and clothing they need. The food and materials found in an area and the type of shelter and clothing needed are largely determined by the **climate** of the area.

Climate is the normal weather that an area has throughout the year. The range of temperatures and the amount of **precipitation** (rain and snow) received during the year are important aspects of every type of climate. Three circumstances may affect the kind of climate an area has: (1) distance from the equator, (2) distance from oceans, and (3) altitude or height above sea level.

Distance from the Equator

Since the most direct rays of the sun shine near the equator, the lands from the equator to the Tropic of Cancer in the north and to the Tropic of Capricorn in the south generally have very warm climates. In fact, the temperature remains about the same all year. There are no seasons of fall, winter, spring, or summer, but many of these areas have rainy and dry seasons. We often call these warm lands near the equator the **tropics** and say that they have a tropical climate.

The areas of the earth near the North and the South Poles generally have a very cold climate. Find the Arctic Circle and the Antarctic Circle on your globe. These two imaginary lines encircle the North and the South Poles. The areas inside these circles are called the **polar regions.** The polar regions do not receive much warmth from the sun because the rays of sunlight that shine there are always very slanted.

Between the tropical regions and the polar regions are the **temperate regions.** Find the area between the Arctic Circle and the Tropic of Cancer. This is the northern temperate region. The area between the Antarctic Circle and the Tropic of Capricorn is the southern temperate region. Lands in the temperate regions usually have four seasons, but the climates in these areas vary. The lands near the tropics usually have warm climates. Those lands near the polar regions usually have cool climates because they are farther away from the warm sunlight received at the equator. The temperate lands, however, do not generally have the extremely hot or cold climates of the tropical and polar regions.

We will learn more about the climates in the tropical, temperate, and polar regions as we find out about some of the lands in those regions.

Distance from Oceans

Another condition that affects the climate of an area is the area's distance from an ocean or other very large body of water. Water does not heat or cool as quickly as land does. While the summer sun quickly warms land areas, oceans slowly absorb the summer heat and stay cooler longer than the land. Land areas near the cooler water do not become as hot as areas away from the water. Then while the land cools quickly in the winter, large bodies of water lose their heat slowly. The lands nearby receive some of the warmth from the water; therefore, their winters are not as cold as those of inland areas.

Ocean water moves in different directions. We call these movements **ocean currents.** The map on the next page shows some of the major ocean currents. Some of the currents are warm, while others are cold. Warm ocean currents begin near the equator where the warm sunlight heats the water. As the water flows away from the equator, it carries warmth to areas in the temperate regions. Lands warmed by ocean currents usually have mild winters.

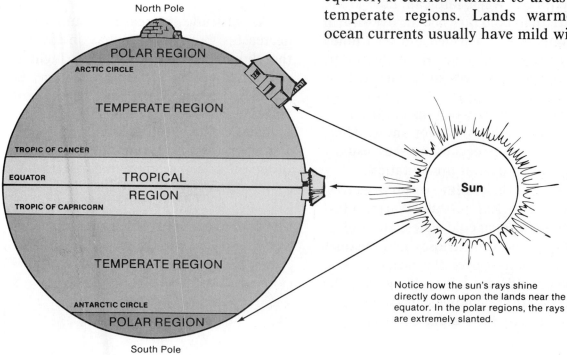

North Pole

POLAR REGION

ARCTIC CIRCLE

TEMPERATE REGION

TROPIC OF CANCER

EQUATOR

TROPICAL REGION

TROPIC OF CAPRICORN

TEMPERATE REGION

ANTARCTIC CIRCLE

POLAR REGION

South Pole

Sun

Notice how the sun's rays shine directly down upon the lands near the equator. In the polar regions, the rays are extremely slanted.

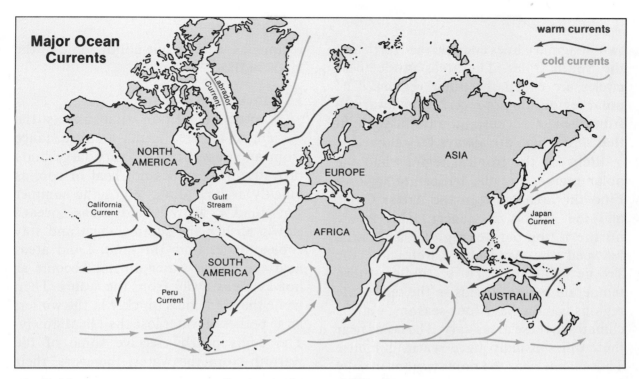

Major Ocean Currents

warm currents

cold currents

Labrador Current

NORTH AMERICA

EUROPE

ASIA

California Current

Gulf Stream

Japan Current

AFRICA

SOUTH AMERICA

Peru Current

AUSTRALIA

Cold ocean currents usually begin in the polar regions and flow toward the equator. In tropical regions cold currents help to cool the coastal areas. In temperate and polar regions, however, the cold currents make the summers cooler and the winters colder.

Besides affecting the temperatures of nearby lands, oceans and seas can also influence the amount of precipitation an area receives. Warm air can hold more moisture than cold air. The air over warm water not only is warmed but also holds moisture that evaporates from the water. As the air rises to blow over land, the air cools. Since the cooled air cannot hold as much moisture as the warm air could, the moisture falls as rain or snow. Thus, lands near warm oceans or seas usually receive a great deal of precipitation.

Lands with cooler waters nearby usually receive less rainfall. Warm, moist winds blowing over cold waters are cooled. As the air is cooled, it loses its moisture, and the rains fall over the ocean or sea. Only dry winds are left to blow over the land. Therefore, lands near cold ocean currents usually have a dry climate.

Altitude

The **altitude** of an area also influences its climate. If you could take a ride in a hot-air balloon, you would be able to feel a definite change of temperature. If it is a pleasant 70° on the ground as you begin the ride, you would begin to feel chilled after a climb of a few thousand feet. By the time you reached an altitude of 15,000 feet, the temperature would drop below freezing.

As altitude increases, temperature decreases. This condition has an effect on the climate of mountainous or highland regions. Two cities near each other, the same distance from the equator and from large bodies of water, may have different climates if they are at different altitudes. If one city is on a mountainside and the other on a low plain, the climate of the

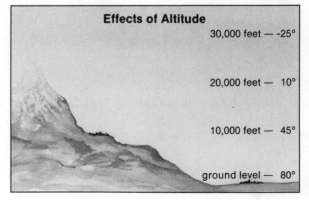

Effects of Altitude

30,000 feet — -25°

20,000 feet — 10°

10,000 feet — 45°

ground level — 80°

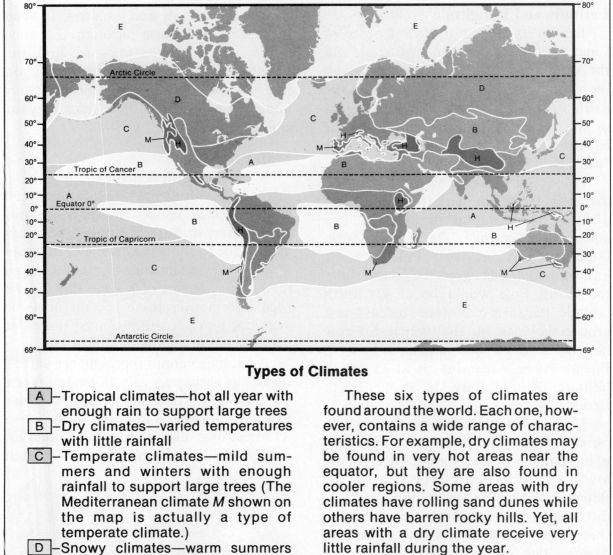

Types of Climates

A—Tropical climates—hot all year with enough rain to support large trees

B—Dry climates—varied temperatures with little rainfall

C—Temperate climates—mild summers and winters with enough rainfall to support large trees (The Mediterranean climate *M* shown on the map is actually a type of temperate climate.)

D—Snowy climates—warm summers and cold winters with enough rainfall to support large trees

E—Icy climates—cold all year

H—Highland climates—variation according to altitude

These six types of climates are found around the world. Each one, however, contains a wide range of characteristics. For example, dry climates may be found in very hot areas near the equator, but they are also found in cooler regions. Some areas with dry climates have rolling sand dunes while others have barren rocky hills. Yet, all areas with a dry climate receive very little rainfall during the year.

The map above shows us where these climates are found on the earth. We will learn more about these climates as we study the different lands of the Eastern Hemisphere.

city on the mountain will probably be colder. Even in the tropical regions near the equator, high mountains may have snow on their peaks while surrounding lands are scorched with heat. In all regions, areas of hills and plateaus usually have cooler climates than nearby low plains.

Altitude not only affects the temperature of an area but also influences the amount of precipitation received.

When warm moist winds blow into a mountainous or highland area, the air must rise to cross that area of high ground. As the air rises, its temperature falls, and the cooled, moist air drops the precipitation as it passes over. Cool dry air is left to blow on the other side of the highlands. For this reason, many highland areas have lush, green vegetation while the inland side of mountain ranges are often dry deserts.

Mapping the Earth

Latitude and Longitude

Besides the equator, the Tropics of Cancer and Capricorn, and the Arctic and the Antarctic Circles, other lines drawn on the surface of a globe help us study the earth. First there are lines of **latitude.** Lines of latitude circle the earth parallel to the equator. Sometimes the lines are called "parallels."

Parallels are labeled according to their distance from the equator, and that distance is measured in degrees. The equator is 0° latitude. The distance from the equator to the North Pole is 90°. A parallel halfway between the equator and the North Pole would be at 45° north latitude. Parallels of latitude run east-west around the earth, but they help us to know how far north or south a place is located. Buenos Aires, Argentina, is at 35° south latitude. Rome, Italy, is at 42° north latitude.

Lines of **longitude** help us to know how far east or west a place is located. Lines of longitude are called meridians, and they are drawn from the North Pole to the South Pole. Meridians are named for their distance from the first or **prime meridian** that passes through western Europe and Africa. The distance from the prime meridian to the meridian on the opposite side of the globe is 180°. New York City lies 74° west of the prime meridian. Tokyo, Japan, lies 140° east of the prime meridian.

Lines of latitude and longitude help us to find locations on a globe or a map.

Sailors use latitude and longitude to keep their ship on course through the seas. Surveyors use these lines to find the boundaries of pieces of property. Can you find the latitude and longitude of your home on a globe or on a map of your city, county, or state?

Map Projections

Since the earth is a sphere, a globe is the most accurate way to represent the earth's surface. Globes, however, are not easy to carry or store. It would take a very large globe to show the details of the state of Missouri, and imagine one large enough to show the streets of Kansas City! If we need information about specific areas or locations on the earth, we must use a flat map instead of a globe.

A flat map cannot represent the earth's surface as accurately as a globe, but it can be much more detailed. It is also easier to carry. Drawing a flat map of the earth is something like trying to flatten an orange peel. The round peel must stretch

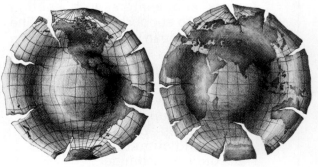

around the edge or it will tear as it is flattened. *Cartographers* (kar TOG ruh furz), or mapmakers, use many different methods to draw the earth's surface on flat maps. Some of these methods are called *projections.*

The Mercator (or cylindric) projection is a common type of world map. It shows distances accurately along the equator, but the land at the top and the bottom of the map is stretched. This makes Greenland

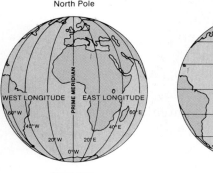

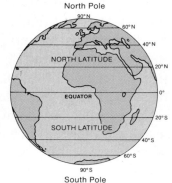

Mercator projection

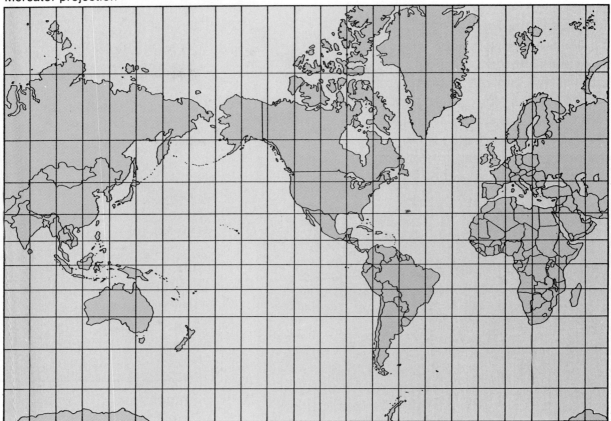

appear larger than South America. Actually, South America is about eight times larger. In the past sailors used Mercator projection maps to chart their courses on ocean voyages.

Interrupted projections look like cut, flattened orange peels. The sizes of the continents are fairly accurate, but it is impossible to find distances between continents because of the breaks in the map.

There are several other types of map projections. Each type is useful for certain purposes. We will use many kinds of maps to help us study the lands of the Eastern Hemisphere.

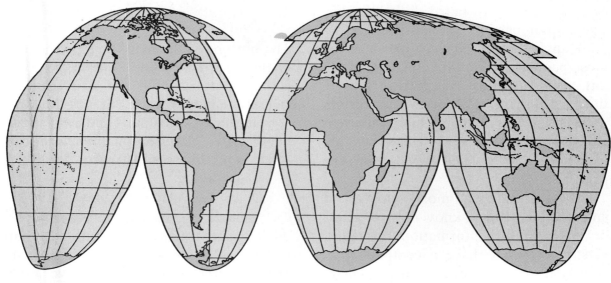

Interrupted projection

Map Information

Maps are useful for many reasons. They may show us the shape and area of continents, countries, states, cities, or your school yard. A map stores a great deal of information that helps us learn about these areas.

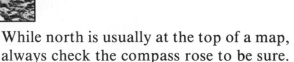

Some maps show us what the surface of the land is like. They show us where there are mountains, hills, plateaus, and plains. This kind of map is called a *physical* or *topographical* map. The map on page vi is a physical map. Other maps show the location and boundaries of countries or states. These are called *political maps.* The map on page 21 is a political map.

Maps may be used to show where the most people live (population map, page xii), where the most rain falls (precipitation map, page 24), or where certain products are raised or manufactured. Road maps show where highways are located so that we can travel from one place to another.

Maps tell us many more things about an area, but we must know how to "read" or interpret the information on maps. First, most maps have a **compass rose,** which tells us the direction on the map.

While north is usually at the top of a map, always check the compass rose to be sure.

The bottom of the map, then, is the part of the area nearest the South Pole. West is on the left side, and east is on the right side of the map when north is at the top.

The **map scale** helps us find the distance between two places on the map. The scale often looks like a small ruler. Its length

scale in miles

0   10   20   30   40   50

on the map usually represents a certain number of miles, kilometers, or feet. By measuring the distance between two points on the map and comparing that distance with the scale, we can find the real distance between those two places on the earth.

The **map key** shows us other information to be found on the map. It may tell us that certain colors on the map show the location of mountains or locations where a certain amount of precipitation falls in a year. It may tell us that a symbol on the map indicates an area where a certain product is manufactured. It may tell us that a star on the map points out the capital city of a state or country. The

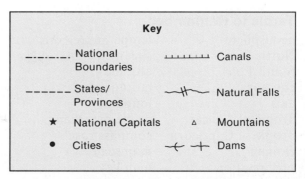

map key tells us the information we need to know to use the map. We will learn to use the information that we find on maps as we study many lands.

Natural Resources of the Earth

Natural resources are the many valuable things that God has placed on the earth for man to use and enjoy. Here is a list of some basic natural resources.

Forests	provide wood for fuel, lumber, paper, and other products
Fuel and mineral deposits	provide fuels and materials for industries
Soil	for growing plants for animal and human food
Sun	provides light and warmth for plants, animals, and man
Water	for growing plants, for animal and human needs, and for water power to produce energy
Wildlife	for food, study, and enjoyment

Some regions of the world have more natural resources than others. People must use the resources that they have in their land to produce the food, shelter, and clothing that they need. Countries that produce more than they need can sell their extra products to countries that do not produce enough.

Natural resources are located all over the world. If we want to find out what types of natural resources are in a certain country, we look at a special kind of map called a *resource map*. Resource maps show the location of mineral deposits and other important natural resources such as deposits of coal and petroleum. Precipitation maps show us how much rain falls in an area, and vegetation maps show us what kinds of plants grow there. From these and other maps we can learn about the various kinds of natural resources an area has.

Section Review
1. What regions lie between the tropics and the polar regions?

2. If a coastal area has a cool, dry climate, what kind of ocean current would you expect to find nearby?

3. Would you expect the temperature to become warmer or colder as you climb up a mountain?

4. What is another name for the lines of latitude?

5. What kind of map shows the location and boundaries of countries or states?

Terms to Remember

hemisphere	temperate regions
North Pole	ocean currents
South Pole	altitude
equator	latitude
axis	longitude
Tropic of Cancer	prime meridian
Tropic of Capricorn	compass rose
climate	map scale
precipitation	map key
tropics	natural resources
polar regions	

Things to Know

1. What is the shape of the earth?

2. The equator divides the earth into what two hemispheres?

3. Every twenty-four hours the earth completes what motion?

4. Every year the earth completes what motion?

5. The climate of an area is affected by what three conditions?

6. What imaginary lines reach from east to west around the earth and help us to measure distances north and south of the equator?

7. What imaginary lines reach from the North Pole to the South Pole and help us find locations east and west of the prime meridian?

8. What part of a map tells us the meaning of the colors and symbols used on the map?

9. What do we call the valuable things that God has placed on the earth for man to use and enjoy?

Things to Talk About

1. What causes the seasons of the year?

2. What is the difference between a Mercator map projection and an interrupted map projection?

3. Explain why a Mercator projection represents distances inaccurately.

4. Why is it often necessary for a compass rose to appear on a map?

5. What are four needs that all people have?

6. Lands near the equator are usually warmer. How is it possible that parts of Colombia, South America, can have snow and freezing temperatures?

7. Why are desert areas often found on the inland side of mountain ranges?

Things to Do

1. Find the latitude of your city on one of the maps in the atlas section. (You may have to estimate the latitude.) There are approximately 69 miles between each degree of latitude. Multiply the latitude of your city by 69 to find out how many miles you are from the equator.

2. Look at the illustrations of compass roses on page 12. Find more styles of compass roses on other maps. Using your imagination and some colored pencils, design your own compass roses. Some can be simple; some can be complicated. See how creative you can be.

3. Look at the list of basic natural resources on page 13. Using encyclopedias or other sources of information, find out what resources your state has. Make a chart that lists or describes these resources.

4. Hold a flashlight about three inches from a sheet of paper. Draw a line around the area on the paper that is lighted when the flashlight is shining straight at the the paper. Now shine the light at an angle toward the paper while still holding the flashlight three inches away. Draw a line around the new area of light. Which area represents the direct sunlight, and which represents the indirect sunlight? Was there a difference in the brightness of the light?

Geography Skills

1. Look at the atlas maps on pages xiv-xv. Find the approximate longitude of Washington, D.C. Find that same line of longitude on the South America map. Which capital city in South America is found at the same longitude?

2. Look at the map of France on page 45. Locate the scale of miles. On a straight-edged piece of paper, mark the distance between Le Havre and Nice. Place the marked paper beside the scale of miles. What is the approximate actual distance between these two cities?

3. Look at the map of Europe on page vi. Find the city of Madrid, Spain. What are its approximate latitude and longitude?

4. Draw a large circle to represent a globe on a piece of paper. On that globe, neatly draw and label these important lines:

   Arctic Circle   Tropic of Cancer
   Antarctic Circle   Tropic of Capricorn
   equator

With colored pencils, shade the tropical regions of this globe yellow. Shade the temperate regions green, and the polar regions blue.

Europe

TWO

Europe

Europe is a continent with many countries. Its people speak different languages and have different cultures. There are many exciting, beautiful, and interesting places. In this unit we will learn about the countries of Europe and the people who live in each one.

Europe is part of a larger landmass that is sometimes called Eurasia (yoo RAY zhuh). The Ural Mountains and the Caucasus Mountains in the Soviet Union separate Europe from Asia. Europe's other boundaries are formed by bodies of water.

Of the seven continents of the world, only Australia is smaller than Europe. Europe is divided into many countries. There are thirty-three European countries in all, and a couple of them are so tiny that you could walk across them in a few minutes.

The heritage of the European peoples sets them apart from the people of other continents. The cultures of ancient Greece and Rome influenced the development of Europe. The Roman Empire controlled a large portion of Europe at the time Christ was on the earth. The Apostle Paul preached the gospel to Europeans. A woman named Lydia became the first European Christian (Acts 16:14).

In later times European men and nations became powerful world leaders. European scientists and explorers increased man's knowledge of the world.

Many great artists, musicians, and writers have been Europeans.

Through the years many Europeans have received the Word of God and preached salvation through Jesus Christ. Others have turned to churches and good works for their salvation or have rejected religion entirely. The countries of Europe are mission fields that need the light of the gospel. This unit will help us to understand more about the heritage of Europe. It will help us to pray more earnestly for the salvation of people in those lands.

European Time Line

European history is often divided into three periods—ancient, medieval (MEE dee EE vul), and modern. Knowing something about these time periods can help you better understand Europe's culture or way of life today. The ancient period began with God's creation of the world and continued until the Roman Empire lost its power.

The medieval period was a time during which Europe was divided into small kingdoms. Knights fought for their rulers, and poor peasants worked on large farms. Most Europeans believed the teachings of the Roman Catholic church.

In the modern period, Europeans began to build strong countries and live in large cities. During the Reformation some preachers broke with the Roman Catholic church and began to point people to the Word of God. New discoveries, inventions, and events influenced the lives of Europeans and continue to affect life on that continent today.

CHAPTER 2

THE BRITISH ISLES

The British Isles are a group of islands near the northwest coast of the continent of Europe. Although they are not actually a part of the continent, they are considered to be a part of Europe.

The total area of all the British Isles is about the same as the area of New Mexico. **Great Britain** is the largest of the islands. It is divided into three parts—England, Scotland, and Wales. The island of Ireland lies west of Great Britain. The two parts of Ireland are Northern Ireland and the Republic of Ireland. Northern Ireland, England, Scotland, and Wales share a single government. Together they are known as the **United Kingdom** (the United Kingdom of Great Britain and Northern Ireland). People often speak of the United Kingdom as Britain. The Republic of Ireland is a separate country with its own government.

	AREA (Square Miles)	POPULATION	CAPITAL	MAIN LANGUAGES	MAIN RELIGIONS	CURRENCY
UNITED KINGDOM	94,226	56,006,000	London	English	Protestant, Roman Catholic	pound
REPUBLIC OF IRELAND	27,136	3,534,000	Dublin	English	Roman Catholic	Irish pound

United Kingdom and Ireland

SHETLAND ISLANDS

ORKNEY ISLANDS

HEBRIDES

Atlantic Ocean

Scottish Highlands

SCOTLAND

Loch Lomond

North Sea

Glasgow • Edinburgh

Londonderry

NORTHERN IRELAND

North Channel

Southern Uplands

Lough Neagh

• Belfast

Pennine Mountains

ISLE OF MAN

Irish Sea

• Leeds

Dublin ★

St. George's Channel

• Manchester

• Liverpool

The Wash

Shannon River

Waterford •

ENGLAND

WALES

• Birmingham

Cork •

Swansea •

• Cardiff

London ★

Thames River

Dover •

Calais •

English Channel

FRANCE

Living in England

When the bell rang to dismiss school, Robert hurried through the door. He quickly walked from the schoolyard to the large factory building a few blocks down the street. He exchanged greetings with a couple of men who were unloading boxes from a *lorry* (truck). As he entered the factory, the hum of the machinery filled his ears. He headed straight for the office at the far end of the building. As he approached, the secretary looked up from her papers. He asked if he could go in, and she smiled and nodded in approval.

"Hello, Robert," his father said as he turned in his big swivel chair. "How was school today?"

"About the same as usual, sir . . . except we studied about the **Industrial Revolution.**"

"Oh? Well, tell me what you learned. I have to go check one of the looms, but you come along."

Robert walked beside his father through the rows of huge machines. He

British English

Even though the British speak the same English language we speak in America, some of the words they use are different. To the British, a truck is a "lorry," gasoline is "petrol," and an elevator is a "lift." Raising the hood of a car is "looking under the bonnet," and listening to a radio is listening to a "wireless."

American Word	British Word
cookies	biscuits
biscuits	scones
sink	basin
closet	cupboard
candy	sweets
dessert	pudding
horn	hooter
trunk (of a car)	boot
drugstore	chemist

had to talk loudly so that his father could hear him over the noise. "The teacher said that the Industrial Revolution was a time when people discovered new and faster ways of doing things. He said that many of the discoveries were made here in England and that the **textile** industry was the first business to make many changes.

That means that the Industrial Revolution was very important for us. Right, Father?"

"That's right. Those inventions made back in the late 1700s and early 1800s made it possible to start producing cloth in factories like this. Since then, other improvements have been made on these machines. Now we can produce hundreds of yards of textile goods in less time than it took to produce a few yards by hand two hundred years ago."

Robert watched his father check several parts of the loom. It looked like such a complicated machine. Robert

remembered the picture of the old hand loom in his history book. This machine, he thought, makes cloth the same way, but it works so much faster. His father finished checking the loom and then called a worker over. After he gave the worker some instructions, they turned the machine on and watched for a few minutes as it swiftly wove the fabric.

His father turned to go back to the office, and as they walked, Robert asked, "Why did England lead the Industrial Revolution?"

His father stopped and thought. "I suppose there are several reasons," he said. "Think of what you know about our country."

Robert and his father talked for several minutes about England and how it became a great industrial nation. These are some of the things they discussed.

Island Advantages

Protection from Enemies

Since England is on an island, the country has several advantages. It is protected by water from enemy attack. The last time England was successfully invaded was in 1066, over nine hundred years ago. At that time William the Conqueror from Normandy (in northern France) fought the English, defeated them, and became their king. Other enemies who have tried to conquer the island country have found the task too difficult. Because they have lived in general safety, the people of England have been able to carry on their businesses peacefully.

Water Transportation

The surrounding water has not only acted as a protection from enemy armies but it has also been an important highway for England. Two hundred years ago there were no efficient ways to transport goods by land. Pack animals and wagons moved slowly. They could not carry large loads. There were no railroads, cars, or trucks. The fastest, easiest, and cheapest way to transport goods was by water. England has many rivers, canals, and good seaports for water transportation. Many English merchant ships carried goods over the ocean to trade with other parts of the world. The English also built a large navy to protect their island and their merchant ships.

Mild Climate

The water around the island strongly affects England's climate. The Atlantic Ocean remains warmer in the fall and winter than the land. The air that passes over the ocean picks up the warmth and carries it across Ireland and Great Britain. This makes the winters in most parts of the islands mild. In some areas the grass is green all year long. This is true even though the British Isles are farther north of the equator than the state of Maine. And, just as the Atlantic is warmer in the fall and winter than the land is, it is cooler in the spring and summer. Therefore, England enjoys cooling sea breezes to combat the summer heat.

The air that comes in over the islands from the Atlantic not only is warmed by the water but it also carries moisture that it picks up from the ocean. As the moist air crosses the islands, and especially as it rises over the hills and mountains on the western coasts of Ireland and Great Britain, it releases much of the moisture.

The Gulf Stream

The precipitation map shows that the western parts of the islands receive much rainfall. Because the winters are usually mild, snowfall is light or nonexistent except in the higher mountain areas. The air is often very humid in England. This damp climate became an advantage to England when the British started to manufacture cotton cloth. Moist cotton fiber is easier to process.

Resources and Needs

Though England is smaller than the state of Alabama, it has about twelve times the number of people. Most of the people live in cities. There are nearly sixty cities that have a population of over 100,000. London, the largest city, is about the size of Chicago. The many people who live in English cities provide the labor needed in factories and businesses. The people also buy and use many of the goods and services produced.

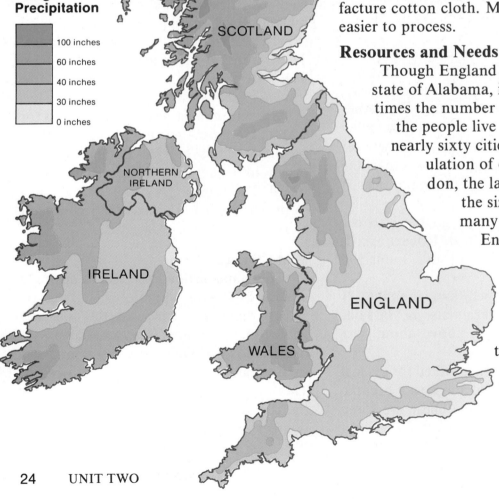

Average Annual Precipitation

100 inches
60 inches
40 inches
30 inches
0 inches

SCOTLAND

NORTHERN IRELAND

IRELAND

WALES

ENGLAND

England has two important materials needed for industry—coal and iron ore. Large deposits of coal in the central and northern parts of the country produce energy. Coal is also processed into coke, a special fuel used in making steel. The presence of iron ore in central England helped to promote the building of large iron and steel industries in the country. Iron and steel are important to a country that is constructing factory buildings and assembling machinery.

England has iron ore and coal, as well as many people to work in businesses and industries. It does not, however, have enough good farmland. English farms cannot produce enough food to feed all the people of the country. England must import much of the food that its people eat.

The country also must import **raw materials** to use in its industries. England imports things such as rubber, wood, textile fibers, chemicals, and leather. British factories use these raw materials to make many kinds of products.

The British Empire

From the discovery of the North American coast by John Cabot in 1497 until the early 1900s, England acquired colonies all over the world. English sea power helped her gain her empire. England built a large navy and fleet of merchant ships. Spanish ships had ruled the seas since the time of Columbus, but in 1588 England won an important victory over the Spanish navy. After this defeat of the Spanish Armada (as the Spanish fleet was called), English ships could travel around the world more safely. The British navy provided protection for England and the colonial empire that she was building.

You remember that the Thirteen Colonies that became the United States had belonged to England. Canada, India, Australia, South Africa, and many other portions of the world were also once a

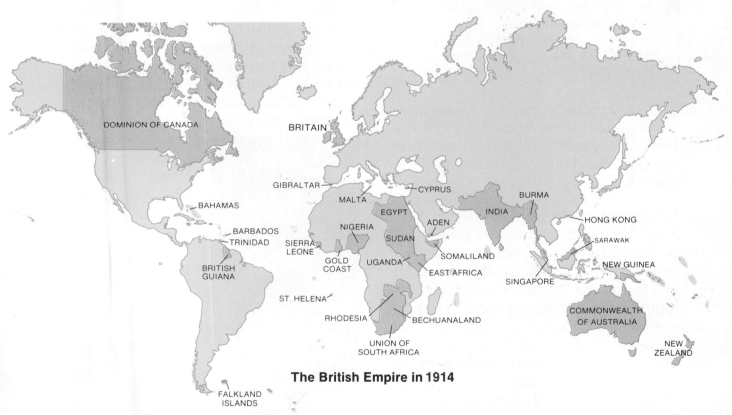

The British Empire in 1914

The British Commonwealth

England with its world empire and strong navy was a powerful leader in world affairs. However, things began to change after World War I (1914-1918). The British government could no longer handle all the problems of the huge empire it had gained. Many of the British colonies wanted independence.

The British Commonwealth of Nations was formed in 1931. This cooperative group helped change the British Empire into an association of free countries. These countries share similar interests because of the influence of the British on their history and development. They continue to work together with Britain for the good of all. Today, a total of forty-four nations are members of the British Commonwealth.

part of England's empire. These lands could provide some of the food and raw materials needed in England. These colonies also bought products made in English factories.

Growth of Trade and Industry

As trade with the colonies grew, many wealthy people in England invested their money in businesses. If the businesses prospered, the investors could make a profit. Some Englishmen opened shipping and trading companies to buy, sell, and transport goods to and from other lands. Some built factories that made imported raw materials into useful manufactured goods. Others opened banks and insurance companies to help finance English business enterprises. England soon became prosperous with all this money-making activity.

The textile or cloth industry was one of the first businesses to grow in England. Spinning thread and weaving cloth on simple home machines had been a slow process. In the late 1700s inventors found ways of building new machinery that would work much faster. At the same time, the newly invented steam engine was ready for use in factories. Coal fueled the steam engines that powered the new machinery in the many new textile factories. Cotton and wool fibers imported from other lands soon became fine cloth ready to be sold around the world.

England's trade with her colonies expanded and so did her industries. English factories used more inventions powered by the new steam engine. During the 1800s, England was leading the world in trade and industry.

Only in this century have other countries been able to surpass England. The expenses of World Wars I and II and the breaking up of the empire hurt the businesses England had built. English trade and industries have also suffered from the competition of younger industrial

The modern textile industry relies heavily on automated machinery.

countries. England is still an industrial country, but it now needs to modernize its factories and businesses. It must improve its technology and production in order to keep up with the advances of other countries.

In 1973 Britain became a member of the European Economic Community (abbreviated EEC and usually called the "Common Market"). This is an organization of European countries that have agreed to trade goods among themselves without charging import or export taxes. They make agreements on their trading policies with outside nations. They also allow workers to move freely among their countries to where jobs are available. Great Britain hopes that her trade and industry will benefit from the advantages of the Common Market.

Robert and his father came to the conclusion that there were many reasons that England became a great industrial country. They were glad that the English people had put their talents and resources to work. From wise investment, England had prospered.

As they walked back to the office, Robert's father said, "In our business here,

we have to be careful with the investments we make. We need good equipment, but we cannot buy big new machines just to make the factory look impressive. That would be unprofitable. We must use good materials and do good work so that our customers will be pleased with our product. When we make wise investments in machinery and materials, we can make a profit."

What Robert's father said can be applied to us as well. We make investments not just with our money, but with our whole lives. We can invest our lives in trying to have a good time or in gaining power, money, or other things. None of those, however, will last. When this life is over, we will have no profit from them. Instead, we should invest our lives in things that will please the Lord Jesus Christ.

The Bible tells us how we may know if we are going to heaven. It also tells us that we should lay up treasures there before we go. We can do that every day by using our talents, our time, and everything we have to serve our Saviour. There is no wiser investment we can make.

> Lay not up for yourselves treasures upon earth, where moth and rust doth corrupt, and where thieves break through and steal: But lay up for yourselves treasures in heaven, where neither moth nor rust doth corrupt, and where thieves do not break through nor steal: For where your treasure is, there will your heart be also.
> (Matthew 6:19-21)

Robert lives in the northern part of England near the city of Leeds. Leeds is a busy industrial city on the banks of the Aire River and on the edge of the Pennine Mountain region. During the Industrial Revolution this area became a center for woolen textile production. Robert's father helps manage a factory that makes cloth from rayon, a synthetic (manmade) fiber.

The English Language

The language that we speak in the United States was developed mainly in England. Around the year 450, three groups of people settled on the island of Great Britain. They were the Angles, Saxons, and Jutes, who were related to the early Germans. They spoke Old English which is sometimes called Anglo-Saxon because the Angles and Saxons were the two largest groups.

Later, churchmen and scholars introduced many Latin words to the English vocabulary. Latin was the medieval language of learning, and it was the language used by the Roman church. Also, when William the Conqueror came from France, the French language became important in England. Although French later died out in England, a great many French words were taken into the English language.

Many of the words we use when we speak English are words from Old English. Many others have come from French or Latin.

Old English (450-1100 A.D.)
dægesēage
(day's eye)
⇩

Middle English (1100-1500 A.D.)
dayeseye, daisie
⇩

Modern English (1500-present)
daisy

Some of the cloth Robert watches come off the big looms in the factory will be used in other Leeds factories to make clothing. Other important products manufactured in the Leeds area are airplanes, cars, and machinery.

Robert and his family like to take little trips away from the city to enjoy the pleasant English countryside. Moors cover

English countryside

parts of Great Britain, including some of the highland area west of Leeds. The moors are still, lonely places. Rain is abundant, but heather and moss are about the only plants that cover the moors. These spots are great places for quiet hikes.

Grain crops grow well in eastern England, but near Leeds there are many small vegetable farms. Dairy cattle graze in green pastures on the rolling hills.

A wondrous sight on the English countryside is an old castle. Robert has taken tours of a few castles that look like pictures from a storybook. He finds it easy to imagine scenes of knights in shining armor in some of these splendid old fortresses.

Old castles add to the historic atmosphere of England.

important to the English. Playing according to the rules and doing one's best is praiseworthy even if the player fails. To the English, acting unfairly or doing less than one's best just "isn't cricket."

Section Review
1. What four lands are included in the United Kingdom?

2. What was the Industrial Revolution?

3. Name two of England's important natural resources.

4. What industry was the first to grow during England's Industrial Revolution?

5. What organization did Britain join in 1973?

Robert enjoys playing and watching sports. His favorite game is soccer, but in England, it is called "football." He also likes cricket, a game in some ways similar to baseball. Good sportsmanship is very

A Trip to London

Sometimes when Robert's family takes a short vacation, they travel to London. Robert always enjoys seeing the wonderful sights of that city.

Buckingham Palace
This past summer while Robert was there, he went to see Buckingham Palace where the Queen lives. He saw the guards

Buckingham Palace

in their red coats and bearskin hats marching near the gates. Then Queen Elizabeth II came out of the palace, waved to the people, and got into a car. Robert watched as she was driven away through the traffic. He was glad to have been able to see the Queen.

Robert, like the other people in the United Kingdom and in the British Commonwealth, looks on his queen with pride. A **monarch** (king or queen) has reigned on the throne of England for over a thousand years. He or she represents the United Kingdom before the other nations of the world. The monarch is a symbol of strength and unity for the British people.

The British Government
The government England shares with Scotland, Wales, and Northern Ireland is called a **constitutional monarchy.** In the days of William the Conqueror, the king possessed absolute power. He could do as he pleased with his kingdom and with the people in it. If the people did not like what

British Parliament buildings

the king did, he would send his soldiers to help them see things his way. After a while, the English people tired of being mistreated by some of their monarchs.

In the year 1215 the English nobles forced King John to sign the Magna Carta. This document made the king and all the monarchs who followed him admit that they were supposed to obey the laws of England just as their people were. Today, the monarch has very limited powers. The British government is guided by the laws of the land and not by the desires of the monarch.

The people of the United Kingdom do not have just one document as a **constitution** as we have in the United States. Theirs is an "unwritten" constitution made up of several documents (including the Magna Carta), their laws, and their traditional rights. Over the years the English people have established a government that protects the rights of its people.

Britain still has a monarch, but the actual governing of the people is done by the British **Parliament,** a legislature in many ways similar to our Congress in the United States. Two groups or "houses" of members meet and discuss the issues of the nation. Then, they pass laws to bring about needed actions. The two groups are the House of Lords and the House of Commons. The members of the House of Commons are elected by the people of Britain. They have most of the authority to take action on the matters of government.

The leading member of the House of Commons is called the **prime minister.** This person is chosen to direct the British government in much the same way as the president leads the government of the United States. The prime minister is assisted by a small group of members from the House of Commons. They are called the cabinet.

Near the Thames

Near Buckingham Palace on the bank of the **Thames River** (TEMZ) are the buildings where the Houses of Parliament meet. Robert likes to be near these Parliament buildings when the clock strikes. The clock tower contains the "Big Ben" bell and a gigantic clock on each of its four sides. The minute hands of the clocks are fourteen feet long.

The Thames River flows through the city of London and on out into the North Sea. London handles much shipping and trade on the busy docks of the Thames.

The city is full of history and of modern activity. Near the Thames sits the famous Tower of London. Part of it was built as a fort by William the Conqueror over nine hundred years ago. Later kings enlarged it and used it as a prison for enemies and criminals. Not far from the Tower, which now serves as a museum, is the busy financial district. There bankers, investors, and all kinds of businessmen complete their transactions.

Westminster Abbey

Many historic places, museums, art galleries, parks, and monuments are scattered throughout London. Several old and beautiful churches are favorite places for Robert to visit. Westminster Abbey is the church in which the kings and queens of England have been crowned for hundreds of years. Many of them are buried there too. Tombs or monuments of other famous people of Britain are in the Abbey as well.

Westminster Abbey was built as a Roman Catholic church by an English

Westminster Abbey

king shortly before William the Conqueror invaded the land. This church building has stood through over nine hundred years of England's history. Well over four hundred years ago, Westminster Abbey turned away from following the Roman Catholic church.

In the 1500s King Henry VIII of England had a quarrel with the pope, the leader of the Roman Catholic church. The pope would not allow Henry to divorce his wife. Henry decided to deny the pope any authority over the people in England. Later, Henry's daughter Queen Elizabeth I set up the new official Church of England, or the **Anglican church.** The Roman Catholic church buildings all over England, including Westminster Abbey, became Anglican churches.

These events occurred during the Protestant Reformation, a time when many people desired to follow the truth of God's Word, the Bible. All the people of England were expected to be members of the Anglican church. Some of the people, however, did not agree with all the teachings of the Anglican church.

Two groups of people, whom you may remember, did not want to be forced to support the Anglican church. One group was the Separatists. They wanted to separate from the Church of England and to worship as they pleased. The Pilgrims who came to America in 1620 were Separatists. Another group in the Church of England wanted to "purify" the church from what they thought were Roman Catholic practices. They were called Puritans.

The officials of the Church of England did not want these Puritans around to cause trouble for them. Rather than stay and be persecuted in England, many of the Puritans came to America in the 1630s and settled in the New England area. From these two groups, the Pilgrims and the Puritans, we gained a great godly heritage in the early days of our American history.

Around 1640 religious persecution stopped in England. The Puritans and other groups could worship as they pleased. In the 1700s and 1800s, many great Englishmen who believed the Bible were able to preach there and go around the world as missionaries spreading the gospel. John Wesley, George Whitefield,

Charles Haddon Spurgeon

Charles Spurgeon (1834-1892) was born into a family that loved the Word of God. Both his father and his grandfather were preachers. The Spurgeon family prayed that Charles might grow up to serve the Lord and that he might be a preacher, too.

As a boy, Charles did good things. He memorized Scripture verses and hymns. He studied hard and did well in school. When he was only six years old, he scolded a man for sinning. Though Charles lived in a good home and did all those good things, he had not asked Jesus to be his Saviour.

When Charles was fifteen years old, he stepped into a little church to get out of a snowstorm. The man who preached that day turned to Charles at the end of the sermon. He told Charles to look to Jesus for salvation. Charles realized that he was unsaved, and he asked Jesus Christ to be his Saviour right then.

Soon Charles began to preach the Word of God. After preaching in a little English town for two years, he went to London. There Charles preached powerful sermons, and the Lord blessed his ministry. Thousands of people came to hear him, and many were saved. Charles also built orphanages, helped the poor, taught other preachers, and wrote many books.

As soon as Charles Spurgeon was saved, he gave his whole life to serving the Lord. God used his life to bless other people. He is remembered as one of England's greatest preachers.

Charles Haddon Spurgeon

William Carey, Charles Spurgeon, and many more preached the Word of God under a government that came to accept and to protect religious freedom.

The Church of England is still the official church in the country. It has many members, although no one (except the monarch) is required to belong to it. Most modern Britons, however, do not find any time for God. Few know Christ as their personal Saviour. This nation, which once sent out many missionaries, now needs to be reminded of its need of Jesus Christ.

The English Channel

While they were in London, Robert's family decided to drive about fifty miles southeast to the city of Dover. There they took a ferry across the **English Channel** to the city of Calais in France. From Calais they could almost see the white cliffs of Dover only twenty-one miles away.

After spending a few hours exploring the French city, they boarded another ferry returning to England. Even on a nice sunny day, the waves in the Channel were high. Robert knew that many swimmers try to cross the English Channel. It looked as if it might be a hard task for anyone to swim over twenty miles through those waves, but he thought he would like to try someday.

Robert's father said that the English Channel has been the scene of many important events in English history. One was William the Conqueror's crossing the English Channel from France to invade England.

His mother remembered, "Our armies quickly came across the Channel to escape capture by the enemy at Dunkirk in World War II."

"That's right," said his father, "but later our armies went back across to invade Normandy on D-Day in 1944. We were then able to defeat the enemy and win the war."

"I know another one!" Robert added. "The English defeated the Spanish Armada here in 1588!"

Robert took a long look across the waters of the English Channel before they left Dover that evening. He thought of what it would have been like to be a sailor on an English ship four hundred years ago.

When Robert and his family returned home to Leeds, Robert thought of what

The English Channel

The Prime Meridian

Lines of latitude and longitude are lines drawn on globes and maps that help us locate our position on the earth. They are especially important to seamen to keep their ships on course. Lines are not actually drawn on the earth or water, but only on maps. Astronomers have learned how to use the position of the moon and certain stars in the sky to determine the position on the earth from which they are seen. The latitude and longitude of that position are charted on maps.

Early navigators took hours to measure, compare, and mathematically figure their longitude. Besides this inconvenience, the instruments used by the early navigators were not precise. Calculations were sometimes as much as two hundred miles off. This particular problem led to many disasters at sea. In 1707 the British navy lost four ships and two thousand men at the mouth of the English Channel because they had miscalculated their position. This catastrophe so affected the British public that Parliament passed the Longitude Act of 1714. This Act offered a reward of twenty thousand pounds to anyone who could discover an accurate method of measuring longitude.

In 1766 the Astronomer Royal from the Observatory in Greenwich, England (just outside London), published the *Nautical Almanac.* This book of charts contained accurate measurements and predictions of the moon's position for a full year. Sea captains found them easy to use. The *Nautical Almanac* soon became popular and was published in several languages. Within a few years it was in use by over seventy percent of the sea-going vessels. Chart makers began supplying maps with longitude in degrees, starting at the Greenwich meridian. This meridian soon came to be called Meridian Zero— and eventually, the prime meridian.

a good time he had had in London. He had learned more about his country by seeing some of the places that are important parts of his English heritage.

Now Robert is looking forward to future family vacations when he can see more of his country. He is saving his pennies and pounds (British money) to buy a camera. He wants to take pictures of everything he sees on his next trip.

Section Review

1. Where does the Queen of England live?

2. Who is the actual leader of the British government?

3. What river flows through London?

4. What is another name for the Church of England?

5. What water passageway separates England from France?

Wales

The Country and Its Language

The small country of Wales lies on the west side of England. Wales is a little smaller than the state of Massachusetts. It is a land of splendid mountain scenery and charming little villages. One village has the longest name of any place in the world. It is . . . Llanfairpwllgwyngyllgogerychwyrndrobwllllandysiliogogogoch.

Unless you are Welsh, you probably cannot pronounce that.

The Welsh language was spoken by some of the early people on the island of Great Britain. Today, about three-fourths of the people of Wales speak Welsh, but most of them speak English as well.

History and Religion

While the Romans occupied Great Britain, they controlled the area of Wales. When the Romans left, the people of that region formed their own small kingdoms and kept to themselves. After William the Conqueror's invasion of England, English kings desired to take over Wales. Edward I, king of England, conquered the land in the 1200s and gave his oldest son the title "Prince of Wales." To this day, the oldest son of the ruling monarch of England is titled the Prince of Wales.

Queen Elizabeth II's son, Charles, is the Prince of Wales today.

In 1536 an Act of Union passed by the English Parliament officially placed Wales under the government of England. Today, as a member of the United Kingdom, Wales sends its representatives to the British Parliament in London to participate in the national government.

The Methodist revivals of the 1700s had a big influence on the Welsh people. The followers of George Whitefield preached throughout Wales with such effect that yet today the largest religious group in Wales is Methodist.

Activities

Until the Industrial Revolution, small farming was the main activity of Wales. When new industries developed, Wales had a very important resource—coal. As new sources of power (gasoline, electricity,

Entering Wales

and so on) developed in the late 1800s, however, the importance of coal declined, and many Welsh coal mines began to close down.

Today the factories and mills of southern Wales still use some coal as fuel in manufacturing metals and chemicals. Cardiff, the capital and largest city of Wales, is a major center for this industrial part of the country. Small farming and tourism are the main activities in the northern part of Wales.

Scotland

The Land of Scotland

Northern Great Britain, along with the Hebrides, Orkney, and Shetland Islands, make up Scotland, which is divided into three regions.

The Scottish Highlands

The **Scottish Highlands** in the north is a rugged area of mountains, shimmering lakes called *lochs* (LAHKS), and moorland. Although it has beautiful scenery, it has little farmland or industry. Fishing is the main activity near the rivers and the sea. Many tourists visit the mountain and lake resorts. Snow skiing and mountain climbing are becoming popular sports.

The Central Lowlands

Most of the people of Scotland live in the central lowland area. There, better farmland and larger towns provide more opportunities for the people to make their living. Scotland's two largest cities are located in this area. Edinburgh (ED in BOOR uh) is the capital of Scotland. From a nearby hill, Edinburgh Castle overlooks the delightful city of stately old buildings and cultural activities. Glasgow is the largest city and the major industrial center of Scotland. Its shipyards along the River Clyde are sometimes busy with the building of large sailing vessels. Steel is also a major product of the city. While Edinburgh has retained a historic beauty,

Edinburgh, Scotland

The Scottish Highland Tradition

Several hundred years ago, the people of the highland areas of Scotland belonged to family groups. These groups were called *clans.* A chief led each clan of family members and other followers. The clan was called by the family name. There were the Campbells, the MacDonalds, the MacKenzies, and many more. Each clan controlled a part of Scotland, and often the clans fought against each other to gain more power.

The highland clans revolted against English rule and were defeated in 1745. For a while the English outlawed the keeping of clan traditions. In the early 1800s, however, the Scottish people began to revive their highland clan heritage.

In Scotland today, many people consider their clan heritage important. Each clan has its own tartan, a plaid cloth often made of wool, which is worn by its members. The traditional dress of Scottish men is the kilt, a skirt made of their tartan. The clan members get together for reunions, and they share the history of their family.

Perhaps the most exciting part of the clan tradition is the highland games. In many parts of Scotland and in several other countries (including the United States), people of Scottish descent meet to watch and to compete in a unique kind of olympics. Events include tossing the caber, a huge tree trunk that strong men lift and try to throw end over end. Another event is throwing a hammer, a long stick with a heavy weight on the end. There are also folk dancing contests and competition between bagpipe bands. The people dress in highland attire, and clan spirit is high. Some of the people even speak Gaelic, the language used by their ancestors in the highlands.

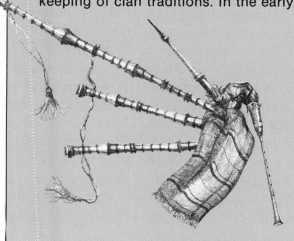

Glasgow has become a modern city of commerce and industry.

The Southern Uplands

The land in the south near the English border is called the southern uplands. In that hilly area, sheep raising and woolen cloth production are important. The southern uplands, like most of Scotland, is not suitable for any kind of heavy farming. Even cattle have a hard time finding enough pasture on the nearly barren hillsides. But God made all kinds of lands. He also provides for His creatures. Flocks of sheep are able to graze on the hillsides of Scotland. Led by the Scottish shepherds, they can find pasture where other animals cannot. The wool from these sheep has helped to build the wool industry in the southern uplands.

Scottish History and Government

Some of the early people of Great Britain escaped Roman control by retreating to the Scottish Highlands. Over a thousand years ago these people began to follow the leadership of a king, and they developed their own government. The Scottish people usually did not get along well with the English people. But because members of the royal families of Scotland and England had married, James VI, King of Scotland, was a cousin to Queen Elizabeth I of England. When she died in

1603 without children, James was her closest relative. Therefore, he received the crown of England.

Since that time, England and Scotland have had the same monarch. The governments of the two countries were officially united in 1707. Today, Scotland sends representatives to the British Parliament that governs all the United Kingdom.

Northern Ireland

 The final piece of the United Kingdom is Northern Ireland, the northeastern part of the large island west of Great Britain. Northern Ireland, too, shares in the national government with England, Scotland, and Wales. The British Parliament is responsible for the welfare of its people. Through the years, strife has developed among the people in Ireland, making peace-keeping a difficult task for the British government. To help us understand why, we must look at the history of the people of the whole island of Ireland.

Irish History

By the time of William the Conqueror, most of the Irish people had accepted the leadership of the Roman Catholic church. At that time, the whole of Ireland was divided into tribal kingdoms, each ruled by a local leader. Soon, however, the rulers of England became interested in taking over Ireland. Henry II, king of England, defeated the Irish in 1170 to begin English rule of the island.

From the beginning, the Irish did not want to be ruled by outsiders. Therefore, the English monarchs placed restrictions on the Irish to keep them from rebelling. After the Reformation when England became a Protestant country, the Irish Catholics became more discontent. Several English rulers took Irish land from troublemakers and gave it to English and Scottish Protestants who went there to live. Most of these Protestants settled in northern Ireland. The descendants of these people are often called Orangemen or Scotch-Irish.

Later, when some Irishmen started a revolt to try to gain independence, the British took over all Ireland's affairs. This made many of the Irish angry. The Irish Roman Catholics, who lived mainly in the southern part of Ireland, wanted complete power over all the island. The Irish Protestants living in northern Ireland feared that if the island were given its own government, the Protestants would be outnumbered. The Roman Catholics would control the government and force their doctrine on all.

In 1921 Britain gave southern Ireland its own government as a member of the Commonwealth. But Northern Ireland wanted to have a separate government protected by Britain. Later, in 1948, southern Ireland declared that it was an independent republic no longer in the Commonwealth and broke all ties with Britain.

Northern Ireland Today

A Cause of Tension

Northern Ireland has remained under British protection as a part of the United Kingdom. Its people, however, are involved in a bitter dispute.

Two-thirds of the Northern Irish people are Protestant—Presbyterian,

Belfast, Northern Ireland

Church of Ireland (like the Church of England), and Methodist. The other one-third is Roman Catholic. Some of the Roman Catholics resent British control and desire a union with the Republic of Ireland, which promotes Roman Catholic interests. The Protestant majority has tried to keep control of the land because they fear Catholic rule and wish to remain part of Great Britain. The Protestants look to Great Britain to keep them separate from the Irish Republic. They wish to protect their religious freedoms and the economic advantages that all the Northern Irish enjoy.

Some terrorist groups, particularly the Irish Republican Army (IRA), have been involved in numerous violent acts such as bombings and shootings. Most of these groups have more interest in political power than in religious issues. The violence has increased the tension between those who want to unite with the Irish Republic and those who want to remain united with Britain. The British government feels much pressure because of this strife. The Protestants of Northern Ireland are concerned that the British will step out and leave them at the mercy of the Irish Republic.

The Christians of Northern Ireland need our prayers. They need the Lord's help to keep their testimony shining amid all the trouble in Northern Ireland. No matter what the conditions, Christians must be "holding forth the word of life" (Philippians 2:15-16).

Cities and Country

Despite all the turmoil, the Northern Irish people try to carry on with their business. Belfast, on the eastern shore near Scotland, is the capital and largest city of Northern Ireland. It is the center of most of the industrial activity of the country. It has a large area of shipyards where ocean-going vessels are built, and it is famous for its production of "Irish linen" cloth. Other industries have developed there and in other cities like Londonderry in the northwest. Small farms and villages occupy most of the remainder of the country.

Lough Neagh, the largest lake in the British Isles, is in the center of Northern Ireland. The Irish say that a giant named Finn MacCool scooped up the ground to form the lake and then threw the soil into the Irish Sea to make the Isle of Man.

Ireland

The Emerald Isle

 "The Emerald Isle" is a phrase often used to describe the island of Ireland. Because of its temperate climate and abundant rainfall, beautiful green grass grows throughout the land. Ireland provides pastureland for cattle and soil for growing crops as well.

Many parts of Ireland have peat bogs. These are areas in which plants have decayed over the years and formed a material called peat. Peat is not nearly as hard as coal, but it does burn. Because Ireland has few trees and lacks coal, the people burn peat in their stoves and fireplaces. Some industries also use peat for fuel. In the past people cut peat from the ground by hand. Now huge machines cut it and shape it into bricks.

Government and Cities

Ireland is no longer a part of the United Kingdom. As an independent country, Ireland has its own president as head of state and its own parliament and prime minister.

A side street in Dublin, Ireland

Dublin on the east coast is the capital and largest city. It is an industrial center, but it also has many fine old buildings, parks, and gardens. Waterford in the south and Limerick in the west are other large Irish towns. Waterford is known for its beautiful cut glassware. The longest river

Irish Potatoes

In the 1800s, many poor Irish farmers raised potatoes as their main crop. Potatoes usually grew well in the Irish soil. Many of the farmers could not afford to raise other crops or raise livestock. Therefore, potatoes were the main food of many Irish families.

In 1845, 1846, and 1848, a plant disease attacked the potato crops, making the vegetable inedible. So many people depended on the potato for food that over a million died of starvation during the Irish potato famine. In order to escape that kind of death, about a million more Irish people left to find livings in other lands. Most of them came to the United States, and many of them settled in our cities of northeastern America. These Irish-Americans brought their culture with them to add to our American heritage.

in the British Isles, the Shannon, flows by Limerick.

Religion and Language

About ninety-five per cent of the people of the Irish Republic are Roman Catholic. The leaders of the church have a great influence in the government of the country. The government supports education for the children of Ireland, but the schools are organized by the church leaders in each area. Therefore, most of the schools are Roman Catholic. Almost all the children of Ireland grow up believing in the traditions of the Roman Catholic church without knowing of God's free salvation.

Although the main language spoken in Ireland is English, Irish Gaelic is the official language. Many street signs are written in Gaelic to emphasize the Irish heritage. *Eire* is the Gaelic name for Ireland.

Section Review

1. What title is given to the oldest son of the king or queen of England?

2. What is the capital of Wales?

3. What is a clan?

4. What parts of the British Isles send representatives to the British Parliament?

Terms to Remember

Great Britain
United Kingdom
Industrial Revolution
textile
raw materials
monarch
constitutional monarchy
constitution
Parliament
prime minister
Thames River
Anglican church
English Channel
Scottish Highlands

Things to Know

1. How many countries are on the British Isles? What are they?

2. What lands constitute the United Kingdom?

3. What surrounds the British Isles to protect them from invasion, provide routes for transportation, and keep the climate mild?

4. Which major industry was the first to develop during the Industrial Revolution?

Top and center: The luxurious interior of the palace of Versailles

Below: A bust of Louis XIV

deliveries of expensive furniture and tapestries to fill the new palace. They heard about the marvelous Hall of Mirrors. It was an enormous room filled with gold and silver furnishings, marble statues, and fragrant orange trees. At night hundreds of mirrors reflected the light of three thousand candles and set the room aglow. The palace of Versailles was a dream world to these lowly people who lived in one-room houses with dirt floors, thatched roofs, and only a few pieces of rough furniture.

When the king moved into his palace in 1682, the people of the village had even more to talk about. Around five thousand noblemen and ladies with their servants moved to be near the king. While the village grew with these new inhabitants, the people watched the activities of the king and the many important people he had invited to live at the palace.

They heard of exciting activities that went on at the palace. There were balls,

	AREA (Square Miles)	POPULATION	CAPITAL	MAIN LANGUAGES	MAIN RELIGIONS	CURRENCY
FRANCE	211,207	54,604,000	Paris	French	Roman Catholic	franc
LUXEMBOURG	999	366,000	Luxembourg	French, German, Letzeburgisch	Roman Catholic	franc
BELGIUM	11,781	9,865,000	Brussels	Dutch, French, German	Roman Catholic, Protestant	franc
THE NETHERLANDS	15,770	14,374,000	Amsterdam, (The Hague)	Dutch	Roman Catholic, Protestant	guilder

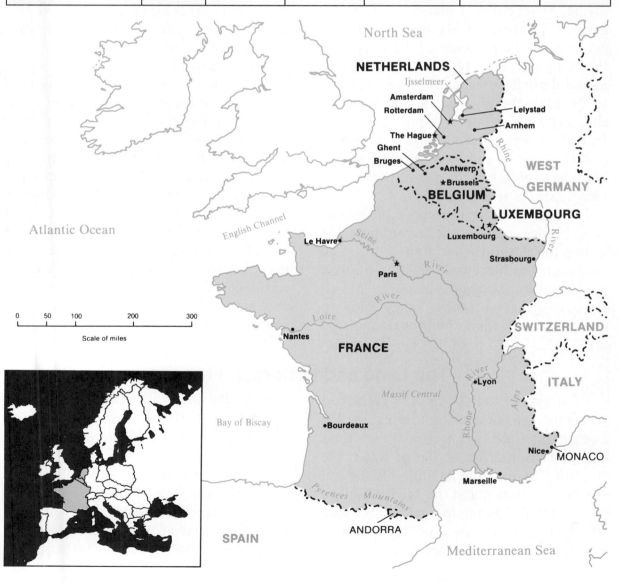

concerts, masquerades, fireworks displays, and all kinds of other entertainment. The guests ate the finest foods at the king's banquets. The ladies and gentlemen of the court paraded around in expensive silk, satin, and lace attire. They all wore powdered wigs, and even the men wore high-heeled shoes. To watch these nobles must have been breathtaking for the commoners in their simple clothes. The poor had to work hard from sunrise to sunset in order to keep their families fed with bread and soup.

So much attention was paid to what the king did or what he desired that Louis was thought by his followers to be almost divine. Strict rules of manners had to be kept at Versailles. Only certain nobility could sit in the presence of the king, and then only in certain types of chairs. It was a special privilege for a noble to be allowed to do such things as hand the king his shirt as he dressed or serve him his dinner. In fact, it was required that if a person saw the tray of food being taken to the king, he should bow to pay respect to the king's meal as it passed by.

Versailles was the showplace of France, and France gained the reputation for setting the cultural styles of the world. The language, the literature, and the lifestyle of Versailles became the envy of all Europe. Rulers of other lands tried to converse in French, build palaces, and

The gardens of the Palace of Versailles

entertain in imitation of the splendor of Versailles. Versailles was the center of fashion, of the arts, of social manners, of elegant cuisine (cooking), and of just about every other aspect of culture. Today, the world still looks to France for leadership in many of these areas.

Now, three hundred years later, Versailles still stands outside Paris as a monument to the glamorous days of Louis XIV and to the greatness of France. After Louis died, however, the expenses and other problems of such extravagant living soon brought to an end the regal activities of the palace. The splendor Louis enjoyed had to be paid for by the hardships of his country. France was left with wonderful memories, but it also has faced many problems in the years since Louis's reign. Despite France's heritage of glory and accomplishment, France is today a country left with many needs.

The Land and History of France

The France that Louis XIV ruled had basically the same boundaries as the country does today. Three of the six sides of France border on bodies of water: the English Channel, the Atlantic Ocean and the Bay of Biscay, and the Mediterranean Sea. The **Alps Mountains** and the **Pyrenees Mountains** form two of the borders between France and other countries. The

final border area to the northeast has no natural barrier. In the past, several enemy armies have entered France through this unprotected area.

Many of the people who watched the building of the Versailles Palace from their nearby village were farmers. Their land, more than that of most of the countries of Europe, is well suited for farming. The northern and western parts of the country, including the area around Paris, are fairly flat with plains and woodland. Although the southern and eastern parts of France have many hills and mountains, some crops are grown, and cattle and sheep raising is important.

France is blessed with a great system of waterways that has made travel easier through the years. The Rhone River flows south into the Mediterranean Sea whereas, the Seine, the Loire, and the Garonne rivers flow to western shores. The Rhine River flows along the border with West Germany, and then to the sea through the Netherlands. It is also a useful waterway for eastern France. Canals now connect these rivers to make them even more useful.

France is as far north of the equator as our northern states of Montana and Maine. France's climate, however, is generally a little warmer. Heat from the Atlantic Ocean and the Mediterranean Sea help to keep the western and southern coasts from getting too cold. But the northeast and the southern mountainous areas have plenty of winter weather. Winds coming over the water from the west bring rain to provide the water needed for crops.

The Arc de Triomphe

France has many geographical advantages to help meet its needs.

Early France

Two thousand years ago, the land of France was called Gaul. The Romans conquered Gaul and built cities, roads, bridges, and other structures throughout the land. When the Roman Empire was weakening in the late 400s, a group of invading people called the Franks entered France. Ruled by their king, Clovis, they set up the first French kingdom. Later, during the rule of Charlemagne (Charles the Great, 768-814), the Franks built a large empire.

The court of Louis XIV (Louis is seated in the center.)

After a few hundred years, a major problem developed between France and England. William the Conqueror, who won control of England in 1066, was from Normandy, an area of northwestern France. William ruled not only England, but a part of France also. Later English kings gained control of more French territory. This situation angered the French kings, who were trying to establish their own control over France.

The French and the English armies began to fight for control of French lands. Because the struggle went on for many years (1337-1453), it was called the Hundred Years' War. At first the English army proved to be much stronger and more skilled, and France was in danger of becoming just a part of the kingdom of England. When things seemed hopeless, a young French woman named Joan of Arc rallied the French armies and led them to victory in battle. Although Joan was later captured and burned at the stake, the French people took courage. They drove the English out of France.

The Age of Louis XIV

By the time that Louis XIV became king, the French kings had much power over a great kingdom. Louis ruled as an absolute monarch. Whatever he ordered was done. He was called the "Sun King" because he had such power and lived in such splendor. The whole world seemed to revolve around him.

Despite all the grandeur, problems arose. Louis did not count the cost of all his activities. The Versailles Palace, which he built, would cost over $1,400,000,000 in our money today. He also sent his armies out to conquer nearby lands. It took much money to provide the supplies for those armies as they fought. Someone had to pay for all that Louis did.

Louis collected taxes to pay for his activities. The rich nobles and the wealthy businessmen, however, did not have to pay most of the taxes. That meant that the poorer people of France had to pay more than their fair share. Of course they were not happy about that. The nobles and the merchants became unhappy, too, because they resented the power that the king had over them. Trouble was stirring for France.

The French Revolution and Napoleon

The trouble broke out in 1789 with the beginning of the French Revolution. That was about seventy-five years after Louis XIV had died. His great-, great-, great-grandson, Louis XVI, was king at the time. The people were tired of seeing their kings and the nobles live in luxury while they faced such poor living conditions. They desired something better, but they could not agree on any plan for their country. There was much fighting and killing. The king and his wife were beheaded by a new device called the guillotine. For several

A guillotine

Napoleon Bonaparte

years there was violence and disorder. It seemed that no government could bring the people under control. Finally, a young military hero, Napoleon Bonaparte, took over.

Napoleon was a brilliant general in the French army. The people wanted his strong leadership for their country. He set French government in order with himself at the head, and then he proceeded to build a French empire. He won more victories with his armies and brought most of Europe under his control. French glory was on the rise again.

Napoleon, however, was not content with what he had. He tried to conquer Russia, but failed. He was finally defeated at the Battle of Waterloo in 1815. His defeat weakened French power and glory.

After Napoleon was stopped, the French kingdom was reestablished, but the people were not satisfied. Throughout the 1800s, France endured several revolts and uprisings. Napoleon's nephew even took power and tried to build a new French empire. He fell from power, however, when he lost a war with Germany in 1870.

France After 1900

When World War I began in 1914, France joined forces with Britain and the United States to stop Germany. Much of

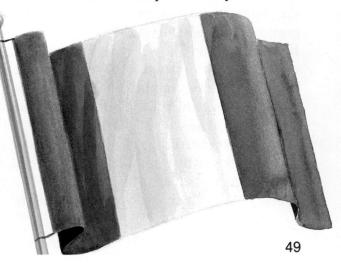

the conflict took place in France, and the land was torn by the warfare.

France had barely recovered from the destruction of World War I when World War II began in 1939. Once again, much fighting took place on French soil. The Germans actually captured France and controlled it until the Allied powers invaded on D-Day, June 6, 1944. The Germans were driven out, and France set up its own free government once again.

Allied forces landing in Normandy on D-Day

The French Government

In the days of Louis XIV, France had what is called an **absolute monarchy.** That means that the king had the authority to oversee all aspects of government as he pleased. There was no constitution to limit his powers. When the French Revolution came in 1789, it was the beginning of many changes in the French government.

Since 1789, the United States has been governed as a republic under one constitution. Even before that date, Britain established its constitutional monarchy. In the same period of time, France has been governed under thirteen different plans. France has survived all the changes, and it is still an important country today. It cannot, however, claim a heritage of a stable government as the United States and Britain can claim.

The government that France has today is called the Fifth Republic. A **republic** is a government in which the people of the country select their leaders. Those leaders govern the country according to a constitution, which is a set of rules for a government. A republic does not have a monarch.

The people of France elect a president, and they elect members to represent them in their Parliament. Unlike the United States and Britain, which have two major political parties, France has many political parties. These groups support different ideas and programs to be carried out by the government. The people can vote for the candidate from the group that they think is the best. Although this multi-party system gives the people many choices, it also makes it hard for any one party or candidate to get the support of most of the people. For this reason, French elections can be confusing. The French people need careful thought and cooperation to make their government work.

Section Review

1. Where did Louis XIV build his new palace?

2. Name the three bodies of water that border France.

3. What two mountain ranges lie along the borders of France?

4. Whose leadership restored order to France after the French Revolution?

5. What kind of government did France have in the days of Louis XIV?

Living in France

The Religion of France

Long before the time of Louis XIV, most Frenchmen accepted Roman Catholicism. During the Reformation period, when many people began to question the teachings of the Roman Catholic church, some Frenchmen accepted the Bible's teachings. France, as a whole, however, rejected the word of the Scriptures.

Life for true Christians in France became difficult. The French Protestants were called **Huguenots** (HYOO guh NAHTZ). The Catholic kings and the church officials were afraid that they would lose their power if the numbers of Huguenots kept growing. For many years there was a struggle between the Roman Catholics and the Huguenots. Thousands of Huguenots were killed. Finally, in 1598, a French king issued an order that the Huguenots would be allowed to live in safety and worship God as they pleased.

Jeanne d'Albret

Jeanne d'Albret was born January 7, 1528. Her uncle was the king of France, and her parents were the rulers of an area in southern France called Navarre. Although most of the French people trusted the teachings of the Roman Catholic church, Jeanne believed the teaching of God's Word.

Many problems faced Jeanne as she grew up and became the new ruler of Navarre. France was in a turmoil over the question of whether the Huguenots would be allowed to worship freely in France. The Roman Catholic leaders desired to stamp out all churches but their own. If Jeanne followed the wishes of the Catholic leaders, perhaps peace would come to her people and, her position and wealth would be secure.

Jeanne, however, did not give in. She trusted in the Lord, and she knew she must do what was right. She determined that she would protect the freedom of her people to worship the Lord and seek His truth in the Scriptures. The Huguenots rallied around their courageous leader as she sought to gain religious freedom for her people and peace for her country.

The Catholic rulers of France tried to force Jeanne to give up her faith. Church officials condemned her for her firm stand. On several occasions, her enemies tried to have her killed. The Lord protected her from danger, however, and she continued to serve Him.

Jeanne never wanted to harm her enemies, but rather to win them to the gospel. Jeanne gave her life to protect the testimony of Christ. She gave her wealth to help support the people in their struggles. She gave her energy to encourage her people as they were persecuted for their faith. She also gave her son to be a leader of the Huguenots.

Jeanne d'Albret died on June 4, 1572. Seventeen years later her son became Henry IV, King of France. As king, Henry passed a law that granted religious freedom for the Huguenots. For a while the Huguenots enjoyed the freedom for which Jeanne had worked and prayed. Later, other French kings took away that freedom. The Huguenots fled to other countries, and France lost the godly heritage it was given by faithful leaders like Jeanne d'Albret.

In 1685, Louis XIV revoked the order that had given the Huguenots safety. Many of them were forced to leave France because they would not submit to the Roman Catholic church. These Huguenots believed that they were to worship God in truth as the Bible said. They had to leave everything they owned in France as they fled to other countries for safety.

Many of the Huguenots were industrious merchants, craftsmen, and businessmen. When they left France, they took their Christian testimonies and their business skills with them. They moved to Britain, the Netherlands, Switzerland, Germany, and other countries. Some of them also came to North America. France lost a talented group of people, but these other countries gained citizens who truly desired to serve the Lord.

Today, Roman Catholicism is still the major religion in France. Most of the people have never heard the gospel. France is a country that needs missionaries to tell the people of God's plan of salvation.

The Economy of France

Before World War I and World War II, France was an agricultural nation. Many farmers working on small portions of land produced the food needed to feed the rest of the people. In cities and towns, workers in small workshops and stores made and sold goods for the local people. Businesses were generally operated by a few members of a family. There were very few large businesses in France.

You remember that Britain gained wealth and power during the late 1700s and the 1800s. That was the time of the Industrial Revolution. While England was building big factories, manufacturing goods, and trading with all parts of the world, the French Revolution and Napoleon's wars kept France busy. Also, France did not have abundant supplies of

coal, as Britain did, to power the steam engines used in factories. France, basically, did not change into an industrial nation as Britain did during the Industrial Revolution.

After 1900, the destruction caused by the two World Wars wiped out many areas of France. As they have rebuilt their country, the French people have had their own Industrial Revolution. Though they lacked coal for fuel, they began to import petroleum and to use electricity to power their machinery. By importing raw materials, using modern technology, and building new and bigger factories, they have developed their production of manufactured goods.

France now has important iron, steel, and aluminum industries. Some of the metal products are used to manufacture automobiles, aircraft, and machinery. France produces textiles and chemical products such as medicines and fertilizers as well as many other goods.

French farmers have begun to use more machinery to increase agricultural production. Today, because of its range of climate, its abundant farmland, and its improved farming operations, France can produce most of its own food. It also sells a great deal to other countries. The wheat

The French countryside

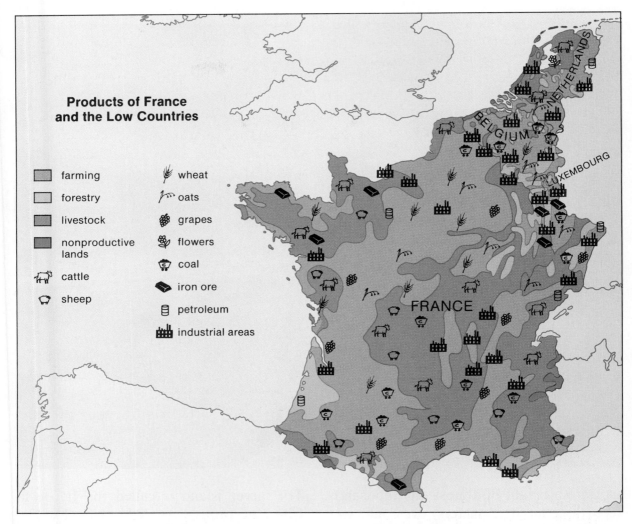

Products of France and the Low Countries

- farming
- forestry
- livestock
- nonproductive lands
- cattle
- sheep
- wheat
- oats
- grapes
- flowers
- coal
- iron ore
- petroleum
- industrial areas

NETHERLANDS

BELGIUM

LUXEMBOURG

FRANCE

grown on France's northern plains is its leading crop. Dairy cattle provide plenty of milk, butter, and cheese, and French-grown fruits and vegetables fill the markets.

Another major product is the wine made from grapes, which grow in many parts of France. The French make money from selling their wines, but they suffer from the effects of alcoholism in their country as well.

Wine is a mocker, strong drink is raging: and whosoever is deceived thereby is not wise. (Proverbs 20:1)

Paris and the important port cities on the coasts of France are centers of world trade. France is a leading member of the Common Market, and in recent years

France has become one of the leading industrial nations of the world. Its businesses and factories, however, need raw materials and technical knowledge to keep them prospering.

Paris

Although it is located in the northern part of France, the city of Paris is "the center" of France. It is the capital city—the center of the French government. It is a great industrial and trading city, and it is the center of French artistic and musical talent and of educational opportunity. Besides all this, Paris is a city full of reminders of the heritage of France.

If we were to take the elevator to the top of the Eiffel Tower and look around

us from a height of almost one thousand feet (three hundred meters), we could see some of the sights that have made Paris such a special city.

The Seine River

First of all, below us flows the busy **Seine River** (SEN). This important waterway has provided transportation for the people of France for hundreds of years. Goods may be carried to and from the Atlantic Ocean at the mouth of the river. Canals also connect the Seine to other rivers; the boats and barges we see below us may be transporting goods to other parts of France or even to Germany and other countries in Europe.

Looking up the Seine, we can see two small islands. They look almost like one huge boat full of buildings pulling a smaller boat down the river toward us. The larger island is called the Ile de la Cité (EEL DUH LA see-TAY, "Island of the City"). It is the place at which the city of Paris began.

The Romans found a few people living on the island when they conquered Gaul (France). The Romans built roads, bridges, and buildings, and soon Paris became an important town for them. Later it grew to spread over both banks of the river. The famous old cathedral of Notre Dame (NAW-truh DAHM, "Our Lady") stands on the Ile de la Cité.

The Left Bank

South of the Seine River on what is called the Left Bank is the students' section of the city. The University of Paris began there over seven hundred years ago. This section of Paris is also called the Latin Quarter because the students used to speak

Latin. Latin was the language of the Roman Empire, and it was the language of scholars for many years.

Napoleon's Tomb is also on the Left Bank in a building called the Invalides (in VAH leed). It once was a soldiers' hospital, but now it is a military museum.

The Eiffel Tower from which we gaze is also on the south side of the river. This tower was built in 1889 for an exhibition held in Paris. At that time it was the tallest structure in the world (986 ft.).

The Right Bank

As we look across the Seine to the Right Bank, we see the Louvre (LOO vruh). This huge building was once the royal palace for French kings. (Louis XIV lived there before he built the Palace of Versailles). Now it is a famous museum with many priceless works of art. The wide street or boulevard called the Champs Élysées (SHAHN zay-lee-ZAY), lined with trees, sidewalk cafés, and small shops, leads over to the Arc de Triomphe (Arch of Triumph). This large monument, begun by Napoleon, stands in the middle of the intersection of twelve streets.

The people of Paris look like tiny ants from our high perch on the Eiffel Tower. They hurry around among these famous landmarks to do their shopping or to take care of their business. They amuse themselves with the many entertainments of their city. Paris restaurants offer the finest foods. The shops and the stores sell expensive perfumes and stylish clothing. Many people spend thousands of dollars just to have the latest fashion from one of the famous Parisian designers.

The sights of Paris: the Eiffel Tower *(left)*, the Arc de Triomphe *(center)*, and the Basilica of the Sacré-Coeur *(right)*

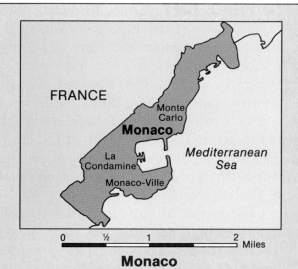

Monaco

Area: 0.7 sq. mi.   Population: 25,000

Picturesque Monaco clings to a small strip of land between the Mediterranean Sea and the mountains of France. Every year nearly one million tourists from all over the world visit the beautiful Monaco terraces and gardens. Frenchmen and other foreigners outnumber the native Monegasques eight-to-one.

Famous for its charming setting, Monaco consists of three sections. Monaco-Ville, sometimes called the Rock, is situated high on a rocky cliff. On the Rock sit government buildings, the cathedral, and the Oceanographic Museum, but it is dominated by the royal palace. Second, La Condamine bustles with the hurried activity of a Mediterranean seaport. An important trading center in Greek and Roman times, Monaco has a secluded harbor that has sheltered many foreign ships from the raging storms on the sea. Finally, Monte Carlo is the chief residential and resort area.

Monaco has been ruled by members of the Italian Grimaldi family since 1304. The reigning prince has absolute authority. If the present Council and Cabinet displease the prince, he may dissolve them and appoint a new one. Prince Ranier III did this in 1959. This prince became famous for his marriage to the late Grace Kelly, a marriage that transformed a Hollywood actress into a real princess.

Paris is often called the "City of Light" because it is such a center of culture and activity. Tragically, Paris is a city of darkness as well because it is a city of millions who need to know Christ as their Saviour.

Then spake Jesus again unto them, saying, I am the light of the world: he that followeth me shall not walk in darkness, but shall have the light of life. (John 8:12)

Section Review

1. What were French Protestants called?

2. What is the religion of most French people?

3. What city is the capital of France?

4. What river flows through the capital of France?

5. Name four famous buildings or structures in the capital city.

The Low Countries

To the north of France in Western Europe lie three small countries, Luxembourg, Belgium, and the Netherlands. Together these three are called the **Low Countries** because their land near the seacoast is flat and near or below sea level.

Throughout their history the Low Countries have often been linked together. Several foreign powers have ruled them in the past, and in World Wars I and II, much fighting took place in these countries.

After World War II the three countries entered into a trade agreement. They decided to let goods be traded among their countries without any tariffs (import taxes). They also agreed to charge the same tariffs on goods imported from other countries. This agreement allowed the BENELUX countries (BElgium, NEtherlands, LUXembourg) to begin producing more and more goods to trade with each other and with the world. They also joined the Common Market when it was formed in 1957.

Luxembourg

Luxembourg (LUK sem BERG) is a beautiful little country of forests, hills, and farmland. With 999 square miles of land, it is smaller than our smallest state, Rhode Island. France, Belgium, and West Germany completely surround Luxembourg; therefore it has no seacoast. A land without a seacoast is called a **landlocked** country.

Despite its scenery, size, and location, Luxembourg is an active industrial country. It must import many raw materials, but it has large steel and chemical industries.

Many of the people of Luxembourg (Luxembourgians) speak two or three

Beaufort Castle, Luxembourg

languages. Letzeburgisch is the most commonly spoken language, while French and German are generally used in writing and in business.

The government of Luxembourg is a constitutional monarchy. There is a parliament, but instead of a king, their ruler is called the "Grand Duke."

Belgium

Shhh! Be very quiet! Watch carefully! The man is scratching one small stone with another. He examines it thoroughly, and then he places the stone with the scratch in a holder. He carefully positions a metal blade in the scratch on the stone. He holds the blade and takes a wooden mallet in the other hand. While we watch, almost breathless with excitement, we see the mallet come down with a firm tap on the blade. It is a perfect cut! If the workman's hand had been unsteady, the rock would have been shattered into pieces. The cut was good, however, and before us lies a diamond cut so that it may be ground and polished into a beautiful precious gem.

The busy city of Antwerp, Belgium, is a very important center of the diamond industry. Dealers from all over the world meet there to buy and sell both rough and cut diamonds. Diamonds are found in all kinds of irregular shapes. It takes highly skilled workmen, like the many in

Antwerp, to carefully cut, grind, and polish them into the beautiful sparkling shapes used in jewelry.

Diamonds are the hardest substance on earth. The diamond cutters are very careful to save all the chips and dust from the diamonds that they are working with. Since only a diamond is hard enough to scratch another diamond, they use the pieces in cutting tools, and they cover the grinding wheels with the dust. Other industries and professional people use diamond pieces, too, to make precision cutting instruments.

Diamonds are precious stones because of their beauty and their usefulness and because they are hard to find. They are a wonderful blessing that God has included in His creation for us to use and enjoy.

Land of Two Languages

Antwerp is an important European port city, handling the shipping and trading of much of Belgium's manufactured goods. The city is inland from the **North Sea** on the Schelde River in the northern part of Belgium. In this area of the country, the people speak Dutch, the language of the Netherlands.

Brussels, the capital of Belgium, is an important industrial center. Also, many international organizations have their headquarters in Brussels. Both Dutch and French are spoken in the city, but the main language spoken south of Brussels is French.

The Dutch-speaking people in northern Belgium are called Flemings, while the French-speaking Belgians in the south are called Walloons. The difference in language has been a problem for the country because each group wants its own language used in education, government, and literature.

Belgium and Its People

Belgium, though much larger than Luxembourg, is only a little larger than the state of Maryland. It has a short coastline along the North Sea, and its climate is temperate. Although the land is low

Lelystad, Netherlands

along the coast and in the north, most of Belgium is rolling hills. Good farmland allows the Belgian people to produce most of the food that they need.

Manufacturing, however, is more important to Belgium than agriculture. Belgium is one of the most highly industrialized countries in the world. The Belgians produce much steel and other metals, chemicals, textiles, machinery, and other goods. They can find few of the raw materials in their own land; therefore, they import most of the materials they need to keep their industries going.

The Belgian government is a constitutional monarchy. The king and parliament try to keep the people working together despite the language problem. Most of the Belgian people, both Flemings and Walloons, are Roman Catholic.

The Netherlands

Jan van Lier and his sister, Anna, are pioneers in the Netherlands. Their family did not move in a covered wagon, and they did not build a log house, but they are pioneers just the same. They moved into a new area and started living in a different way.

Jan's father is a doctor from Amsterdam, the capital and largest city of the Netherlands. The Netherlands is a small country, but it has a large population. Therefore, many areas of the country are crowded with people. A few years ago Jan's father decided that the family should leave

the crowded city and move to a new area, and that is what they did.

A New Land

The van Lier family moved to East Flevoland, an area of the Netherlands that did not exist until a few years ago. This land did not exist because it was beneath the waters of the Zuyder Zee, the "Southern Sea." This was an arm of the North Sea that extended into the country.

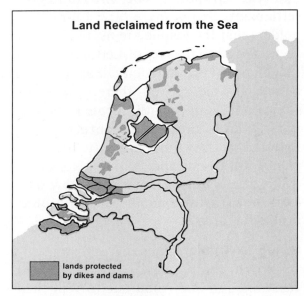

Land Reclaimed from the Sea

lands protected by dikes and dams

Because the people of the Netherlands needed more land in which to live and grow their food, they decided to drain part of the Zuyder Zee. The task was begun back in the 1920s by building a nineteen-mile-long barrier dam to shut out the waters of the North Sea. The Zuyder Zee became a huge lake now called Ijsselmeer (Lake Yssel). Then workers began to build **dikes,**

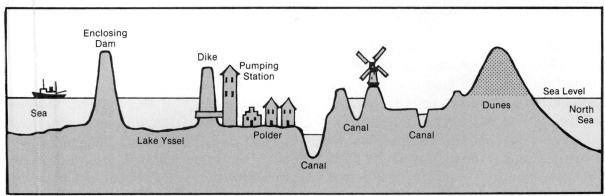

strong walls of stone and earth, around sections of the lake. Big electric pumps drained the water out of these sections until the land inside them (polders) was dry. In some places the land of the **polders** is many feet below the surface of the lake, but the strong dikes and the pumps keep unwanted water out.

It has taken many years for the building of the dikes, the draining of the water, and the preparing of the land for settlement. Now there are four large polders that the people are using. The van Liers moved to the city of Lelystad in East Flevoland. This new city was planned before anyone moved there. The wide streets and conveniently located schools, parks, and shopping centers make Lelystad a busy, modern city but with plenty of room and without excessive traffic. Jan's family has a nice, new one-story house with a small yard in a quiet residential area.

Going to Amsterdam

When their family takes a short vacation, Jan and Anna like to visit their grandparents in Amsterdam. After they leave Lelystad, they drive for over twenty miles through the polders. Beside the road are new farmhouses with carefully cultivated fields. Many crops grow in this land that not long ago was the bottom of the sea. Finally, they cross a bridge into North Holland, the section of the country that contains the city of Amsterdam.

Before long they are driving on the narrow, crowded streets of the city. People on bicycles are everywhere. Jan and Anna have their own bicycles at home in Lelystad, but they are glad that they can ride them in a town where the traffic of cars, trucks, and buses is not so heavy.

A large canal connects Amsterdam with the North Sea, making the city a busy port. Over one hundred smaller canals cut through the city. As Jan and Anna ride

Amsterdam, Netherlands

over the bridges, they see boats full of sightseers and many small barges carrying goods on the canals below.

Their grandparents' house is much different from their house in Lelystad. The house is nearly four hundred years old. It is three stories high, but it is very narrow. The houses on both sides are built against it with no room between. In front there is a sidewalk, and in back is a tiny yard with a high fence.

Inside the house, the children love to climb the narrow stairs up to the attic to look through all the odds and ends that Grandmother has saved. There is a small window at the front of the attic. Jan once asked his grandfather why there was a beam sticking out over the window. Grandfather explained that because the stairs in the house are so narrow, large pieces of furniture must be pulled up to the second and third story of the house. A rope is attached to a pulley on the beam, and the furniture is hoisted up and brought through an open window.

Anna likes to help her grandmother and her mother in the kitchen. Grandmother makes delicious *gehaktballen* (minced meatballs), and Jan especially likes her apple tarts. On very special occasions they may have a dinner of smoked eel.

Importance of the Sea

The Dutch people (people of the Netherlands) live in a land that was made prosperous by the sea. In the 1600s, Dutch sailors began trading with America and with the Far East. Their ships brought spices and raw materials from around the world.

You probably remember the name *Henry Hudson*. He sailed for the Dutch in 1609 and discovered the Hudson River that flows into New York harbor. Because of his voyage, the Dutch were able to claim the area that is now the state of New York. They called the colony New Netherland, and they built the city of New Amsterdam on Manhattan Island. Do you know what the name of that city is today? The British later gained control of the colony, but the Dutch continued to carry on trade with America and all parts of the world. Today the city of Rotterdam in the Netherlands is the busiest port in the world. The transporting of goods in merchant ships is an important part of the country's business.

A miniature of a Dutch village

The North Sea has also been a great supplier of seafood for Dutch fishermen. In the past the Dutch sold their fish to much of Europe. Although the fishing industry is not as important as it was in the past, many Dutchmen still pull their living from the sea.

A Low Land

The Netherlands have benefited by being close to the sea, but the people have to work hard to keep the sea from covering their land. *Netherlands* means "low lands," and that name is well suited to the country. Not only the polders of the Zuyder Zee but also about one-third of the land is below sea level. During storms, the sea often threatens to flood any unprotected lowland. Strong dikes help keep back the water so that the people remain safe on dry land.

For hundreds of years the Dutch have been building dikes to protect their land from water. They learned how to construct windmills that use the power of the winds to drain their polders of unwanted water. (They also used the power of windmills to grind their grain.) Most of the pumps now use other sources of power to keep the land dry, but a few hundred old windmills are still working. They provide beautiful and interesting scenery on the Dutch landscape.

Another beautiful feature of the Dutch landscape is flowers. Tulips, daffodils, and

Tulips are probably the most famous product of the Netherlands.

other flowers grow by the thousands near the coast. The color of the blooming fields is breathtaking. The blooms are cut off, and the bulbs are sent around the world to be planted in window boxes and flower gardens. More flowers grow inside heated glass greenhouses. All year round these provide lovely cut flowers for florists in many countries.

The Dutch People

The people of the Netherlands speak the Dutch language. Often, their country is called "Holland." Actually, that is the name of two regions on the west coast of the Netherlands. North and South Holland contain many large cities and have much industry and commerce, whereas most of the other areas of the country are rural.

The people who live in the rural areas sometimes dress up in the native costumes of the Dutch. Wooden shoes were once the standard footwear in the Netherlands. Some field workers still wear them to keep their feet dry as they walk on the damp ground, but now wooden shoes are mainly a curiosity for tourists.

The Netherlands is a constitutional monarchy. It is ruled by the queen (or king) who is aided by her ministers and a parliament called the States General. Queen Beatrix became the monarch in 1980 when her mother, Queen Juliana, stepped down from the throne after having reigned for thirty-two years. Although Amsterdam is the official capital of the Netherlands, the government actually operates from a city called The Hague.

The Netherlands has had a long heritage of religious freedom. You will remember that the Pilgrims went to live in the Netherlands before they came to America. Today the Netherlands still offers religious freedom, but few of the Dutch people truly know the Saviour. Many do not even go to church, while many others follow the teachings of their churches and do good works. They need to know that it is "not by works of righteousness which we have done, but according to his mercy" that He will save us (Titus 3:5).

Section Review

1. What does *BENELUX* stand for?

2. What two languages are spoken in Belgium?

3. What do we call sections of land that have been enclosed by dikes and drained of water?

4. Besides cars, trucks, busses, and trains, what other two means of transportation are used in Amsterdam?

5. What structures were once used to pump water and grind grain?

Terms to Remember

Alps Mountains	republic	Low Countries	dikes
Pyrenees Mountains	Huguenots	landlocked	polders
absolute monarchy	Seine River	North Sea	

Things to Know

1. What did Louis XIV build at Versailles?

2. What natural barriers form five of France's six boundaries?

3. What kind of government does France have today?

4. What is the religion of most French people?

5. What is the capital of France?

6. What countries are the Low Countries?

7. What do we call walls built to keep water out of polders?

Things to Talk About

1. How were the lives of Louis XIV and the noblemen different from the lives of the common people of France?

2. What is a republic?

3. What situation was the cause of the Hundred Years' War?

4. How did taking away the freedom of the French Huguenots hurt the country of France?

5. While England was having its Industrial Revolution, what was going on in France?

6. Why are Luxembourg, Belgium, and the Netherlands called the Low Countries?

Things to Do

1. Give a report on one of the following people:
   a. Louis XIV
   b. Napoleon Bonaparte
   c. Joan of Arc
   d. Clovis
   e. Charlemagne
   f. Charles De Gaulle

2. Find the correct ending to each of the following statements.
   a. Louis XIV was the king of
      (1) England.
      (2) France.
      (3) Ireland.
   b. Louis XIV built his palace at
      (1) Calais.
      (2) Verdun.
      (3) Versailles.
   c. The common people of France lived in
      (1) small houses.
      (2) castles.
      (3) palaces.
   d. One of the borders of France is formed by
      (1) the Pacific Ocean.
      (2) the English Channel.
      (3) the Caribbean Sea.
   e. In the Hundred Years' War, France fought against
      (1) Germany.
      (2) England.
      (3) Spain.
   f. After the French Revolution in 1789, order was restored to France by
      (1) Napoleon.
      (2) Joan of Arc.
      (3) Louis XIV.
   g. France's government today is
      (1) a republic.
      (2) a constitutional monarchy.
      (3) an absolute monarchy.
   h. In the days of Louis XIV, French Protestants were called
      (1) reformers.
      (2) Anglicans.
      (3) Huguenots.
   i. Most of the people of France are
      (1) Roman Catholics.
      (2) Anglicans.
      (3) Huguenots.
   j. France changed from an agricultural nation into an industrial nation
      (1) during the time of Louis XIV.
      (2) at the same time as England.
      (3) after World Wars I and II.
   k. The smallest of the Low Countries is
      (1) Belgium.
      (2) the Netherlands.
      (3) Luxembourg.

l. The governments of all three of the Low Countries are
   (1) republics.
   (2) constitutional monarchies.
   (3) absolute monarchies.

m. Flemings and Walloons live in
   (1) Belgium.
   (2) the Netherlands.
   (3) Luxembourg.

Geography Skills

Use the maps on pages 45 and 53 to answer the following questions.

1. What eight countries have borders with France? (Hint: Two are very small.)

2. What is the large highland region of southern France called?

3. Le Havre is the port city at the mouth of what river in France?

4. What grain crops are grown in France?

5. What is the major natural resource of Luxembourg?

6. What fuel or mineral resources does the Netherlands have?

7. What are the major industrial cities of Belgium?

8. In what regions of France would you be likely to find sheep grazing in pastures?

CHAPTER 4

GERMANY, AUSTRIA, AND SWITZERLAND

The Divided Land of Germany

The central region of Europe is called Germany. Hundreds of years ago this region was the home of groups of people who wandered from place to place looking for food and other provisions. These groups were the Germanic tribes from whom the region gets its name.

Through the years, rulers gained control of portions of Germany. Each ruler had his own little kingdom. Many strong leaders tried to unify Germany into one nation that they could rule. The small kingdoms, however, were careful to keep their own power. Germany remained divided until a little more than one hundred years ago.

In 1871 Germany was finally united. Otto von Bismarck, the prime minister of one of the German kingdoms, Prussia, used the military strength of his kingdom

	AREA (Square Miles)	POPULATION	CAPITAL	MAIN LANGUAGES	MAIN RELIGIONS	CURRENCY
WEST GERMANY	95,976	61,543,000	Bonn	German	Protestant, Roman Catholic	mark
EAST GERMANY	41,768	16,724,000	East Berlin	German	(restricted) Protestant, Roman Catholic	mark
AUSTRIA	32,374	7,574,000	Vienna	German	Roman Catholic	schilling
SWITZERLAND	15,941	6,463,000	Bern	German, French, Italian, Romansch	Protestant, Roman Catholic	Swiss franc

to unify Germany. The German kingdoms united under the rule of the Prussian king, and the new German nation was formed.

Germany remained a united country until the end of World War II (1945). At that time the Allied countries (the United States, Britain, France, and the Soviet Union), which had defeated Germany, took over temporary control of the country. They intended to help Germany establish a good government and become a peaceful country. The Soviet Union, however, forced the eastern part of Germany to become a Communist country in 1949, while West Germany became a free republic. Now Germany is once again a divided land—the two countries of West Germany and East Germany.

The best way for you to learn about a place is to see it for yourself. You can probably describe many interesting things about the places you have visited on family vacations or other trips. It would be nice

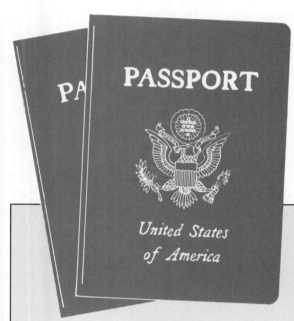

Passports

A passport is an official government document that an individual carries when traveling to another country. The passport proves the identity and citizenship of the person who carries it. It gives him permission to travel outside his country. It also requests the foreign government to give safe passage and protection to the traveler while visiting in that land. A passport is usually needed when one leaves his own country.

To obtain a passport, one must follow these steps.
1. Get an application from the Post Office.
2. Fill out the application.
3. Go back to the Post Office with the application and the following items:
   a. Proof of U.S. citizenship—your birth certificate (identifies the place of birth)
   b. Proof of identity—identification papers or an identity witness (an adult who knows the applicant)
   c. Two recent photographs—both must be alike, of the applicant alone, from a front view, without sunglasses or hat

4. Pay for the passport processing.
5. The postal clerk will mail the application to the Department of State.
6. The passport will be mailed in a few weeks.

A person should carry his passport at all times when he is in a foreign country. New passports are valid for ten years and then must be renewed.

Some countries also require a visa, especially for persons staying in the country for long periods of time. A visa is an official approval of the passport from the country to be visited.

if we could take the whole class to Europe to see the countries that we are learning about. But even though such a field trip is not possible, we can try to imagine what it would be like to visit another land.

Let's imagine taking a vacation to Germany. We can leave our school behind for a little while and enjoy the wonders of a faraway place. Since we already know a little about France, let's fly to Paris and begin our trip there.

Day 1
Arrival in Europe

Europeans travel a great deal by train. The railroads provide fast transportation for passengers going almost anywhere in Western Europe. In Paris, we board an express train bound for Strasbourg, a French city near the West German border. Speeding along at nearly 100 m.p.h., we watch the changing French countryside from our comfortable compartment.

In a few hours we reach an area of France known as Alsace-Lorraine. In the past, this strip of land along the border was claimed by both France and Germany.

Since World War I the area has belonged to France.

Soon we arrive in the city of Strasbourg, and we decide to find a place to eat lunch. As we roam the streets near the station, we find that there are both French and German newspapers and magazines on the stands. While sitting at a sidewalk café, we overhear some people at another table speaking in German. Others around us are speaking French. After eating a quick lunch, we are ready to go back to the station and board our train for Germany.

Entering Germany

As our train begins to move, an officer comes through our railcar to check our **passports.** On the edge of the city, we cross the **Rhine River,** the boundary between France and West Germany. The Rhine is a very important river in Europe. We will see more of it later in our trip, but now we take a train ride through the beautiful **Black Forest.**

The Black Forest is an area in the southwestern corner of West Germany.

Castle above the Rhine River

DENMARK

Baltic Sea

North Sea

EAST
GERMANY

NETHERLANDS

POLAND

Hamburg

Elbe River

Bremen

Weser River

Berlin

Hanover

Potsdam

Wittenberg

Düsseldorf

Leipzig

Cologne

WEST
GERMANY

Dresden

Eonn

Mainz

Frankfurt

CZECHOSLOVAKIA

LUX.

Main River

Rhine River

Nuremburg

Alsace-Lorraine

FRANCE

Stuttgart

Strasbourg

Black Forest

Danube River

Bavarian Alps

Munich

Key

SWITZERLAND

AUSTRIA

———— highway

+++++++ railway

———— river

0   20   40   60   80   100

Scale of miles

Dark green fir trees cover the mountainsides, and the valleys are shadowed by towering oak trees. This area is a favorite spot for tourists. Its little villages have small shops that sell cuckoo clocks and many other carved wooden items. Some of the old farm houses still have thatched roofs so that visitors may see what life was like in the Black Forest many years ago.

After enjoying an afternoon of beautiful scenery, we reach the busy city of Stuttgart in the early evening. Like many cities in Germany, Stuttgart suffered much damage from bombing during World War II. Since then, however, the city has been rebuilt and has become a modern industrial city. We will spend our first night in a hotel here in Stuttgart.

Day 2

The next day we wake up ready to see more of Germany. After a light breakfast at the hotel of freshly baked rolls, jam,

The mountains of West Germany

and fruit juice or hot chocolate (often called a Continental breakfast), we board an express train headed north to Frankfurt. We speed past hills, fields, and forests as we enter this central region of Germany. We pass Heidelberg and Darmstadt, and soon come to Frankfurt on the Main (MYNE) River. It was raining when we left Stuttgart, but now the sun is beginning to shine. We are glad because it is hard to go sightseeing in the rain.

Frankfurt, West Germany

Frankfurt is an important city of finance, trade, and travel. Many bank headquarters are located here, and several industries have their trade fairs and conventions here as well. Planes from all over the world fly into Frankfurt's international airport, and many railroads and highways converge in the city.

A Rhine River Cruise

From Frankfurt, we travel by train along the Main River. On the shore where the Main River joins the Rhine River sits the city of Mainz (MYNTZ). Johann Gutenberg lived in Mainz over five hundred years ago. He developed a movable-type printing press. The first Bible printed on such a press was made in his shop about the year 1455. In Mainz we board a steamer moored at the riverfront. We soon begin a delightful cruise down the Rhine.

Our journey down the Rhine from Mainz to Bonn is full of spectacular scenery. Ancient castles atop green hillsides keep watch over the river below. A tower perched on a small island in the Rhine stands guard over the river traffic as it has for hundreds of years. Vineyards cover many of the hillsides, and charming villages rest on the banks of the river. Our cruise seems to be through the pages of a fairy-tale book rather than down a real river. It is no wonder that the Grimm

The Grimm brothers' story "Rapunzel"

brothers collected some of their well-known tales as they traveled around the German countryside.

At one bend in the Rhine River, the current used to be especially treacherous. The famous legend of the Lorelei says that a beautiful maiden sat on the cliff above this bend. Sailors, when they saw her beauty and heard her song, forgot to guide their vessels and were dashed against the rocks.

The City of Bonn

All too soon we pass this picture-book land to enter the busy modern world again. Our boat approaches the city of Bonn. Ludwig van Beethoven, the great music composer, was born in Bonn in 1770. Many great classical musicians were born in Germany. Germans have a great love for music. All over the country, concerts and operas delight German audiences. Bonn has a special Beethoven Festival every two years.

Since 1949, Bonn has been the capital city of West Germany. From the Rhine we can see several of the modern government buildings. A constitution called the Basic Law is the foundation of the West German government. The Parliament (legislature) has two houses just as our Congress and the British Parliament do. One is the Bundestag (BOON dus TAHG) and the other, the Bundesrat (BOON dus RAHT). A president acts as head of state representing West Germany in official actions. The chancellor (prime minister), chosen by the Bundestag, is actually the political leader or head of government.

On to Düsseldorf

Once past the city of Bonn, we soon see the tall spires of the beautiful cathedral at Cologne. Through that large German city we speed on to Düsseldorf. Although the Rhine wanders on farther through about fifty miles of Germany, and then through the Netherlands to the sea, we will end our cruise here at Düsseldorf. This city is the center for much of the business of the Ruhr Valley to the north. In that river valley connecting with the Rhine, several cities blend together to form one huge industrial area.

We may see some children along the streets of Düsseldorf turning cartwheels. The fine art of *radschlagen* (cartwheel turning) is a part of their physical education in school. Tradition says that many years ago the ruler of Düsseldorf and his new bride were in a carriage, and one of the wheels broke. A boy of the city came to the rescue by taking hold of the hub with one hand and turning cartwheels with the other. The carriage with its human wheel took the couple safely home. Now a cartwheel-turning contest is held every year to determine the new champion of Düsseldorf.

Camping Out in Germany

From this point on we will explore Germany by driving where we want to go. Before we pick up our vehicle, let's quickly do some shopping in some of the shops of Düsseldorf. German cities now have supermarkets much like ours in the United States, but many German people still prefer to shop in the little specialty shops. First, we find a bakery that sells bread and rolls. There are so many kinds to choose from, it is hard for us to decide what we want. Next, we go to a store that sells meat. All around us there are sausages of every description. Wurst (sausage) is a favorite food of the Germans. They eat beef sausage, pork sausage, liver sausage, and many other kinds. Some kinds are hard, and others are soft enough to spread with a knife. We will buy several different kinds. Quickly, let's stop by another store where we can buy some soft drinks and other articles needed for our meal.

The vehicle we have reserved is ready to go, so now we will drive on out of the city into the peaceful German countryside. East of Düsseldorf we find a good place to camp for the night. The Germans are great outdoorsmen. Many miles of hiking routes and nearly two thousand camping sites provide recreation throughout the country. We quickly set up our camp and eat our German supper around a campfire. Then we are ready to get into our tents and sleeping bags for a much-needed rest.

Day 3
On the German Autobahn

For our next day's activity, we will drive northeast to Hamburg. Germany has a superhighway system much like our interstate highways. Their highway system is called the *autobahn*. There is a high speed limit on these roads, and so we can swiftly travel on our way. High speeds do cause a problem, though. Every year many Germans die in highway accidents.

A German bakery

Hamburg, West Germany

drive to the North Sea coast. The northern coasts of Germany are popular vacation spots. If we see any large ships out at sea, they may be going to or from Hamburg. We will turn toward that city now.

Hamburg and Hannover

Hamburg is the largest port city of Germany, but it is nearly seventy miles from the sea on the Elbe River. Shipbuilding and trading activities keep the docks along the Elbe busy. Hamburg was the birthplace of another famous German musician, Johannes Brahms. After a drive through the city and a visit to some markets, we must move on our way.

South of Hamburg is the city of Hannover. That will be our stop for tonight. Every April, Hannover is the scene of the International Industrial Fair. Businesses from all over the world display their latest products and equipment. At that time the city is full of visitors and business activity. Now, however, Hannover is a pleasant place to get some rest for the night. We have a big day ahead of us. Tomorrow, we will drive through East Germany to the city of West Berlin. We will find out what it is like to travel in a Communist country.

The northern region of Germany through which we now travel is not as hilly as the central part of the country. The area near the North Sea looks a great deal like the low marshy plains of the Netherlands. In fact, some of the coastal area is bounded by dikes and drained by windmills or pumps just as the low areas of the Netherlands are.

Rather than going straight to Hamburg, let's turn north at Bremen and

Section Review

1. When did Germany become one united nation?

2. What country had the greatest influence on the eastern portion of Germany after World War II?

3. What is the tree-covered, mountainous area of southwestern Germany called?

4. Name four cities that lie along the banks of the Rhine River.

5. What city is Germany's largest port?

Day 4

Going Behind the "Iron Curtain"

After a good night's rest in Hannover, we are ready to find out what life is like behind the **"Iron Curtain."** The "Iron Curtain" is an expression used to indicate the boundary between the free countries of Western Europe and the Communist countries of Eastern Europe. Fences, mine fields, armed guards, and attack dogs keep those people behind the Iron Curtain from escaping to the West. The Iron Curtain separates West Germany from East Germany. On our way to West Berlin, we must stop at a checkpoint before we are allowed to enter East Germany.

The guards at the checkpoint thoroughly check our passports and survey our vehicle. We tell the guards that we are traveling to West Berlin on a sightseeing trip. After about an hour of waiting, they tell us that we may proceed. They warn us, however, that we must travel straight to West Berlin. We are allowed to stop only in designated places.

Traveling along the East German autobahn, we look across the fairly flat countryside. East Germany has more good farmland than West Germany. The farms are owned and run by the government. The workers live together in farm communities. The government provides their supplies, and the people do the farmwork that the government tells them

to do. The East German farmers cannot move unless the government gives them permission. They must stay on the farm and work. East Germany does not have as much farm machinery as many free countries do, and so much of the work must be done by hand with hoes and pitchforks. The buildings we see are very drab, and some are in need of repair.

The autobahn goes to West Berlin with very few places to stop along the way. If we tried to explore some other route, the police would soon be questioning us. Therefore, we hurry on our way to the entrance to West Berlin.

In West Berlin

Again we must pass through a check at the border before we can enter into West Berlin. The Communists want to make sure that we are not helping anyone escape from East Germany into this free city. After a careful search, they allow us to go on through. In minutes, we are traveling down the broad, modern avenues of West Berlin. Everything here is like the busy cities of West Germany. We would never guess that we are one hundred and ten miles inside the Communist border.

People hurry here and there on the sidewalks. Stores and shops sell all kinds of modern things. Restaurants, theaters, and amusement spots are open for West

West Berlin

West Berlin

Berlin

French Zone

Berlin Wall

British Zone

WEST BERLIN

EAST BERLIN

U.S. Zone

Soviet Zone

West Berlin is like an island inside East Germany. It is free rather than Communist, and it is considered to be a part of West Germany.

The city of Berlin is divided into two parts, East Berlin and West Berlin, much like Germany is in two parts. The whole city of Berlin was the capital of Germany when it was a united country. At the end of World War II, when Germany was divided, Berlin was in the middle of the area controlled by the Soviet Union. Because the other Allied countries (the U.S., Britain, and France) did not want the Soviet Union to control all of this important city, they divided Berlin into four sections.

The Soviet Union was not content to control only the eastern section of Berlin. The Communists tried to cut off the western sections of Berlin from the free countries in the West. For eleven months beginning in 1948, the Soviet

Union would not allow needed food, fuel, and other supplies to be transported by railroad or vehicle through East Germany to West Berlin.

The other Allied countries saved West Berlin by organizing an airlift. Planes flew night and day from West Germany to West Berlin with the needed supplies. The Soviet Union finally allowed free movement of goods from the West to West Berlin along specific routes. The courage of the West Berliners during that time of trial helped to keep West Berlin free.

Another tense situation arose in 1961 when the Communists built a fence around West Berlin. Until that time, people had been able to travel freely from East Berlin to West Berlin.

Hundreds of thousands of people escaped the Communist rule of East Germany by entering West Berlin either to live there or to arrange travel to a free Western country.

In order to stop this loss of people, the Communists hurriedly put up a barbed wire wall. It was soon reinforced with a cement wall and carefully guarded. The Berlin Wall separated East Berlin from West Berlin so that those in the East had no way of escape. Many families were separated from members on the other side of the wall.

The Berlin Wall still stands as a barrier to freedom today. People in West Berlin are allowed short visits in the East, and elderly people from the East are allowed visits to West Berlin. But, the Berlin Wall is a symbol of the force that communism uses to control human freedoms.

Berliners to enjoy. French, British, and American military forces still protect West Berlin, but the citizens have their own city government. They also participate in the West German national government. Also, the West Berliners are free to stay or move away as they please.

A Ride in East Berlin

East Berlin is the capital of East Germany. We may take a brief visit to the other side of the wall. Foreigners may enter East Berlin through "Checkpoint Charlie." After passing the check, we drive down the streets of East Berlin.

There is a distinct difference between the two parts of the city. Although there are stores, modern buildings, and broad avenues, the lively activity is missing in East Berlin. There, stores sell mainly the common articles needed by the people. There is little variety. The buildings are drab, and since not many East Germans can afford cars, we see less traffic on the streets. East German soldiers are always on patrol in the city. Still, East Berlin is a showplace for communism. Compared to other cities in the Communist countries, East Berlin is prosperous.

In East Berlin and the rest of East Germany, school children study the doctrines of communism. Beginning in the fifth grade, they learn the Russian language.

East Berlin is closing up quickly for the night. The people will disappear into their apartments for the evening, making the streets nearly deserted. We must make our way back to Checkpoint Charlie. We go through a search again before we can re-enter West Berlin.

In the free city we find that the streets are as full of activity as ever. Neon lights flash on signs overhead while streams of cars hurry down the streets. The two million people who live in West Berlin's 185 square mile "island" are enclosed by a wall, but they are free.

"Checkpoint Charlie"

Berlin in World War II

Berlin was the capital and the center of activity during World War II. Today, most Germans wish to forget that their country brought so much destruction to themselves and to the rest of the world. Adolf Hitler, a man controlled by selfish desire for power, used his exciting personality to gain the following of much of the German population in the 1930s. He set out to conquer the world. Deceived by his promises of glory and a good life, the German people followed Hitler's leadership.

From 1939 until 1945, World War II brought death to millions and devastation to Europe. Hitler declared the Jews in Germany to be enemies of the new empire. Thousands were taken from their homes and put into concentration camps. Some were forced to work, but many were put to death.

When Hitler was defeated, the German cities were left in ruins from the bombings of Allied planes. After a long battle with the Russians, Berlin was left a pile of rubble. But Berlin and the other cities of Germany have been rebuilt. The women of West Berlin pitched in to clear away the debris. Four hills in West Berlin were formed from the piles of rubble. One, the Teufelsberg, is nearly four hundred feet high. It is used for skiing in the winter.

There is very little left here in West Berlin to remind us of the war's destruction. Tonight we stay in this modern city rebuilt from the ruins. Tomorrow will be our last day of touring Germany.

Day 5

We will spend our final day in Germany by traveling to the southern area of Germany, which is called Bavaria. We leave West Berlin bright and early this morning. Of course, we have to pass through a checkpoint to exit. By now, we are almost used to the inconvenience. And, once again we are passing through the East German countryside.

Martin Luther and the Reformation

If we were allowed to take a side trip, we could stop at Wittenberg. That city was the place where Martin Luther nailed a list to the church door in 1517. The list proclaimed many errors of the Roman Catholic church. Luther's action started what is known in history as the Protestant Reformation. Many people considered Luther's ideas, and they began to look to the Scriptures for the truth.

Most of the people of Western Europe, including those in the area of Germany, were faithful supporters of the Roman Catholic church. Luther and his followers, armed with the truth of God's Word, began

Nuremburg, West Germany

to protest against the wrong teachings of the church. These protesters were called **"Protestants."** In northern Germany, where Luther preached, many heard the message of salvation by faith and accepted Jesus Christ as their Saviour. Other men arose to preach the gospel in other areas of Europe. Although most of Europe clung

Protestant Memorial Church in Speyer

to Roman Catholicism and rejected the truth of God's Word, the Protestant Reformation brought to light the gospel that the Roman Catholic church had hidden.

Today, the northern part of Germany, including East Germany, is mainly Protestant, while the southern part is mainly Roman Catholic. Under the Communist government in East Germany, however, all religions are discouraged. Those East Germans who still choose to go to their churches rarely receive any government favor. They usually do not receive job promotions or any extra benefits.

The Protestants who followed Luther were called Lutherans. The Lutheran denomination is still very strong in Germany, although few of the Lutheran churches there still follow Luther's teachings and the truth of Scripture. Many German Lutherans seldom go to church. To them, the church is mainly a place to gather for christenings (infant baptisms), weddings, and funerals. They also attend services at Christmas and Easter.

On to Bavaria

Passing the turn-off to Wittenberg, we drive on to the southern border of East Germany. There, for the last time we must

A Wife for Luther

Martin Luther is by far Germany's most famous preacher. You probably have read several stories about Luther and his stand for the Word of God. Luther was a Roman Catholic priest before he realized that the Bible teaches that salvation comes by faith in the Lord Jesus Christ. The Roman Catholic church teaches that priests should not marry. Luther found that the Bible does not place that restriction on preachers of the Word. In fact, the Bible teaches that marriage is "honourable" (Hebrews 13:4), and Luther decided that he would be married.

Luther was forty-two years old when he married the twenty-six-year-old Katherine von Bora. Katherine had been a nun who had heard about Luther's preaching. She accepted the truth of God's Word for herself. Along with eight other nuns, she escaped from the convent in a wagon loaded with empty barrels. She lived with a family for two years until Luther asked her to be his bride.

Katherine became a good wife for Martin Luther. For a woman in the 1500s, Katherine was well educated. She could read and write in German, and she knew some Latin. She worked hard around the house, cooking and cleaning. She looked after the farm animals and also raised fruit and vegetables.

The Luthers had six children—as well as a number of "guests." Several orphaned nephews and nieces came to live at the Luther house also. College students boarded there, and many guests stopped by to talk to Martin Luther. Katherine stayed busy feeding and caring for the many people under their roof.

Martin Luther called his wife "Katie," and they grew to love each other very much. Katie encouraged her husband as he worked for the Lord. She often wrote to him when he was away from home preaching. She took good care of him when he was ill. Luther was very thankful for the fine wife the Lord had given him.

pass through a Communist checkpoint. Our vehicle is thoroughly searched, and then we are free to go. Now that we have experienced the kind of captivity known by those behind the Iron Curtain, we will be much more appreciative of our freedoms.

Traveling south now toward Munich, we find the land much more hilly than it was near Berlin. We pass by Nuremberg and then cross the **Danube River.** Soon we approach the city of Munich. We are so hungry after the long drive from Berlin that the first thing we look for is a place to eat. The air is chilly here in this high country. Did everyone bring some warm woolen clothing such as the people here in Munich wear? We find a restaurant and sit down to a satisfying meal. We will order a German favorite, *wiener schnitzel,* a breaded veal cutlet.

The Bavarian Alps

The afternoon is quickly passing. If we do not go on to the Alps now, we will not be able to see them before night falls. We can come back and see some of Munich after dark.

We travel south into the foothills of the Alps mountain range. The air is getting colder as we pass through several villages. Many of the houses in these villages are bright and colorful, with paintings right on the sides of the buildings. Some of the people are dressed in their native Bavarian clothing.

Along the road in the country we see some little shrines. Roman Catholic farmers and travelers often stop for a moment's worship before these small crucifixes attached to posts. Sorrowfully we think of how these people do not know that Christ paid all the penalty of our sins on the cross. They think they must help pay for their sins by works such as this. The Bible says that "they that worship him

Castle Neuschwanstein, Füssen, West Germany

[God] must worship him in spirit and in truth" (John 4:24). Most of these German people do not know the truth of God's Word.

Snow now covers the mountains around us as we climb the roads of the Alps. We pass near a beautiful "fairy tale" castle, Neuschwanstein. We get out to take some pictures of the beautiful scene. We wish we had time to take the hour hike up to the castle for the tour, but it is getting late and a cold wind is blowing. Anyway, this is as far as we can go in the Alps without crossing the border into Austria. We must hurry back to Munich to see the city and then catch our plane.

The Sights of Munich

It is dark by the time we reach the city, but the buildings are brightly lit. We drive by the Olympic Village that was used for the Olympics in 1972. We decide to stop and take the elevator up to the top of the Olympia Tower, a tall structure that looks almost like a huge needle pointing upward. From the top we see the stadiums below, and we look out over the city of Munich. We see the towers of old church buildings and the lights of modern skyscrapers. The view is breathtaking.

We drive to the center of town and take a walk around some of the older buildings. We see the famous clock on the town hall. It is too bad that we did not get here in time to see the figures of knights on horseback go into action as the clock struck. We stop now for a bite to eat before we drive to the airport.

Our trip has passed so quickly. Soon we will be on our way back to the United States. We wish that we could have stayed longer. There is so much more in this country that we would like to see. At least, though, we now know a little about this land of Germany.

Section Review

1. What is the boundary between the free countries and the Communist countries of Europe called?

2. In which part of Germany is West Berlin located?

3. Who was the leader of Germany during World War II?

4. What Protestant denomination is very strong in Germany?

5. What mountain range lies in the southeastern region of Germany?

Austria

Southeast of Germany lies the mountainous country of Austria. The people in this land speak German, but their country is different from Germany.

Austria is just a little larger than the state of South Carolina, and the Alps mountain range covers over two-thirds of the land. The Danube River flows out of West Germany and through the northern section of Austria. This northern area around the Danube and a small area along the eastern border with Hungary are the only Austrian lands flat enough for productive farming. Dairy cattle, however, can feed in the mountain pastures of southern and western Austria.

A Religious People

The people of Austria live in a country of natural mountain barriers, but religious celebrations often bring them together. Over ninety per cent of the people are Roman Catholics. Many of them faithfully follow the teachings of their church, and many believe in following old customs that they think will bring them good luck.

Every year the Austrian towns have big celebrations on religious holidays and other occasions. During these days the people participate in the religious ceremonies and in all kinds of superstitious activities. Some believe they must drive evil spirits away by making noise or that they must hide from them by wearing disguises. When cattle are brought down from mountain pastures in the fall, they are "disguised" in colored headdresses to protect them from the spirits. Some people believe that a barefoot walk in a field at certain times will bring protection from lightning or from witches.

The Austrian people are very religious. They believe in God. They know of Christ and His good life. But many do not know that Christ died to save them from judgment and eternal death. They believe their religious works will get them to heaven. Few missionaries are in Austria to tell the people about the salvation God has provided through Christ Jesus. Those people need to be shown the peace and the joy that they can have in their hearts when they accept Christ as their Saviour.

Education in Austria

Going to school in Austria is different from going to school in America. From the first through the fourth grades, most children attend a general elementary school. In the fifth grade they either continue with a general education or they enter the Gymnasium. In Austria that is not a building for sports activities. It is a school that will help to prepare the students to go to a university.

The students know that it is very important to go to the Gymnasium and to do well there. Austrian young people want to be able to go to a university. The students spend long hours doing their homework. Many families even hire a tutor to help the students learn more. Then, when they have finished their work at the Gymnasium, they must take an important test. They must remember the things they have learned in their twelve years of schooling. If they fail their final exam, they cannot go on to a university. From the beginning, the young students seem to realize that their future depends on how well they do in their schoolwork.

Austrian History

Austria was once a German kingdom much like Prussia. You will remember that Prussia gained control of surrounding lands to form the country of Germany. Austria also gained control of surrounding lands in east central Europe. In the 1800s, Austria was united with Hungary to form the Austro-Hungarian Empire. This empire covered much of what is now Austria, Hungary, Rumania, Yugoslavia, Czechoslovakia, and Poland.

When World War I began in 1914, Austro-Hungary sided with Germany. These countries were called the Central Powers. The Allies (Britain, France, and the United States) defeated the Central Powers to end World War I. When the

Cutting hay in the Austrian Alps

war was over, Austria and Hungary were separated and much Austrian territory was taken away from the country. Austria was left the small country that it is today.

A few years later, Hitler wanted Austria to be a part of his German empire. He took over the country before World War II began. He then forced the Austrians to support him during the war. When he was defeated, Austria regained her independence.

Austrian Government and Economy

The government of Austria today is much like that of West Germany. The people elect a president to be the leader of the country. The two-house parliament led by the chancellor actually determines most of the actions to be taken by the government.

Because so much of Austria is covered by mountains, the people must make good use of the land and the resources they have in order to make a living. One resource that Austria has is the forests that grow on the mountainsides and in the valleys. The trees provide wood pulp that is used in the paper-making industry. Another resource that Austria has is mountain streams and rivers. Hydroelectric plants use the running water to produce electricity. The mountains themselves have become important to the Austrian tourist industry. Good conditions for skiing bring tourists to the Austrian slopes nearly year round. Trees, flowing water, and mountains would not seem to be very important materials for the Austrians to

Lipizzaner horses

Lipizzaner Horses

In a majestic 250-year-old hall in Vienna furnished with chandeliers and other ornaments of gold and ivory, people from far and near sit around a dirt ring. The dirt floor is a striking contrast to the surroundings. But, the performance on that floor far outshines the splendid surroundings.

In the ring a group of Lipizzaner horses perform with wonderful grace and strength. Vienna is the home of these fine animals of the Spanish Riding School. Here the horses and the riders show their amazing skill to the delight of the audiences.

The Lipizzaners are a carefully kept Spanish breed of horses. They are dark when they are born, but after a few years their coat usually changes to white. When the stallions are about four years old, they begin their schooling.

The Spanish Riding School has been training the Lipizzaners and giving performances for over four hundred years. It takes about four years to train the horses, but it takes six or seven years to train their riders. When they are both ready, the horse and rider will move together in the ring as if they are one form.

In the riding hall the well-trained Lipizzaners move to the rhythm of orchestra music by the great artists of Vienna. The riders sit perfectly balanced on the animals through every drill. The horses move in a high-stepping trot. They stand on their hind legs in a pose called the *levade*. They take a flying leap in the air called a *capriole*. Only the very strongest horses learn to perform a graceful kind of hop on their hind legs called a *courbette*. The audience is thrilled by their display of ability. The Lipizzaners are, indeed, special horses.

work with. But the Austrians use these simple materials to make a living in this modern world.

Leisure Time

Sports are not as important in Austria as they are in other countries. (However, some of the Austrians do enjoy skiing on the slopes of their snow-covered Alps.) The schools have physical education classes, but there are usually no school soccer teams or basketball teams. Instead of playing sports after school, the teenagers often meet for a while in a local coffeehouse. There they sit, talk, and drink soft drinks, tea, or coffee until it is time to go home and begin their homework. The adults also enjoy meeting in the coffeehouses on occasion for a conversation with friends or for an opportunity to read the newspaper.

Vienna

The city of Vienna is located on the banks of the Danube River in eastern Austria. With a population of about one and a half million, Vienna is the center of government and culture for the country.

Vienna, Austria

In years past, emperors reigned from this magnificent capital city. They entertained in grand style in their beautiful palaces. Vienna became the home of many talented musicians who wrote and performed for Austrian leaders and foreign guests. Beethoven, Haydn, and Mozart are just a few of the great musicians who worked in Vienna.

The people of Vienna still love music. Performances of operas and concerts are an attraction to music-loving tourists from all over the world. In fact, Austria gains much income from tourists who come to enjoy the music and the sights of Vienna.

The Vienna Opera House

The Alps

Before the mountains were brought forth, or ever thou hadst formed the earth and the world, even from everlasting to everlasting, thou art God. (Psalm 90:2)

God created the different landforms of the world. We may view beautiful scenes of sweeping plains or rolling hills. But to many people, the most fascinating features of the earth are the towering mountains.

The Alps cover a large region of south central Europe. Although they are not among the highest mountains of the world, they clearly display the splendor of God's creation. The Alps extend from eastern France through Switzerland, northern Italy, southern Germany, and Austria.

A mountain is an area of land that rises high above its surroundings. Mountains located close together in a group are called a mountain range. When mountains are close together, travel from one side to the other may be very difficult. Roads must be built through the lowest gap between the mountain peaks. Such a passageway is called a mountain pass.

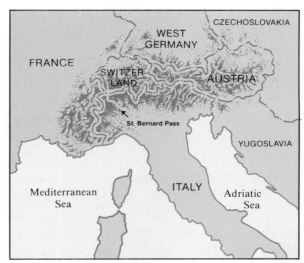

The St. Bernard Pass provides a way through the Alps from Italy to Switzerland. People have traveled over this pass for hundreds of years. In the Middle Ages, monks lived in a monastery beside the pass. They trained big St. Bernard dogs to help travelers who might be lost in the snow.

Even passes are difficult to cross. Roads must twist and turn rather than climb too steeply up to the pass. Snow and ice cover the roads at times. Loose

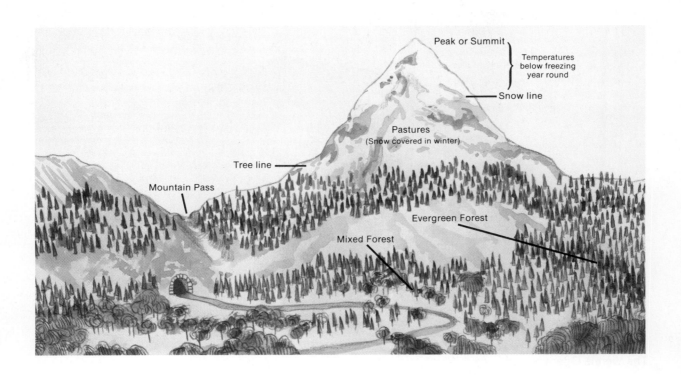

rocks tumble down to block the way. To avoid these problems, in some places road builders have tunneled through mountain barriers. The St. Gotthard Road Tunnel in Switzerland is one of the longest highway tunnels in the world (10.14 mi.).

Switzerland

To the west of Austria and still south of Germany lies the country of Switzerland. Like Austria, it is a mountainous land, but it is less than half the size of that neighbor. The towering Alps cover two-thirds of Switzerland, while the Jura Mountains extend along much of its northwestern border with France. Between these two mountain ranges is a small area of green hills and sparkling blue lakes.

Life in Switzerland

Switzerland is a scenic little country. But, other than great beauty, it has few natural resources. There are no coal mines or sources of petroleum in the land to provide fuel for factories and power plants. Most of the land is not flat enough for farming. The people must import much of the food that they eat. Switzerland lacks the metal ores and other materials usually needed for big industries. Besides these problems, the beautiful mountains make transportation difficult and expensive.

The Swiss people have learned to overcome the difficulties of living in their mountainous land. Over the years they have built industries and businesses that use few raw materials. With the money they make, they buy the food and other materials they need.

One profitable industry for which the Swiss are famous is watchmaking. From a small piece of steel they can make the parts for many watches. The watchmakers carefully assemble the watches so that they keep accurate time. Swiss watches have a reputation for fine quality.

Switzerland does have plenty of dairy cattle. Two important Swiss products come from the milk they produce. One is what we call Swiss cheese. Actually, the

Switzerland is one of the most beautiful and scenic countries in the world.

Swiss make two kinds of cheese, and both of them have holes. They are Emmental and Gruyere. If you ask for Swiss cheese in Switzerland, the people will wonder what kind you mean. The other important milk product is Swiss chocolate. Milk chocolate was invented in Switzerland in 1878. The cacao beans from which chocolate is made are imported from tropical regions. The Swiss add their own milk to make delicious chocolate candy.

Tourism is also very important to Switzerland. People from all over the world like to spend their vacations in this beautiful land of mountains and lakes. Snow skiing, mountain climbing, tobogganing, and boating are a few of the activities that attract visitors to Switzerland. There are plenty of things to do all year round. Many come just to relax and breathe the brisk, cool mountain air. As the tourists pay for their hotel rooms and fine meals and buy Swiss products to take home, they help Switzerland make the money it needs to import goods from other countries.

Like Austria, Switzerland has many mountain streams and rivers. From their water power, the Swiss generate electricity. The electricity provides power for their cities and factories so that they do not need to import large amounts of coal or petroleum for fuel. Even the Swiss trains run on electricity.

Language and Government

There are three official languages spoken in Switzerland—German, French, and Italian. Although one of these is the main language in each part of the country, most people can speak at least two. Another language, Romansk, is also spoken in some areas of Switzerland.

Switzerland is divided into sections called cantons. Each canton is much like one of our states. The Swiss national government, like our national government, directs the whole country. They have a two-house legislature, a judicial or court system, and an executive branch. The executive branch is led by a group of seven men called the Federal Council. These men take turns being president for one year each. Although the president leads the Council for the year, he is not a well-known political figure like our American president. In fact, most of the Swiss people would not know the name of their president.

The Swiss people, however, are concerned with governing and protecting their country. They vote on many of the issues and laws that affect their canton or their whole country. All able-bodied men from age twenty to fifty are trained to defend their country in case of an attack. Being prepared has helped the Swiss to remain safe inside their mountain fortress for over 150 years.

Cities of Switzerland

Geneva

The area of land between the Alps and the Jura Mountains contains most of the larger cities of Switzerland. In the southeast of this area near the French border is Geneva. John Calvin, the Protestant reformer, preached in this city in the 1500s. Later, many Huguenots fled to this area to escape persecution in France. Today Geneva is the home of many international organizations.

Zurich

In the northern area is Switzerland's largest city, Zurich. Now it is a place of business and commerce, but during the Reformation it was also the center of Ulrich Zwingli's preaching. Zwingli was another early Protestant reformer. Although the Reformation reached Switzerland, many of the people rejected God's Word. Today, few of the Swiss people know the true way of salvation.

Edelweiss

Edelweiss is the national flower of Switzerland. In German, the word means "noble white." The white-flowered plant is less than a foot tall. It grows well in the rocky soil of the Alps. High in the mountains it can receive the sunlight that it needs to help it grow.

Daring young men have climbed the mountains to pick an Edelweiss for their sweethearts. Some of these climbers have been hurt or killed in their attempt to prove their love.

Edelweiss, the national flower of Switzerland

Bern

Between Geneva and Zurich lies the capital city of Bern. It is said that a nobleman named this city for the first animal he killed in a hunt nearby. That animal was a bear. The city now keeps a number of bears in a large outdoor area. Children love to visit the bear pit to watch the animals play.

Lugano

One area of Switzerland lies south of the Alps on the Italian border. There the city of Lugano seems quite different from the other cities of Switzerland. Its climate is much warmer because (1) it is on lower ground, (2) it is a little farther south and therefore nearer the equator, and (3) it is near enough to the Mediterranean Sea to receive some of the warming winds from over that body of water. The people of Lugano mainly speak Italian, and their city is much like many cities of Italy. We will learn more about that European country in the next chapter.

Section Review

1. What important river flows through Austria?

2. What natural resources are a great benefit to Austria?

3. What is the main religion of the Austrians?

4. The Alps mountain range covers an area of what five countries?

5. What city is the capital of Switzerland?

	AREA (Square Miles)	POPULATION	CAPITAL	MAIN LANGUAGES	MAIN RELIGIONS	CURRENCY
PORTUGAL	35,553	10,008,000	Lisbon	Portuguese	Roman Catholic	escudo
SPAIN	194,896	38,234,000	Madrid	Castilian Spanish, Catalan, Galician, Basque	Roman Catholic	peseta
ITALY	116,303	56,345,000	Rome	Italian	Roman Catholic	lira
GREECE	50,944	9,898,000	Athens	Greek	Greek Orthodox	drachma

A Spanish port on the Mediterranean Sea

Many times the Bible calls the Mediterranean simply "the sea." The Mediterranean was the scene of several well-known events in the Bible. A great fish in the Mediterranean gave Jonah his underwater voyage. Paul's missionary journeys took him sailing over Mediterranean waters many times.

Although we have no record of Christ sailing on the Mediterranean, He spent His life on earth in Palestine, the land on the eastern shore of the sea. No doubt He often viewed this great sea to the west as he stood on the hilltops of Judea and Galilee.

In Bible times and still today, the Mediterranean is a sea of world commerce. The ancient Phoenicians, Greeks, and Romans founded cities along the seacoast. They sent trading ships to buy and sell products. Today, ships from around the world carry on trade in the harbors of the Mediterranean.

The Mediterranean Sea is over two thousand miles long. It reaches from the **Strait of Gibraltar** in the west to the shores of the Middle East. If the Mediterranean Sea were placed in the United States, it would reach from Denver, Colorado, all the way to Washington, D.C. At its deepest point, the sea extends down over 14,000 feet. The Mediterranean covers an area of over one million square miles or about one-third of the area of the United States.

The lands that border the Mediterranean have a temperate climate, but they are unlike most other lands in the temperate regions of the world. Lands with a Mediterranean climate usually have mild, rainy winters and hot, dry summers. Olives grow well only in lands with such a climate. The map below shows where olive trees are found in the Mediterranean area. The climate map (page 9) shows that these areas also have a Mediterranean climate.

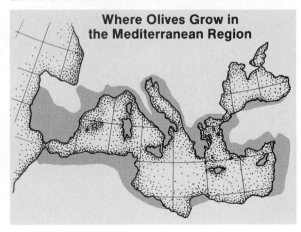

Where Olives Grow in the Mediterranean Region

SPAIN, PORTUGAL, ITALY, AND GREECE   91

Venice, Italy

In this chapter we will learn about four Mediterranean countries in Europe— Spain, Portugal, Italy, and Greece. Portugal does not actually touch the Mediterranean, but it is similar to the other three countries that border the sea. The geography and culture of all four countries have much in common. Let's find out what these lands are like.

Spain

A noisy crowd fills the large, round outdoor stadium in Seville, a city in southern Spain. Although it is a hot summer day, the heat of the late afternoon sun does not seem to bother anyone. A trumpet sounds and two mounted officers ride across the arena. The crowd watches and cheers as three matadors in glittering apparel walk behind followed by other men, some mounted, some on foot. They receive the key to the bullpen from the president of the bullfight, and now the action begins.

A bullfight is a traditional event in Spanish cities. The Spanish people are fond of many sports. They especially enjoy soccer. But, to them, bullfighting is a special art. A highlight of many of their festivals from March to October is a bullfight featuring some of Spain's best matadors.

From the unlocked pen, the first bull charges out into the arena. One of the men on horseback begins to provoke the bull with a long lance. The angry bull attacks while the horseman dodges the bull's sharp

horns. Those horns often injure the horse and sometimes hurt the rider as well.

Now that the bull is excited, one of the men on foot takes over. As the bull charges at him, he moves so that he may stab the bull in the neck with a pair of long, sharply pointed sticks called banderillas. This is a hazardous job. After the bull is maddened by the pain of four pairs of banderillas, the final act begins.

The matador enters the ring to face the raging bull. He carries a red muleta (cape), which he skillfully waves before the bull. The bull charges, but the matador gracefully steps aside. The sharp horns barely miss the matador, but his bravery delights the crowd. The more graceful and daring the matador, the more the crowd enjoys the fight. This dangerous contest between man and bull goes on until, in a final charge, the matador plunges his sword into the bull's neck. The fight is over for the bull, but there are five more bulls waiting in the pen. Each of the matadors will fight two before the event is over.

Bullfighting has gained little popularity except in Spanish-speaking countries. It is a dangerous sport. Many men are injured in the arena, and some are killed. People often criticize the cruel treatment of the animals. Yet, the Spanish people continue to admire the bravery and the skill of the matador, and they enjoy the tradition and the excitement of the bullfight.

The Land of Spain

A piece of land that is almost surrounded by water is called a peninsula. Spain is located on the **Iberian Peninsula.** This land is attached to the rest of Europe only along the northeast border. The Mediterranean Sea and the Atlantic Ocean surround the rest of the peninsula. Spain shares the Iberian Peninsula with the country of Portugal.

Although Spain's mountains are not as high as the Alps, Spain is a mountainous country. The Pyrenees Mountains divide Spain from France, while several other mountain ranges spread throughout the central areas of the country. In fact, the entire central area of Spain is a **plateau,** a level area with a high altitude. Only the coastal areas have land near sea level.

Spain's climate varies from area to area. The southern and eastern coastal areas have a Mediterranean climate. These areas have hot, dry summers and mild, dry winters. Most of Spain receives little rainfall during the year. Only the land along the Atlantic coast receives enough rain to raise abundant crops. Other areas must irrigate or use the moist soil near rivers for their crops. The central plateau's dry summers are very hot, while the winters are very cold in the high altitudes.

History and Government

If you know who Columbus, Balboa, Magellan, Ponce de Léon, Cortés, and Pizzaro were, you know something about a glorious part of Spain's history. These men explored and conquered new worlds for Spain. In the 1500s, Spain was a rich and powerful country.

Spain's good times did not last, however. Soon other European countries opposed Spain's rise to power. Parts of the great Spanish Empire desired to be free from Spain's control. Shipments of wealth from the New World declined. Spain fought to keep its power, but by 1600 that power was slipping away.

By 1900 none of Spain's western empire remained. The Spanish government was weak, and the people were poor and discontented. Few industries had begun in Spain; most of the people worked on the land.

From 1936 to 1939 the Spanish fought a civil war. Many people died in a struggle to determine the kind of government Spain should have. General Francisco Franco's forces finally won control of the country. Franco made himself **dictator** of Spain. A dictator is a ruler who takes complete control over a country. Franco ruled Spain for over thirty years.

When Franco died in 1975, the dictatorship ended and Juan Carlos became king of Spain. King Juan Carlos I has helped Spain to gain new freedoms. The people now have a voice in government.

The Spanish Inquisition

King Ferdinand and Queen Isabella, who sent Columbus on his voyages, wanted all of Spain to follow the teachings of the Roman Catholic church. They established a court called the Spanish Inquisition. This court tried people who were suspected of being unfaithful to the Roman church. Those who would not submit to the church were tortured and put to death. Hundreds of people were burned at the stake because they would not give up their beliefs.

Would you be willing to stand up for your beliefs, even if it meant torture or death?

Fear none of those things which thou shalt suffer. . . be thou faithful unto death, and I will give thee a crown of life. (Revelation 2:10)

For over two hundred years the Spanish Inquisition forced Catholicism on the people of Spain. Today almost all the people of Spain are Roman Catholic. They know the traditions of the church, but they do not know the way of true salvation.

Missionaries are allowed to preach in this country that was once closed to the gospel. Spain is now an open mission field that needs to be harvested for Christ.

The Spanish People

In the center of the country lies Spain's capital and largest city, Madrid. Madrid is the center of government activity and also a beautiful city of Spanish culture. Tall, modern buildings and splendid old buildings stand beside pleasant tree-lined

The streets of Madrid, Spain

streets. From one until three in the afternoon, businesses close and the schools take a break for a siesta, a nap during the hottest part of the day. After their siesta, the people of Madrid return to their activities. They eat their supper around ten o'clock at night. Often they visit with friends in cafés or take walks through the brightly lit city until after midnight.

The people in Madrid and those in most of Spain speak the Spanish language called Castilian. This is the same Spanish language that is spoken in most of Central and South America. There are, however, three other languages spoken in Spain: Catalan, Galician, and Basque. The people in the area around Barcelona, an important port city on the Mediterranean, often speak Catalan. The people in the northwest corner of Spain speak Galician. And, a group of people called the Basques, who live on both sides of the border with France, have their own language. The Basques are an unusual group of people who have customs that are neither Spanish nor French.

Spain is slowly becoming a modern country. Although many farmers still use hand tools, some are beginning to use machinery. Many people sell small handicrafts or fruit and vegetables on the streets of the towns, but new industries are growing.

Section Review

1. What is the name of the peninsula on which Spain is located?

2. What mountain range divides Spain from France?

3. What is the capital of Spain?

4. What little country lies between Spain and France?

5. Who was the dictator who ruled Spain for many years?

Andorra

Area: 188 sq. mi.   Population: 31,000

Sandwiched between France and Spain, the small, peaceful country of Andorra (an DOR uh) lies high in the Pyrenees Mountains. Once called a "political curiousity," it is still a suzerainty. (A *suzerainty* is supposedly owned by another country.) Andorrans pay a small tribute to the rulers of both Spain and France. The small country also combines the best of both its neighbors. Among the things that attract tourists to Andorra are its majestic scenery, ski resorts, health spas, and opportunities for mountain climbing and hunting.

Sheep are an important source of income. Visitors may see sheep grazing on the grassy hillsides of the high mountain valleys. The most important occupation, however, is the sale of European goods at a minimal cost. Tourists and nationals brave the winding mountain passes to get a tax-free bargain. Swiss watches, electronic equipment, French perfumes, Swedish crystal, Irish linen, and much more sell inexpensively in Andorra's shopping paradise.

Portugal

"Depressa, depressa! Hurry, hurry!" Several boys run along the beach shouting that another fishing boat is returning. The women and children nearby drop their activities and run down to the water's edge. Some fishermen from the seaside town of Nazaré, Portugal, are coming home with their catch of fish.

The fishermen, most of whom wear black stocking caps, heavy shirts, and bright plaid trousers, row their wide little boat to the shore. The boat drags a net full of fish behind it in the water. When the boat hits the sand bottom, several fishermen jump out to carry the net ropes to the waiting crowd. Everyone takes hold of a rope and helps to pull the heavy net to the shore. Soon a silver pile of flapping *carapau* (mackerel) lies at their feet.

The barefoot fishwives line up to fill their baskets with fish. Then each one places her filled basket on her head and rushes up to the town to sell the *peixe fresco,* fresh fish. The fishermen divide up some of the fish to take to their homes for supper, and they send the rest to sell at the fish auction. Before they go home for the night, the fishermen spread their nets on the sand to dry, while they sit to mend any holes in the nets.

Three methods of fishing: trawling *(left)*, line fishing *(center)*, and trapping *(right)*

Though the sea was calm today, these fishermen often risk their lives in the waves of sudden storms. For hundreds of years Portuguese fishing crews have braved the waters to bring home their catch. Many families, however, have mourned for their men who have been lost at sea.

Fishing is an important Portuguese industry. The fishermen catch sardines, *carapau,* and tuna near their coasts. Small fishing fleets sail across the Atlantic to the waters off Newfoundland to catch the Portuguese favorite, cod. The Portuguese eat most of the fish that they catch, but they also can many of the sardines to export.

The Land of Portugal

The country of Portugal lies on the west coast of the Iberian Peninsula. The land is one-fourth the size of its only neighbor, Spain. The northern half of the country is mountainous while the southern half has broad plains and plateaus. Sea breezes from the Atlantic help Portugal to have mild temperatures in both summer and winter. Snow rarely falls except in the high mountains. Most of the country enjoys a mild Mediterranean climate.

Portugal's Past

Although Portugal is much like Spain in many ways, the Portuguese people have a distinct heritage of their own. They have fought to maintain their independence for over eight hundred years.

In the 1400s Prince Henry the Navigator helped Portuguese sailors learn to use charts and instruments to sail in new waters. Portuguese explorers led the way to new discoveries. Bartholomew Diaz reached the southern tip of Africa, the Cape of Good Hope, in 1488. Ten years later Vasco da Gama sailed all the way to India and back. His voyage was the beginning of many years of Portuguese trade with the East. Pedro Cabral claimed Brazil for Portugal in 1500. Today, the main language of Brazil is still Portuguese.

Government and Economy

Portugal was a monarchy until 1910. It then became a republic, but the government was weak. In 1932 the Portuguese accepted the strong leadership of a dictator, Antonio Salazar, who firmly ruled Portugal for over thirty-five years. The country has since returned to a republican form of government. However, Portugal still faces many problems.

Portugal is a poor country. It has few industries to provide income for its people. In recent years it has given independence to its African colonies. These lands had once supplied Portugal with valuable resources.

Portugal does have some resources of its own. Two are fish and cork. Cork comes from the bark of the cork oak tree. Every nine years cork harvesters carefully strip the bark in large sheets off these trees. Cork oaks grow only in a few lands of the western Mediterranean area. Portugal is the world's foremost supplier of cork.

Cities and People

Two of Portugal's most important cities are Lisbon and Oporto. Lisbon, the capital, is a major European seaport on the Atlantic coast. The city lies at the mouth of the Tagus River. Phoenician traders settled there over two thousand years ago. An earthquake and fire destroyed much of Lisbon in 1755, but the people rebuilt it into a beautiful city. The other important city, Oporto, lies at the mouth of the river Douro. It is an important center for craftsmen and businesses.

Nearly all the Portuguese people have two things in common. They speak the Portuguese language, and they are members of the Roman Catholic church. Like the people of other countries, the Portuguese need to hear God's message of salvation.

Italy

The bright sun shines down on a group of excited tourists. They are listening to their Italian guide tell them about the wonderful things they are seeing in the city of Rome. Now they stand in the awe-inspiring Colosseum.

The guide explains, "Roman emperors built this huge arena over nineteen hundred years ago. Fifty thousand people once walked up marble staircases, past marble statues, and sat on marble seats to watch events on the oval-shaped field below. Sometimes an awning was stretched over the top to shade the spectators or keep them dry during a rain. In the center gladiators fought each other to the death, or wild animals were unleashed against unarmed victims. At other times the field was flooded to provide a lake for mock sea battles."

The tourists walk around the remains of the Colosseum. Over the years the beautiful marble has been carried away for use in other buildings. The floor of the arena is missing, revealing the passageways and cages for wild animals below. Although the Colosseum is in ruins, these tourists can almost imagine the place filled with a crowd of ancient Romans cheering wildly for their favorite gladiators.

Many early Christians faced death in the Colosseum. Because these brave Christians had refused to bow down and worship the Roman emperor, they were

Left: Venice, Italy **Right:** The Roman Colosseum, inside *(top)* and outside *(bottom)*

slain by the swords of gladiators or by the claws and teeth of wild beasts. The testimony of these martyred Christians inspired many people to believe in the Lord Jesus Christ.

The tourists follow their guide back to the tour bus. They could spend all morning exploring the Colosseum, but many more spectacular sights await them in the city of Rome.

The Roman Empire

Rome's ancient heritage is one of greatness. For about five hundred years, Rome ruled an empire that extended all the way around the Mediterranean Sea. The Romans built many roads, bridges, and buildings in their empire. They developed a government and laws to keep their empire under control, and Roman soldiers guarded the borders of the empire and kept peace within the land.

It was during the early days of the Roman Empire that the Lord Jesus Christ lived on earth. Under the order of the Roman emperor, Augustus Caesar, Joseph and Mary went to Bethlehem to be taxed, and there Jesus was born. Over thirty years later Roman soldiers crucified Jesus. After His resurrection and return to heaven, the news of the gospel was carried throughout the Roman Empire. Early Christians used the roads and ships of the Empire as they spread the story of salvation. In the book of Acts we learn about the missionary journeys of Paul. On his last journey, he was taken to Rome, where he was able to preach about the Saviour.

Christian worship was strange to the Romans, who worshiped many gods. The Roman emperors began to fear that the Christians would destroy their power. Christians would not obey the emperor if it meant that they must disobey God. Soon the Roman government began to persecute faithful Christians. Christians in many parts of the Empire were put to death. In the city of Rome, crowds came to watch as Christians were thrown to the lions in the Colosseum.

The Romans, however, could not kill the testimony of the martyred Christians.

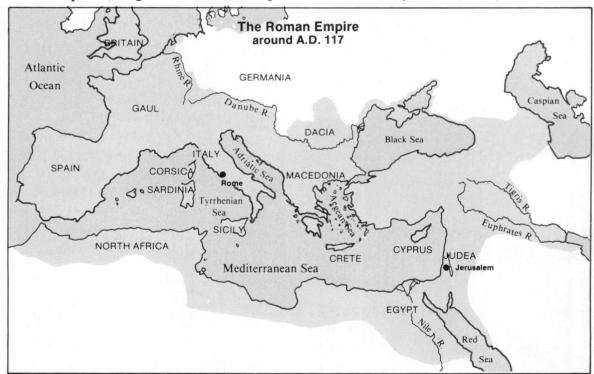

Clement of Rome

Very little is known about Clement. We are not even sure about the years of his birth and death. We do know that he lived in Rome at the end of the first century. He also was one of the leaders of the congregation of Christians that was growing in that city. He probably knew the Apostle Paul, and he may have known Peter as well.

What we do know about Clement comes to us because of a letter he wrote. You know that the Bible contains two letters that Paul wrote to the church at Corinth—I and II Corinthians. Later, after Paul's death and about one hundred years after the birth of Christ, Clement also wrote to that same church. Clement's letter was copied, and a few manuscripts have survived.

Clement's letter gave encouragement and instruction to the Corinthian Christians. Though not inspired Scripture, the letter is one of the oldest and best writings of the early Christians. The letter displays its author's love for and knowledge of the Word of God. It also shows his genuine concern that fellow-Christians maintain a godly testimony.

Clement's knowledge of the Word of God allowed him to quote Scripture that would help the Corinthians. We should carefully study the Bible so that we can use it not only for instruction in our own lives, but also for encouraging and helping others.

Despite the persecution, more and more people accepted Christ as their Saviour. Finally, in the year 313, the emperor Constantine made Christianity legal. Persecution stopped. Soon many people were accepting Christianity because it was the thing to do. Some truly repented of their sins and asked Christ to be their Saviour. Others merely acted like Christians so that they would fit in.

The power of the Roman government decreased. Barbarian tribes from northern Europe began to attack the Empire. In the year 476, one of these groups of invaders was able to take control of the city of Rome. Rome's empire was gone, and for nearly fourteen hundred years, the Italian peninsula was not united under a government of its own. Finally, in 1871 Italy became a united nation with its capital at Rome.

Modern History and Economy

The young country of Italy had many problems. There was little industry, and the people were poor. In 1922, a man named Benito Mussolini gained control of the government. He strengthened Italy so that he could conquer more lands. He joined Hitler in fighting against the Allies in World War II. Italy and Germany were both defeated. Afterwards, Italy faced the big job of rebuilding its country and government.

In the years since World War II, Italy has made much progress. The automobile, machinery, and textile industries have grown in the busy cities of northern Italy. Farming methods have improved so that Italians produce most of their own food. Tourists from all over the world come to Italy to enjoy the wonders of ancient Rome, the art and culture of Italy, and the warm Mediterranean climate.

The Leaning Tower of Pisa

Geography

The geography of northern Italy has helped that half of the country to prosper. The Alps form Italy's borders with France, Switzerland, and Austria. Even along the short border with Yugoslavia, the terrain is rugged. The mountains in the north provide swift streams that produce electricity for the cities in the north. The mountains also act as a barrier to keep out some of the cold winter winds from northern Europe.

South of the Alps lies the broad Po River valley. This is the most fertile farming region of Italy. The busy city of Milan and most of the industrial areas of the country are in this river valley. Between the Po and the city of Rome lies an area rich in beauty and historical interest.

From about the year 1300 until 1600, many great artists and writers lived and worked in Rome and northern Italy. This time period of history is called the **Renaissance,** meaning "rebirth." It was a time when art and learning made great advances after years of slow progress in the Middle Ages. In Italy wealthy men paid artists to design and decorate beautiful buildings. Some men became famous for their wonderful paintings and sculptures that adorned palaces and churches. Italy's cities display many of these Renaissance treasures.

South of Rome and on the large islands of Sardinia and Sicily, Italy is less prosperous. The **Apennine Mountains,** which extend from northern Italy

Venice

Venice is an unusual city. Unlike most cities, Venice is built on many low islands in a swampy lagoon. In Venice you do not ride in cars or busses over paved streets. To travel there you ride in motorboats or in gondolas (long black boats) through the many water passageways of the city. Gondoliers wearing blue and white shirts and flat black hats guide their gondolas through Venice's canals.

Buildings, built on piles of mud and supported by debris, logs, and rocks, line the islands of Venice. The waters

of the Adriatic Sea wash against the foundations of many buildings that were built during the Renaissance. Saint Mark's Cathedral and the Doges' Palace are two of the most famous and beautiful buildings of the city.

Every year thousands of tourists come to view Venice and ride in a gondola on the Grand Canal, the main waterway through the city. At the Grand Canal Market, merchants and shoppers bargain for precious lace and other crafts. Sidewalk cafes are filled with laughter and music. Children feed the ever-present pigeons that fly around and perch on buildings, statues, and sidewalks. Venice is an exciting city unlike any other in the world.

throughout the length of the country, cover practically all southern Italy. Sardinia and Sicily are very mountainous as well. Although the soil is very poor in these mountain regions, farming is the main activity. There are few industries and few large cities. Thus, most of the people of southern Italy live under poorer conditions than the people in the north. The different needs in the two parts of Italy present many problems for Italy's young parliamentary government.

Growth of Roman Catholicism

The church that grew in Rome after the fall of the Roman Empire became a very important influence. The attacks of invaders caused the people to look to their religion for refuge. The people trusted the church leaders to help them find safety and salvation. The church leaders, especially the bishop of Rome, began to use their influence to make themselves wealthy and powerful. Traditions that

Vatican City

Area: 0.17 sq. mi.   Population: 728

The pope is the leader of the Roman Catholic church. He lives in Vatican City. Vatican City is actually a tiny country inside the city of Rome. Its area is only one-sixth of a square mile; it is the smallest country in the world. The pope rules Vatican City, and from there he leads all the members of the Roman Catholic church around the world.

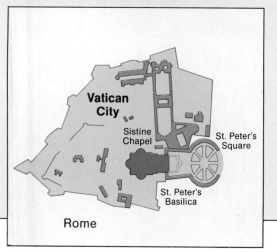

San Marino

Area: 23.4 sq. mi.   Population: 21,000

Nearly seventeen hundred years ago, Marinus and his small band of followers climbed silently and slowly up the steep side of Mount Titano. They were weary from dodging the persecutions of the Roman emperor Diocletian. They hoped that here, secluded and secret, they would at last be free to worship the true God of heaven.

A stonecutter by profession, Marinus set to work fortifying the crude settlement atop the craggy slope of the mountain. Searching for the best possible protection, he decided to build stone walls around Mount Titano. Soon stone buildings and castles filled the secured refuge.

Diocletian discovered the hideaway, but was unable to capture the determined believers in their new stronghold. The settlement grew and prospered, for Marinus was a faithful and fair leader in this young republic. After the death of Marinus, the people honored him as a saint and a hero. They renamed the country after him, San Marino.

Today, thousands of tourists visit Europe's smallest republic each year. Collectors eagerly purchase the unique postage stamps printed in San Marino. Although closely tied to surrounding Italy, the people of San Marino are proud of their independence and traditions.

developed became more important than the teaching of Scripture. Soon, many of the people of Europe were following the false teachings of the church in Rome. They looked to its bishop, the pope, as the supreme authority for their religion.

Today, over 580 million people all around the world look to the Roman Catholic church for salvation. These people believe that by being members of the church and by doing the traditional good works that the church teaches them to do, they will be able to go to heaven.

that Christ rose from the dead, they do not know that His death on the cross paid all the penalty for their sin. They are a very religious people, but they are lost.

The Land of Greece

Like Italy, Spain, and Portugal, Greece is located on a peninsula. The name of the peninsula on which Greece is located is the **Balkan Peninsula.** The map below shows that the Balkan Peninsula is surrounded on three sides by water: the

Adriatic Sea on the west, the Mediterranean on the south, and the Aegean and Black seas on the east. Greece is the land on the southern edge of this peninsula, and the country also includes about three thousand islands in the seas nearby.

Greece is a rocky, mountainous country. Although it has a pleasant Mediterranean climate, only small areas of land are suitable for farming. Still, farming is one of the main activities of the Greeks. They grow fruits and vegetables, wheat, and tobacco on their small plots of ground. Most Greek farmers are poor because they do not have the land or the machinery to produce large crops.

Greece is a country surrounded by water. For thousands of years the Greeks have been fishermen and sea traders. Today, the shipping industry is one of Greece's most profitable businesses. Thousands of Greek ships sail the waters of the Mediterranean and around the world carrying out their business.

Greek Democracy

Greece is a country famous for its ancient heritage. Several hundred years before Christ was born, the people of

The mountainous landscape of Greece

Greece developed a great culture. Some Greeks discovered new ideas in math, science, and medicine, while others became great artists and writers.

Wise leaders helped the Greeks to form a new type of government. Instead of having kings rule all the affairs of the people, the Greeks learned to govern themselves. The citizens met at certain times to elect their leaders and to vote on how matters should be handled. This kind of government by the people is called a **democracy.** The ancient Greek democracy did not last because of wars and the conquest of Greece by the Roman Empire. Yet we remember that Greece first used the democratic form of government.

Athens

Athens is the capital and largest city of Greece. It is a modern city with many broad streets and new buildings, but it also has some reminders of the glorious days of ancient Greece. In the center of the city is a hill called the **Acropolis** (*acro* means "high"; *polis* means "city"). The city was first built on top of the Acropolis. Later the city grew around the foot of the hill, and the Acropolis became a place for worship. The people built beautiful temples on top of the Acropolis. The most famous temple is the **Parthenon.** The remains of the Parthenon still stand on the Acropolis above the city of Athens. Many tourists come to Athens to see the Parthenon and visit the many museums filled with sculptures and other articles made by the ancient Greeks.

The Greek Alphabet

Many of the European people we have studied so far speak languages other than English. We have read of lands where French, Dutch, German, Spanish, Portuguese, Italian, and other languages are spoken. Unlike English and these other foreign languages, the Greek language uses a different alphabet. There are twenty-four letters in the Greek alphabet, and many of them are similar to our letters. In fact, our word *alphabet* comes from the first two Greek letters—alpha and beta.

A α   B β   Γ γ   Δ δ   E ε
Z ζ   H η   Θ θ   I ι   K κ
Λ λ   M μ   N ν   Ξ ξ   O o
Π π   P ρ   Σ σ ς   T τ   Υ υ
Φ φ   X χ   Ψ ψ   Ω ω

Greek Mythology

Before the time of Christ, the Greeks worshiped many gods and goddesses. (The worship of many gods is called polytheism.) They worshiped a god of the sun, a god of the sea, a goddess of wisdom, and many more. The people made up **myths** or stories about their gods. The people also made statues and built temples to honor these gods.

In the book of Acts we read that the Apostle Paul visited the city of Athens (Acts 17:15-34). He found the people worshiping their many gods. They had even built an altar to "the unknown god" just in case they had left out a god. Paul told them about the one God they needed to know and about His Son, Jesus Christ, who had died and risen again for them.

Land and Sea

Another Greek city that Paul visited was Corinth. The water of the Gulf of

Malta

Area: 122 sq. mi.   Population: 343,970

Sea-drenched sailors drifted in the tossing waves near the rocky shore. Some swam, and others grabbed pieces of their broken ship while anxious survivors watched from the shore. Numbering themselves, they found that every sailor, soldier, prisoner, and passenger had been saved from the Mediterranean storm, just as the prisoner Paul had assured them.

Hours later, the exhausted group huddled around campfires on the cool beach of the island of Melita. As the fires burned low, Paul began to gather more firewood. Suddenly a poisonous snake hidden in the sticks bit Paul's hand. Unable to help, the islanders watched Paul, expecting him to die within minutes. Instead, Paul shook the snake off into the fire and continued working. The astounded natives and the ship's passengers knew that Paul's God had protected him from both the raging storm and the poisonous snake.

Hearing of the miraculous incident, Publius, the ruler of the island, invited Paul and his escort to stay at his home.

While there, Paul discovered that Publius' father was very sick and close to death. Paul called out to God, and the ruler's father was healed.

The Bible tells us in Acts 27 and 28 of these adventures of the Apostle Paul on the island of Melita. Today that same island is called Malta. Located sixty miles south of Sicily, Malta served as a strategic British naval base during the world wars. In 1974 Malta became a self-governing republic.

Corinth nearby nearly cuts mainland Greece into two parts. A narrow strip of land near the city of Corinth is all that held the land in one piece. Today, however, a four-mile-long canal, the Corinth Canal, cuts off the southern part of Greece. This area, called the Peloponnesus, is now an island connected to the rest of Greece only by bridges. The Corinth Canal helps Greek ships sail swiftly from one side of Greece to the other.

Most of Greece's three thousand islands are tiny and uninhabited, but several hundred of them have beautiful little fishing villages. Crete, south of Greece in the Mediterranean, is the largest of the Greek islands. Crete is a mountainous island with a mild climate. Olives, grapes, and citrus fruits grow well in Crete.

Section Review

1. On what peninsula does Greece lie?

2. What is the Greek name for the high hill in the city of Athens?

3. What famous temple is found in Athens?

4. What are stories about Greek gods called?

5. What is the largest Greek island?

Terms to Remember

Mediterranean Sea
Strait of Gibraltar
Iberian Peninsula
plateau
dictator
Renaissance
Apennine Mountains
icons
Balkan Peninsula
democracy
Acropolis
Parthenon
myths

Things to Know

1. What strait lies at the western end of the Mediterranean Sea?

2. What two countries are located on the Iberian Peninsula?

3. What is the name given to a person, such as Franco, Salazar, or Mussolini, who takes over a country and rules by force?

4. What mountain range extends along the Italian Peninsula?

5. What country is located within the city of Rome?

6. What are Greek stories about gods and goddesses called?

7. What is the main religion of Greece today?

8. What is a government in which the people rule themselves called?

9. On what peninsula is Greece located?

Things to Talk About

1. How did the Mediterranean Sea get its name?

2. Describe a Mediterranean climate.

3. What is a dictator?

4. Why is northern Italy more prosperous than southern Italy?

5. What is a democracy?

Things to Do

1. Using a Bible with maps in it or a Bible atlas, find the cities of Greece that the Apostle Paul visited. (Also see Acts 16:11-12; 17:1, 10, 15; 18:1, 18; 21:1-2—Rhodes is a Greek island.)

2. Alpha and omega are letters of the Greek alphabet. Use a dictionary to find their significance and then read Revelation 22:13. What does the Lord's statement, "I am Alpha and Omega" mean?

3. Some of the English words we use are formed from Greek words. For instance, *bio* comes from a Greek word meaning "life," and *graph* or *graphy* means "writing." We use the word *biography* to mean a writing about someone's life. Here are some other parts of words that come from Greek.

acro- high
poly- many
-ism belief
geo- earth
tele- far
-logy science or study
hemi- half
-phon- or *-phono-* sound
-phobe fear
micro- small
-the- or *-theo-* god
-scope seeing
mon- or *mono-* one
-archy ruling
-sphere ball

Here are some English words we might use. Can you find their meanings from the word parts above?

a. geo-logy

b. acro-phobia

c. tele-phone

d. micro-scope

e. hemi-sphere

f. poly-the-ism

g. mon-archy

What other words can you form using these words parts? What are their meanings?

Geography Skills

Look at the atlas maps and the map on page 90 to find the answers to these questions.

1. Of the four countries, Spain, Portugal, Italy, and Greece, which has regions farthest to the north?

2. Which of these countries is the farthest east?

3. Through which of these countries does the prime meridian pass?

4. What sea lies between Greece and Turkey?

5. What mountain range lies along the northern border of Italy?

6. The Italian Peninsula is shaped somewhat like a boot. What island is the "boot" of Italy ready to "kick"?

7. What mountain range extends along the length of Italy?

8. What are the names of the three seas (parts of the Mediterranean) that surround the Italian Peninsula?

9. What group of Spanish islands lies near the Gulf of Valencia?

CHAPTER 6

SCANDINAVIA

Hetta Anders lives in the far north of Europe. Her home is in the town of Karasjok, Norway. Karasjok is nearly two hundred miles north of the Arctic Circle. Hetta enjoys the short summers in her land because the winters are long and cold.

Hetta's people are called **Lapps.** The Lapps have lived in northern Europe for many years. In the past, most Lapps made their living by herding reindeer. The Lapps ate reindeer meat and drank reindeer milk. They wore clothing made from reindeer hides and rode in sleds pulled by reindeer.

Some of the Lapps today still tend large herds of reindeer. Many other Lapps, like

	AREA (Square Miles)	POPULATION	CAPITAL	MAIN LANGUAGES	MAIN RELIGIONS	CURRENCY
NORWAY	125,181	4,131,000	Oslo	Norwegian, Lapp	Protestant	krone
SWEDEN	173,731	8,331,000	Stockholm	Swedish	Protestant	krona
DENMARK	16,629	5,115,000	Copenhagen	Danish	Protestant	krone
ICELAND	39,768	236,000	Reykjavik	Icelandic	Protestant	króna
FINLAND	130,119	4,850,000	Helsinki	Finnish, Swedish	Protestant	markka

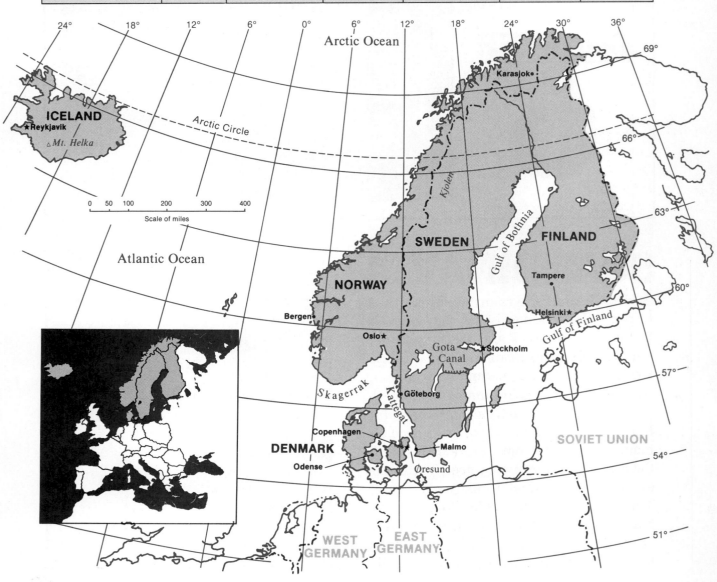

Hetta's father, live in towns and work in other businesses. Many are miners or lumbermen. Some who live on Norway's coast are fishermen. The area where the Lapp people live in northern Europe is often called Lapland. Find Lapland on the map on page 109. Lapland covers a portion of four countries. One is Norway. What are the other three?

Hetta's life would not seem too unusual to you. She lives in a comfortable house in Karasjok with her parents, her older brother, Erik, and her little sister, Inga. She goes to school, and she enjoys playing with her friends. She usually speaks the Norwegian language, but sometimes she speaks the old Lappish language with her family.

Hetta and her family often dress in traditional Lapp clothing. Their shirts and dresses are made of warm, blue cloth decorated with lots of red trim. The women and girls wear unusual bonnets while the men and boys wear unusual pointed hats. These hats are lined with soft duck feathers called eiderdown.

Last spring, Hetta's brother, Erik, was old enough to go with their Uncle Nils as the reindeer moved north to new pastures. Uncle Nils still owns and cares for a herd of reindeer. The herds must

Reindeer

move across the frozen **tundra** (northern grasslands) to find their food. They eat mosses and small plants that grow under the snow. In the fall the men herd the reindeer back to the winter pastures.

Caring for the reindeer is hard work. Erik skied through the snow for hours every day keeping the herd together. He loaded and unloaded supplies on reindeer sleds as they moved to new camps. He helped put up the shelter in which they ate and slept. It looked like an Indian teepee covered with reindeer hides. Occasionally he was allowed to drive the snowmobile. That was his favorite job.

Land of the Midnight Sun

In the land above the Arctic Circle where Hetta lives, the sun never sinks below the horizon on some days of the year. There is daylight for all twenty-four hours of the day. The sun shines in the sky even at midnight. For this reason the land of the far north is often called the "Land of the Midnight Sun."

You remember that the tilt of the earth on its axis causes us to have different seasons during the year. The tilt of the earth also causes the polar regions to have

seasons of light and darkness. During the summer months the lands near the poles have long days and short nights—and sometimes no nights at all. During the winter these lands have long nights.

If you use your classroom globe and a light, you can demonstrate how the length of days and nights varies in different parts of the world. First, point the North Pole toward the light as the earth is tilted in the summer season of the Northern Hemisphere. You notice that the light does

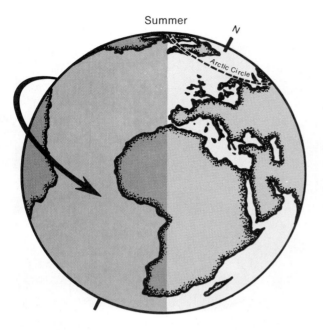

Summer

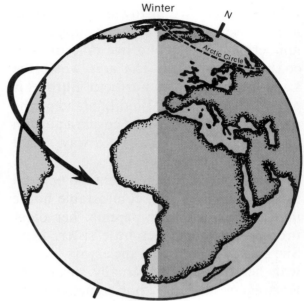

Winter

not reach all the way to the South Pole. However, the light shines beyond the North Pole. Now spin the globe around as the earth rotates on its axis every day. Watch the area near the North Pole. The light shines continuously on the northern polar region. Now watch the area near the South Pole as you spin the globe. That area remains in the shadows, and the light does not shine on it at all.

Now move the globe around the light as the earth revolves around the sun. Stop occasionally and notice where the light reaches in the polar regions. Stop when the North Pole is pointed away from the sun. Notice that the light does not reach any of the northern polar region, but it covers the southern polar region. When the earth is in this position, the North is having its dark winter while the southern polar region is having the midnight sun.

Where Hetta lives, the midnight sun begins about May 22 and ends around July 23. For those two months, Hetta's family stays busy. They do not sleep much during those days. Instead, they work and play outside and enjoy the warmth of the sun. Although the sun shines all day, it never climbs high in the sky. Those slanted rays

of sunlight do not greatly warm the air. A hot day in Lapland would be any day that the temperature climbs above 50°F.

For two months during the winter, the sun never shines on Hetta's home in Karasjok. Those cold, dark days are good for staying indoors to read or sew. But when she walks to school, the glow of the Northern Lights in the sky and the whiteness of the snow-covered ground make it easy for her to find her way. Hetta does not mind the long, dark winters in Lapland. She enjoys the extra sleep she gets during those long nights.

Norway, where Hetta lives, is one of the **Scandinavian** (SKAN duh NAY vee un) countries. Norway and Sweden lie on the Scandinavian Peninsula. To the south of these two countries lies the small country of Denmark. Norway, Sweden, and Denmark all have a similar history, language, and culture. Denmark, therefore, is usually considered a Scandinavian country along with the other two. Finland and Iceland are also sometimes grouped with the Scandinavian countries because of their similar heritage. In this chapter we will learn about these five countries of northern Europe.

Norway

Land of Fjords

Norway is a long and narrow country on the west coast of the Scandinavian Peninsula. Its long coastline along the Atlantic Ocean and the North Sea does not have many straight, sandy beaches. Instead, it has many deep, narrow bays called **fjords** (FYORDZ).

The "Troll's Tongue" overlooking a fjord

Glaciers carved the deep fjords along Norway's coast. Frozen glaciers slide slowly down the mountains toward the sea. Because large glaciers are so heavy, they can move with such a force that they scrape the earth like huge bulldozers.

Sea water fills many of the valleys that were hollowed out by the glaciers. These fjords, enclosed by steep hills and cliffs, harbor peaceful little villages at their heads.

The Vikings

About a thousand years ago, the villages of these fjords were the homes of Viking warriors. **Vikings** sailed from the Scandinavian countries in swift, long boats to raid the towns of Europe. They explored Iceland, Greenland, and a new land they called "Vinland." Today we know that Vinland was the east coast of Canada. The Vikings found America about five hundred years before Columbus.

Today's Norwegians are not Viking warriors, but they are still brave sailors and explorers. Fleets of fishing boats sail from the fjords of Norway to catch fish in the stormy waters of the North Sea and the North Atlantic Ocean. Other Norwegians sail in huge cargo ships that carry goods to all parts of the world. Within the last century, Norwegians have led explorations of both the North and the South Poles.

Climate

Norway is over one thousand miles long. The northern third of the country is above the Arctic Circle. Because the country is so far north, it would be expected to have a very cold climate. The warming effect of the Atlantic Ocean, however, keeps much of Norway's weather from being bitterly cold. You remember that the Gulf Stream, the warm water current in the Atlantic Ocean (p. 24), brings a mild climate to the British Isles. That same current flows on by the shores of Norway. The warm current keeps the water in the ports from freezing during the winter. Ships can sail into Norwegian ports all year long, even most of the ports north of the Arctic Circle.

Norway is a country of rugged hills and mountains. The mountains are beautiful, but they block the warm sea air from reaching the inland parts of Norway. For that reason, the winters in the interior parts of the country are much colder than they are along the coast. Most of the people of Norway live where the climate is warmer. Few people besides the Lapps enjoy living in the colder parts of the country.

Travel and Sport

The deep fjords, the rugged mountains, and the cold weather make land travel difficult in Norway. Roads and railroads must be built over or around the fjords and mountains. Ice and snow often block passages on these land routes. Travel by boat or airplane is usually much faster and cheaper.

Much snow falls in the mountains of Norway. Although the snow makes normal travel difficult, the Norwegians enjoy skiing down the mountain slopes. Even the small children learn to ski. Ski jumping is a favorite competition for the skillful Norwegian skiers.

The Oslo City Hall, Norway

The Cities

Oslo, the capital and largest city, is located at the head of a large fjord in southern Norway. Hills surround this busy harbor city. Workmen build large ships at the docks, while nearby factories and businesses bustle with activity. A large portion of Norway's people live in or near Oslo.

The large fishing port of Bergen lies on the west coast. Norwegian fishermen from near and far bring their catch to sell in Bergen. They also buy many of their fishing supplies from the city shops. Fish canning factories pack the fish for export to many parts of the world.

Government and Religion

Norway has been an independent country since 1905. Before that time, it was ruled first by Denmark and then by Sweden. Today, Norway is a constitutional monarchy ruled by its own king and its parliament called the *Storting*.

Nearly all the people of Norway belong to the Lutheran church. Lutheranism is the dominant religion in all the Scandinavian countries. Most of the people of these lands believe that their church membership will be enough to please God. They do not realize that they must personally trust Jesus Christ, who paid the penalty for their sins.

Sweden

To the east of Norway lies the country of Sweden, the largest of the Scandinavian countries. Like Norway, Sweden is a long, narrow country. It reaches beyond the Arctic Circle in the north, and its southern tip stretches to within sixty miles of East Germany. The **Baltic Sea** and the **Gulf of Bothnia** form Sweden's eastern border. A small arm of the North Sea called the Kattegatt (KAT ih GAT) separates Sweden from Denmark on the southwest. At the narrow strait of Øresund (UR uh SOOND), the southwestern part of Sweden nearly touches Denmark's islands.

Northern Sweden

Evergreen forests cover most of the northern part of Sweden. Some of the Lapps in the far North who no longer herd reindeer work in the lumber industry. Sweden produces much lumber and many wood products.

Although most Swedes live in the southern part of the country, a few others besides the Lapps brave the cold winters of the North. Working in the industries there can bring good profits. Along with the wealth of the forests, northern Sweden

Scene from Stockholm, Sweden

holds rich iron ore deposits. Most of the ore that is mined travels by railroad over the mountains and through Norway to the sea. Ships wait in Norwegian ports to transport the ore to steel mills all over Europe.

Another treasure of northern Sweden is its swift mountain streams. As the mountain snows melt, the water flows southeast toward the Gulf of Bothnia. The Swedes have built many large hydroelectric plants that use the water power

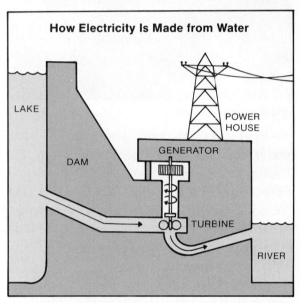
How Electricity Is Made from Water

to produce electricity. Power lines carry this electricity to furnish heat and light for homes all over Sweden. Their factories and trains also use electricity instead of power from other fuels. Sweden's neighbor, Norway, uses a great deal of hydroelectric power produced by its own mountain streams.

Southern Sweden

The population of the whole country of Sweden is about the same as that of New York City. Most of the people live in the lowlands and hills of southern Sweden. Most of Sweden's farmland lies in that southern area. Swedish farmers use the small portions of fertile land available to grow practically all the food the country needs. They grow many kinds of grain and lots of potatoes, a crop that grows well in cool countries.

Sweden's large cities lie in the southern region, where the climate is milder. Stockholm (STAHK HOLM), the capital and largest city of Sweden, spreads over

Stockholm, Sweden

several islands and the banks of a waterway between Lake Malaren and the Baltic Sea. For this reason, the city is sometimes called the "Venice of the North." Instead of Italian gondolas, however, ferryboats and bridges help to transport goods, vehicles, and people to all parts of the city.

Stockholm has many beautiful old and new buildings and lovely parks. The king of Sweden lives in the Royal Palace, a favorite site for tourists to visit.

Businesses thrive in Stockholm. Banks, stores, and offices carry on brisk activity. Factories produce metal and wood products, machines, automobiles, and food products. Stockholm is also a busy port city. But unlike the western ports of Scandinavia, eastern ports in the Baltic Sea freeze over during the winter. For a couple of months, the ships at Stockholm's docks are unable to move out of port without the help of an icebreaker ship.

On Sweden's west coast, the large port city of Göteborg (YUR tuh BORE ee) remains ice-free. Göteborg carries on a heavy sea trade all year long. It is also Sweden's main fishing port. The Göta Canal provides a water passageway from Göteborg through southern Sweden.

Malmo lies at the southern tip of Sweden. Its nearness to Denmark and Germany makes the city a transportation center. From Malmo, goods from nearby European countries pass quickly into Sweden.

The Swedes

Many Swedes and other Scandinavians have blond hair, blue eyes, and fair skin. The languages spoken in Sweden, Norway, and Denmark are so similar that their peoples can usually understand each other. Scandinavians are often called Nordic peoples. *Nordic* means "northern," and you can see from a look at their countries on a globe that these people are indeed from the North.

In the later 1800s thousands of Swedes and Norwegians went to the United States. Most of them moved to the farms and forests of the north-central states, especially to Illinois, Wisconsin, Minnesota, North Dakota, and South Dakota. These Scandinavians helped to settle the American frontier. Some of their blond-haired descendants still live on those northern farms. A few of them even speak a bit of the Scandinavian language of their forefathers.

What Do You Call Them?

A person from Germany is called a German. Someone from Sweden is a Swede. But a fellow from Ireland is an Irishman, and one from Spain is a Spaniard. Do you know what to call a person from these lands?

Switzerland	Japan
Finland	Denmark
Greece	Egypt
Hungary	India
Turkey	Italy
Poland	France

Gustavus Adolphus

Gustavus Adolphus was one of the greatest kings of Swedish history. He became king in 1594 when he was only seventeen, and he reigned until 1632. He was well-educated, brave, and hard-working. More importantly, he was a Christian king who cared about the spiritual welfare of his people.

Gustavus lived about a hundred years after the time of Martin Luther. The preaching of the Protestant Reformation had brought the light of the gospel to much of northern Europe, including Gustavus's land of Sweden. He was determined to keep that light shining.

In the early 1600s, Roman Catholic rulers of Europe sought to reconquer northern Europe for their religion. Protestant rulers fought to protect their lands from these attacks, but they lacked the necessary military strength.

When Gustavus saw that northern Europe was in danger of being cut off from the gospel and controlled by the Roman Catholic church, he took quick action. He gathered his well-trained but small Swedish army and sailed for Germany. After recruiting more Protestant soldiers, he faced still larger enemy armies. Yet he won victory after victory.

Gustavus was always concerned that he and his men were justly fighting for freedom and the truth. He spent much time reading the Bible and praying, both alone and with his men. He made sure that his men behaved honorably both on and off the battlefield. He knew that each battle was the Lord's and that they must follow His commands.

When Gustavus died in battle, his men began to lose courage, thinking their cause was lost. The singing of an old hymn, however, reminded them that God was their strength. They re-entered the battle and defeated the Roman Catholic army.

The religious wars in northern Europe continued for several years. When they ended, many areas remained free to accept the truth of God's Word. Gustavus Adolphus's faith and courage had helped to keep the light of the gospel shining in northern Europe.

Section Review

1. What animal is very important to the Lapps?

2. What two countries lie on the Scandinavian Peninsula?

3. What is the capital of Norway?

4. Who were the Scandinavian sailors who discovered America?

5. Name three resources God has given to northern Sweden.

6. Why is *Nordic* a good word to describe the people and lands of Scandinavia?

Denmark

The Land of Denmark

To the north of Germany and below the Scandinavian Peninsula lies the small country of Denmark. The total area of Denmark is about half that of the state of Maine. Its area is composed of islands in the North and Baltic Seas and the **Jutland Peninsula** that extends northward from West Germany.

Unlike Norway and Sweden, Denmark is a flat country. The highest hill in Denmark is only 568 feet above sea level. Also unlike its neighbors to the north, Denmark has an abundance of farmland. Mountains, forests, and frozen tundra cover large areas of Norway and Sweden, but few trees grow on Denmark's wide, level ground. This leaves plenty of room for pastures and fields.

Because Denmark is a small, flat country, its climate is nearly the same in every region. There are no cold, mountainous areas. The air from over the North Sea generally brings mild temperatures to all parts of the country.

Copenhagen

About one-fourth of Denmark's people live in or around the city of Copenhagen (KOH pun HAY gun). Nearly half of Denmark's industry is located in the Copenhagen area as well. Copenhagen lies on Denmark's largest island, Zealand.

Copenhagen is not only a large industrial city, but also an important center of governmental and cultural activity. It is a city of charm and beauty. Tall, gabled houses line the narrow, old streets of Copenhagen, while new concrete and glass buildings sit beside the modern, wide boulevards. Rows of delightful shops selling all kinds of merchandise tempt shoppers and tourists.

One of the most exciting spots in Copenhagen is the Tivoli Gardens. Tivoli is an amusement park holding a wealth of entertainment. Visitors find everything from carnival rides to musical concerts. Parades, circus acts, and fireworks provide additional excitement. Refreshment stands and fine restaurants offer plenty of food for those who are hungry. Tivoli was built in 1843, and it is still a major attraction in Copenhagen.

Sitting on a rock in Copenhagen harbor, a statue of the Little Mermaid watches the ships sail by. Hans Christian Andersen wrote a fairy tale about this imaginary creature that longed to be human. Perhaps you have read some of Andersen's fairy tales. He was born in

Copenhagen, Denmark

Denmark's third largest city, Odense. The stories he wrote over one hundred years ago still delight people of all ages.

Food and Farms

One of the favorite foods of Danes (people from Denmark) is an open-faced sandwich called smørrebrød (SMUR uh BRER), meaning "smeared bread." To make smorrebrod, you spread butter on one thin slice of bread. Then you pile on some kind of meat. The Danes use pork, beef, shrimp, sardines, smoked eel, and many other tasty toppings.

Although Copenhagen and the other cities of Denmark bustle with activity, small villages and farms cover most of the land. While traveling through the countryside of Jutland, you might occasionally see old farm buildings with thatched roofs. The pastures are full of dairy cattle and the barnlots are filled with hogs and chickens. Northern Europe enjoys Denmark's fresh milk and butter as well as its bacon and eggs.

Transportation

Because Jutland and the islands of Denmark are separated by the sea, travel between the areas of the country could be difficult. Danish ferryboats, however, usually make trips from place to place very easy. Ferryboats carry passengers, cars and trucks, and even trains from one port to another in Denmark. They also travel to and from Sweden, Norway, East and West Germany, and several other European countries. You can travel from Denmark to Sweden without leaving your car or train compartment.

Greenland

Denmark is a small country, but a very large island belongs to Denmark. Thirteen hundred miles away from Denmark in the North Atlantic Ocean lies the largest island in the world, Greenland. Greenland is over fifty times larger than Denmark, yet it has only one per cent of the number of people Denmark has.

Over two thirds of Greenland lies above the Arctic Circle. An ice cap about a mile deep in some places covers nearly all the island. Only small areas around the coast are not covered by the thick ice.

Practically all the people of Greenland live in towns along the southwest coast. The climate there is cold but not nearly as harsh as in the other parts of the island. (In central Greenland on the ice cap, winter temperatures average -25°F.)

Eskimos were living in Greenland when early Viking settlers from Iceland arrived

The Population of Greenland and Denmark

people per sq. mile

uninhabited

1 or 2

60-124

125-250

on the island. A Viking named Eric the Red settled in Greenland in 985. About fifteen years later his son, Leif Ericson, sailed to the southwest to find the shores of Vinland. The Greenlanders, however, did not have the boats and people needed in order to settle Vinland. Soon that new land was forgotten, and the Viking settlements on Greenland also failed for lack of supplies.

The people of Greenland today are the descendents of the Eskimos and of later Danish settlers who moved to the land. Fishing is their main occupation, but some of them still hunt seals, foxes, and polar bears as the Eskimos did in the past.

Iceland

To the east of Greenland and just below the Arctic Circle lies the island country of Iceland. From its name one would think that it must be a frozen wasteland much like the ice-capped Greenland. On the contrary, Iceland stays about as warm in the winter as our New England states do. The waters of the Gulf Stream flow around Iceland, keeping the winter temperatures mild despite its northern location. The summers remain cool with temperatures generally in the 50s.

Icelanders

Vikings settled Iceland in the 800s. Today most Icelanders are the descendants of those early adventurers. They speak the Icelandic language, which is almost identical to the language of the Vikings.

Most Icelanders live in the cities and towns around the coast. There they find jobs in Iceland's main industries, fishing and fish processing. Sheep and dairy cattle graze in scattered pastures, but most of Iceland's interior is covered with volcanic mountains. The soil is poor, and glaciers cover some areas. The rugged mountain landscape and beautiful waterfalls along swift-moving streams provide some spectacular scenery.·

Volcanoes and Hot Springs

Iceland has several active volcanoes, including Mount Hekla. Because of its

Scenic Iceland

Hot springs

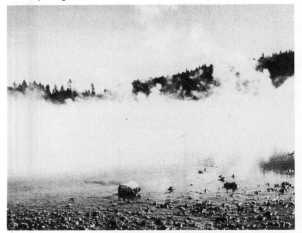

fiery eruptions, Scandinavians once thought that Mount Hekla was the door to hell. Iceland also has many hot springs. Streams of steamy water shoot up into the air from some of the springs. We take our English word *geyser* from Iceland's most impressive shooting spring, the Great Geysir.

Iceland makes use of its hot springs. The hot water is piped to many towns. Most of the homes and buildings in Reykjavik (RAY kyuh VEEK), the capital and largest city, are heated by the spring water. The hot water even fills an outdoor swimming pool in Reykjavik. There Icelanders swim year-round despite the winter temperatures. Few fruits and vegetables can be grown outdoors during Iceland's short, cool growing season. Water-heated greenhouses, however, can grow plenty of such foods for the islanders. Even tropical fruits such as bananas grow with the help of the spring water's heat.

Finland

The last of the five Scandinavian countries is Finland. Finland lies at the northeast end of the Baltic Sea. The shores of the Gulf of Bothnia and the Gulf of Finland bound the country on two sides. Sweden and Norway share borders with Finland in the northern region, and a long border in the east separates the Finns from the Soviet Union.

Though farther away from the Atlantic Ocean than the other Scandinavian countries, Finland still receives some warmth from the waters. The air is not warmed enough, however, to keep the ports of Finland from freezing over during the winter. Because of that problem, Finland builds great icebreakers. These ships plow through the ice, allowing other ships to pass through the frozen seas.

Land of Lakes and Forests

Finland's only mountains are in the far northwest corner. The rest of the country abounds in wooded hills and peaceful lakes. The glaciers that carved the fjords of Norway also formed most of the lakes in Finland and on the Scandinavian Peninsula. Huge glaciers carved out valleys in these lands. When the glaciers melted, water filled in the low areas, leaving thousands of shimmering lakes.

The thick forests of Finland are the country's greatest resource. Logs cut in the forests are floated down the streams and across the lakes to sawmills and paper mills. The sawmills saw the wood into lumber for buildings. The paper mills use wood pulp to make paper.

A lovely Finnish lake

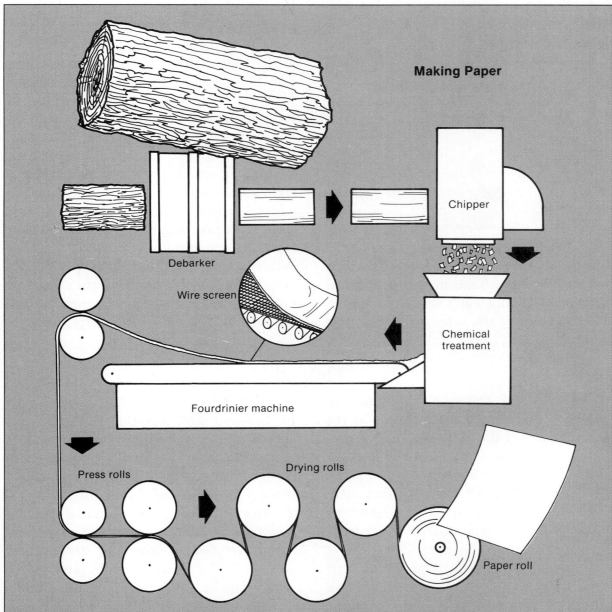

Making Paper

Debarker

Chipper

Wire screen

Chemical treatment

Fourdrinier machine

Press rolls

Drying rolls

Paper roll

Papermaking began in China nearly two thousand years ago. The fact that paper could be made from trees was not discovered, however, until 1851. Before that time most paper was made from cloth. Now most of the paper we use is made from wood pulp.

Several processes have been found to make pulp, a solution of water and wood fibers. Some is made by grinding the wood into small particles. Most is made by cutting the wood into small chips and cooking them in chemicals until they soften into fibers.

The wood pulp then enters a large machine in which a thin layer of pulp settles on a wire screen. The wire screen lifts the pulp layer out of the water. Many rollers dry and press the wet sheet of pulp into a sheet of paper. At the end of the machine the paper is wound onto large rolls that are sometimes thirty feet wide. The huge rolls are then taken to a cutting machine, and the paper is cut into the desired size. These rolls are made into the smaller paper products we use every day.

Capital and Government

As with Norway and Sweden, most of the population lives in the southern part of the country where the weather is milder. The capital city of Finland, Helsinki (HEL SING kee), lies on the southern coast. This modern industrial and cultural center looks much like the other Scandinavian capitals.

Finland has been an independent country only since 1917. Russia controlled Finland for a hundred years. Before that it had belonged to Sweden. Now Finland has a government of its own with leaders elected by its people. Because of its position by the Communist Soviet Union, Finland must carefully guard its independence.

Section Review

1. What very large island belongs to Denmark?

2. What peninsula is a part of Denmark?

3. What people settled Iceland?

4. What is Finland's most valuable resource?

5. What country lies to the east of Finland?

Terms to Remember

Lapps	Vikings
tundra	Baltic Sea
Scandinavia	Gulf of Bothnia
fjords	Jutland Peninsula
glaciers	

Things to Know

1. Who are the people who live in extreme northern Scandinavia?

2. What are the areas in the North called wherein the climate is very cold and only small plants will grow?

3. What is the name for a deep, narrow bay that was carved by a glacier?

4. What sea touches Denmark, Sweden, and Finland?

5. To what country does Greenland belong?

6. Who were the sailors and fighters who lived in Scandinavia about one thousand years ago?

7. The Soviet Union touches which Scandinavian country?

Things to Talk About

1. Why do the polar regions of the earth have seasons of light and seasons of darkness?

2. Why is the climate along Norway's coast much milder than the climates of other lands at that latitude?

3. In what ways is Denmark like or unlike Norway and Sweden?

4. Why is Copenhagen an important city?

5. Why must Finland be careful to defend its freedom?

Things to Do

1. Read about the explorations of Roald Amundsen or Fridtjof Nansen, and give a report to your class.

2. Get a book of Hans Christian Andersen's fairy tales, and make a poster that describes a scene from one of the stories. Find out if your classmates can guess the name of the fairy tale that you chose.

3. Try a Scandinavian meal of smørrebrød.

Geography Skills

Use the world map in your atlas, the map on page 110, and a globe to help you answer the following questions.

1. What Scandinavian capital city is found at 18° East longitude?

2. Which two capital cities in Scandinavia lie at about the same latitude?

3. Is Iceland nearer to Texas or to Alaska? (Use a globe for this question.)

4. What gulf lies south of Finland?

5. Using the scale of miles, find the distance between Copenhagen, Denmark, and Helsinki, Finland.

6. What is the capital of Iceland?

7. If there is a scale of miles on your globe, find the distance between the northern tip of Greenland and the North Pole.

8. If a plane were flying from Juneau, Alaska, to London, England, in which Scandinavian country might it stop for fuel? (Use a globe for this question.)

CHAPTER 7

THE SOVIET UNION

The Russian Empire faced serious problems in 1917. The Russian armies were fighting against Germany in World War I. The soldiers lacked food and supplies, and many were left dead or wounded after enemy attacks. The people in Russian cities also lacked food. Many were starving to death. The **peasants** (poor farmers) of the Russian countryside were unhappy. They could not raise enough food on their small plots of land to feed everyone. The government tried to take away what food they raised to feed others, leaving the peasants without enough food to feed themselves and their families.

Everyone in Russia had problems, and they blamed their ruler, Nicholas II.

Nicholas II was the last **czar** of Russia. (Czar [ZAR] is the Russian word for

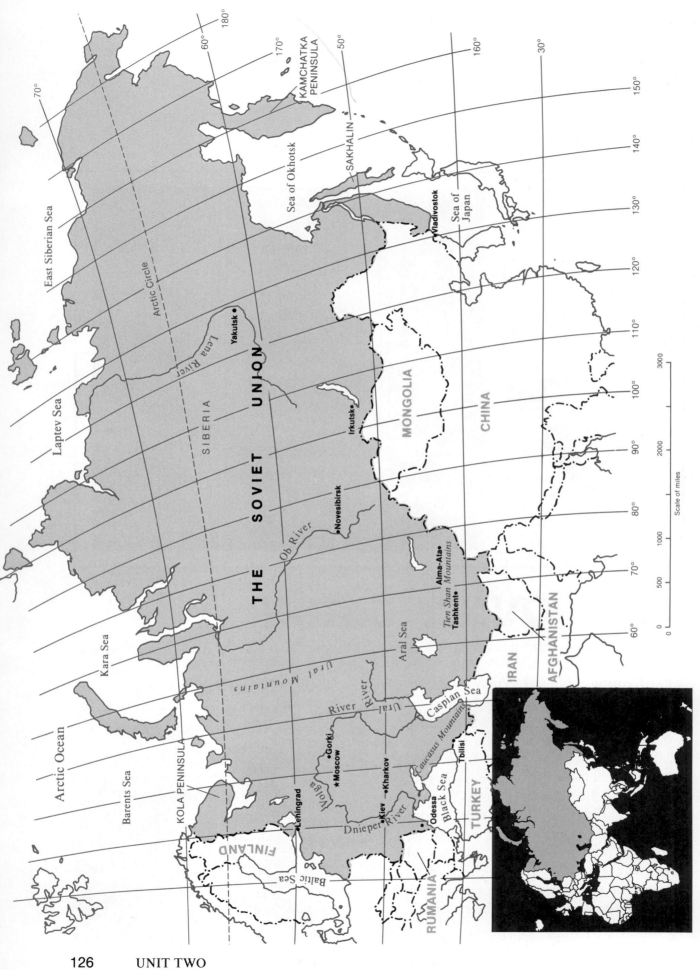

THE SOVIET UNION

SIBERIA

East Siberian Sea

Laptev Sea

Arctic Circle

Lena River

Yakutsk

KAMCHATKA PENINSULA

Sea of Okhotsk

SAKHALIN

Vladivostok

Sea of Japan

Kara Sea

Arctic Ocean

Barents Sea

KOLA PENINSULA

Irkutsk

MONGOLIA

CHINA

Ob River

Novesibirsk

Ural Mountains

Aral Sea

Alma-Ata

Tien Shan Mountains

Tashkent

IRAN

AFGHANISTAN

Ural River

Ural River

Caspian Sea

Caucasus Mountains

Tbilisi

TURKEY

Gorki

Moscow

Volga

Kiev

Kharkov

Leningrad

Dnieper River

Odessa

Black Sea

FINLAND

Baltic Sea

RUMANIA

Scale of miles

0   500   1000   2000   3000

"caesar" or "ruler.") For hundreds of years, powerful czars ruled Russia harshly. They built large armies, a huge empire, and beautiful palaces for themselves, while the common people faced many hardships. Wealthy landowners treated the peasants like slaves, forcing them to work long, hard hours on the land while barely providing for their needs. The czar's police kept watch over all the people to make sure that they were obeying his orders. No one could speak or write anything against the government for fear of being arrested. People who displeased the czar were often sent to live in **Siberia,** the bitterly cold northeastern part of Russia. The people had no part in their government. They could not change things by law. Change was coming, however, and in 1917 the people were ready to fight for that change.

Czar Nicholas II tried to satisfy his people. He wanted to be a good ruler, but his country faced many serious problems. During World War I, Nicholas lost control. In March of 1917, the soldiers and the people prepared to revolt. Nicholas was forced to abdicate (give up his rule). A new republican form of government replaced the rule by the czar. A constitution guaranteed basic freedoms for the people and established a legislature where the people were represented.

Although the new government was founded upon good principles, it could not solve all the country's problems instantly. The people, however, were impatient. They wanted everything to get better immediately. The soldiers wanted to stop fighting. The city-dwellers wanted food, and the peasants wanted more land for themselves.

Amid all this discontent appeared a Russian man named Nikolai Lenin. Lenin believed that man could bring about a

A public library in the western Soviet Union

Nikolai Lenin

perfect world where everyone would live peaceably and all needs would be provided. Lenin wanted to lead a revolution so that he could begin to set up this new world in Russia. He promised the people "Peace, Land, and Bread." Many followed him in hopes of gaining their desires.

In November of 1917, Lenin's revolution took place. His followers helped him gain control of the government. The country was now called the Union of Soviet Socialist Republics (U.S.S.R. or Soviet Union for short), and its new government was called a **Communist government.** Lenin quickly used his power to wipe out all opposition to this "Communist Revolution."

Today the Soviet Union is a large and powerful country. It still has a Communist government, but its people never received the peace and the possessions that they wanted. In this chapter we will find out what life is like under the Communist government in the Soviet Union.

The Land of the Soviet Union

One Country on Two Continents

The Revolution of 1917 brought the first Communist government to the largest country in the world. The Soviet Union covers nearly one-sixth of the world's land area. It is larger than the whole continent of South America. From the Baltic Sea on its western border, it stretches six thousand miles east to the shores of the Pacific Ocean. That is twice the distance from Los Angeles to New York City. The area of the United States would fit inside the Soviet Union about two and one-half times.

A large portion of the country lies north of the Arctic Circle. Many areas are farther north than the most northerly part of Alaska. The icy waters of the Arctic Ocean border the long northern coast of the Soviet Union. In the south, however, the Soviet Union's desert area near its border with Iran and Afghanistan is on the same latitude as the state of Nevada.

The Soviet Union stretches across two continents. The **Ural Mountains,** which reach from near the Arctic Ocean southward toward the **Caspian Sea,** and the **Caucasus Mountains** divide the continent of Europe from that of Asia. (Because Europe and Asia are joined together along this long border, they are

The Soviet Union has made many advances in technology and transportation.

128   UNIT TWO

A modern residential section of Moscow

sometimes called by the combined name of Eurasia.) Although three-fourths of the Soviet Union is in Asia and only one-fourth is in Europe, about three-fourths of the Soviet people live in the European part of the country. The capital and most of the large cities lie in the European section. Most of the industrial and commercial activity takes place there as well. Also, the culture of most Soviet

people is more European than it is Asian. For these reasons, the Soviet Union is usually considered a European country rather than an Asian country.

Why do most of the people live in the European portion of the Soviet Union? The major reasons lie in the different climates and topography of the regions.

Climate

Because the Soviet Union covers such a vast area, it contains many regions with many different climates. Even within the European section, a wide variety of climates can be found. The western area near the Baltic Sea has a cool but mild climate. Although it is far away from the equator, this region receives just enough sea breeze to keep its winters from becoming too severe. The Baltic air also keeps the summers cool and pleasant.

The southern area near the **Black Sea** enjoys a warm, mild climate almost like

Largest Countries in the World	
Country	Area (sq. miles)
Soviet Union	8,649,490
Canada	3,851,809
China (People's Republic)	3,691,000
United States	3,615,123
Brazil	3,286,470
Australia	2,967,909
India	1,269,339
Argentina	1,068,296
Sudan	967,494
Algeria	919,591

Apartment houses in the Soviet Union

that of the Mediterranean countries you learned about in Chapter Five. Most of the European section, however, finds little help to moderate its temperatures. In the long winters, cold winds blow, and temperatures often fall below 0°F. Summers can become quite warm. The climate in the area near Moscow is similar to that of Minnesota.

The Asian portion of the Soviet Union contains the huge area known as Siberia. Siberia covers nearly all the eastern part of the country from the Arctic Ocean to the mountains of central Asia. The climate of Siberia is colder than that of any other settled place in the world. Summer lasts only about one month in Siberia. During the long winters, the temperature can drop lower than -80°F in some areas.

To the southwest of Siberia lies a large desert region. This area east of the Caspian Sea has hot summers and cool winters. Very little rain or snow falls in this desert region or in the wide areas of Siberia. There are no oceans and few seas near these lands of central Asia to provide moisture for precipitation.

The Soviet Union not only has a wide variety of climates, but it also has a varied topography. Vast plains, rolling hills, and high mountain ranges are features of this country.

The Country and Its People

The Soviet Union is divided into fifteen parts that it calls "republics." These republics do not have their own independent representative forms of government. They are regions controlled by the Communist government of the Soviet Union from the capital, Moscow.

By far, the largest Soviet republic is the Russian Soviet Federated Socialist Republic, or **Russia.** Over half of the Soviet people live in Russia, most of them in the European portion of that land. Most of the people who live in that Soviet republic may be correctly called Russians. They speak the Russian language and share the culture and heritage of the people living in European Russia.

Often, all the Soviets are called Russians, but many of the Soviet people are of other **nationalities.** Each nationality

130   UNIT TWO

LITHUANIAN S.S.R.

MOLDAVIAN S.S.R.

ESTONIAN S.S.R.

LATVIAN S.S.R.

UKRAINIAN S.S.R.

BELORUSSIAN S.S.R.

ARMENIAN S.S.R.

GEORGIAN S.S.R.

AZERBAY-DZHAN S.S.R

TURKMEN S.S.R.

UZBEK S.S.R.

KIRGIZ S.S.R.

TADZHIK S.S.R.

KAZAKH S.S.R.

RUSSIAN SOVIET FEDERATED SOCIALIST REPUBLIC

S.S.R is the abbreviation for Soviet Socialist Republic

has a language of its own and a heritage that links the group together. There are about one hundred nationalities in the Soviet Union. Fourteen other large national groups besides the Russians have their own republics within the Soviet Union. The map above shows the names of these groups and the location of their republic within the country.

Even though many languages are spoken by the Soviet people, Russian is used in every republic as the official language. The Soviets use the Cyrillic alphabet (see chart) to write their language. Any Soviet who wants to get a good education or any kind of a high position in government or business must learn to speak Russian well. Any official you might meet in the Soviet Union, whether he be Estonian, Ukrainian, Georgian, Uzbek, Tartar, Jew, or any other nationality, will know Russian along with his own language. Although the Russians and their language seem to dominate the Soviet Union, the other groups are also very proud of their own nationalities.

Cyrillic Alphabet

Cyrillic	English	Cyrillic	English	Cyrillic	English
а	a	к	k	х	kh
б	b	л	l	ц	ts
в	v	м	m	ч	ch
г	g	н	n	ш	sh
д	d	о	o	щ	shch
е	ye	п	p	ъ	*
ё	yo	р	r	ы	y
ж	zh	с	s	ь	*
з	z	т	t	э	e
и	i	у	u	ю	yu
й	y	ф	f	я	ya

*Not pronounced

Section Review

1. What does *U.S.S.R.* stand for?

2. What man led the Communist Revolution in Russia?

3. How does the size of the Soviet Union compare with the size of the United States?

4. What features divide Europe from Asia?

5. What is the name of the cold eastern region of the Soviet Union?

The Communist Government

Marx and Lenin

When Lenin led the Communist Revolution in 1917, the goal of the Communists was to establish a better world. Lenin had read the books of Karl Marx. Marx believed that someday men would stop fighting in wars. They would learn to share everything that they produced so that everyone's needs would be met. Marx did not believe in heaven or in God. He thought that man was good enough to make this world perfect on his own.

Lenin set up the new Communist government with hopes of building the kind of world Marx had written about. Although the Communists had promised that the Soviet people would control their new government, Lenin and a few other Communist leaders ruled the country. Instead of letting the people own their own factories, stores, and farmland (capitalism), the government took over all businesses and farms (socialism). Many peasants refused to give up their property, and thousands were executed.

Lenin's new Communist government closely watched the people to make sure they obeyed its commands. Lenin established a secret police force to keep watch over people who might cause

trouble for the Communists. (Today that secret police force is called the K.G.B.) People who tried to fight against the Communists, and even those who openly disagreed with them, were threatened, put into prison, or sent to concentration camps in Siberia. The Soviet people were not free to speak what they thought about the government. The newspapers and magazines were censored. Only articles that supported the Communist government were printed.

Shopping in the Soviet Union

Since the government owns the businesses, the stores of the Soviet Union do not have distinctive names. If you lived there, instead of shopping at "Brown's Grocery" or "Highland Pharmacy," you would go to "Grocery Store number fifty-six" or "Pharmacy number two."

There are no advertisements, commercials, or billboards persuading people to buy a certain brand of toothpaste or to shop at a new store. The Soviet people do not have a choice about the products that they buy. They must buy whatever the government produces or do without. Often they must settle for merchandise of poor quality.

These conditions still exist in the Soviet Union. People must be very careful if they disagree with the government. K.G.B. agents carefully watch the lives of those who might criticize their government. Only approved stories are printed in newspapers and magazines. Crime, accidents, and other kinds of bad news are rarely reported on radio or television. The government wants everyone to believe that all things are going well in this Communist country.

Atheism in the Soviet Union

Lenin's government forced the idea of **atheism** on the people of the Soviet Union.

Pictures of Communist party leaders line the streets in preparation for a Soviet parade.

Atheism is the belief that there is no God. The Bible says, "The fool hath said in his heart, There is no God" (Psalm 14:1). The Communists did not believe the Bible. They tried to close down the churches. The people, however, did not give up their religion easily. Most of the Soviet people belonged to the Russian Orthodox church. This church is much like the Greek Orthodox church we read about in Chapter Five.

Today, many old church buildings in the Soviet Union are used for club houses, museums, and even barns and warehouses.

Christians in the Soviet Union

Christians in free countries like the United States do not suffer much persecution. We may be laughed at for our beliefs. We may even lose our friends or a job because of our refusal to do things that are ungodly. But we still can meet together in our churches and witness to others for Christ without fear of being tortured or put in prison. Christians in some other lands do not have the freedom to practice their faith in Christ as we do. It is not easy to be a Christian in countries like the Soviet Union.

Nicholai Khrapov was from Tashkent, the capital of the republic of Uzbekistan in the southern part of the Soviet Union. He was saved when he was twenty-one years old. He began to preach the gospel and write poetry and literature to help Soviet Christians.

The Communist government of the Soviet Union persecuted Nicholai for serving the Lord. They put him in a prison camp for twelve years because he preached to others about Christ. Nicholai was treated harshly, but when he was released, he continued to preach God's Word. He was imprisoned again and again for his faithfulness to Christ. He suffered in concentration camps for twenty-eight years. He died in 1982. Nicholai lived for Christ in a land where Christians are truly persecuted for their faith.

Many Christians in the Soviet Union have been imprisoned for witnessing for Christ, for printing Bibles and Christian literature, for holding Bible studies, and even for telling their own children about Christ and teaching them from the Bible. Some children have been taken away from their Christian parents. They are put in schools that try to make them atheists. Young Christians who are soldiers in the Soviet army are sometimes tortured and beaten until they renounce Christ or die. Christians are watched carefully by the K.G.B. Bibles and religious books, when found, are taken from Christians, and sometimes their houses or jobs are taken from them as well. They are questioned, beaten, and sometimes imprisoned for telling others about their Saviour.

We should pray for the Christians in the Soviet Union. They need the Lord's strength to face such sufferings. They also need our prayers that their testimonies will reach the hearts of Soviets who have been taught that there is no God.

Remember them that are in bonds, as bound with them; and them which suffer adversity, as being yourselves also in the body. (Hebrews 13:3)

But and if ye suffer for righteousness' sake, happy are ye: and be not afraid of their terror, neither be troubled; For Christ also hath once suffered for sins, the just for the unjust, that he might bring us to God, being put to death in the flesh, but quickened by the Spirit. (I Peter 3:14,18)

Nicholai Khrapov

Life in the Soviet Union

On a Collective Farm

In the eastern part of the Ukrainian Republic, about five hundred miles south of Moscow, lies a huge **collective farm.** Boris and Irina Trifonov live and work on this farm with five hundred other workers. In the Soviet Union, farmers are not allowed to own and manage their own farms. Instead, they must work for the government, raising the crops or livestock that they are told to raise. All the farmland is controlled by the government. The farmland is divided into huge farms called collectives. Usually, between one hundred and one thousand workers farm each collective. Collective farms cover much of the western part of the country. The eastern part has far less agricultural land, but it contains some state-owned farms as well.

Boris and Irina live in a small cottage grouped with many others into a small village on the collective. Although they have electricity, they have no plumbing inside their house. They must carry water from a hydrant down the street. The streets and roads of the collective are not paved.

In the spring and fall, rains make these paths very muddy. In the dry summer months, dust fills the air whenever machinery passes by.

Boris drives a tractor for the farm. Irina works in the fields planting, hoeing, and picking the corn and sugar beets. The Trifonovs work many hard hours from the time of spring planting until the last crops are harvested. No matter how tired they are when they come home from the fields, though, they always work in their private plot before they sleep.

Behind their house, Boris and Irina have about an acre of land that they use to grow vegetables and to keep a cow and a few pigs and chickens. Were it not for the food they raise on this plot, they would not have much good food to eat. They receive very low wages for their work on the collective, and even though the food in the state-operated market is not expensive, it is of poor quality. When they have a day off from work, they take some fresh vegetables, eggs, butter, and perhaps a pig to a larger village to sell. (They have to walk or borrow a horse and cart to get

there because they have no car.) From the money they receive, they buy clothing and other needed items. Once, after saving their money for over a year, they bought a radio. That radio is their most prized possession.

The part of the Ukrainian Republic where the Trifonovs live is covered with rolling hills and flat plains. A region of this prairie land called the **steppe** (STEP) covers much of the southwestern portion of the Soviet Union. Once the steppe land was a sea of tall grass and wildlife, much like the Great Plains of North America were. Much of the steppe, like the Great Plains, is now cultivated farmland.

In Siberia

Boris and Irina have two grown sons, Viktor and Andrei. Neither of the boys wanted to stay on the collective farm. Farm life was too hard and boring. They wanted to earn more money and enjoy the comforts and pleasures of city life. Their parents encouraged them to go, but leaving the farm was not easy. The Soviet Union does not allow anyone to move without special permission. Citizens are not free to live where they please.

So that he could move, Viktor signed up to go work in a lumbermill in Siberia. He now lives in the city of Yakutsk. He receives high wages for working in this cold land, but life there is not as easy as he had hoped. The winters are long and bitterly cold. Viktor goes to work at the mill when temperatures are far below zero. Only when the temperature drops to -58°F does the activity of Yakutsk come to a halt. At that temperature machinery breaks down and steel tools shatter.

Permafrost poses another problem for Viktor and the others living in Siberia. The ground in most of that region stays permanently frozen. Only for a month or two in the summer do the top few inches of dirt thaw out. Only hardy plants survive

Police taking Soviet Christians to court

in a land with such a short growing season. Digging in ground that is frozen solid is almost impossible. The warmth of buildings built on the soil, however, melts the permafrost. Many of the older buildings in Yakutsk are sinking into the mud as they melt the permafrost around them.

Viktor and his wife live in a new apartment building in Yakutsk. They have two small rooms of their own, but they share a bathroom and kitchen with three other apartments. Although Viktor's wages are high, they enjoy very few luxuries. Better housing, good furniture and appliances, and stylish clothing are rarely available to the working people of the Soviet Union. Viktor and his wife are saving their money for a vacation. They want to spend a few weeks in a resort by the warm Black Sea so that they can warm up for a while.

Siberia, though a cold land, contains a wealth of resources for the Soviet Union. Mines yield gold, diamonds, uranium, and coal. Petroleum resources lie beneath the ground, and evergreen forests provide lumber and paper products. The main resource that Siberia lacks is enough people willing to brave the cold in order to claim its wealth. That is why the Soviet government pays Siberian workers well.

The Communist government also sends many prisoners to work in Siberia. Prisoners are forced to work in the bitterly cold climate with little food or clothing to give them strength and warmth. Many Soviet Christians have been sent to Siberian prison camps to suffer because of their faith in Christ.

In Moscow

In the Soviet Union, no matter what a person's job is, he works for the government. Factory workers, farmers, waitresses, scientists, teachers, and store clerks all receive their pay from the Soviet government. Under Communist socialism, the government is supposed to make sure that all its people receive the things that they need so that everyone may live comfortably. There are not supposed to be wealthy and poor people in a Communist country.

The Trifonovs' other son, Andrei, has found that all people in the Soviet Union do not live under the same conditions. In order to leave the farm, Andrei joined the army. He wanted to go to college, but his education in the little farm school was too poor to help him pass the entrance test. Neither could his parents afford a tutor to help him prepare. Instead, he served in the army for three years.

The hard work as a soldier ended, and Andrei was allowed to live in a city. He was assigned a job as a factory worker in Moscow, the capital and largest city of the Soviet Union. During breaks at work he listened to speeches given by Communist party members. They were always trying to encourage the workers to do a better job for the good of the homeland. Though the speeches were boring, Andrei soon realized that if he

Moscow

Moscow is the center of Soviet life, and the Kremlin is in the center of Moscow. *Kremlin* means "fortress," and one look at the great walls, towers, and gates will tell you that it was built to be a fort.

This fort surrounds the cathedrals and palaces of the czars. For several hundred years, the czars ruled Russia from their splendid quarters inside the Kremlin. In 1712 Czar Peter the Great moved the capital from Moscow to his new city on the Baltic, St. Petersburg (now Leningrad). The Kremlin in Moscow, however, still served as the czar's home in that important Russian city.

When the Communists took over the Russian government in 1917, they made Moscow the capital again. They turned the plush buildings of the Kremlin into their government headquarters. Today, the highest leaders of the Communist party meet in the Kremlin buildings to determine the policies that will dictate the lives of the Soviet people.

East of the Kremlin, just outside its walls, lies a large open area called Red Square. On special days the government organizes spectacular parades that march through the square. Government leaders and authorized visitors watch as thousands of people march by carrying red flags and banners praising the Communist party. Rows of soldiers also march in the parade with a procession of hundreds of tanks and trucks bearing military equipment. Most Soviet citizens are not allowed to watch the parade from Red Square, and so they watch it at home or in some gathering place on a television.

In Red Square next to the Kremlin wall is Lenin's tomb. On most days, crowds of Soviet people are forced to line up to visit the tomb. They wait in line for hours to file by the tomb of their first Communist leader.

The unusual but beautiful St. Basil's Cathedral stands at one end of Red

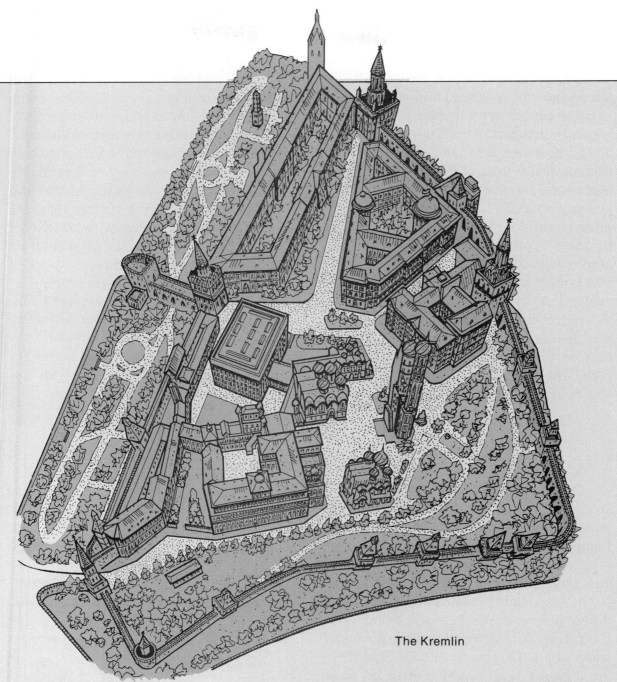

The Kremlin

Square. Each of its eight colorful onion-shaped domes is different. St. Basil's is no longer a church building. The Communist government has made it into a museum.

Shoppers in Moscow try to find needed goods in the Soviet Union's largest department store, GUM (from the Russian for "State Department Store"). Although it is in a grand building and contains many shops, its supplies of popular goods often run out.

More trucks and busses than cars fill the streets of Moscow. The Soviet Union makes few cars, and only a small number of people can get them. Most people ride the busses or the subway to work. Many of them dream of someday owning a car.

Moscow is the center of Soviet government and industry. It is also a city of abundant cultural activity. Besides many museums and art galleries, Moscow provides many drama, opera, ballet, and concert performances. The Soviet government keeps a tight control over all the fine arts. Artists are not free to perform works of which the Communist party does not approve.

wanted to advance to a better job, he would have to join the Communist party like those other workers had.

Only members of the Communist party are given better jobs, and only they may become factory managers or government leaders. Andrei knew that important party members receive chauffeur-driven cars, plush country houses, and even the chance to travel to other countries. They also are able to shop in special stores that have all kinds of good merchandise not available in other stores.

Andrei is also married, and his wife now spends several hours after work each evening just shopping for the food they need. The lines in stores are always long, and needed items are often unavailable.

Andrei and his wife live in a small, old apartment with her parents. The young couple would like a place of their own, but there is a housing shortage in Moscow. They put their name on a list to receive a new apartment, but they will probably have to wait for several years. Andrei and his wife have a baby girl, but they are unable to spend much time with her. Soviet mothers usually work while little children spend their days in government-operated nurseries or with their grandmothers.

Andrei hopes that by joining the Communist party he and his family will eventually be able to live more comfortably. Right now, things are not any better for him in Moscow than they are for his parents back on the collective farm.

Time Zones

The Soviet Union is a wide country stretching nearly halfway around the world. When the sun comes up in Leningrad, it is already going down in Vladivostok. When it is noon in Leningrad, it is 7:00 P.M. in Vladivostok.

In the United States there are four different time zones between Maine and California. The Soviet Union is so much wider than the United States that there are eleven time zones. The map on page xii shows how the Soviet Union is divided into time zones.

Over one hundred years ago, it was decided that the world should be divided into time zones. This would allow people to know what time it was in other lands. Men divided the world into twenty-four time zones. Most countries use these zones, but some do not. It is usually easy for us to find out what time it is in lands that use these time zones.

There are two basic rules for finding the time in other time zones. The first is that for every time zone you move to the east, you add one hour to the time. For instance, Tashkent is three time zones east of Moscow. If it is 2:00 A.M. in Moscow, you would add three hours to that Moscow time. It would be 5:00 A.M. in Tashkent.

The other rule is that for every time zone you move to the west, you subtract one hour from the time. Helsinki, Finland, is one time zone west of Leningrad. If it is 4:00 P.M. in Leningrad, it is 3:00 P.M. in Helsinki. Question: New York is eight time zones west of Moscow. If it is 6:00 A.M., Tuesday in Moscow, do you know what time it would be in New York?

Terms to Remember

peasants
czar
Siberia
Communist government
Ural Mountains
Caspian Sea
Caucasus Mountains
Black Sea
Russia
nationalities
atheism
permafrost

Things to Know

1. What kind of a government does the Soviet Union have?

2. What is the belief that there is no God called?

3. What is the huge, cold eastern region of the Soviet Union?

4. What is the capital of the Soviet Union?

5. What mountain ranges divide Europe and Asia?

6. Who was the leader of the Communist Revolution in Russia?

Section Review

1. What is a large farm controlled by the Soviet government called?

2. What is the rolling prairie land of the Soviet Union called?

3. In what region of the Soviet Union is Yakutsk?

4. What is ground that remains frozen all year long called?

5. If it is 9:00 P.M. in one time zone, what time would it be two time zones to the west?

7. What is the largest republic in the Soviet Union?

8. What are the two seas on the southern border of the Soviet Union?

9. What were the Russian rulers called before the Communist Revolution?

Things to Talk About

1. Are all people who live in the Soviet Union Russians? Why or why not?

2. What are some of the things that might happen to a Christian in the Soviet Union if he tried to witness to others for Christ?

3. Soviet children are taught to respect Lenin greatly, almost as if he were a god. Why is this wrong?

4. What is different about the lives of Boris and Irina Trifonov and their sons from the life of your family? What is the greatest need that the Soviet people have?

Things to Do

1. Find and read stories about Christians who live in Communist countries. How are their lives tormented under Communist rule? How is their faith in the Lord strengthened?

2. Learn the names and conditions of some Christians who are at present being persecuted in a Communist country. Make a prayer card for them, and pray for them regularly. In addition, it may be possible for you to write them letters.

3. Your teacher will give you materials and instructions to make a time-zone wheel. After you have put the wheel together, you will be able to find out what time it is in just about any place in the world. To find out what time it is in a city listed on the wheel, simply follow this procedure. Find a city on the wheel for which you know the correct time. Align the name of that city with the proper time on the larger circle. Then look at the name of the city for which you wish to find the time. The time on the larger circle that corresponds to that city is the correct time. Every time a city comes to the midnight position, it is the next day in that city (Wednesday—Thursday, etc.). Use the time-zone wheel you made or the time-zone map to help you answer these questions.

   a. If it is 10:00 A.M. in Athens, Greece, what time is it in New York?

   b. If it is 11:00 P.M. in Sydney, Australia, what time is it in Los Angeles?

   c. If it is noon in Chicago, what time is it in Moscow?

d. When people in Halifax, Nova Scotia, are eating breakfast, what are people in Honolulu, Hawaii, probably doing?

e. The time zone of your home is the same as the time zone of which of the cities on the wheel?

f. If it is 6:00 A.M. at your home, what time is it in Tashkent, U.S.S.R.?

Geography Skills

Use the maps in the atlas and on page 126 to help you answer the following questions.

1. What ocean lies to the north of the Soviet Union?

2. The city of Leningrad is near what degree of latitude?

3. What sea lies between the city of Vladivostok and Japan?

4. Using the scale of miles, how far is it from Moscow to Yakutsk?

5. Name two rivers that flow into the Caspian Sea.

6. List the Asian countries that lie along the southern border of the Soviet Union.

7. List the European countries that lie along the Soviet Union's western border.

CHAPTER 8

EASTERN EUROPE

The last section of Europe that we will learn about is made up of seven countries—Poland, Czechoslovakia, Hungary, Rumania, Bulgaria, Yugoslavia, and Albania. These countries of Eastern Europe are in many ways similar to one another, yet each has many distinctive features of its own.

These Eastern European countries stretch from the Baltic Sea in the north to the Balkan Peninsula by the Adriatic and Black Seas in the south. Along with East Germany and the Soviet Union, these lands lie behind the Iron Curtain. You remember that the Iron Curtain is the name given to the border between the free countries of Western Europe and the Communist countries of Eastern Europe (see Chapter 4). As in East Germany, Communist governments took control of these seven countries after World War II. The Soviet Union's strong influence has kept the people of these lands from overthrowing their Communist rulers. Because of communism, life in these countries is much like life in the Soviet Union.

Climate

The climate in these lands is not as mild as that of most of Western Europe.

	AREA (Square Miles)	POPULATION	CAPITAL	MAIN LANGUAGES	MAIN RELIGIONS	CURRENCY
POLAND	120,725	36,556,000	Warsaw	Polish	(restricted) Roman Catholic	zloty
CZECHOSLOVAKIA	49,370	15,420,000	Prague	Czech, Slovak	(restricted) Roman Catholic, Protestant	koruna
HUNGARY	35,919	10,691,000	Budapest	Magyar	(restricted) Roman Catholic, Protestant	forint
RUMANIA	91,699	22,649,000	Bucharest	Rumanian, Magyar, German	(restricted) Eastern Orthodox, Roman Catholic, Protestant	leu
BULGARIA	42,823	8,944,000	Sofia	Bulgarian	(restricted) Eastern Orthodox, Islam	lev
YUGOSLAVIA	98,766	22,826,000	Belgrade	Serbo-Croatian, Slovenian, Macedonian, and others	(restricted) Eastern Orthodox, Roman Catholic, Islam	dinar
ALBANIA	11,100	2,846,000	Tiranë	Albanian, Greek	(restricted) Islam, Eastern Orthodox	lek

Eastern Europe lies far away from the waters of the Atlantic Ocean. Only small areas of the region are near enough to large bodies of water to receive much warmth in the winter and cool breezes in the summer. While mountainous areas are generally cooler, the level plains can have extreme hot and cold temperatures.

Land and Resources

Eastern Europe has a wide variety of landscape. There are broad plains, rugged mountain areas, thick forests, and flower-sprinkled meadows. Some areas contain rich farmland. Other areas have a large supply of mineral resources. Elsewhere the soil is poor and resources are scarce. In each area the people have to work hard to use the resources that God has given to their land.

Eastern European Agriculture

A large number of the people of Eastern Europe work in agricultural jobs. In some

Baltic Sea

POLAND

Gdansk

Oder River

•Poznan

Vistula River

★Warsaw

EAST GERMANY

•Lodz

•Wroclaw

WEST GERMANY

★Prague

•Plzen

CZECHOSLOVAKIA

Ostrava•

•Cracow

Danube

Brno•

Carpathian

SOVIET UNION

River

•Bratislava

AUSTRIA

★Budapest

HUNGARY

•Szeged

Cluj•

RUMANIA

Mountains

Zagreb•

YUGOSLAVIA

Dinaric Alps

Transylvanian Alps

Belgrade★

Bucharest★

•Sarajevo

Adriatic Sea

BULGARIA

Black Sea

Balkan Mountains

★Sofia

•Plodir

Skopje•

Tirane★

ALBANIA

Scale of miles
0   50   100   200   300

145

of the countries, the people work on collective farms like those in the Soviet Union. Some of the countries, however, allow farmers to own small farms of their own. The large collective farms use some modern machinery to care for their crops. But on most farms much of the work is done by hand. Often women work hard all day in the fields planting, hoeing weeds, raking hay or grain, or picking fruits and vegetables. The men usually drive trucks and tractors or supervise work crews.

Look at the agricultural charts on the following pages. These charts show us what countries in the world produce the most of certain items. Why does the United States, or the Soviet Union, or China often produce the largest quantities of these products? These large countries have much more farmland and more people to raise food items. Smaller countries like those in Eastern Europe have neither the land nor the people to raise such large crops. Yet for their small size, some of these countries produce very large crops.

Corn

The chart below shows the leading corn-growing countries. Which two coun-tries in Eastern Europe raise large crops of corn? Look at a world map or a globe and find the approximate latitude of these two countries. Iowa and Illinois are the two leading corn-growing states in the United States. At what latitude are those states found? At what latitude are the other leading corn-growing countries found? What do you think would be the reason that the Soviet Union produces a smaller amount of corn than the other countries?

Rye

Rye, a grain similar to wheat, grows well in cool climates like those of northern Europe. For two thousand years, Europeans have ground rye into flour for bread. Rye bread is dark brown and much heavier than the wheat bread that we generally eat. Eastern Europeans still eat a great deal of rye bread. Americans usually prefer to use the rye they raise as feed for livestock.

This chart shows the leading rye-producing countries. Which country grows the most rye? Why do you think the Soviet Union grows more rye than corn? Which Eastern European countries grow large quantities of rye?

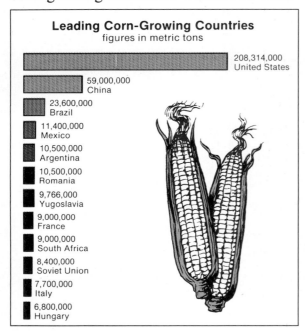

Leading Corn-Growing Countries
figures in metric tons

- 208,314,000 United States
- 59,000,000 China
- 23,600,000 Brazil
- 11,400,000 Mexico
- 10,500,000 Argentina
- 10,500,000 Romania
- 9,766,000 Yugoslavia
- 9,000,000 France
- 9,000,000 South Africa
- 8,400,000 Soviet Union
- 7,700,000 Italy
- 6,800,000 Hungary

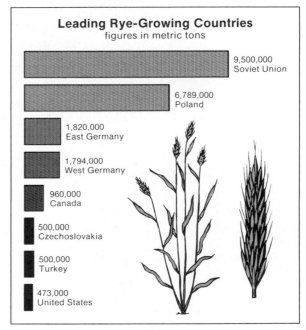

Leading Rye-Growing Countries
figures in metric tons

- 9,500,000 Soviet Union
- 6,789,000 Poland
- 1,820,000 East Germany
- 1,794,000 West Germany
- 960,000 Canada
- 500,000 Czechoslovakia
- 500,000 Turkey
- 473,000 United States

Farmers in Communist-controlled Eastern Europe often use almost primitive methods of farming.

Ham and Potatoes

The potato also grows well in cool climates and in poor soils. This important vegetable grows in many countries. Potatoes contain many vitamins and minerals, and potatoes can be prepared in many ways. How many ways have you eaten potatoes?

Potatoes have been grown in Europe for only about four hundred years. Spanish explorers found them growing in South America. They brought them back to Europe where they became a popular food. Which Eastern European country listed on this chart grows more potatoes than the United States?

Farm livestock provides meat for us to buy and eat. Eastern Europe's farms have cattle, hogs, and chickens just as American farms do. When the hogs are butchered, the people enjoy ham, sausage, and bacon. Which Eastern European countries raise many hogs?

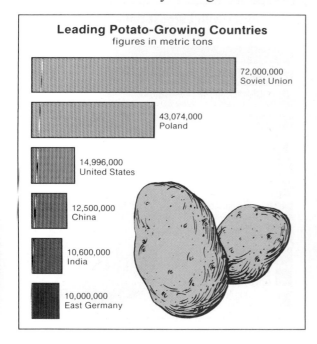

Leading Potato-Growing Countries
figures in metric tons

- 72,000,000 Soviet Union
- 43,074,000 Poland
- 14,996,000 United States
- 12,500,000 China
- 10,600,000 India
- 10,000,000 East Germany

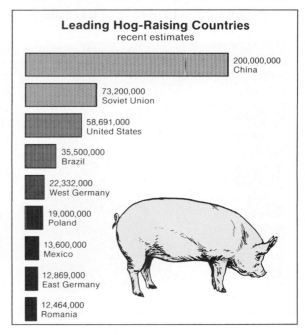

Leading Hog-Raising Countries
recent estimates

- 200,000,000 China
- 73,200,000 Soviet Union
- 58,691,000 United States
- 35,500,000 Brazil
- 22,332,000 West Germany
- 19,000,000 Poland
- 13,600,000 Mexico
- 12,869,000 East Germany
- 12,464,000 Romania

Resources for Industry

In our modern world, countries must produce more than just agricultural products. They must develop industries that will provide goods that their own people can use and goods that can be traded to other countries.

Industries need raw materials and fuels to use in their production. Countries that have large supplies of raw materials or fuels may use them to develop their own industries, or they may sell these resources to other countries. Countries with abundant natural resources have a great advantage over countries in which resources are scarce.

Unlike the United States, the Soviet Union, and some other countries, smaller Eastern European countries do not have an abundance of natural resources. Some of the countries, however, do have supplies of a few raw materials or fuels that have helped them build up industries and trade.

Coal

Coal is an important fuel in many countries of the world. Coal is often used to produce electricity. Burning coal heats water to produce steam. The pressure of large amounts of steam makes the wheels of turbines spin. The turbines turn huge generators that produce electricity. That electricity can then provide energy for homes and factories.

Another important use of coal is for making coke, a special fuel used for making iron and steel. When coal is heated to extremely high temperatures, it is purified. Unwanted materials in the coal change to gasses, leaving behind the solid coke. Countries that have supplies of both coking coal and iron ore have an advantage in the iron and steel industry.

Besides using it as a fuel for industry, many Europeans burn coal to heat their houses and other buildings. Which Eastern European country has large coal resources?

Mineral Resources

Minerals that can be made into metals or chemicals provide raw materials for many industries. Countries that have mineral deposits can use them to supply their own industries, or they can sell them to other countries.

The mineral ore **bauxite** contains aluminum. Since aluminum is used in the

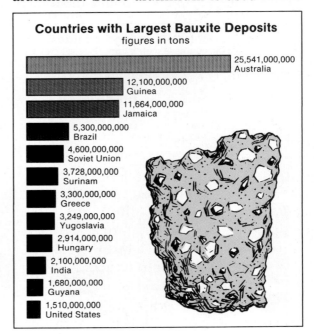

Countries with Largest Coal Deposits
figures in short tons

256,840,000,000	Soviet Union
246,100,000,000	United States
109,130,000,000	China
65,410,000,000	Australia
65,190,000,000	West Germany
49,600,000,000	United Kingdom
42,990,000,000	Poland
27,880,000,000	South Africa
27,670,000,000	East Germany

Countries with Largest Bauxite Deposits
figures in tons

25,541,000,000	Australia
12,100,000,000	Guinea
11,664,000,000	Jamaica
5,300,000,000	Brazil
4,600,000,000	Soviet Union
3,728,000,000	Surinam
3,300,000,000	Greece
3,249,000,000	Yugoslavia
2,914,000,000	Hungary
2,100,000,000	India
1,680,000,000	Guyana
1,510,000,000	United States

Yugoslavia is one of the Eastern European nations attempting to increase its oil production.

manufacture of many products, bauxite is a valuable resource for a country to have. This chart shows the leading bauxite-mining countries of the world. Which two Eastern European countries have deposits of bauxite?

In areas of Eastern Europe in which raw materials are available and industries have grown, the people live in cities with most of the conveniences we enjoy. In other areas farming continues to be the only way that the people can make their living.

Eastern European Nationalities

Many different nationalities live in the Eastern European countries. In the past they have desired independence for themselves. They wanted to rule themselves in their own countries, enjoy their own customs, and follow their own religions. For hundreds of years these nationalities have fought among themselves and against other nations to win or to keep their freedom.

Today these peoples are without freedom. Strong, harsh Communist governments control their lives. They are not allowed to speak freely or move about as they please. Neither are they free to hear the gospel. Even though some of the people continue to practice a form of religion, only a few have ever heard that Jesus died to pay all the penalty for their sins. Most of them do not know that by accepting Jesus Christ as their Saviour, they may have eternal life.

Christians Behind the Iron Curtain

The few Christians who live in these countries face many difficulties. They risk their safety when they tell others about the Lord Jesus. If the Communist governments find out that they have been witnessing for Christ, they are often threatened, beaten, or put into prison. Communist teachers and officials encourage children to tell the authorities about the activities of their Christian parents so that they may be punished for their work for the Lord.

The governments do not allow Bible studies to be held in homes. Yet Christians happily invite their neighbors to hear the

Word of God. They know the Lord wants them to tell the lost about the Saviour.

Few of these Christians have their own Bibles. Since Bibles cannot be legally printed in Communist countries, missionaries from free countries try to take them copies when they visit. Many of the people memorize large portions of Scripture. In that way they may carry God's Word in their hearts even if they do not have a Bible to carry in their hands.

Despite all these risks and hardships, dedicated Christians in these lands continue to witness to others and to teach their children about the Lord. They eagerly attend church services where the gospel is preached. Often they must walk several miles to reach the meeting halls.

We should pray for these Christians. We should also pray that we will keep our religious freedom in America. What if our government were to take away our privilege to worship freely, witness, and have a Christian education? Would we still stand for the Lord as these Christians in Communist countries do?

Section Review

1. What kind of government do the countries of Eastern Europe have?

2. Where were potatoes first grown?

3. What important metal is found in bauxite?

4. What are three uses for coal?

5. What is the western border of the Communist Eastern European countries often called?

Poland

The Slavs

Hundreds of years ago, a large group of people known as the **Slavs** moved from Asia into Eastern Europe. Over the years, these Slavic people separated into several national groups that still live in Eastern Europe. Included in these Slavic groups are the Russians, the Poles, the Czechs, the Bulgarians, and the Yugoslavians. The languages that these people speak are similar. They are called Slavic languages.

People Without a Country

A group of the Slavic people moved into the broad plain south of the Baltic Sea. About one thousand years ago, this group established its own kingdom called Poland. For many years the Poles ruled their large and powerful country. However, in the 1700s, Poland's neighbors became stronger. Russia, Austria, and the German state of Prussia agreed to divide Poland into parts, and each country took a portion for its own. The Poles were not strong enough to stop these greedy neighbors. Soon they were without a country of their own. The Poles still lived on the same land, but that land was ruled by three other countries.

Natural Boundaries

Look at the area that is Poland on a topographical map. The country's northern border is formed by the Baltic Sea. Its southern border is formed by mountains. Seas and mountains make good natural boundaries for countries. Such boundaries are easier to defend against enemies than borders in open countryside.

Poland does not have natural boundaries on its eastern and western borders. Through the years, many enemy armies have crossed through the fields and plains along these borders to attack the Polish people and capture their land. This lack of natural boundaries on these sides has left Poland unprotected from foreign invasions.

A palace in Poland

The Polish people struggled for many years to regain their independence. Finally, at the end of World War I in 1918, the country of Poland was reestablished. The Poles rejoiced in their freedom, but their new country was not strong. Adolph Hitler began World War II by moving his German armies into Poland from the west. Armies of the Soviet Union also marched into Poland from the east. The Poles could not stop these strong enemies from destroying Polish cities and taking over the countryside.

Conquered by Communism

When World War II ended, the Poles set up their country once more. This time, however, the Soviet Union forced them to accept a Communist government. The Poles have tried to change their government, but the Soviet Union makes sure that the Communist government remains in control. The Polish people are not free to speak, work, travel, or govern themselves as they please.

The Polish People

The Poles are a busy people. Many of them are farmers. After the Communist government took over, Polish farmers refused to allow the government to take away their own farms. They did not want to be forced onto large collective farms like those in the Soviet Union. Finally,

the government allowed the farmers to keep small farms of their own. Many of these private Polish farms cover only ten or twelve acres, yet they are very productive. From the charts we looked at earlier in this chapter, we know that Polish farmers produce a large amount of rye, potatoes, and pork.

Many Poles work in industry. Poland has large amounts of coal and enough natural resources to supply many of its industries. The Poles produce a great deal of iron and steel and manufacture a large amount of machinery.

Warsaw, Poland's capital and largest city, was almost completely destroyed during World War II. Since the war, its people have carefully rebuilt the city.

Warsaw, Poland

Many of the newer buildings are identical to the ones that were standing before the war. As in the Soviet Union, few cars are in the city streets. Most people cannot afford a car. Their pay must buy food and other necessities that are often very expensive in this Communist land.

The Polish people enjoy festive occasions. Most Poles still cling to the Roman Catholic religion despite the disapproval of the Communist government. Church holidays provide opportunities to celebrate. The Poles who live in the mountains along the southern border

Casimir Pulaski

Madame Curie

Thaddeus Kosciusko

of the country dress in their traditional costumes. All over the country, women prepare their special dishes. *Keilbasa,* a favorite sausage, and *bigos,* a meat and cabbage dish, might be part of a special supper.

Famous Poles

Though the Polish people have faced many hardships through the years, they have accomplished great works. Two Polish military leaders helped the United States to win its independence during the Revolutionary War. Casimir Pulaski offered his help to Ben Franklin, and he was allowed to organize the first American cavalry unit. Thaddeus Kosciusko also served well in the Revolutionary Army. He was awarded American citizenship for his aid, but he returned to Poland to try to save his country from being divided by its neighbors.

Another famous Pole was Marie Sklodowska who married a Frenchman, Pierre Curie. Madame Curie and her husband conducted scientific research on radioactive materials. During their research, Madame Curie discovered two elements. One was radium, and the other was polonium, named for her home country. The Curies received great honors for their work. Marie Curie is the only person who has ever received the Nobel Prize in both physics (1903) and chemistry (1911). (Nobel Prizes are the world's highest honors awarded each year to people of great accomplishment.)

Czechoslovakia

Czechoslovakia (CHEK uh sluh VAH kee uh), like Poland, was settled by Slavic people. These people were united together in one country for the first time at the end of World War I. Before that time, they were divided into three main groups.

A Union of Three Peoples

The Bohemians (boh HEE mee unz) lived in what is now the western part of Czechoslovakia. About seven hundred years ago, the Bohemians ruled a strong kingdom of their own. Then rulers of other lands tried to win control over **Bohemia.** The people tried to maintain their independence, but they were not strong enough to keep the greater powers of Europe from taking over.

Moravia, in the central area of Czechoslovakia, had a great kingdom of its own a few hundred years before Bohemia did. It, too, fell to the control of stronger powers. The eastern area of Czechoslovakia was **Slovakia.** The Slovakians never had a strong country of their own.

The desire of these three peoples for independence led them to unite in 1918. Under the leadership of Tomas Masaryk, a great national leader, the new Czechoslovak nation was established.

The Bohemians and the Moravians both spoke a Slavic language called Czech. Often both people were referred to as Czechs. By combining the Czechs and the Slovakians together, they came up with the title for their new country.

The Czechoslovak Nation

The Czechoslovaks prospered in the early years after World War I. Masaryk became president of the well-organized republic. Industries were begun, and Czech farms produced good harvests. But Adolph Hitler wanted control of this prosperous area. Before World War II began, he had taken over most of the country. Once again these people had lost their independence.

When Soviet armies came to drive the Germans out of Czechoslovakia, the Soviets brought communism with them. When the war was over, the people tried to reestablish their free government, but Soviet pressure was too great. In 1948 a Communist government took over Czechoslovakia.

The Czechs are not happy with their government. They want more freedom. In 1968 when the people tried to gain some freedom from the Communist restrictions, the Soviet Union sent tanks and troops into Czechoslovakia. The people were forced to submit to the authority of communism. The people there continue to live without the kind of freedoms we enjoy in America.

Geography and Activity

Czechoslovakia has large coal deposits and some mineral resources. By importing other needed materials, it has become the leading industrial country in Eastern Europe. Most of the country's industry, however, is located in the cities in the western section. The eastern part of the country is more agricultural. The Communist government took the farmland away from the farmers and organized state-owned collective farms. The production on these collectives is low.

Unlike the flat land of Poland, Czechoslovakia is a land of hills and mountains. The Danube River flows along a portion of its southern border. The Vltava (or Moldau) flows north through the city of Prague. Prague, the capital and largest city, is a wondrous old town. A hilltop castle overlooks a large area of the city in which most of the buildings are hundreds of years old. Surrounding this historic area are the modern industrial sections of the city.

Top: The historic Lesser Town of Prague, Czechoslovakia **Bottom:** A winter scene in Czechoslovakia

John Huss

Over six hundred years ago, a boy named John was born in Hussinecs, a little village in Bohemia. John of Hussinecs later shortened his name to John Huss. He became a great preacher of the truth of God's Word. He was faithful to Christ, although his faithfulness meant death.

John lived over one hundred years before the time of Martin Luther and the beginning of the Protestant Reformation. He lived in a time when most of the people throughout Europe were depending on the Roman Catholic church for salvation. John went to the University of Prague, and he studied to become a priest. He was a good scholar. He soon became a popular teacher at the university as well as a priest.

In John's study of the Bible, he learned that Christ is the Head of the church, not the Roman Catholic pope. Huss found that many other teachings of the Roman Catholic church were not Scriptural. He preached the truths he found in God's Word to the Bohemian people. Many grew to love this man who brought them the Truth.

The Roman Catholic rulers and churchmen, however, were angered by this one who dared to show the errors of their religion. They told Huss to go to a meeting at Constance (in Germany) to talk about the situation. He was promised that he could return safely to Bohemia if he went.

John went to Constance, where the pope and many rulers of Europe were gathered. Those people, however, called him a heretic. They put him in chains and kept him in a dark cell for months. When he was finally brought before the meeting, they accused him falsely of teaching errors. He asked that they show him from Scripture the errors he was teaching. Of course, they could not, but they accused him more.

At last in July of 1416, they condemned him to death. He prayed for the Lord to forgive them. He declared that he was glad to die for the truth of the gospel. They took him outside the town and burned him at the stake.

That the trial of your faith, being much more precious than of gold that perisheth, though it be tried with fire, might be found unto praise and honour and glory at the appearing of Jesus Christ: Whom having not seen, ye love; in whom, though now ye see him not, yet believing, ye rejoice with joy unspeakable and full of glory: Receiving the end of your faith, even the salvation of your souls.(I Peter 1:7-9)

A Christmas Tradition

Like the Poles, the Czechoslovaks enjoy celebrations. A special event for them is their Christmas Eve supper. Instead of turkey or ham, the Czechoslovaks' traditional meal includes a big carp, a large freshwater fish. To make sure that it will be fresh, some Czechoslovaks buy their carp alive a few days before Christmas. They let it swim in the bathtub until it is time to prepare it.

Section Review

1. What is Poland's capital?

2. What three peoples live in Czechoslovakia?

3. What is the capital of Czechoslovakia?

4. When did Czechoslovakia become a Communist country?

5. What famous Pole made great contributions to science?

Hungary

Hungary, like Czechoslovakia and Poland to the north, was once a strong kingdom. One hundred years ago it was part of the great empire of Austria-Hungary. Today like its northern neighbors, it is a weakened Communist country.

Hungary lies on a broad plain that stretches from both sides of the Danube. Hungary's greatest resource is her fertile black soil. Lacking other resources, Hungary has remained more agricultural than Czechoslovakia. Grains, fruit, and vegetables grow well in Hungary. Today those foods are raised on collective farms run by the Communist government.

Hungary is about the size of the state of Indiana. Its capital and largest city is Budapest (BOO duh PEST). Budapest is actually two cities in one. Buda sits on the hills of the west bank of the Danube River, while Pest lies across the river on the east bank. Budapest is a mixture of old and new buildings and activities.

The Hungarians are not a Slavic people like many of the nationalities of Eastern Europe. They are the descendants of another group of early settlers called the Magyars. Their Magyar, or Hungarian, language is similar to the language spoken by the Finns.

Like the other Eastern European countries, Hungary was forced by the Soviet Union to accept a Communist government after World War II. Hungary, too, has tried to rebel against Communist control. Soviet troops marched into Hungary in 1956 to stop an uprising. The Hungarians are forced to obey the Communist government that strictly controls their way of life.

Hungary's Parliament building

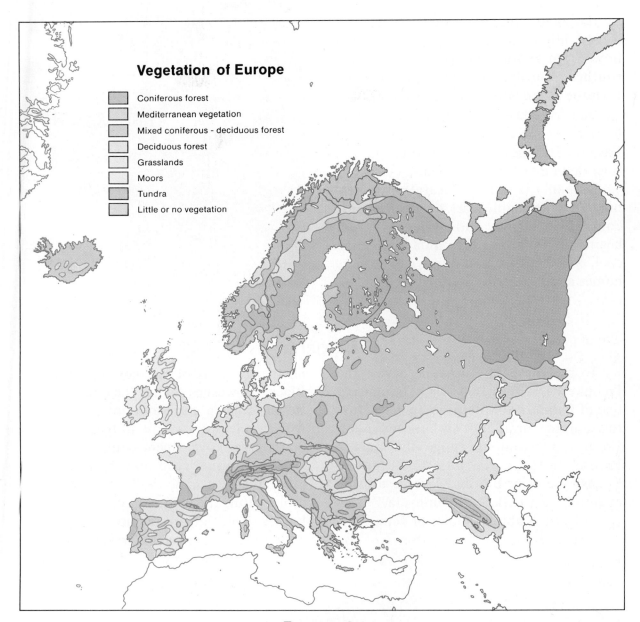

Vegetation of Europe

- Coniferous forest
- Mediterranean vegetation
- Mixed coniferous - deciduous forest
- Deciduous forest
- Grasslands
- Moors
- Tundra
- Little or no vegetation

Rumania

The Rumanians claim to be descendants of the ancient Romans who conquered, settled, and ruled this land by the Black Sea. Today they are a people ruled by communism. They live without the freedom to speak what they think, move about as they please, or worship as they choose without government supervision. They read in newspapers and magazines only what the government wishes them to read. They buy in government stores only the limited products produced by government factories. Communism controls their lives.

Some Rumanians have heard the gospel, despite the government's control. Dedicated Rumanian Christians share the news of salvation with others. They also rejoice in every opportunity they have to hear more of God's Word. They want to serve the Lord faithfully in their land.

Rumania is over twice the size of Hungary. The Transylvanian Alps and the **Carpathian Mountains** provide a contrast

to the landscape of broad plains and rolling hills. The Danube River, which flows from Yugoslavia, forms most of the southern border of the country. The Danube then turns north across the Rumanian coastal plain to the Soviet border. From there this great river of Eastern Europe flows east through the river delta into the Black Sea.

Rumania is rich in natural resources, but half of its people work on government-controlled farms. Industries are just beginning to grow. Rumania has some coal, but it also has natural gas that its homes and industries use for fuel.

Bulgaria

To the south of Rumania, across the Danube River, lies Bulgaria. The narrow line of **Balkan Mountains** stretches across this country for about two hundred miles. From this mountain range the Balkan Peninsula gets its name. Bulgaria, Yugoslavia, Albania, and Greece are the countries on the Balkan Peninsula.

Bulgaria is about the size of Tennessee. The Danube provides water for the northern plains of the country, and the Black Sea washes against the eastern coast. Bulgaria has a large amount of farmland with fertile soil. Many Bulgarians work on the large government-controlled farms.

One unusual crop that the Bulgarians grow is roses. The Valley of Roses in central Bulgaria contains billions of rose bushes. The Bulgarians pick rose blooms early in the morning before the sun dries

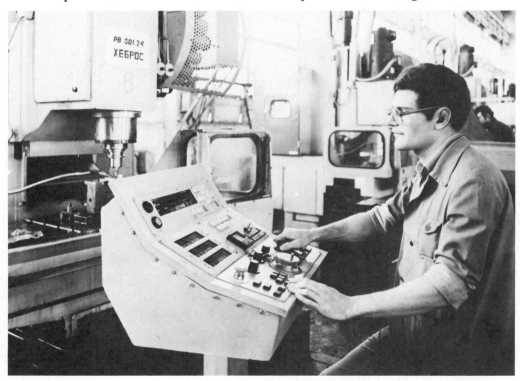

Bulgaria has borrowed from Western technology in an attempt to improve its industry.

them. The petals are crushed to produce a liquid called rose attar. Rose attar gives a beautiful scent to perfumes and other sweet-smelling items. It takes about five thousand petals to produce a single ounce of rose attar.

The Bulgarian language is written in the Cyrillic alphabet as is the Russian language. If you should ever talk to a Bulgarian, be careful how you shake your head. To a Bulgarian, a head-shake sideways means yes, and a nod up and down means no.

Communists took control of the Bulgarian government after World War II. The Soviet Union remains very supportive of the Bulgarian government, which strictly controls the lives of its people.

Yugoslavia

Yugoslavia lies on the western side of the Balkan Peninsula by the **Adriatic Sea.** This rocky, mountainous country has only a small area of good farmland. That area is in the northeastern section near the Danube River. The remainder of the country, although very rich in various mineral resources, serves mainly as pastureland for the cattle, horses, goats, pigs, and other animals raised by the Yugoslav people.

Yugoslavia, which is about the same size as the state of Wyoming, is divided into six or more regions. The people speak several different languages. Some use the Latin alphabet while others use the Cyrillic alphabet to write their language. Most of the Yugoslav people are religious even though the Communist government discourages all religions.

Although Yugoslavia contains a mixture of cultures, most of its people are descendants of the Slavic people that

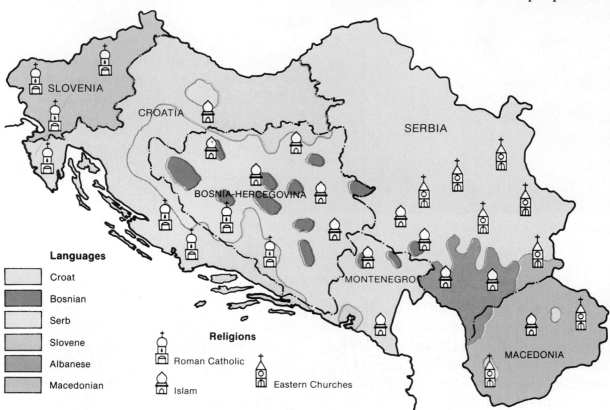

SLOVENIA

CROATIA

SERBIA

BOSNIA-HERCEGOVINA

MONTENEGRO

MACEDONIA

Languages
- Croat
- Bosnian
- Serb
- Slovene
- Albanese
- Macedonian

Religions
- Roman Catholic
- Islam
- Eastern Churches

moved into Europe hundreds of years ago. For many years these southern Slavs were ruled by outsiders: the Turks, Austrians, Hungarians, and Bulgarians. At the end of World War I in 1918, these Slavic peoples formed their own country called the Kingdom of the Serbs, Croats, and Slovenes. In 1929 they changed the name to Yugoslavia, which means "Land of the South Slavs."

After World War II, Marshal Josip Tito gained control of the Yugoslav government. He became a powerful dictator who forced communism on his people. Although he did not follow the Soviet Union's wishes for his new Communist country, Tito did take the freedom of the Yugoslav people from them. Tito strictly ruled Yugoslavia until his death in 1980. The Communist government of that country continues to forbid its people the freedom to change their lives.

Beautiful Yugoslavian countryside

Albania

Albania is the smallest of the Eastern European countries. Squeezed between Yugoslavia and Greece, Albania sits on the eastern shore of the Adriatic Sea. It is a mountainous little country that isolates itself from the rest of the world.

A Communist dictator named Enver Hoxha took control of Albania during World War II and ruled until 1985. At first the Soviet Union aided the little Communist country. Later Communist China became Albania's protector. Then

Dubrovnik, Yugoslavia

Albania decided to shut itself off from outside influence.

The Albanian government allows no Americans or Soviets to visit Albania. Only a few tourist groups from other countries are permitted inside Albania. Albanians cannot visit other countries. All churches have been closed, and no Bibles can be brought into the country.

The Communist government strictly controls the Albanian people. Most of them work on collective farms, but the soil is poor and harvests are meager. The people live in poverty with little to eat and unsatisfactory housing. A few trains and busses provide long-distance transportation. In the towns most people walk or ride bikes. In the countryside, horses, donkeys, and ox carts are common. Only Communist party leaders have cars.

None of us would like to live in a Communist country. We should be very thankful for the freedom that we still have to worship, speak, and move as we please in our country. God ordains the powers of the world, and we must remember that we are to obey the government that rules over us (Romans 13:1-7; I Peter 2:13-15; Matthew 22:21).

If we lived in one of the Eastern European Communist countries, what would we Christians do when the government treated us wrong? Should we rebel if such a government took away our property or forced us to work for very low wages? Although we could and should try to change the laws peacefully, we should not rebel.

In the Bible we read about the life of Daniel. Daniel was captured and taken to another country. In that country he was forced to work. Though he longed to live in his own nation, he faithfully served the government that ruled him. Only when that government demanded that he disobey God did he take a stand against his rulers. Daniel continued to pray to God in spite of the new law that prohibited such prayer. Daniel was thrown into the lions' den because he stood for God, but God used Daniel's testimony to glorify Himself.

Communism in Eastern Europe

Why does communism control the countries of Eastern Europe? There are several reasons.

1. The Soviet Union has a strong influence over these countries.
    a. The Soviet Union desires to increase its power by gaining control of other countries.
    b. The Soviet Union desires to control regions between itself and the strong, free countries of Western Europe.
2. Before World War II, the countries of Eastern Europe were very weak. After the war these lands lacked a strong government to fight against communism.
3. Communist governments establish great military strength. Once they come to power, it is very difficult for the people to overthrow them.

Throughout history God's people have often suffered hardships because of their faith. We must determine that we will stand for our Lord no matter what people or governments do to us. If we were ordered not to pray, not to tell others about Christ, or not to meet together to worship the Lord, we should obey God's Word. Like Daniel, however, we should submit to governmental authority except when it demands disobedience to God. In this way, our testimony can bring glory to our Saviour, Jesus Christ (I Peter 4:15-16).

Section Review

1. Rumania lies on the coast of what sea?

2. What mountain range stretches across Bulgaria?

3. What alphabet is used in Yugoslavia besides the Latin alphabet that we use?

4. What dictator ruled the Communist government of Yugoslavia for many years?

5. What small Eastern European country has completely closed all churches in its land?

Terms to Remember

rye	Slovakia
bauxite	Carpathian Mountains
Slavs	Balkan Mountains
Bohemia	Adriatic Sea
Moravia	

Things to Know

1. What is the name of the ore that contains aluminum?

2. What was the name of the large group of people that settled in Eastern Europe? This group included the Russians, Poles, Czechs, Bulgarians, and Yugoslavians.

3. What country strongly influences the countries of Eastern Europe?

4. What kind of government do all the countries of Eastern Europe have?

5. Name the three lands that united to form Czechoslovakia.

6. Name three ways in which coal can be used.

7. What sea lies between Yugoslavia and Italy?

8. What mountain range is found in Bulgaria?

Things to Talk About

1. Why do large countries often produce more agricultural products than small countries?

2. Why is it important for a country to have supplies of raw materials and fuels?

3. How does coal help to provide electricity?

4. Why is it important for a country to have natural boundaries?

Things to Do

1. Imagine what it would be like to live in a Communist country. Write a short story about life in a land where atheism is taught in school, where Christians are persecuted, and where people are not free to worship, speak, or even move about as they desire.

2. Bring some rye flour for your classmates to see and some rye bread for them to sample.

Geography Skills

Use the maps in your atlas and in this chapter to answer the following questions.

1. What two countries of Eastern Europe have borders along the Black Sea?

2. How many countries of Eastern Europe share a border with the Soviet Union?

3. The Danube River's source is in West Germany. It flows through Austria and its capital city, Vienna. Through what Eastern European capitals does the Danube flow?

4. What mountain range extends along the coast of Yugoslavia?

5. What kind of vegetation covers most of Scandinavia?

6. What kinds of vegetation are generally found in Poland?

THREE

Asia

Asia is the largest continent on the earth. In part because of its great size, Asia displays an amazing variety of features. It reaches from the polar region in the north to the tropical region in the south. It holds wide deserts as well as dense rain forests. Both the highest and the lowest points of land on earth are found on the Asian continent. It contains not only prosperous industrial countries, but also backward, poverty-stricken countries in which most of the people struggle to make a living by farming or herding. In some lands the people live with basic freedoms, while in others they live under the harsh rule of communism or dictators.

Asia covers over seventeen million square miles of land and is the home of nearly three billion people. It was the home of ancient civilizations and the birthplace of most of the world's religions. It was the setting for Christ's first coming to earth as our Redeemer, and it will be the site of His return when He comes again to rule as King of Kings and Lord of Lords.

Over half of the people on the earth live in Asia. Although there are many large cities, most of the Asian people are villagers or farmers. Many do not have any education; many do not have enough food. Most of the people of Asia have never heard the gospel.

Although this great continent of Asia may seem very far away from our homes, it certainly demands our attention. Its land and its peoples play an extremely important role in the events of the world today. Let's take this opportunity to learn about this wide and varied continent.

CHAPTER 9

THE MIDDLE EAST

In this chapter we will explore sixteen countries of the Middle East. Some other countries of northern Africa and Afghanistan are often included as a part of the Middle East, but we will learn more about those lands in later chapters.

The Middle Eastern region has been important in history. It is the area wherein most of the events of the Bible took place. The Middle East has also been a place of trade between the peoples of Europe and those of eastern Asia. The region received its name because it is "in the middle," that is, between Europe and the Far East (eastern Asia).

Today, the Middle East is a center of commerce, but it is also a center of conflict and changing situations. Events in the Middle East make headlines in world news broadcasts and publications. The petroleum resources of some of the Middle Eastern countries bring billions of dollars of trade and investments to the region. The peoples of these lands are involved in many quarrels and fights with each other, and their governments face many problems. So that we may understand more about the accomplishments and the difficulties of the people in these lands, let's consider the countries of the Middle East.

	AREA (Square Miles)	POPULATION	CAPITAL	MAIN LANGUAGES	MAIN RELIGIONS	CURRENCY
ISRAEL	8,019	3,960,000	Jerusalem	Hebrew, Arabic, English	Judaism, Islam, Christianity	shekel
LEBANON	4,015	2,598,000	Beirut	Arabic, French, English	Christianity, Islam, Druze	pound
CYPRUS	3,572	653,000	Nicosia	Greek, Turkish	Eastern Orthodox, Islam	pound
SYRIA	71,498	9,739,000	Damascus	Arabic, Kurdish, Armenian	Islam, Eastern Orthodox	pound
JORDAN	37,737	3,420,000	Amman	Arabic, English	Islam	dinar
SAUDI ARABIA	829,996	10,443,000	Riyadh	Arabic	Islam	riyal
KUWAIT	6,830	1,652,000	Kuwait City	Arabic, English	Islam	dinar
BAHRAIN	240	393,000	Manama	Arabic, English	Islam	dollar
QATAR	4,247	267,000	Doha	Arabic	Islam	riyal
UNITED ARAB EMIRATES	32,278	985,000	Abu Dhabi	Arabic, English	Islam	dirham
OMAN	82,030	978,000	Muscat	Arabic	Islam	rial
SOUTH YEMEN	128,559	2,086,000	Aden	Arabic	Islam	dinar
NORTH YEMEN	75,290	5,744,000	Sana	Arabic	Islam	riyal
TURKEY	301,381	49,155,000	Ankara	Turkish, Kurdish, Arabic	Islam, Eastern Orthodox	lira
IRAQ	167,924	14,509,000	Baghdad	Arabic, Kurdish, Persian	Islam	dollar
IRAN	636,293	42,490,000	Teheran	Persian, Turkish, Kurdish	Islam, Zoroastrianism	rial

20° 30° 40° 50° 60° 70°

50°

SOVIET UNION

Black Sea

Caspian Sea

40°

Istanbul

THRACE

★Ankara

Mt. Ararat
(16,945 ft.)

ANATOLIA

TURKEY

Aegean Sea

★Teheran

AFGHANISTAN

CYPRUS

SYRIA

Euphrates River

Tigris River

•Isfahan

Mediterranean Sea

LEBANON

Jerusalem

ISRAEL ★

IRAQ

IRAN

30°

JORDAN

PAKISTAN

Aqaba

ARABIAN

KUWAIT

Persian Gulf

EGYPT

Red Sea

**SAUDI
ARABIA**

BAHRAIN

QATAR

Gulf of Oman

Tropic of Cancer

•Medina

Riyadh★

PENINSULA

N

**UNITED ARAB
EMIRATES**

RUB' AL KHALI

OMAN

20°

Jidda• ★Mecca

W   E

S

NORTH
YEMEN

SOUTH
YEMEN

Arabian Sea

★

Aden

10°

Equator

0°

0   200   500   1000   1500
Scale of miles

Indian Ocean

Israel

The Land of Israel

For the Lord thy God bringeth thee into a good land, a land of brooks of water, of fountains and depths that spring out of valleys and hills; a land of wheat, and barley, and vines, and fig trees, and pomegranates; a land of oil olive, and honey; a land wherein thou shalt eat bread without scarceness, thou shalt not lack any thing in it; a land whose stones are iron, and out of whose hills thou mayest dig brass. (Deuteronomy 8:7-9)

In these verses God told Moses and the children of Israel about the land that was promised to them. In Numbers 34:1-12 God told them what would be the borders of their land. Under the leadership of Joshua, the Israelites marched into the land. They conquered the Canaanite peoples who were living there and established their own nation.

Today much of that "promised land" belongs to the modern nation of Israel. It is a small country about the size of the

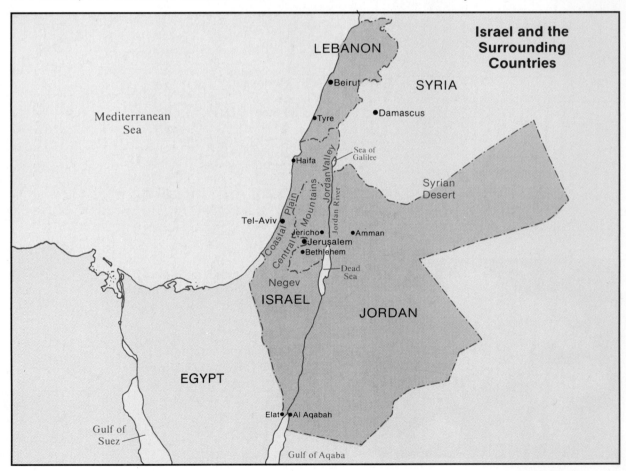

Israel and the Surrounding Countries

Mediterranean Sea

Sea level

Dead Sea

state of Massachusetts. The land has four basic geographical areas: the coastal plain, the central mountains, the Jordan valley, and the Negev (the southern desert region).

Most of Israel has a mild Mediterranean climate. The summers are warm and sunny while the winters bring gentle rains to the coastal areas. Much of the central mountain area and the Negev, however, receive little rainfall. Water is a precious resource in these dry areas of Israel. Wells and springs are as important for the farmers and herders today as they were in Abraham and Isaac's time.

The eastern border of Israel follows the Jordan River from the **Sea of Galilee** to the Dead Sea. The Sea of Galilee (called Lake Kinneret today) is as busy today as it was when Christ was on earth. Small fishing boats still glide over its waters, but now they are joined by pleasure boats and sightseeing cruise boats.

The **Jordan River** flows out of the Sea of Galilee and through a deep, junglelike valley. It crosses a desert plain and flows into the Dead Sea. The shore of the Dead Sea is the lowest area of land on the earth. It is 1,290 feet below sea level.

The Bible calls the **Dead Sea** the "Salt Sea" (Numbers 34:3; Deuteronomy 3:17). The water that flows into the Dead Sea cannot flow out. Instead it evaporates, leaving behind minerals that make the water very salty. The Dead Sea is so much saltier than the ocean that no fish can live in it. Plants do not grow in or near the salty water either. Anyone can swim in the Dead Sea. The water is so thick with

minerals that people do not sink in it. Swimming in the Dead Sea is not very pleasant, however. The water tastes terrible, and the salt often irritates the skin.

The People of Israel

In Bible Times

> Now the Lord had said unto Abram, Get thee out of thy country, and from thy kindred, and from thy father's house, unto a land that I will shew thee: And I will make of thee a great nation, and I will bless thee, and make thy name great; and thou shalt be a blessing: And I will bless them that bless thee, and curse him that curseth thee: and in thee shall all families of the earth be blessed. (Genesis 12:1-3)

About four thousand years ago, Abraham journeyed to the land that God had promised to him and his family. The book of Genesis tells us of Abraham's life in that land. There his sons, Ishmael and Isaac, were born. Isaac's sons, Esau and

Jacob, were born there, and so were Jacob's twelve sons.

God promised to make a great nation from Abraham's family. God also promised that the Lord Jesus Christ would come through Abraham's family.

God changed the name of Jacob, Abraham's grandson, to Israel. Jacob's sons and their families were called the children of Israel, the Israelites. They were also called the Hebrews. While Joseph was a ruler in Egypt, all the children of Israel moved from the Promised Land, Canaan, to Egypt to find food during a famine.

During their stay in Egypt, the number of Israelites grew to millions. The Egyptians made them work as slaves, but, of course, the Israelites longed to be free. God sent Moses to lead them back to the Promised Land.

Because of their lack of faith, there was a forty-year delay and the death of a generation before God allowed Joshua to lead the Israelites across the Jordan River and into the Promised Land. For many years judges sent by God ruled the Israelites. The people, however, wanted a king. God permitted King Saul, King David, and King Solomon to rule over all the Israelites and to build a great kingdom.

After Solomon's death the nation was divided into two kingdoms, Israel and Judah. Wicked kings ruled Israel, and the people turned away from God. The people of that kingdom were conquered and scattered by the Assyrians. Later the Chaldeans conquered the kingdom of Judah. The people were transported to Babylon where they lived in captivity for seventy years before they were allowed to return to the Promised Land. About five hundred years later, Christ was born.

At the time that the Israelites returned to the land, they began to be called **Jews.** First the Greeks (Macedonians) and then the Romans took control of the Jews and their land. The Jews looked for the Messiah, the promised Saviour to set them free from these conquerors. They looked for a mighty hero who would give them the victory. When Jesus came, few recognized Him as the Messiah. They did not realize that He first had to come to pay the penalty for their sins by conquering sin and death.

Since Bible Times

Few of the Jews accepted Jesus as the Son of God, the Saviour of men. They chose instead to continue looking for a Messiah to set them free from their difficulties. Because they revolted against Roman rule, the Romans destroyed Jerusalem shortly after the time of Christ. The Jews were then scattered throughout Europe, Asia, and northern Africa.

Nazareth, Israel

For hundreds of years the Jews had no homeland of their own and lived in areas far from **Palestine** (the Promised Land). Palestine was filled with other peoples. Finally after years of longing to be back in the land God gave to them, they began to move there. About a hundred years ago, Jews from many countries began to return to the land of Palestine. At first only small numbers of Jews returned to the land. Then in the 1920s and 1930s many more Jews left their homes

Jerusalem as seen from the Mount of Olives

abroad to help build a Jewish nation. Thousands of Jews fled to Palestine during World War II to escape Hitler's persecution in Europe. After the war, in 1948, the modern nation of Israel was established.

When the Jews returned to Palestine, the Arab people who were living there and in the neighboring areas did not want the Jewish people there. They tried to drive the people away by attacking the Jewish cities and settlements. The new nation has fought against its unfriendly neighbors in several wars. Israel has maintained a

Bethlehem, Israel

strong army to protect its cherished homeland.

Not all the people who live in Israel today are Jews. Many are Arabs or people of other nationalities. Whether Jewish or not, all the people who live in Israel are called Israelis. Jews live in countries all over the world, but many Jews are still returning to Israel.

The Israelis have worked hard to make their country strong. They have built new cities and towns in which businesses are growing. They have irrigated a great deal of farmland so that they can produce large crops of citrus fruits, wheat, cotton, olives, and vegetables. They have built homes and schools for the growing Israeli population.

Judaism

Following the Law

Judaism is the religion of the Jews. They accept the Old Testament as their sacred Scripture, but they do not regard the New Testament as a part of their Bible.

Very devout Jews, called Orthodox Jews, follow carefully the laws of the Old Testament and many other rules for their worship. Some of these rules are found in the Talmud, a book of interpretations of Jewish laws. These Orthodox Jews diligently strive to keep all these traditional laws. They eat only *kosher* foods, foods that are proper according to dietary laws of the Old Testament. They will not eat pork or other animal meats that the Old Testament calls unclean (Leviticus 11). When they pray, Orthodox Jews often wear prayer shawls and small boxes attached to their foreheads or arms by a strap. These boxes, called *tefillin* or phylacteries, contain Scripture verses. The Orthodox Jews think that by wearing them they follow the instruction of Deuteronomy 6:8. As with the Pharisees Christ condemned in the New Testament, however, most of these practices are just an outward show of religion for these Jews. They think that works will win them favor with God, yet they reject the message of His Word (Matthew 23).

> Knowing that a man is not justified by the works of the law, but by the faith of Jesus Christ, even we have believed in Jesus Christ, that we might be justified by the faith of Christ, and not by the works of the law: for by the works of the law shall no flesh be justified. (Galatians 2:16)

The Bible tells us that the laws of the Old Testament were given to the Israelites to teach them how sinful man is and how holy God is. No one can obey all of the law, so men must have faith in God to be delivered from sin. Jesus Christ, God's Son, fulfilled all the law and made the perfect sacrifice for sin. It is by faith in Christ, not by following laws, that all are saved.

The Apostle Paul was a Jew who tried to follow all the laws of that religion. When Paul was converted, he realized that those works were not what would save him. Instead, he said that he must "be found in him [Christ], not having [his] own righteousness, which is of the law, but that which is through the faith of Christ, the

The northern coast of the Sea of Galilee

Bar Mitzvah

When a Jewish boy reaches the age of thirteen, he is considered to be a man. A special religious ceremony called a bar mitzvah usually marks the occasion. *Bar mitzvah* means "son of the commandment," and it signifies that the boy is now responsible for his own religious life. The ceremony generally takes place on the Saturday following the boy's birthday.

At the ceremony the boy reads from one of the Books of Moses (the first five books of the Old Testament). He also may give a speech to demonstrate his knowledge of the Old Testament Scriptures and of the Jewish traditions. Afterwards the family and friends enjoy a special feast prepared by his parents. Also, family members and guests give the boy presents to honor his arrival at religious manhood.

---

righteousness which is of God by faith" (Philippians 3:9).

Not all the Jews are Orthodox. Some have little regard for the religious beliefs of Judaism. They wish simply to have a strong nation of Jews in Israel. Today all the Jews of Israel and those living in other countries need to learn that they must have Christ's righteousness through faith.

The Language of the Jews

The Old Testament was written mostly in Hebrew, the language of the ancient Israelites. By the time of Christ, the Jews were speaking other languages. The Hebrew language was used only in religious instruction. After the time of Christ, when the Jews were scattered around the world, they learned to speak the languages of those lands. When the new nation of Israel was established in recent years, its people spoke many languages. They decided that they would all learn to speak Hebrew once again. Jews who returned to the land received instruction in the language. Today most Israelis speak Hebrew, although Arabic

Hebrew Alphabet

Hebrew character	Name	Hebrew character	Name
א	Aleph	ל	Lamed
ב	Beth	ם מ	Mem
ג	Gimel	ן נ	Nun
ד	Daleth	ס	Samekh
ה	Hay	ע	Ayin
ו	Waw	ף פ	Pay
ז	Zayin	ץ צ	Tsade
ח	Kheth	ק	Qof
ט	Teth	ר	Resh
י	Yod	שׁ	Sin or Shin
ך כ	Kaph	ת	Taw

and other languages are commonly used, especially by those who are not Jewish.

Jerusalem

The land in and near Israel is often called the Holy Land. Most of the events of the Bible, both the Old and the New Testaments, took place in this area, and so it is a special land to both Jews and Christians. Jerusalem, the capital of Israel, is often called the Holy City. Because King David established his capital there, it is the "City of David" as well. Solomon built the Temple there for the worship of God, and there Christ ministered and was sentenced to death. Christ also has promised to return to earth and establish His perfect kingdom at Jerusalem. In addition, it is considered a holy city by the Moslems (also called Muslims), followers of another religion about which we will learn shortly.

Today there are two parts to the city of Jerusalem. One part is the Old City, the area in which the people of Christ's day lived. Many of the buildings in the Old City are hundreds of years old. A few of the buildings were probably standing at the time of Christ. Many churches have been built over places at which people think events of the Bible occurred. No one,

The "Holy City," Jerusalem

however, really knows the exact location of these events.

The Old City is surrounded by stone walls that were built about five hundred years ago. On the eastern side of the Old City is the large area where the Temple once stood. Only one part was left standing when the Romans destroyed the Temple. That wall is called the Wailing Wall, and it is the most precious place for the Jews. They often go there to pray.

The Wailing Wall

To the west of the Old City lies the modern city of Jerusalem. Government buildings, apartment buildings, schools, businesses, and broad streets in this part of the city are filled with hard-working Israelis.

When Israel was established in 1948, the Israelis were not allowed to have the Old City as a part of their country. Jews were not allowed in the Old City at all. They did, however, build their modern city nearby, and they waited for the time when they could reclaim their ancient capital.

In 1967 war broke out between the Arabs and the Israelis. It lasted six days. During the war Israel claimed the Old City for its own. Now the Jews, and anyone

else who wishes, may visit the famous sites of the Old City. Tourists from all over the world eagerly come to visit this Holy City in the Holy Land.

Government and Economy

Israel has a parliament called the knesset with a prime minister and cabinet to lead its government. The elected parliament appoints a president to be the ceremonial leader of the country. The government has supervised the country's agricultural development and industries. Organization and hard work have helped the Israelis to produce almost enough food to feed the growing nation. People in businesses and industries also labor diligently to provide the necessary goods and services for the country.

Section Review

1. What are the four geographical regions of Israel?

2. What two bodies of water lie along the eastern border of Israel?

3. What is the name of the Jews' religion?

4. What language do most Israelis speak?

5. What part of the Jewish Temple in Jerusalem remains?

Lebanon, Cyprus, Syria, and Jordan

Lebanon

To the north of Israel along the Mediterranean Sea lies the little country of Lebanon. Lebanon is a mountainous country smaller than the state of

Connecticut. Once its mountains were covered with forests of cedar and fir trees. The cedars of Lebanon were prized as lumber for great buildings. The forests were cut down centuries ago, and today only a few of the famous trees remain on the mountainsides.

Solomon used the cedars of Lebanon to build the Temple in Jerusalem about three thousand years ago. Hiram, king of Tyre, a city in Lebanon, helped Solomon get the materials needed for the buildings in Jerusalem.

The people who lived in the area of Lebanon during Bible times were called Phoenicians. They were great sailors and merchants. The Phoenicians sailed over the Mediterranean, trading with the people of distant lands.

Today most of the people of Lebanon are Arabs. While about half of the Lebanese are Moslem, the other half are Christians. This does not mean that half of the people of Lebanon are true Christians. Often the word *Christian* is used to mean a person who follows any religion that acknowledges Jesus as leader or example. All Roman Catholics, Greek Orthodox, and Protestants consider themselves "Christians" in this sense. Most of these Christians in Lebanon are Maronites. Their religion is similar to Roman Catholicism. We know that true Christians are only those who have accepted Jesus Christ as their Saviour. There are a few true Christians in Lebanon who are trying to preach the gospel in that land.

Lebanon is a country in which business and agriculture have prospered. Regrettably, the people of Lebanon in recent years have not been able to live together peacefully. Religious and political differences have brought fighting and destruction. Neighboring countries have also added to Lebanon's troubles. The beautiful capital of Beirut has been attacked several times. Artillery fire has wrecked many of the tall modern buildings along the coast, but the Lebanese continue to rebuild.

The people of Lebanon need peace for their country but more desperately need peace in their hearts. We should pray for the true Christians in Lebanon, that they may be good testimonies in this land of turmoil.

The wreckage that was once Beirut, Lebanon

Cyprus

This large island in the eastern Mediterranean Sea holds a wealth of fruit trees. Groves of lemon, orange, grapefruit, and olive trees thrive in the Mediterranean sunshine. Apricot, cherry, and peach trees blossom in the spring. Many other fruits and grains grow well in the soil of Cyprus.

The island is a beautiful spot with pleasant scenery, but its people are not content. Most of the Cypriots speak Greek and belong to the Greek Orthodox church. Although they are hundreds of miles away, they wish to be closely associated with the

A Syrian shepherd and his sheep

land of Greece. A large group of Cypriots, however, have a Turkish heritage. They speak Turkish, and they are Moslems. The different desires of these two groups have led to bitter and violent struggles on the island.

Syria

North and east of Lebanon lies the much larger country of Syria. Although about the size of the state of North Dakota, the country has only a few large cities. The ancient city of Damascus is its capital. We remember that Saul of Tarsus (Paul) was on the road to Damascus when he was converted (Acts 9). The city is also known for its fine craftsmen.

On Damascus streets lined with shops and stalls, one may find potters and silversmiths at work. Woven rugs and embroidered cloth are on sale. The people are eager to sell their vegetables, baskets, leather items, and much more to the passersby. **Bazaars** similar to those of Damascus fill the streets of many of the larger towns of the Middle East.

The **Euphrates River** flows through the northeastern corner of Syria, providing water for the farmers in that region. Dams on the river hold more water that is used to irrigate additional farmland. A large portion of the country, however, is desert with few sources of water.

In the desert areas of Syria and other countries of the Middle East lives a type of people called the **Bedouins** (BED oo inz). Bedouins are nomadic. That means that they wander from place to place to find pasture for their flocks and herds. They live in black tents made from goat or camel hair. They eat the fruit that grows in the oases where they often feed and water their animals. They also eat a large amount of yogurt made from the milk of their goats and camels. Some still wish to live in their simple way, wandering across the land just as their ancestors did for thousands of years. More and more of the Bedouins, however, are giving up their nomadic life to settle in the villages of the Middle East.

The Syrians are an Arabic people. Most of the Syrians are also Moslems. They dislike having the Jewish nation of Israel for their neighbor. There has been much fighting between the Syrians and the Israelis.

Jordan

East of Israel is the kingdom of Jordan. Jordan is an Arab nation ruled by a king. Most of the Jordanians are Moslems, and many of them live in small villages. There are a few large cities, of which Amman, the capital, is the largest.

The land of Jordan has few resources. There are few areas that receive enough rainfall to support crops. Much of the land is rocky desert and highland that provide only small areas of pasture for the Bedouins' sheep and goats.

Only a few rivers flow year-round in this country. Other streams may flow after a rain, but then they dry up after a few days or weeks of heat. (Temperatures sometimes rise to 120°F in parts of Jordan.) The dry valleys through which the streams of rainwater flow are called **wadis.** Wadis are commonly found in many of the dry areas of the Middle East. They often have steep sides that have been worn into cliffs by the occasional rushing water.

Except for a short coast at Aqaba on the gulf at the north of the Red Sea, Jordan is a landlocked country. It is surrounded by other countries and has no port other than at Aqaba. There Jordan sends and receives goods that are transported by water.

When the nation of Israel was established in 1948, Jordan gained an area of Palestine called the West Bank. This area to the west of the Jordan River includes the Old City of Jerusalem along with Bethlehem, Jericho, and many other Biblical sites. During the 1967 Arab-Israeli War, the Israeli armies took control of the West Bank. Many of the Arabs living in that area fled across the Jordan River, and some went to Syria and Lebanon. These Palestinian Arab refugees have fought against Israel in attempts to regain Palestine for themselves. Today the West Bank, though technically a part of Jordan, is ruled by the Israelis.

Old customs still exist in modern Syria.

The Countries of the Arabian Peninsula

A Desert Region

The large **Arabian Peninsula** lies between the continent of Africa and the rest of Asia. The peninsula is so large that it would cover the area of the United States from the Mississippi River to the Atlantic Ocean. Although the peninsula is surrounded by water on three sides, it is a very dry area. The air from over the seas loses its moisture as it rises over the hills near the coasts. The interior areas receive very little rainfall. The climate is so dry that there are no lakes, rivers, or forests in Arabia.

In southern Arabia lies a huge desert called the Rub' al Khali (ROOB ahl KHAH-lee), the "Empty Quarter." This area, almost as large as Texas, consists of miles and miles of endless sand. The Rub' al Khali often goes without rain for several years at a time. Day after day the blazing

Camels

The camel is a remarkable animal. God created it with features that enable it to live in desert lands. Because it has helped man travel though dry regions in which other animals cannot survive, the camel has been called the "ship of the desert."

The camel has an amazing ability to conserve water. Although it may drink twenty or more gallons of water at a time, it can travel for days without a slurp. The water is not stored in the camel's hump as once was believed. Instead, God made the animal's body so that it would recycle the water it drinks without losing much of it. The camel can also eat scrawny desert shrubs and drink salty water unfit for man and most other animals. Despite its diet, the camel produces milk to feed its young and its owners.

God also gave the camel other features to help it live in the sandy deserts. It has two sets of eyelashes to keep the sand from blowing in its eyes. It has big, soft feet that keep it from sinking into the loose sand as it walks. And the camel's long neck allows it to eat shrubs on the ground and still reach leaves from low trees.

A camel can travel up to 100 miles a day in the desert, and it can carry a heavy load. Camel caravans—long lines of camels—carried the goods of countless traders across deserts in the past. Today airplanes and special desert vehicles have almost replaced the camel as a means of transportation. Yet when other vehicles fail, a camel is still a reliable carrier of shipments in the desert.

There are two kinds of camels: the dromedary and the Bactrian. The dromedary has only one hump and is common in the hot desert regions of the Middle East and North Africa. The Bactrian camel has two humps and lives mainly in the cooler desert regions of central Asia.

sun shines on the shifting ridges of sand in the great desert. Travel is difficult in the Rub' al Khali. One may comfortably travel across this region only by plane.

In the past, most of the people of the Arabian peninsula were nomadic Bedouin herders and traders. Some of the villages were the homes of merchants and craftsmen who traded with the Bedouin tribes.

A few farmers lived in oases where they raised fruit and small areas of crops.

Mohammed and Islam

About six hundred years after the time of Christ, a man named **Mohammed** (moh HAM id) lived in Mecca, an important trading center on the Arabian Peninsula. Mohammed believed that he had been given revelations from a god named Allah. He then taught others about the way he believed they could achieve salvation. He wrote down many of his teachings in a book called the **Koran.** Mohammed's followers, the **Moslems,** believe that the Koran is the holy book. It gives them instruction for following their religion, called **Islam.**

Soon Mohammed's ideas were accepted by the people of the Arabian Peninsula. These Moslems believed that they must convert the people of other lands to their new religion. The Moslem armies conquered most of the Middle Eastern peoples as well as the people of North Africa. As they conquered, they forced these peoples to accept their Islamic religion. The Arabic language and culture were spread throughout these areas. That is the reason that many of the peoples of the Middle East are Arabs.

The Moslems took their religion into Eastern Europe and far into Asia. The map below shows where many Moslems live today. There are about eight hundred million Moslems who are living without the knowledge that salvation comes only by faith in Jesus Christ. Instead, these people believe that they must perform at least four of the following five actions if they are to go to heaven.

1. Proclaim, "There is no God but Allah, and Mohammed is His prophet."
2. Pray five times a day
3. Give alms (money) to the poor
4. Fast
5. Make a pilgrimage (religious journey) to Mecca if possible

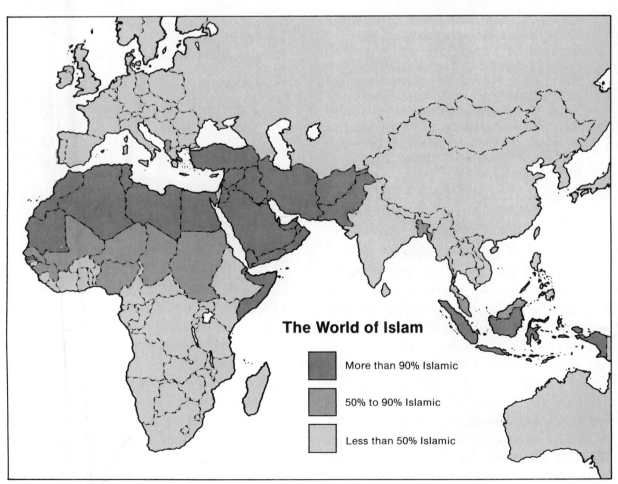

The World of Islam

More than 90% Islamic

50% to 90% Islamic

Less than 50% Islamic

The Islamic Religion

1. **Proclaim, "There is no god but Allah, and Mohammed is His prophet"**

   Every day Moslems recite this statement of their belief. The Moslems believe in one god. Their god is called Allah. They believe that Mohammed was Allah's special prophet sent to teach men submission to Allah.

2. **Pray five times a day**

   The Moslems call their churches mosques. Near their mosques stand towers called minarets. Five times a day, every day, a call is given from the top of the tower. When the call to prayer is given, Moslems stop what they are doing, spread their prayer rugs on the ground, face in the direction of Mecca, drop to their knees, bow their heads to the ground, and pray their required prayers.

3. **Give alms to the poor**

   Moslems believe that it is their duty to help the poor. They often give money to beggars sitting by the wayside.

4. **Fast**

   For one month each year—a month they call Ramadan—Moslems go without food or water from dawn until dusk. They eat and drink only during the hours of darkness. As a sacrifice to Allah, they go all day in their warm climate without a drink to quench their thirst.

5. **Make a pilgrimage to Mecca**

   Every Moslem desires to make a journey to Mecca at least once in his life. For those who live far away from Arabia or for those who are very poor or sick, the journey may be impossible. Those who are unable to go are excused, but thousands of Moslems are able to make the trip each year at the appointed time.

   Mecca is Mohammed's hometown. In the past only Moslems were allowed into this city, which is very sacred to them. There, inside the Great Mosque, is a cube-shaped building called the Kaaba. In the wall of the Kaaba is a Black Stone that the Moslems believe Allah sent to earth. The Moslems circle the Kaaba seven times, and they try to touch or kiss the Black Stone. The Moslems are careful to follow all of the many rules for their pilgrimage to Mecca. When they go back to their homes, they are honored by their neighbors who have not yet made their journey to the Moslem holy city.

The Kaaba at Mecca's great mosque

The Nation of Saudi Arabia

Over fifty years ago the people of the Arabian Peninsula were members of different tribes without a united government of their own. Then a man named Ibn Saud led a movement to establish an Arabian country. The different peoples united under Saud's leadership, and they named their country after the new ruling family, Saudi Arabia. The Saudi government has been controlled by a king, an absolute monarch. The king is a member of the Saud family, and his power is not limited by a constitution. He has full authority to run the government. He rules most of the Arabian Peninsula. Only a few small countries on the eastern and southern sides of the peninsula have never become a part of Saudi Arabia.

Until recent years Saudi Arabia was a land of poor Bedouins and villagers. Oil was discovered there in the 1930s, and since then the petroleum industry has grown rapidly. New wealth from oil has brought great changes to the people of Saudi Arabia.

In the past few children were able to attend school. Now with money earned from the sale of oil, Saudi children receive free education. The Saudis have built airports, hospitals, roads, and modern cities. Many drive their own luxury cars.

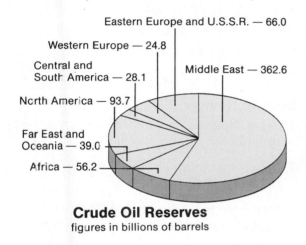

Eastern Europe and U.S.S.R. — 66.0
Western Europe — 24.8
Central and South America — 28.1
Middle East — 362.6
North America — 93.7
Far East and Oceania — 39.0
Africa — 56.2

Crude Oil Reserves
figures in billions of barrels

Most of the Saudis are no longer Bedouins or villagers. Instead, they work in the oil industry or in the businesses of the cities.

Although life has changed for many Saudis, some things have remained the same. The Saudis are still devoted to Islam. In fact, the Saudi government protects and promotes its religion, and it prohibits any other religious worship. Saudis are threatened with the penalty of death if they become Christians, and foreigners are not allowed to witness for Christ.

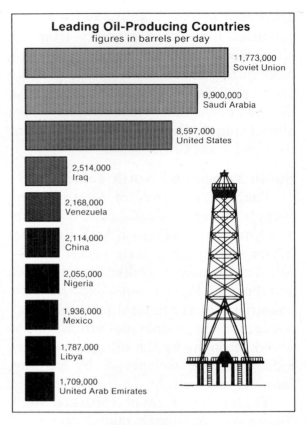

Leading Oil-Producing Countries
figures in barrels per day

11,773,000 Soviet Union
9,900,000 Saudi Arabia
8,597,000 United States
2,514,000 Iraq
2,168,000 Venezuela
2,114,000 China
2,055,000 Nigeria
1,936,000 Mexico
1,787,000 Libya
1,709,000 United Arab Emirates

Many Saudis have begun to wear clothes like those we wear in America, but others continue to wear the kind of clothes worn for centuries in that land. Not only the Bedouins, who continue to live in their tents in the desert, but also many of the people of the cities have kept the same desert clothing. The long, flowing garments that the Saudis wear keep them cool during the hot days. They also keep them warm when the desert cools at night.

Eastern Arabian Nations

The small countries of Kuwait, Bahrain, Qatar, United Arab Emirates, and Oman lie on the eastern side of the Arabian Peninsula by the **Persian Gulf** and the Gulf of Oman. They have hot, dry climates, and their peoples are Moslem Arabs.

Like Saudi Arabia, these countries were once poor desert lands. Most of their people made their living by trading, fishing, and herding until oil was discovered in the area. Today these little countries have large incomes from oil industries. Like Saudi Arabia, they are modernizing their countries and providing for the physical needs of their peoples. Also like Saudi Arabia, these countries are almost completely without a testimony for the Lord Jesus Christ.

South Yemen and North Yemen

The two countries of South Yemen (People's Democratic Republic of Yemen) and North Yemen (Yemen Arab Republic) lie on the southwestern corner of the Arabian Peninsula. Unlike Saudi Arabia and the small Persian Gulf countries, these countries lack the natural resource of oil. Because these people do not have the wealth brought by the oil industry, they must continue to survive by herding, farming, and trading.

The highland areas of North and South Yemen receive enough rainfall to grow a few crops. Coffee grows well in that area, and much of it was once shipped from the port of Mocha on the Red Sea. For that reason, coffee is sometimes called mocha.

Most of the people of these countries are poor farmers who belong to different Moslem tribes. These Arabic-speaking groups find it difficult to get along with each other. South Yemen became a Communist country in 1969. The Communists also wish to control North Yemen, but the northern Yemenis are fighting to keep their independence.

Section Review

1. What kind of tree from Lebanon was used to build Solomon's Temple?

2. What two countries have a strong influence on Cyprus?

3. Name the seven countries that lie on the Arabian Peninsula.

4. Who founded the religion of Islam?

5. What is the holy book of Islam?

Turkey

Location

Only two countries in the world contain land in both Europe and Asia. One is the Soviet Union, which covers large areas of both Europe and Asia. The second is Turkey. Most of Turkey lies on a large peninsula in western Asia. That peninsula is often called Asia Minor or Anatolia. The remainder of Turkey lies in Europe and is called Thrace.

A narrow channel of water from the Black Sea to the Aegean Sea separates Thrace from Anatolia. At the western end of this water passageway is the narrow strait called the Dardanelles. The water widens into the Sea of Marmara between the Dardanelles and the Bosporus Strait at the eastern end. The waterway between the Black Sea and the Mediterranean is an important transportation route. Also, overland trade from Europe and Asia has often gone through this area where the two continents nearly touch.

A City and Empires

A few hundred years before the time of Christ, a Greek village called Byzantium began on the European shore of the Bosporus Strait. About three hundred years after the time of Christ, the Roman emperor Constantine made the city his eastern capital. The name was changed to Constantinople. When Rome's power collapsed, Constantinople grew in strength and wealth. For about a thousand years, the city was the capital of an area of Eastern Europe and the Middle East called the Byzantine Empire.

Moslem conquerors brought an end to the Byzantine Empire. A group of Asian peoples called the Turks invaded Asia Minor. The Turks converted to Islam, and they were eager to conquer new lands for their religion. Constantinople struggled for many years to keep the attackers away. Finally, in 1453 the Turks were successful. They made Constantinople the capital of their Moslem empire, the Ottoman Empire. A Moslem ruler called a sultan controlled the Turks from the city on the Bosporus until the 1920s.

Modern Turkey

In 1923 a Turkish soldier named Mustafa Kemal helped establish a new government for his land. Kemal helped his people to modernize their way of life. He promoted better education and better government. His people gave him the title of *Ataturk,* which means "Father of the Turks." Kemal Ataturk also changed the name of Constantinople to Istanbul, and he moved the capital to Ankara in the middle of Anatolia.

Despite improvements that were made in Turkey while Ataturk was president, many of the Turkish people still live in poverty. Ankara, Istanbul, and several cities along the coast of Turkey are large and hold opportunities for the people to live comfortably, work, and get a good education. The rural areas, however, are not as prosperous.

Mountains and hills cover much of Anatolia. Although the soil is good for farming, there is not enough rainfall in the interior of the country to grow many crops.

A mosque in Istanbul, Turkey

An explorer searches for the remains of Noah's Ark on Mt. Ararat.

Some of the land is irrigated, but much of it is pastureland where herds of sheep and goats graze. The people live in villages or scattered farmhouses made out of mud bricks. Many of the villages still do not have electricity or plumbing. While cars are common in the cities, most of the people in the countryside still travel in horse-drawn wagons or use donkeys to carry their loads while they walk. Most of the farmers use simple tools and farm animals to do their work instead of modern machinery.

Farmers in the coastal areas of Turkey grow much fruit. In the interior, wheat is the main crop. The sheep raised in Turkey provide mutton, the most common meat eaten by the Turks, and a Turkish breed of white goats grows a coat of popular, soft wool known as mohair.

Bible Geography

Turkey's most famous mountain is **Mount Ararat.** Mount Ararat is 16,945 feet high and it is located near Turkey's border with the Soviet Union. Genesis 8:4 tells us that Noah's ark came to rest "upon the mountains of Ararat."

The Apostle Paul was from Tarsus, a city in Asia Minor. Paul visited many cities in Asia Minor on his missionary journeys. In chapters two and three of Revelation, the Apostle John wrote God's warnings and promises to seven churches located in Asia Minor. In those early days of Christianity, many true Christians lived in this area that today is the country of Turkey. Now, however, the darkness of the Islamic religion keeps the people of Turkey from knowing Jesus Christ as their Saviour. Almost all Turks are Moslems. They are trusting in the teachings of the man Mohammed rather than trusting in the grace of God through His Son, Jesus Christ.

Iraq

Mesopotamia

And the name of the third river is Hiddekel: that is it which goeth toward the east of Assyria. And the fourth river is Euphrates. (Genesis 2:14)

This Bible verse speaks of two of the four rivers that flowed out of the Garden of Eden. Hiddekel is the ancient name of the **Tigris** River. Today, these two rivers, the Tigris and the Euphrates, flow through the country of Iraq to the Persian Gulf.

Most of the Middle East is very dry. The whole area has little rainfall, few areas of good farmland, and few rivers. The area around the Tigris and Euphrates Rivers is one of the few fertile areas in the Middle East. In ancient times the area was called *Mesopotamia,* which means "the land between the rivers."

Some of the world's early civilizations grew in the Mesopotamian area. Abraham

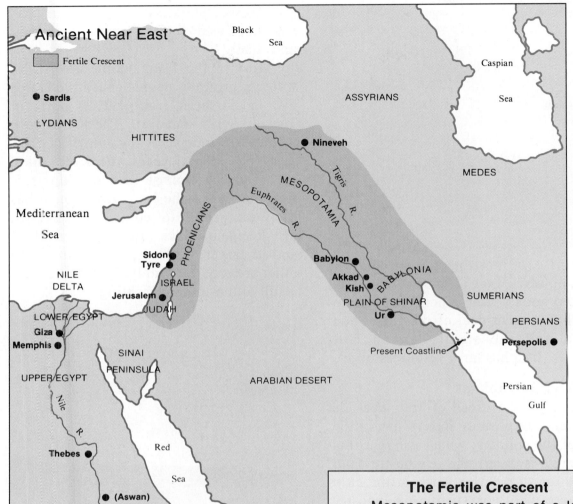

Ancient Near East

◻ Fertile Crescent

Black Sea

● Sardis

LYDIANS

HITTITES

Caspian Sea

ASSYRIANS

● Nineveh

MESOPOTAMIA

Tigris R.

Euphrates R.

MEDES

Mediterranean Sea

PHOENICIANS

Sidon ●
Tyre ●

ISRAEL

Jerusalem ●

JUDAH

NILE DELTA

LOWER EGYPT

Giza ●
Memphis ●

SINAI PENINSULA

UPPER EGYPT

Nile R.

Thebes ●

● (Aswan)

Red Sea

Babylon ●
Akkad ●
Kish ●

BABYLONIA

PLAIN OF SHINAR

Ur ●

Present Coastline

ARABIAN DESERT

SUMERIANS

PERSIANS

● Persepolis

Persian Gulf

was from a city called Ur (Genesis 11:31), which was beside the Euphrates River. The Chaldean Empire grew around the city of Babylon in Mesopotamia. King Nebuchadnezzar conquered the Jews and carried many of them away to Babylon as captives. Daniel was one of those captives who lived in Mesopotamia.

Agriculture in Iraq

After several thousand years of farming in Mesopotamia, Iraqi farmers have worn out the soil near the rivers and irrigated areas. As a result, today's Iraqis find it difficult to grow large crops. Iraqi farmers must use fertilizer. They must also allow some of their fields to lie fallow for a few years. By careful cultivation, the Iraqis

The Fertile Crescent

Mesopotamia was part of a larger area that stretched along the eastern coast of the Mediterranean Sea. Because the coastal area received rainfall and was watered by the Jordan River, and because the Tigris and Euphrates Rivers flowed through Mesopotamia, this large crescent-shaped area contained most of the good farmland in the Middle East. For that reason, this area is often called the "Fertile Crescent."

grow good crops of wheat, barley, rice, cotton, and vegetables.

The most important crop in Iraq is dates. Groves of date palms along the Tigris and Euphrates near the Persian Gulf produce many tons of dates. Dates are an important food for the desert-dwelling

The two main rivers of Iraq: the Euphrates *(below left)* and the Tigris *(below right)*

Bedouins. To most people around the world, however, they are a tasty ingredient in baked goods. Iraq exports many dates as well as a great deal of oil. Like Saudi Arabia and the small Persian Gulf countries, Iraq has large resources of oil.

People and Problems

Although the areas of Iraq near the Tigris and Euphrates Rivers are fertile, most of the country, which is larger than California, is desert and dry pastureland. Except for those who work in the cities and those who work in the oil industry, most Iraqis are farmers and herders. Almost all the Iraqis are Moslems, and many of them are very poor. Money from the oil industry is beginning to bring

improvements to Iraq, but the country still has many needs such as schools, hospitals, and roads.

Most of the Iraqi people are Arabs. Another group of people called the Kurds live in northern Iraq and in parts of Turkey, Syria, and Iran. The Kurds wish to have an independent country of their own. For several years, the Kurds have been fighting against Iraq to gain their freedom. While the Iraqi government has been struggling to control the Kurds, disagreements have arisen between Iraq and its larger neighbor, Iran. Along with other areas of the Middle East, this region is full of tension and fighting.

Iran

Past and Present

Iran (today's name for ancient **Persia**) was once the center of the great Persian Empire. This empire conquered the Chaldean Empire that held Daniel captive in Babylon. The Persian ruler Cyrus allowed the Jews to return to Palestine after seventy years of Babylonian captivity (II Chronicles 36:22-23). The Roman Empire conquered Persia, and later Arabs took control of the land and brought their Islamic religion.

Today Moslem religious leaders have taken control of Iran's government. Although nearly all Iranians are Moslems, they are divided into many groups with different religious and political ideas. Disagreements between these groups have caused violence and discontent throughout Iran. Leaders have wrongfully blamed American influence and other foreigners for the problems of the country, causing many Iranians to hate the United States.

The Land

Iran is a land of mountains and deserts. The southern regions of the country are extremely warm, while winters in the northern mountainous areas can be very cold. The southern border lies along the Persian Gulf and the Gulf of Oman. The north of Iran is bounded by the Soviet Union and the Caspian Sea.

For many years the Soviet Union has greedily watched this important region. If the Soviet Union could gain control of Iran, it would have access to the oil-rich Persian Gulf area and gain important seaports on those shores. Such threats increase the tension in this land of confusion.

The People

The Iranian people are mainly poor, although a prosperous oil industry and a few other businesses have brought wealth to some. The nearly barren desert and mountain areas provide some pasture for goats and sheep. Living in tents, some herders wander with their flocks from pastureland to pastureland. Others keep their animals in areas near their village houses. Farmers use well water to irrigate their crops of wheat, cotton, and barley. Craftsmen fashion useful and decorative articles for local use or for export.

Iranian villagers construct most of their buildings from mud bricks. Typical houses have two or three rooms with an enclosed courtyard. Cooking is done over a fire in the courtyard, and a donkey or ox may be kept in that area as well. There are no tables or chairs in the houses. The people sit, eat, and sleep on rugs and cushions. Most Iranians eat a few basic foods such as rice, curdled milk, and large, round, thin loaves of bread. These living conditions and foods are common to many areas of the Middle East.

Iran also has several large cities where the living conditions are more modern and comfortable. Cities such as Teheran and Isfahan have areas of houses and apartments much like those in American and European cities. Bazaars, markets, and restaurants offer many kinds of food for sale. *Shish kebab*—chunks of lamb meat, onions, and peppers broiled on skewers and seasoned with spices—is a favorite dish of the Iranians.

The most famous product of Iranian craftsmen is their beautiful rugs. The women spend hundreds of hours in their homes or in small workshops weaving the woolen carpets by hand. These Persian rugs have colorful and complicated designs. Because they are stiff when they are finished, the rugs are spread out on the walkways for a few days. The foot traffic that tramples and soils the rugs, also helps to improve their texture. When the carpets have received enough of a beating, they are taken to a stream or pool where they are scrubbed and rinsed. After drying in the sun, they are ready for sale at a bazaar or for shipment around the world. People pay hundreds or even thousands of dollars for these rugs, which are not only useful but are also prized as works of art.

The Middle East, A Region of Turmoil

The Middle Eastern area we have discussed in this chapter has many unique and important features. The Middle East is a strategic region of the world. It is at the crossroads of three continents. Throughout history, traders and armies have traveled through this region as they passed from Europe, Asia, and Africa.

Powerful nations have sought control of this area where early civilizations of the world developed. Today, nations continue to watch and try to influence the events in this critical political region.

The Middle East is a holy land to three religious groups—the Jews, the Moslems, and Christians. Most of the events of the Bible took place in this region, making it a special place to those of us who truly believe in Jesus Christ and in the truth of the Scriptures. Yet today, most Middle Eastern people are Moslems or Jews who follow their religions of good works.

Religions of the World

Religion	Estimated Numbers
"Christian" *	998,775,000
Islam	587,336,000
Hindu	475,940,000
Buddhist	254,841,000
Confucian	158,137,000
Shinto	57,156,000
Jewish	14,319,000

*Includes: Roman Catholic 580,914,000
Protestant 338,397,000
Eastern Orthodox 79,464,000

The Middle East is a poor region. Its land receives little precipitation and has few rivers. Some of its people still wander across the deserts to find trading opportunities or pastures for their animals. Irrigation is necessary in most areas where farming is successful. The Middle Eastern area contains great wealth in its oil resources, and some of its people have grown rich, yet many continue to live in poverty.

The Middle East is a region of hatred and violence. Fighting takes place almost constantly. The Israelis and their Arab neighbors struggle against each other. Islamic sects often fight against one another. Cyprus, Lebanon, Iraq, and Iran suffer from internal warfare and discontent. Terrorism threatens the peace and safety of many in the lands of the Middle East. It is indeed a region of turmoil, and yet the greatest need of the people of those lands is for the Saviour. The Lord Jesus Christ can bring peace to the lives of individuals in the Middle East regardless of the strife that surrounds them.

Section Review

1. On what two continents does the country of Turkey lie?

2. What city is the present capital of Turkey?

3. What two important rivers flow through the country of Iraq?

4. What was the ancient name for the region that is now the country of Iran?

5. What two bodies of water lie to the south of Iran?

Terms to Remember

Sea of Galilee	Arabian Peninsula
Jordan River	Mohammed
Dead Sea	Koran
Jews	Moslems
Palestine	Islam
Judaism	*Persian Gulf*
bazaars	Mount Ararat
Euphrates River	Tigris River
Bedouins	Persia
wadis	

Things to Know

1. What country of the Middle East has been settled mainly by Jews?

2. What is the religion of most of the Middle Eastern countries?

3. What language do the Israelis speak?

4. What natural resource has brought wealth to several Middle Eastern countries in recent years?

5. What are the followers of Mohammed's religion called?

6. Name three important rivers of the Middle East.

7. The area that was once the land of Persia is now what country?

8. What animal provides transportation in the deserts of the Middle East?

Things to Talk About

1. Why do you think the Dead Sea got its name?

2. News broadcasts, books, and magazines often speak about "Christian" religious groups, "Christian" countries, or people they call "Christians." Does this always mean that the people spoken of are true Christians who know Christ as their Saviour? Why or not?

3. Is the Koran truly holy as our Bible is? Why or why not?

Things to Do

1. Look up these Bible verses to find the events that occurred at or on the Sea of Galilee.

   a. Matthew 4:18-20

   b. Matthew 14:22-33

   c. Luke 5:1-11

   d. Luke 8:22-25

   e. Mark 4:1-2

2. What events took place at the Jordan River?

   a. Joshua 3:10-17

   b. II Kings 5:9-14

   c. Matthew 3:13-17

3. Read Revelation 2 and 3. The following passages were written to churches in which cities of Asia Minor (modern Turkey)?

   a. Revelation 2:1-7

   b. Revelation 2:8-11

   c. Revelation 2:12-17

   d. Revelation 2:18-29

   e. Revelation 3:1-6

   f. Revelation 3:7-13

   g. Revelation 3:14-22

4. Answer these questions about camels.

   a. Who wore clothing made of camel hair? (Matthew 3:4)

   b. Who drew water for camels? (Genesis 24:19)

   c. Who owned three thousand camels? (Job 1:3)

5. Make a collection of newspaper and news magazine articles on recent events in the Middle East. As a class, use them to make a Middle East bulletin board display or a scrapbook. Change the bulletin board or add to the scrapbook news articles about the countries studied in later chapters. Briefly discuss the significance of each article that is posted.

Geography Skills

Use the atlas pages along with the maps in this chapter to complete the following:

1. Through what three countries does the Euphrates River flow?

2. What countries share a border with Israel?

3. The Persian Gulf touches what Middle Eastern countries?

4. At what latitude does the capital of Turkey lie?

5. At what longitude does the capital of Israel lie?

6. Find Mount Ararat on the topography map. What is its height?

7. What country in the Western Hemisphere lies at the same latitude as Israel?

8. If you were five hundred miles north of Jerusalem, in what country would you be?

CHAPTER 10

SOUTHERN ASIA

India

On a stormy night in 1947, several thousand people gathered around a large building in New Delhi, India. Inside, a large crowd sat in the assembly hall decorated with green, white, and orange banners. The meeting began at 11:00 P.M., and excitement grew as the minutes passed. Jawaharlal Nehru, one of the many speakers that night, told the people, "At the stroke of the midnight hour, when the world sleeps, India will awake to life and freedom."

The people sat in silence as the clock struck twelve times. Someone broke the stillness by blowing on a conch shell. Then cheers filled the hall and the streets as the people celebrated their independence. The date was August 15, 1947, the birthday of the modern country of India.

No Longer in the British Empire

For nearly two hundred years the British had controlled this large area of southern Asia. The forests and the fields

	AREA (Square Miles)	POPULATION	CAPITAL	MAIN LANGUAGES	MAIN RELIGIONS	CURRENCY
INDIA	1,269,339	730,572,000	New Delhi	Hindi, English, and other regional languages	Hinduism, Islam, Christianity, Sikhism	rupee
PAKISTAN	310,403	94,780,000	Islamabad	Urdu, English, and other regional languages	Islam, Hinduism	rupee
BANGLADESH	55,598	96,539,000	Dacca	Bengali, English	Islam, Hinduism	taka
AFGHANISTAN	249,999	14,177,000	Kabul	Persian, Pushtu	Islam	afghani
SRI LANKA	25,332	15,647,000	Colombo	Sinhalese, Tamil, English	Buddhism, Hinduism	rupee
NEPAL	54,362	16,169,000	Katmandu	Nepali	Hinduism, Buddhism	rupee
BHUTAN	18,147	1,386,000	Thimbu	Dzongka	Buddhism	ngultrum

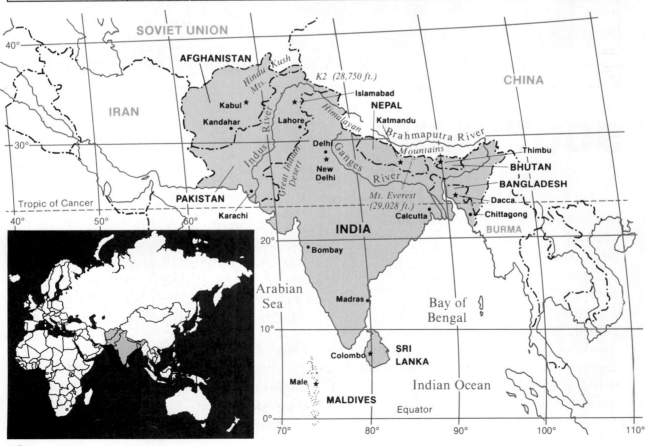

of India provided raw materials for the factories of Britain. British officials and businessmen governed and employed the Indians. British businesses profited from the riches of India. But in 1947, British rule was ended. India was free to rule itself and to profit from its own businesses. The people of India rejoiced, but their new country faced many difficulties.

Many People with Many Ways of Life

India is a large country. It is one of the ten largest countries in the world, but it is also a very poor and crowded country. There is only one country, China, that has more people than India. India's cities do not have enough houses and apartments for all the people who live in them. Many people sleep in tents and shacks, or on sidewalks. There are so many farmers in India's countryside that each one rarely has more than a few small fields in which he may raise his crops. The farmers cannot afford to buy modern machinery for their small fields. Instead, they use hand tools and wooden plows pulled by oxen. Though these Indian farmers work hard, their harvests are usually small because they lack machinery.

The land of India includes a wide variety of landscapes and a wide variety of people. In the **Himalaya Mountains** (HIM uh LAY uh) of northeastern India, the people have features and customs similar to those of the Chinese. The Indians who live in the northwestern desert region have much in common with the people of the Middle East. The villagers of central and southern India have distinctive customs. Even the rich and poor people in the cities of India have their own special ways of life.

In 1947 the leaders of India faced the task of uniting all the peoples of that country. The new government needed the support of the Indians who lived in the mountains, deserts, plains, and forests. It needed the support of those who lived in small villages and those who lived in large cities. However, three big problems kept India from becoming a strong, united country. One was that the people of India

Many of the people of India live in deep poverty.

speak many different languages. Another was that transportation and communication are difficult in such a large and poor land. Finally, most of the people of India followed one of two religions, Islam or Hinduism, and the Moslems and the Hindus hated each other. In the years since Indian independence, these problems have not been completely solved, and they still affect India's prosperity.

The Language Problem

The peoples of India speak hundreds of different languages. Most Indians know only the language that is spoken in their area. News and government affairs must be translated into all these languages if everyone is to understand. The leaders of India realized that the country must have one official language that everyone should learn. Although English was used and taught by the British in many areas, the new Indian leaders chose an Indian language. **Hindi,** a language spoken in the north central area of the country, became India's official language. Today about one-third of the Indian people can speak Hindi. India still lacks enough schools and teachers to teach everyone how to read and write, and so it may be a long time before all Indians know Hindi.

Many Indians live in poverty.

An Indian farmer and his wife

Many People in a Large Land

The large land of India is shaped somewhat like a kite. The country is over one thousand miles long and more than one thousand miles wide. With over a million square miles, India is about one-third as large as the United States. In that area live about 700 million people, three times the number of people in the United States. Although many people live in India's crowded cities, many more live in villages scattered throughout the land.

Most Indians do not have cars, and travel by bus, train, or plane is too expensive for the common people. Although the cities have highways, railroads, and airports, only narrow paths reach many of the villages. Most of the villagers live their whole lives without ever leaving their own villages. Even in the cities, some of the poorer people live and work in the same area and never see other parts of the city only a few blocks away.

Because India is so large and transportation is so difficult, many of the people never learn about life outside their small area. They do not understand the problems of other Indians. The leaders of

India must try to understand the needs of Indians in all parts of the country, and they must try to meet those needs.

Two Religions

Hinduism is the traditional religion of India, but some Indians are Moslems. Moslem invaders conquered and ruled India several hundred years before the British came to control the land. The Moslems converted some of the Indians to their Islamic religion, but most of the people remained **Hindus.** Many of the beliefs of the Hindus and the Moslems were different. Even though they lived together in the same land, these people did not live peaceably.

In 1947 the British tried to help India deal with the problems of these two religions. The Moslems refused to be ruled by Hindus, and the Hindus refused to protect the Moslems. Therefore, the Moslems were given their own separate country.

Most of the Moslems lived in two areas of India. These two areas were separated from India in 1947, and they became the country of Pakistan. Pakistan set up its Moslem government at the same time India set up its Hindu government. Problems remained, however, because there were still some Moslems who lived inside the boundaries of India and some

Hindus who were then inside the new land of Pakistan. Many of the Moslems fled India to live in Pakistan, but others remained in India. Strife continued between these Moslems in India and the Hindus. Riots and fights were common. Another problem was that several million Hindus from Pakistan fled to India. Most went to the cities, which were already crowded. These refugees had no homes or jobs. The new leaders of India had to help resettle these refugees, stop the fighting between Moslems and Hindus, and deal with all the other problems of the country.

Despite the difficulties facing the leaders of India in 1947, they were able to establish their new government. They adopted a constitution much like the Constitution of the United States. A president and parliament members were elected. Jawaharlal Nehru was chosen as prime minister. All of India's problems were not solved right away, but the people began to work together.

Today India is still a poor country. It still has problems in language, transportation, and communication, and there is still strife between the religious groups. Yet, India is a country with many advantages and resources. Let's take a closer look at the people of India and at the heritage and the opportunities of this Asian country.

Life in India

Making a Living

Most of the people of India are very poor. In the villages they live in small mud and straw houses. The farmers try to raise enough food to keep their families fed throughout the year. Rice is the main crop grown in India, but many other crops grow well in India's rich soil and warm climate. Wheat, cotton, tea, vegetables, sugar cane, bananas, and pepper are other important agricultural products.

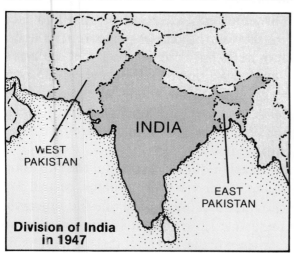

Division of India in 1947

WEST PAKISTAN

INDIA

EAST PAKISTAN

The farmers depend on the monsoon rains to help their crops grow. Monsoon winds blow from over the **Indian Ocean,** the Arabian Sea, and the **Bay of Bengal,** bringing moist air to India during the summer months. Many areas of the country receive large amounts of rain during the monsoon season. One area of eastern India often receives over four hundred inches of rain during a year, and most of it falls during the summer months. Although they do not need that much rain, Indian farmers hope that the monsoon rains will come at the right time to help their crops. If the rains come too late or too early, their crops may be ruined and their families may go hungry.

Other Indians make their living by making and selling jewelry, woven rugs, shawls, pottery, woodcarvings, metal utensils, and other goods. Such items are displayed in booths and workshops that lie along the streets of villages and cities. Poorer people who live in the cities of India often work for low wages as servants or factory workers. Others who have a good education can find work in offices and businesses.

Construction of irrigation canals in India

Hinduism

Over 80 percent of the Indian people are Hindus. Hinduism is the traditional religion of India, and its teachings have helped to shape India's culture. Hindus worship many gods and practice many rituals that they think will help them live a better life. Hindus believe that people are divided into different groups called **castes.** Some castes are higher or better than others. Each person is born into the caste of his parents, and he remains in that same caste for his entire lifetime. Young people cannot marry anyone who is not in the same caste as they are.

Hindus also believe in **reincarnation.** Reincarnation is the belief that after a person dies, he is reborn and lives another life on earth and dies again. After that he goes on to live and die over and over again. Hindus believe that people may be reincarnated as animals as well as humans. For that reason, many Hindus do not eat meat. They think an animal might be someone they knew in a previous life.

Hindus believe that if they live a good life they will be reincarnated as something better than what they are. People born into low castes work hard to please the Hindu gods so that they will be reborn into a higher caste after they die. They think that if they are bad during their life they may be reborn in a lower caste or as an animal. The chief goal of Hindus is to live each life so well that they will be reborn again and again into higher and higher castes. They think that finally they will become so good that they will escape from life on earth and become one with the "world soul." They will no longer be reincarnated into bodies.

The Hindus believe that if they do good works, their next life will be better. We know that we have only one life on earth. The Bible says that "it is appointed unto men once to die, but after this the judgment"

The Ganges River

The Ganges (gan JEEZ) is one of the largest rivers in the world and the most important river in India. Beginning in an ice cave in the Himalayan Mountains, it travels over fifteen hundred miles across India before emptying into the Bay of Bengal. The Ganges supplies irrigation water for India's farms. The river is also very muddy. It carries an estimated 900,000 tons of sediment daily.

The Ganges is very sacred to the Hindus. According to legend, the river is the goddess Ganga who came to earth, and the water is holy. Hindu temples line the riverbanks, and stairs lead down to the water. Pilgrims bathe in the the water and believe the holy water will cleanse their souls. Some pilgrims come to the Ganges for healing. Others come to die in the river in hopes of entering paradise immediately. After the cremation of loved ones, pilgrims sometimes sprinkle the ashes in the Ganges. For those who cannot make the journey to the river, Hindus bottle the water and carry it home. Although the water is dirty, the Hindus believe the impurities will not hurt them. They use the water for drinking, cooking, and washing. Diseases such as cholera have been spread by the filthy water.

A Hindu prayer asks for cleansing from the waters of the Ganges. When Christ encountered the Samaritan woman at Jacob's well, however, he told her about "living water." "But whosoever drinketh of the water that I shall give him shall never thirst; but the water that I shall give him shall be in him a well of water springing up into everlasting life" (John 4:14). As Christians we know that only the blood of Christ cleanses us from sin. Hindus in India trust in the water of the Ganges in vain.

(Hebrews 9:27). When we die, we are not going to be reborn as an animal or as another person. Hindus hold to the false idea of reincarnation without realizing that the new birth they truly need is a spiritual birth. They need to be born again through faith in Jesus Christ.

> Jesus answered and said unto him, Verily, verily, I say unto thee, Except a man be born again, he cannot see the kingdom of God. (John 3:3)

The people of India need to know that Jesus came to die for their sins. Only if they receive Him as their personal Saviour will they be truly born again. Then after their death, they can live forever with Him in heaven. Each of us also must have a spiritual rebirth, or else we will face eternal judgment for our sins. Have you been born again by accepting Christ as your Saviour?

Taking Christ's gift of salvation not only assures us of a home in heaven but also gives us the right purpose for living in this life—to bring glory to our Saviour. We should faithfully serve the Lord all of our life and praise Him for providing a home in heaven for us when we die.

Food and Clothing

The food eaten by Indians and the clothes they wear might seem very strange to us. One of the main foods of most Indians is a pancake-like bread called chapaty. Indians also eat lots of rice and vegetables. Most eat with their fingers instead of using knives, forks, and spoons. Although many Hindus are vegetarians (people who do not eat meat), others will eat fish, pork, or goat meat if they can afford it.

The Hindus will not eat beef because to them the cow is a sacred animal. But the cow provides milk and milk products for them to eat, and its manure is used as fuel for their cooking fires and as a building material for their mud houses. Cattle are allowed to roam freely through the streets of villages and cities. Because they are protected, there are more than 200 million "holy" cows in India, more than in any other country.

Although some Indians wear the kind of clothing we wear in America, many continue to wear the loose, cool clothes of traditional India. Over half of India lies south of the Tropic of Cancer near the equator. Because the land receives direct sunlight and warm ocean breezes, its climate is quite warm. Only the high mountains of northern India have a cooler climate. The people usually wear clothes made of cotton because it keeps them cooler in India's hot weather.

Indian clothing requires little sewing. Most of the garments are made by wrapping long pieces of cloth around the body. The most common women's garment is the **sari** (SAH ree). The *sari* is about six yards of cloth that is wrapped and tucked around the waist to form a skirt. The long end is then draped over the shoulder and sometimes over the head. Men wear a *dhoti* (DOH tee), a shorter length of cloth wrapped around the waist and legs to form a kind of short trousers. Blouses, shirts, and jackets may be worn with these clothes. In some areas, men also

Dhoti

Sari

wear a turban made by winding many yards of cloth around the top of their heads.

Indian women like to wear lots of jewelry. Bracelets often cover their arms, and rings or jewels pierce their noses. The women also often wear a spot of dark powder on their foreheads to enhance their beauty and to indicate their caste.

Animals, Minerals, and Industry

As well as being crowded with people, India is the home of many animals. Domestic animals such as cattle, buffalo, sheep, and goats live near the cities and villages. Many wild animals roam in the forests. Monkeys, deer, tigers, and leopards search for their meals in the dark woods, while poisonous snakes, like the deadly cobra, slither around trees and rocks. The Indians have tamed elephants and trained them to carry logs and heavy loads. Some elephants remain wild in the jungles.

Animals are abundant in India, and so are many other natural resources. Forests once covered a large portion of the country. Although many trees have been cut through the years, India's remaining

Pandita Ramabai

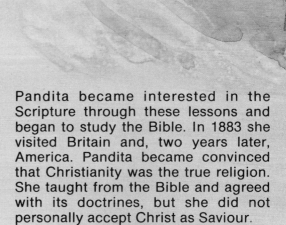

Pandita Ramabai was born in India in 1858 to an unusual family. Her father, a high caste Hindu teacher, disagreed with other Hindu leaders of that time. He believed that women should receive the same quality of education as men. Therefore, he taught his daughter to read and memorize the religious literature of India.

Young Pandita traveled all over India with her family. Her father earned his living lecturing on the Hindu religion. They visited holy Hindu shrines and made many offerings to the Indian gods. But they found none of the spiritual comfort or physical help that they desired. After her parents died in a famine, Pandita married an Indian lawyer and had a daughter. However, within two years, her husband died, leaving her a widow with a small child.

The condition of Indian widows was very difficult. Girls married very young, as early as the age of nine, to men who were twenty or thirty years older. Often these young wives became widows before they were twenty. A widow in Hinduism held a lowly place. She had to shave her head, wear special garments, and could associate with very few people. Pandita's situation was

not as bad as some, for she was older. Still, she felt compassion for the other widows who suffered under the rules of Hinduism.

Shortly after her husband's death, Pandita began studying English with a Christian schoolteacher from Britain.

Pandita became interested in the Scripture through these lessons and began to study the Bible. In 1883 she visited Britain and, two years later, America. Pandita became convinced that Christianity was the true religion. She taught from the Bible and agreed with its doctrines, but she did not personally accept Christ as Saviour.

With the help of some American friends, Pandita returned to India and began a home for the child widows. Starting with only two, the home grew rapidly. Soon Pandita realized that she needed more than a "head knowledge" of Christianity, and she personally accepted Christ as Saviour. She began to lead her students to Christ as well. This offended many Hindus who had supported her, and they withdrew their help. With the help of God, however, Pandita continued her home.

Pandita's home flourished. As many as nineteen hundred girls lived at the home at one time. They helped support themselves by operating a farm and weaving cloth. The home also ran a printing press, a school, and a church. By the time of her death in 1922, Pandita Ramabai had taken in and helped over three thousand people. She not only relieved their physical and social suffering but also gave them the message of salvation through Christ alone.

Cities of India

Calcutta, Bombay, and Delhi are the three largest cities of India. Calcutta, the largest, is located on the shore of the Hooghly (HOOG lee) River near the northern coast of the Bay of Bengal. The Hooghly is part of the delta area of two great rivers of India, the Ganges and the Brahmaputra (BRAH muh POO truh). Crowds of people fill this city, whose streets are lined with old and new buildings and rich and poor dwellings. Calcutta is a port city harboring trading ships from near and far. Most of India's coal and mineral

of India's cotton crop to produce large amounts of cotton cloth.

Delhi (DEL ee) is actually two cities in one. The narrow, crowded streets of Old Delhi have been filled for over three hundred years with the displays of merchants and craftsmen. The small shops and stalls boast all kinds of goods from food and cloth to jewelry and carvings of wood and ivory. Along the wide boulevards of neighboring New Delhi, the British built their capital city in the 1920s. In the government buildings the leaders of India rejoiced over their independence in 1947, and today's leaders deal with their country's problems.

resources are transported through this city. Calcutta's factories transform jute, a fibrous plant grown in nearby areas, into large quantities of rope and burlap material.

All the way across the country from Calcutta lies Bombay on the coast of the Arabian Sea. This second largest city of India is a major port city and a commercial center. Like other Indian cities, it contains European-style buildings built by the British: Hindu temples, Moslem mosques, modern hotels, office buildings, as well as slum areas. Bombay's textile mills use most

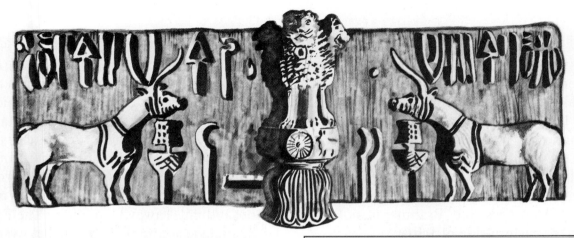

forests provide rich woods for furniture and wood carvings. India has large supplies of coal, iron ore, bauxite, copper, and many other minerals. India also has several large rivers, which not only provide water for farmland but also are sources of energy. Dams are being built to supply hydroelectric power to many areas of the country, but many villages in other areas still have no electricity.

Though India has many resources, its people still live in poverty. Only a few large industries are prospering in the country. One is the textile industry. Its factories take the cotton grown in the fields of India and turn it into cotton cloth. There are a few large iron and steel mills. Indian factories also produce fertilizer, cement, paper, and some other products. Still, most of the goods needed by the people are produced in the homes and small workshops. While this keeps the people busy and provides their basic needs, most Indians do not enjoy the many luxuries that we enjoy every day and often take for granted.

We should thank the Lord for the comforts that we enjoy. Many other people around the world do not even know what it is like to have such things as a refrigerator, a kitchen sink, an electric light, or a car. We are blessed to live in a land where we can work at many factories and businesses that help to provide such comforts for us.

The Maldives

Area: 115 sq. mi.   Population: 114,469

A group of about two thousand little islands lies three hundred miles southeast of India's southern tip. These islands, the Maldives, have formed an independent republic since gaining their independence from the British Empire in 1965.

Only a few more than two hundred of the islands are inhabited, and the largest of the islands has less than five square miles of area. The Maldives sit in the Indian Ocean near the equator. Their climate is hot and humid. In recent years European tourists have discovered the islands to be a pleasant spot for a tropical vacation.

The Maldivian people are poor, and many have little education. Most of the people work in the fishing industry, or they raise tropical fruits and nuts. They must import their rice, other foods, and many supplies. Almost all Maldivians are Moslems.

Section Review

1. What country had ruled India before its independence in 1947?

2. What mountain range lies to India's northeast?

3. What is the official language of India?

4. What is the traditional religion of India?

5. What three bodies of water border India?

Pakistan and Bangladesh

In 1947 two new independent countries were born in southern Asia: India and Pakistan. Pakistan consisted of two areas of land that were over one thousand miles apart. The larger part, West Pakistan, lay to the northwest of India along the Indus River Valley. The smaller part, East Pakistan, contained most of the delta area of the Ganges and Brahmaputra Rivers on the eastern side of India.

A Divided Country

The only thing West Pakistan and East Pakistan had in common was their religion. These two areas were separated from India because the majority of their peoples were Moslems. Other than the Islamic religion, these two areas were very different. Their peoples spoke different languages. There were more people crowded into small East Pakistan than there were in all of West Pakistan, which was nearly six times larger. The climate of West Pakistan was hot and dry, while East Pakistan received large amounts of rain. The needs and the activities of the people in the two areas were different.

It was very difficult for the Pakistani government to rule both parts of the country. Transportation and communication between the areas was expensive and unreliable. The people of more heavily populated East Pakistan complained because their government operated from Karachi, the capital city that was over one thousand miles away from them. The East Pakistanis also complained that the government was controlled by West Pakistanis and that they neglected the needs of their distant region.

The Pakistani government had to face not only the discontent of East Pakistan but also the wrath of India. Hatred between the Indian Hindus and the Pakistani Moslems continued after the two countries were separated in 1947. Fights over border areas between the two countries kept tension high. In 1971 when East Pakistan revolted against the united government, India sided with the smaller land. India joined in a war against the West Pakistanis that won independence for East Pakistan. The new little country declared itself to be the free country of Bangladesh.

Pakistan Since 1971

After 1971 West Pakistan by itself was the country of Pakistan. Its area, which is a little larger than Texas, stretches from the shores of the Arabian Sea northeastward to the Himalaya Mountains. Although most of the country receives little rainfall, water from the melting snow in the mountains flows down the Indus River to the sea. This river and its tributaries provide water to irrigate the fertile plains of Pakistan. Beyond the irrigated land lie dry, rocky hills and plains.

Peshawar, Pakistan

Pakistan is an agricultural country. Farmers in the Indus Valley grow wheat, rice, corn, and other grain crops along with vegetables, sugar cane, and cotton. Because they lack machinery, farmers use water buffalo and oxen to pull their plows and wagons. Fields are small and so are the harvests. The Pakistanis barely produce enough food to feed themselves.

Other than water for hydroelectric power and natural gas deposits, Pakistan has few profitable natural resources. Most of its industries are those that process its agricultural products. The cotton textile industry is its largest business. Sugar refining factories and food-canning factories also employ a large number of workers.

Since most of the Hindus have left Pakistan, nearly all the people in the country are Moslems. As in the Middle Eastern countries, the teachings of this religion rule the lives of the people. Although they are Moslems, they are divided into different groups whose opinions differ on some religious and political issues. Sometimes bitterness and fightings arise between the groups.

The new city of Islamabad, completed in 1967, is Pakistan's capital. Its population, however, is small compared to the older cities of Pakistan. The streets of these and other cities throughout southern Asia are often crowded with all kinds of vehicles. Some are wagons and carts drawn by horses, camels, oxen, or water buffalo. Bicycles and bicycle-taxis called pedicabs wind their way through the streets dodging the animals as well as occasional cars, trucks, and busses. Bazaars lining the sidewalks offer hand-made articles of every description. The Pakistanis may use many languages as they buy and sell their wares. Only a small portion speak the official language, **Urdu.** Most continue to speak the traditional languages of their regions.

The Pakistanis face problems of religious and political tension. Their government is weak, and their peoples have many needs. Their greatest need is for the Saviour. Very few Pakistanis have

Pakistani women must veil themselves in public.

ever heard the good news of salvation through Jesus Christ. Their land is controlled by Islamic teaching. They will never know of God's love for them unless Christians find a way to take the gospel to them.

Bangladesh

On the eastern side of India, Bangladesh has struggled with its own problems since 1971. This little land with a very large population is one of the poorest countries in the world. Many of its people are often hungry and without proper shelter. The Bangladeshis are also Moslems. Not only do they suffer under poor conditions in this world but many also have no hope of heaven because they do not know Christ as their Saviour.

Bangladesh lies in the low land of the Ganges and the Brahmaputra River Delta. Monsoon rains water the jungles and fields and fill the delta area with high waters. In recent years storms and floods have swept through the country, killing thousands of people and destroying crops and buildings. After such disasters even more have died from famine because of the loss of crops.

As in India and Pakistan, most of the people of Bangladesh rely on agriculture for their living. Rice and jute grow in the lowlands, and tea grows on the hills. Tigers and snakes lurk in the jungles, but many of the elephants have been trained as work animals. The many fish that swim in the rivers help to provide needed food for the Bangladeshis.

Dacca is the capital and largest city of Bangladesh. Many of its people work in the jute mills along the riverbank. Others sell books, cloth, spoons, buttons, and a variety of other things along the city streets. Those with good jobs in banks, offices, and businesses live in fine houses in some areas of the city. The poor, however, live in make-shift dwellings in vacant lots and along the roadsides. The next flood or bad storm may wash them away.

Jute

Jute is second only to cotton as a source of natural fiber. Its fiber can be spun into coarse and inexpensive thread that has a variety of uses. It can be made into burlap, and sometimes fine jute thread can be woven into imitation silk. Jute fibers are more commonly used for making gunny sacks, carpets, twine, rope, cheap cloth, and wrappings for cotton bales.

India and Pakistan produce most of the world's jute. The plant, native to India, grows from eight to fifteen feet high. Fiber comes from the bark and is removed by soaking the stalks in water until the bark softens. Later the stalks are thrashed, and the fiber is stripped from the stalks. Then the fiber is wrung out and dried. In 1870 jute was brought to the United States where it is grown along the coast from Texas to South Carolina.

Section Review

1. What new country with two parts was formed in 1947?

2. What river flows through West Pakistan?

3. What name did the eastern part of Pakistan take when it became independent in 1971?

4. What is the language of Pakistan?

5. What is the capital of Pakistan today?

Elephants are used as work animals in Sri Lanka.

Afghanistan

Wedged between the countries of Pakistan, Iran, and the Soviet Union lies the mountainous Moslem country of Afghanistan. Afghanistan is a backward country. Most of its people are farmers or wandering tribesmen. Only a small portion of the people can read and write. There are few large cities and few large industries to provide business and income for the Afghans.

Nonetheless, Afghanistan is located in a very important area. To the west are the oil-rich Arab countries of the Middle East. To the south across Pakistan are the warm waters of the Arabian Sea. To the east is the **Khyber Pass,** the ancient passageway to India. To the north is the powerful Communist country of the Soviet Union.

The Soviet Invasion

The Soviet Union has kept a watchful eye on this neighbor to the south. The Soviets do not want countries along their borders to be hostile toward them. To ensure that Afghanistan would remain a friendly neighbor, the Soviet Union sent troops into the country in 1979. A weak Communist government had taken over the land, and the Soviets rushed in to help the Communists stay in control.

When the Soviets entered Afghanistan, they found that the Afghans did not give in easily. The Afghans are devout Moslems, and they do not want to give up their faith in Allah (their god). They do not want a Communist government to take away their religion and teach atheism. The Afghans are also loyal tribesmen. Most live in small villages or in movable tents. They belong to tribal groups that have a common heritage and common customs. They are accustomed to ruling themselves and handling their own affairs. The Afghans do not want to give up their independence to submit to the strict rule of a Soviet-controlled, Communist government.

After the 1979 invasion, Afghanistan's cities quickly lost control to the Soviets. The rural tribesmen, however, fiercely resisted the Soviet armies. They used their small weapons to make quick attacks against the invaders. Then they scattered themselves to hide in the mountains and villages. The Soviets sent more troops, and they even bombed villages to try to force the Afghans to surrender their country to Communist control. Refusing to give in, the determined Afghans fought on for their freedom.

Land and People

Afghanistan is a rugged country covered with mountains, deserts, and barren plains. The largest mountain range, the **Hindu Kush,** extends over the northeast section of the country to the capital city, Kabul (KAH bool). Smaller ranges spread through other parts of the country. Two large desert regions lie in the southern portion of the country, and rocky plains cover other areas.

Most of the people of Afghanistan are farmers or herders. They water their crops and animals with the water that flows from the mountain areas. Few areas of the country receive enough rainfall for agriculture, but plenty of snow falls in the mountains during the winter. When it melts, its streams provide hydroelectric power along with water for farmers. Winters are very severe in the mountainous areas, but the snow and cold temperatures quickly pass. Spring arrives early in Afghanistan, and the summers are long and hot. The Afghans grow wheat and other grain crops for their own needs, and they raise fruit and cotton for export. The herders raise sheep, goats, camels, donkeys, cattle, and horses.

Sri Lanka

In 1972 the teardrop-shaped island at the southern tip of India changed its name from **Ceylon** (say LAHN) to Sri Lanka (sree LAHNG-kuh). Ceylon was the name the Europeans called the island, but Sri Lanka is its ancient name, which means the "Resplendent Land." This island in the Indian Ocean is indeed filled with splendor.

Sri Lanka lies near the equator. Its tropical climate and abundant rainfall help it to grow thick forests and many valuable tropical plants. Sri Lankan plantations grow tea, rubber, coconuts, cacao, cotton, and spices. Mines in Sri Lanka produce beautiful rubies, sapphires, and other precious stones. The coastal plain and inland mountains provide beautiful scenery, and many ancient buildings and shrines are of special interest to tourists and religious pilgrims.

Most of the Sri Lankan people are villagers or farm workers. Many of them are Hindus, but the majority of the people are Buddhists. Buddhists are followers of a religion called **Buddhism** that began in India about twenty-five hundred years

Buddhist temple in Sri Lanka

ago. They follow the teachings of a man who was called the **Buddha.** He believed that he had found the true meaning of life. He believed that all misery and suffering in the the world was caused by men following their own selfish desires. He taught that if men would give up their selfish desires and instead be gentle, kind, and generous to others, everything would be better.

While it is true that sin is the cause of misery and death, the Buddha did not teach men the true meaning of life. The Bible says that trying to be good will never bring peace with God. Christ died to pay for our sin, and we must believe that it is not the good things we do that save us but the complete sacrifice that He made on the cross.

But God commendeth his love toward us, in that, while we were yet sinners, Christ died for us. Much more then, being now justified by his blood, we shall be saved from wrath through him. (Romans 5:8-9)

Knowing Jesus Christ as our Saviour and living to serve Him gives true meaning to life. The Buddhists of Sri Lanka, however, do not know the Saviour. Instead, they follow the teachings of Buddha, and they try to be good.

Nepal and Bhutan

Nepal and Bhutan are two countries located in the Himalaya Mountains. Both of them have borders with India on the south and with the Tibet region of China on the north. Most of the people of these lands are farmers who grow their crops in terraced fields on the sides of the mountains and in the valleys. They also

Nepal

Climb Up Everest

Tenzing Norgay

Edmund Hillary

On May 29, 1953, Edmund Hillary and Tenzing Norgay did what no other human had ever done—they stood on the summit of Mount Everest. After the Nepal government first permitted exploration in 1920, sixteen people had died trying to scale the mountain before the task was accomplished.

Everest is a great challenge to a mountain climber. It is climbable a few weeks a year in the late spring and in the fall. Like most tall mountains, it has rugged terrain, but Everest also has severe weather—fierce winds and bitterly cold temperatures. At -40°F the perspiration on a climber's feet could freeze and cause frostbite. Blinding snowstorms and avalanches also pose threats to climbers.

Everest's high altitude causes even more problems. Since the oxygen level is only a third of what it is at sea level, it is hard to breathe. Legs become heavy and the simplest tasks difficult. If the body is not used to such high altitudes, the climber could become unconscious in just a few minutes without oxygen equipment.

If the real obstacles are not scary enough, there are also imaginary ones. In the Himalayan region tales abound about the "Abominable Snowman," a creature five feet high and covered with reddish hair.

Despite all this, Edmund Hillary, a beekeeper from New Zealand, and Tenzing Norgay, a Sherpa tribesman of Nepal, both made it to the top. The climb took more than two months. Even though only two reached the summit, several other team members contributed to the expedition. To supply food and materials, fellow climbers set up a series of camps along the route. As the trail got higher, each camp had fewer members. The last camp at 27,900 feet had only two members, Hillary and Norgay. Teamwork was vital.

Physically exhausted, the two men finally reached the summit. Using his ice ax as a pole, Tenzing flew the flags of the United Nations, Britain, Nepal, and India. Then in the snow he buried gifts to Buddhist gods, and Hillary buried a crucifix. After the climb was over, Queen Elizabeth II of Britain knighted the New Zealander. The conqueror of Everest became *Sir* Edmund Hillary.

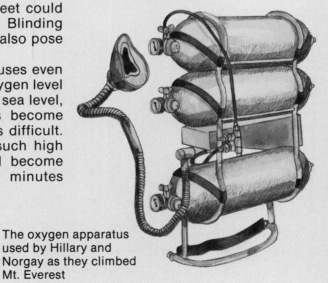

The oxygen apparatus used by Hillary and Norgay as they climbed Mt. Everest

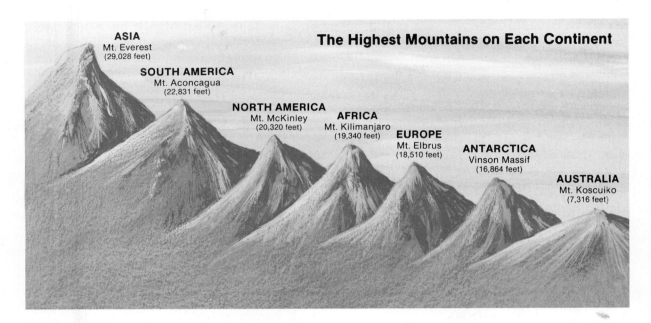

The Highest Mountains on Each Continent

ASIA
Mt. Everest
(29,028 feet)

SOUTH AMERICA
Mt. Aconcagua
(22,831 feet)

NORTH AMERICA
Mt. McKinley
(20,320 feet)

AFRICA
Mt. Kilimanjaro
(19,340 feet)

EUROPE
Mt. Elbrus
(18,510 feet)

ANTARCTICA
Vinson Massif
(16,864 feet)

AUSTRALIA
Mt. Koscuiko
(7,316 feet)

raise cattle and yaks, long-haired mountain oxen. The mountain people use yaks as pack animals to carry mail and supplies to the villages of Nepal and Bhutan. In these mountainous countries there are few roads and almost no railroads and motor vehicles. Animals provide most of the transportation.

Nepal is a little larger than the state of Arkansas, and it is ruled by a king. Katmandu, the capital and only large city of Nepal, lies on a small plain in the central part of the country. All around Katmandu, mountains and valleys spread out covering the land. The highest ridge of mountains extends along Nepal's northern border. There **Mount Everest,** the highest mountain in the world, rises to a height of 29,028 feet.

Most of the Nepalese people are Hindus. It is illegal for them to accept any other religion. If a Nepalese person accepts Christ as his Saviour, he may be put in prison.

Bhutan is only about one-third the size of Nepal, and it too is ruled by a king. The climate in the Himalayan regions is very cold in the mountains, but the valleys and the plains may be quite warm. Most of the Bhutanese people are Buddhists. They worship at Buddhist temples and shrines, and they follow the teachings of Buddhist monks who live in monasteries.

Section Review

1. What passageway through the mountains lies to the east of Afghanistan?

2. What country's troops invaded Afghanistan in 1979?

3. What mountain range lies in the northeastern portion of Afghanistan?

4. What is the island that was once called Ceylon now called?

5. What two countries lie in the Himalaya Mountains?

Terms to Remember

Himalaya Mountains   *sari*
Hindi   *Urdu*
Hinduism   Khyber Pass
Hindu   Hindu Kush
Indian Ocean   Ceylon
Bay of Bengal   Buddhism
castes   Buddha
reincarnation   Mount Everest

Things to Know

1. What is the world's highest mountain range?

2. What is the chief religion of India?

3. The two Moslem areas that separated from India in 1947 are now what two countries?

4. What country did the Soviets invade in 1979?

5. What island country lies to the south of India?

6. What Indian began a religion now popular in Bhutan and Sri Lanka?

7. What is the world's highest mountain?

Things to Talk About

1. What three problems faced India when it became independent?

2. What is reincarnation?

3. Why was Pakistan separated from India in 1947?

4. Why did East Pakistan want independence from West Pakistan?

5. What difficulties does a Himalayan mountain climber face?

Things to Do

1. Make a list of all the things you (or your parents) use during the day that you think a poor Indian villager might not have.

2. Mount Everest is certainly a well-known mountain. It is far higher than the mountains of Palestine. Yet, many of the small mountains of that Middle Eastern region have great importance in the Bible. Find the name of the mountain in each of these Bible verses.

   a. Genesis 31:21

   b. Exodus 19:18

   c. Deuteronomy 32:49

   d. Joshua 13:11

   e. I Samuel 31:1

   f. I Kings 18:20

   g. II Chronicles 3:1

   h. Lamentations 5:18

   i. Luke 21:37

Geography Skills

Use the map on page 194 to complete the following.

1. Find the Indian cities of Calcutta, Bombay, and Delhi on your map.

   a. Which one of the three cities is farthest north?

   b. Which is the farthest east?

   c. Which is not near a sea coast?

2. Find the Maldives islands to the south of India. What is their capital?

3. What capital city of a southern Asian country lies very near the Tropic of Cancer?

4. What large desert region lies along the India-Pakistan border?

5. What three countries have a border with Afghanistan?

6. The second highest mountain in the world, K2, lies in northern India.

   a. What is its height?

   b. How much higher than K2 is Mount Everest?

CHAPTER 11

SOUTHEAST ASIA

What would happen if for some reason your family had no bread to eat for a whole year? Or instead, what if there were no corn, no potatoes, or no beans on your table for a long time? If the one food that your family eats the most could not be obtained, would your family starve? Although you might miss that food, you would still find plenty of other good things to eat. In America we eat a wide variety of foods. There is no one food that we could not live without.

In Asia, however, many people eat one basic food, **rice.** The people eat rice for breakfast, lunch, and supper. Without rice,

many of the people of Asia would go hungry. Many Asians eat as much rice in a week as most Americans eat during a whole year. They eat rice with vegetables, rice with fish sauce, rice with chicken curry, rice soup, and rice cakes.

The people of the area that we call **Southeast Asia** grow much of their own rice. Because it is very important to their diet, the growing of rice is a vital part of their lives. Let's take a look at how it is grown in Southeast Asia. While we learn about growing rice, let's also find out about the people who grow it and the lands where it is grown.

	AREA (Square Miles)	POPULATION	CAPITAL	MAIN LANGUAGES	MAIN RELIGIONS	CURRENCY
BURMA	261,789	37,061,000	Rangoon	Burmese	Buddhism	kyat
THAILAND	198,456	50,731,000	Bangkok	Thai, English, Chinese	Buddhism, Islam, Christianity	baht
MALAYSIA	127,316	14,995,000	Kuala Lumpur	Malay, English, Chinese, Tamil	Islam, Buddhism, Hinduism	ringgit
VIETNAM	128,401	57,036,000	Hanoi	Vietnamese, Cantonese	(restricted) Buddhism, Confucianism, Roman Catholicism	dong
LAOS	91,429	3,647,000	Vientiane	Lao, French	(restricted) Buddhism, Animism	kip
KAMPUCHEA (Cambodia)	69,898	5,996,000	Phnom Penh	Khmer	(restricted) Buddhism, Christianity	rief
INDONESIA	735,268	160,932,000	Jakarta	Bahasa Indonesia, native languages, English	Islam, Christianity, Hinduism	rupiah
PHILIPPINES	115,830	53,162,000	Manila	Pilipino, English, Spanish	Roman Catholicism, Protestantism, Islam	peso

Growing rice is different from growing most other crops. Most kinds of rice grow only in fields that are covered with water. To grow rice, a farmer needs an abundant supply of water for his fields. Southeast Asia is well-suited to growing rice because it receives heavy rains during the **monsoon** season. Southeast Asia also has many rivers whose waters can be used to irrigate nearby lowlands. On the map of Southeast Asia, find the **Irrawaddy** (IR uh WAHD ee), the **Mekong** (MAY KONG), and the **Red** rivers. These and other rivers help to water the rice fields of Southeast Asia.

In Southeast Asia the monsoon rains begin in May or June. At that time warm, moist winds blow over the region from the southwest. Nearly every day for about five months sudden downpours bring heavy rain. Before this rain begins, the Southeast Asian farmer prepares his fields for the new crop. He builds or repairs low dikes made of hard-packed dirt that will enclose the water in the fields. A water-covered rice field is called a **paddy.**

After the rains begin, the farmer plows one of his small, water-covered fields and plants his seed rice there. The seed rice is a portion of last year's crop that was saved to be used as this year's seed. While the seed rice sprouts in its small field, the farmer prepares his other fields by plowing them and getting rid of all weeds. His faithful water buffalo pulls the simple, iron-tipped wooden plow through the mud and shallow water.

After about one month, the rice in the seedbed has grown into a thick patch of green plants over a foot tall. At this time the young plants are carefully pulled up by the roots and tied into bundles. The farmer carries the bundles to the prepared fields. The rice plants are divided into small clumps and pressed into a small hole in the mud made with a poke of the farmer's thumb. He presses the mud around the base of the plant to keep it in place. After all the young plants have been transplanted, the farmer carefully watches his crop grow until harvest time in November or December. He keeps animals and birds out of the fields, and he keeps the water at the right level in the paddies.

An Indonesian woman prepares a rice offering to take to the temple.

Indonesian farmers sifting rice

Not only the farmer but also his whole family help with the rice crop. Boys help plow the fields. Women and girls help to transplant the seedlings, and small children scare birds and animals away from the paddies. At harvest time, everyone helps to bring in the year's crop. The paddies are drained and allowed to dry while the grain ripens. Then, dressed in baggy trousers or colorful loose skirts and wearing wide straw hats to shade them from the sun, the Southeast Asians cut down the golden stalks of rice.

After the harvested rice has dried for a few weeks, the farmer threshes it. **Threshing** is separating the grains of rice from the stalk. The hooves of the farmer's oxen or water buffalo or perhaps the feet of his family members trample over the harvested rice plants until the threshing is complete. Then, a portion of the crop is set aside for next year's seed rice while the rest is taken to a mill nearby or sold to a local shopkeeper.

A hull and an inner skin cover the threshed grains of rice. A milling process removes these outer shells, leaving behind the good kernels of rice. In the past farmers milled their own rice by grinding the grain between stones. In some remote areas this is still done, but most rice is now milled by machines. If there is a mill in a nearby village or town, the farmer takes his rice there to be milled. The miller keeps a large portion of the farmer's crop as the fee for milling the remainder of the farmer's grain. The farmer then takes his rice home to feed his family until next year's rice crop is harvested.

If there is not a mill nearby, the farmer sells his grain to a village shopkeeper. The shopkeeper transports the rice to the nearest mill. He then sells the milled rice back to the local people. The farmer hopes that the money he receives for his crop will be enough to buy grain at the market for his family's needs during the year.

The greatest fear of the rice farmer is that the rainfall will be too little or too much. If the monsoon rains come too early or too late or if the rainfall is too heavy or too light, the crop may be ruined. If his harvest is poor, his family may go hungry during the year. On the other hand, if the rains are better than normal, the farmer may have an abundant crop. There may even be some extra grain to sell to the miller or the rice merchant.

Because so much depends on the success of the rice crop, the Southeast Asian farmer tries to make sure his crop is good. Southeast Asians have a wide variety of religious beliefs, but nearly all of them believe in spirits. They think spirits control the rains, the soil, and the rice plants. The farmer may consult a local wise man to find the best date to begin his plowing. He would not want to offend the spirits by plowing on the wrong day. He also may leave offerings of rice cakes or other food near the fields to please the spirits. Besides these superstitions, the farmer may take part in village celebrations where the local people perform rituals that they hope will ensure a good rice harvest.

Now that we have learned about rice farming in Southeast Asia, we must find out more about that portion of the world. What is the land of Southeast Asia like?

Land and Life in Southeast Asia

Location

Southeast Asia is made up of a small section of the Asian continent and thousands of islands to the south and east. The total land area of Southeast Asia is about half the size of the United States. All of Southeast Asia, except for the northern section of Burma, lies in the tropics. The equator crosses several islands of Indonesia, and much of that country lies in the Southern Hemisphere.

Climate

Because Southeast Asia is located in the tropics and because its lands are near large bodies of warm water, the climate of this area is very warm. Only highland areas have cool temperatures. In most places temperatures remain above 70°F all year long. Instead of summers and winters, Southeast Asia has rainy seasons and dry seasons. The rainy seasons are the time when the monsoon rains come. A few months of clear skies and pleasant temperatures follow the rains. Around February the temperatures rise, and everything becomes dry. These dry seasons end when the monsoon rains come again.

Vegetation and Animal Life

Because of the warm and rainy climate, much of Southeast Asia is covered with thick rain forests. Some areas have been cleared to make room for rice fields, rubber plantations, and other agricultural areas. Many of the trees are cut down for use as lumber, but in many areas the jungles are still very dense. Tigers, wild

elephants, and snakes still roam about in many jungle regions.

Rural Housing and Transportation

Many of the villagers in the countryside build their houses on stilts. It is wise for them to have their houses above the

Stilt houses in Singapore

ground for two reasons. One is that heavy rains often bring flood waters to lowland areas, but such houses remain safe and dry. The other reason is that they need protection from snakes and other creatures that might crawl into their homes. The area under the houses also provides a good place for the farm animals to rest.

Thick jungles and heavy rains have made road building difficult in Southeast Asia. Aside from a few highways, the roads of the region are mainly narrow paths through the jungles. In rural areas most people either walk to get around or else they ride in small boats on the many

A Vietnamese fishing village

streams and rivers. Many people even build their stilt houses over the edge of a river. River water for drinking, washing, and transportation is handy.

Monsoons

The monsoon winds of Asia bring seasonal times of rain and drought to much of the southern and eastern parts of the large continent. The heating and cooling of air over Asia and over the Indian and Pacific oceans cause these winds to blow. Although similar winds blow over the other continents, Asia's monsoon winds blow with more regularity, and they determine much of Asia's agriculture.

In the summer warm, moist air from over the oceans blows inland, dropping its moisture as it goes over the land. The farmers of Southeast Asia and other affected regions depend on these rains to support their rice crops.

In the winter cold, dry winds blow from over central Asia out toward the oceans. During the winter monsoon, most of the Asian countries receive little rainfall. The rice farmers hope that when this winter monsoon is ended the summer winds will bring the right amount of rain at the right time to give them a bountiful crop.

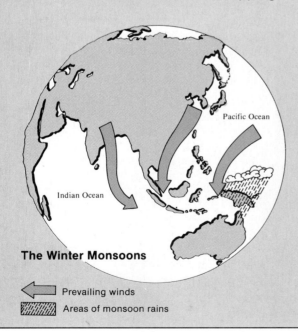

The Winter Monsoons

Indian Ocean
Pacific Ocean

⬅ Prevailing winds
▨ Areas of monsoon rains

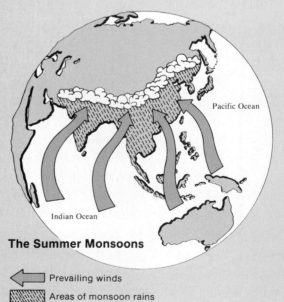

The Summer Monsoons

Indian Ocean
Pacific Ocean

⬅ Prevailing winds
▨ Areas of monsoon rains

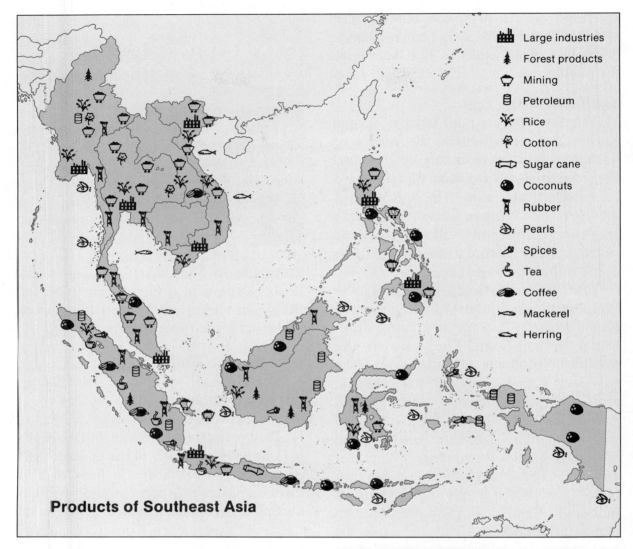

Products of Southeast Asia

Legend:
- Large industries
- Forest products
- Mining
- Petroleum
- Rice
- Cotton
- Sugar cane
- Coconuts
- Rubber
- Pearls
- Spices
- Tea
- Coffee
- Mackerel
- Herring

Life in the Cities

Most of the people of Southeast Asia live in rural areas where they work on farms or in small villages. There are, however, several large cities in Southeast Asia. Life in the cities can be quite different from life in the countryside. Businesses have grown in the large trading centers, and many people have moved from their farms and villages to find jobs and better opportunities in the cities.

The large cities of Southeast Asia are often overcrowded. New apartment buildings and houses cannot keep up with the growing population. Newcomers from the countryside often live in hastily built shacks on the edges of the cities. Bicycles, motorcycles, and pedicabs weave their way down the streets among cars, trucks, and busses. Often, heavy traffic creates bewildering traffic jams.

Small shops and large department stores line the city streets. Merchants sell everything from handwoven baskets to stereos and televisions. Peddlers walk the streets carrying trays of food or trinkets. At open-air markets, fruits, vegetables, rice, meats, and handcrafted items of all descriptions lie on display for the shoppers who stroll by.

Southeast Asia's cities are busy centers of trade and activity. Most of the cities are located on seacoasts or rivers where they serve as ports to trading ships. Small and large factories process or manufacture all kinds of products. Large banks finance businesses of all kinds in that corner of the world.

Southeast Asia's Past

Whether they are poor farmers, village workers, or city dwellers, the people of Southeast Asia have a unique heritage. Their lands lie to the east of India and to the south of China. The ancestors of the Southeast Asians came from these neighboring regions. Many of their customs and beliefs are still similar to those of the Indians and the Chinese.

After Vasco da Gama, the Portuguese explorer, sailed around Africa and reached India in 1498, European trading ships began to sail east. They sought the wonderful products of India, Southeast Asia, and China. They took spices, silk, gems, and other precious goods back to Europe. In the 1700s and 1800s, European countries gained complete control of all the lands of Southeast Asia except for Thailand. The Dutch controlled the East Indies, which today are the islands of Indonesia. The British took over the area that is Burma and Malaysia, while the

A Vietnamese soldier

The people of Southeast Asia are bound by the superstition of pagan religions.

French took Laos, Vietnam, and Cambodia (Kampuchea). Spain controlled the Philippines until 1898 when the United States acquired those islands.

Governments Today

Since World War II all of these Southeast Asian countries have gained their independence. They have also struggled to use their resources to provide for the needs of their peoples. Many of the governments have been too harsh or too weak to help these countries prosper. Communism has overcome three of the countries: Vietnam, Laos, and Kampuchea. Communist armies now control those lands where the people have lost all their freedoms. Communism threatens the remainder of the Southeast Asian countries. They need wise governments to help them keep their people free.

Section Review

1. What is the basic food of many Southeast Asians?

2. What are monsoons?

3. Name three important rivers of Southeast Asia.

4. What is unusual about many houses of Southeast Asian villagers?

5. What Southeast Asian country was never controlled by a European nation?

Mainland Southeast Asia

Part of Southeast Asia lies on the mainland of Asia, while the remainder of the region is made up of islands. Mainland Southeast Asia lies on the **Indochinese Peninsula,** which extends from the south of China. The mainland contains the countries of Burma, Thailand, Kampuchea, Laos, Vietnam, and a portion of the land of Malaysia. The **South China Sea,** the **Strait of Malacca,** the **Andaman Sea,** and the Bay of Bengal surround the Indochinese Peninsula on three sides. Before we look to the island countries of Southeast Asia, let's discover more about the countries of the mainland.

Burma

The Land

The Southeast Asian country of Burma lies on the eastern shore of the Bay of Bengal. Burma is about the size of our state of Texas. It shares borders with the countries of Bangladesh, India, China, Laos, and Thailand.

Rice is an important crop in Southeast Asia.

Burma is shaped something like a kite with a long tail. From the top of the kite to the bottom of the tail, Burma is about one thousand miles long. That distance is about the same as the distance between New York City and Miami, Florida. Northern Burma is at the same latitude as Florida, and southern Burma reaches the same latitude as that of the northern coast of South America.

Mountains lie along most of Burma's borders, providing the land with strong natural barriers. Waters from the high mountains near China and India meet to form the Irrawaddy River. This great river flows through the central lowlands of Burma, acting as an important water highway.

The People

The people of Burma are called Burmese. They belong to several different tribal groups. The largest group is the

Thai farmer growing coffee

Burmans, and others are Karens, Chins, Kachins, and Shans. Many Burmese look much like the people of China. Most of the people speak the language of the Burman tribe, which is called Burmese, although other tribal languages are common.

In Rangoon, the capital and largest city of Burma, as well as in the other small cities and towns of Burma, many of the Burmese dress in the same kinds of clothes that we wear in America. Others wear the traditional clothing of the land. The *longyi* is made of several yards of material sewn together to make a very large skirt. The Burmese often wear their *longyis* with one end pulled between their legs and tucked into the waist to form an odd-looking pair of trousers. Men wear jackets with their *longyis* while women wear blouses.

Most Burmese people are Buddhists. We learned in the last chapter that Buddhism is a religion founded in India by a man called the Buddha. The Burmese people faithfully follow the teachings of Buddha. Almost all Burmese boys enter a Buddhist monastery when they are about ten or eleven years old. When a boy enters the monastery, his family provides a spectacular but solemn ceremony on the day he becomes a monk. Family and friends watch as the boy gives up his costly clothes and jewelry worn for the occasion. The boy will then wear the yellow-orange robe of a Buddhist monk.

Some boys will remain monks for their entire lives. Others will live at the monastery for a few months and then return to their families. At the monastery the monks may own nothing but their robe and a bowl from which they eat. Every morning they walk through the town or village with their bowls to receive food from the people. The monks never thank the people for the food. The Buddhist people believe that they are being allowed to do a good work when they help feed the monks. The monks must eat all their food before noon because they are required to fast during the afternoon and evening.

Buddhist monks study and meditate on the teachings of Buddhism. They think that such good works will help them to become perfect. One such work is offering sacrifices at Buddhist temples called **pagodas**. The Shwedagon Pagoda in Rangoon is one of hundreds of Buddhist pagodas found in Burma. Gold covers the Shwedagon, which is the most popular shrine in the whole country. The gleaming spire reaches over 350 feet into the air. At the pagoda, monks and other worshipers meditate before hundreds of statues of the Buddha. They offer flowers and trinkets in sacrifice. They light candles or even wash the statues in belief that such rituals will help them achieve peace in their lives.

Although these Buddhists are sincerely trying to live a good life and do good deeds, they will never receive the peace they seek. Good deeds cannot pay for their sins. Only God's gift of salvation through Jesus

Christ will satisfy their need. These people need to know the Saviour.

> For they being ignorant of God's righteousness, and going about to establish their own righteousness, have not submitted themselves unto the righteousness of God. For Christ is the end of the law for righteousness to every one that believeth. (Romans 10:3-4)

The Government

Britain considered Burma to be a part of India during the days of the great British Empire. In 1937 Britain made Burma a separate dominion under her rule, and in 1948 Burma became an independent republic. Since gaining its independence, Burma has had difficulty maintaining a stable government. Most of its people are poor farmers, and many of its tribal peoples have not been contented. Communist **guerrillas** (soldiers in small groups that fight in the countryside) occasionally terrorize villages. Burma's government faces many problems that threaten the country's freedom and keep Burma from prospering.

Thailand

The name *Thailand* (TYE land) means "land of the free." Unlike the other

A Thai mother carries her child on her back.

Left: the traditional dress of the king of Siam
Below: the current king of Thailand, King Bhumibol and his wife, Queen Sirikit

countries of Southeast Asia, Thailand was never colonized by another country. For hundreds of years, Thailand was called Siam. Many great kings ruled the country of Siam. Siam became a constitutional monarchy in 1932, and its name was changed to Thailand in 1939.

King Bhumibol has reigned over the country since 1946. The people of Thailand love their king and his wife, Queen Sirikit. Royal visits and ceremonies are always colorful and exciting events. The Thai king, however, now takes little part in running the government. Thailand's constitution gives authority to a parliament and prime minister, but the leaders of the Thai government have faced many difficulties. On several occasions military leaders have taken temporary control of the government to preserve order in the land.

Many refugees fled to Thailand during the Vietnam War and after the Communist takeover of South Vietnam, Laos, and Cambodia in 1975. Thousands of defeated soldiers and poor homeless people escaped from the Communists to seek refuge in Thailand. While Thailand was a place of freedom, it did not have the ability to care for all these new people. Conflicts between the refugees and the Thais have added greatly to the problems of the country's government.

Thailand is about four-fifths the size of Burma, its neighbor to the northwest. Like Burma, Thailand has a long "tail" that extends southward along the narrow Malay Peninsula. Mountains lie along Thailand's western and northern borders, and the Mekong River flows along much of the country's northeastern border with Laos. The Chao Phraya River flows through central Thailand, emptying into the Gulf of Siam near the capital city, Bangkok.

Most of the Thai people are farmers, and the most important crop in Thailand is rice. The country has plenty of good

An open market in Thailand

farmland. It also has rivers and coastal areas teeming with fish and forests filled with **teak, bamboo,** and **rattan.** Teak is a heavy hardwood that grows in tropical

Rattan is used in making many products.

regions. Because of their strength and beauty, teakwood lumber and furniture are highly prized. Bamboo is a stiff grass that grows into a tall, straight stem. Some types of bamboo may grow over one hundred feet tall and nearly one foot in diameter. The Thais use bamboo in many ways. They use it to build or make houses, furniture, baskets, boats, cages, and hundreds of other useful items. The Thais also use rattan. Rattan, made from the stems of a certain palm tree, is a woody material that is usually woven into mats, ropes, baskets, or furniture.

The trees of Southeast Asian forests are valuable resources, and so are the elephants that live in the region. After a little training, elephants can, like living tractors and forklifts, drag and lift heavy teak logs. Unlike heavy machinery, elephants can easily work in remote areas of thick jungle where there are no roads. While elephants do not usually work for peanuts, they are easily satisfied with a meal of tender leaves and tree bark. They like to take a break during the hottest part of the day to enjoy a cooling bath in a nearby stream.

Elephant Excitement

Many of the work elephants of Thailand meet once a year in a big round-up. This gathering is something like a western rodeo with elephants instead of horses and cattle. People from far and near come to watch the huge animals skillfully perform.

Special events fill the day of the round-up. To begin the activities, over one hundred well-trained elephants parade before the crowds. Their trainers, called *mahouts* (muh HOUTZ), sit proudly on the shoulders of their beasts. The *mahouts* give commands by using their feet to nudge the elephants behind the ears.

A small group of elephants demonstrates the way in which wild elephants are caught and tamed. A few of the animals pretend to be wild. The others chase these creatures until men riding the backs of the trained elephants can rope the savage beasts by their hind legs.

In other events the elephants show off their speed, skill, and agility. Imagine lying on the ground, as some of the spectators do, and having four or five eight-thousand-pound animals step over you! One misstep and you could be squashed.

Between races and log-lifting demonstrations, Thai dancers, wearing colorful costumes, perform many traditional Thai dances.

Perhaps the most exciting elephant race is one that takes great speed and trunk coordination. Several elephants line up ready to run when the signal is given. They race to a line several yards away; then they stop and pick up a banana or other small article with their trunks. They turn and hurry back to the point at which they began and place the article in a small circle on the ground. Then they gallop back and pick up another article and return it to the circle. The round trips are carried on until the last article, a red flag, is returned.

Elephants

The elephant is the world's largest land animal. There are two kinds of elephants: the African and the Indian. The African elephant is larger, fiercer, and more difficult to tame. It may weigh up to fourteen thousand pounds. The Indian elephant, one of the most intelligent animals in the animal kingdom, is smaller. More properly called the Asiatic elephant, a trained Indian elephant can stand on its head, roll over, or dance. When trained to work, it is productive for most of its 65 to 70 years.

God created the elephant with single incisor teeth on each side of the upper jaw. The elongated teeth form a pair of tusks that may weigh up to 295 pounds. The tusks are often used as ivory to make many kinds of carved items. The elephant's outstanding feature, a remarkably long snout, forms a flexible trunk with nostrils at the tip. The elephant uses his trunk to carry food and water to his mouth, to spray himself during a bath, to lift, and to smell. Since his trunk is very sensitive, the elephant protects it. Faced with danger, the elephant will always curl back its trunk and keep it out of the way as it fights or runs.

At times elephants may seem almost human. They frequently help each other. If one elephant is injured, two others will get on either side and, keeping the injured elephant upright, help it away.

The first elephant to return with the red flag wins.

Malaysia

Attached to the Indochinese Peninsula is the narrow **Malay Peninsula.** The southern portion of the peninsula, called Malaya, was a part of the British Empire for nearly one hundred years. In 1963 Malaya joined with three other British colonies, Sabah, Sarawak, and Singapore, to become the independent country of Malaysia. Sabah and Sarawak are regions located on the north side of the island of Borneo. The small island of Singapore withdrew from Malaysia and became a separate country in 1965.

Four hundred miles of the South China Sea divide West Malaysia on the mainland from East Malaysia on Borneo. More than miles of sea, however, divide the people of Malaysia. Different backgrounds, religions, and ways of living make cooperation difficult in the country. Hatred between Malaysia's people has brought rioting and strife to their land.

Its Many People

On mainland Malaysia a large number but not a majority of the people are native

The cities of Southeast Asia are often crowded.

A worker draws latex from a rubber tree.

Malays. These people, whose ancestors have lived in the area for hundreds of years, are mainly farmers and plantation workers. Over five hundred years ago, the Malays became Moslems. The Malays have made their Islamic religion the state religion of Malaysia.

Another large group of people on the mainland is the Chinese. Many Chinese immigrants came to the area about one hundred years ago. They came to work in the tin mines and on the rubber plantations and to start new businesses in the cities. The Chinese have remained in Malaysia, and they continue to carry on their own traditions. Most follow the teachings of the Chinese philosopher Confucius. They worship their ancestors and various spirits. The Chinese have become successful in the businesses of Malaysia, but the native Malays despise their prosperity. The Chinese, in return, wish to gain more control of government from the Malays.

A smaller group of people from India immigrated to Malaysia about the same time that the Chinese came. The Indians are mainly Hindus, and most of them are poor workers in the industries of Malaysia.

The people of several native tribes inhabit the regions of Sabah and Sarawak in East Malaysia. Some of these people are Moslems. Others have their own traditional types of spirit worship. They are mainly farm and plantation workers, and their island regions have fewer people, cities, industries, and modern advantages than mainland Malaysia.

The Country's Resources

Malaysia's two most important natural resources are tin and rubber. Malaysian mines produced great quantities of tin ore to supply much of the world with that useful metal. The importance of Malaysia's tin is tapering off, however. Aluminum and other metals are replacing tin for use in making cans and other articles. Also Malaysia's tin mines have used most of the ore that was easily reached. Further mining will be more expensive.

Malaysia's other major resource did not grow naturally in that country. The British brought rubber trees to the land about one hundred years ago. The trees grew wild in the jungles of South and Central America and in Africa, but harvesting the rubber there was difficult. The trees brought to Southeast Asia thrived. The plantations of Malaysia were soon producing more rubber than was produced anywhere else.

Rubber is a very useful and necessary resource. It is used for making everything from pencil erasers and rubber bands to automobile tires and soles for shoes. In fact, the events of World War II made many people realize how important rubber is.

In 1941 during the war, Japan gained control of much of Southeast Asia, including Malaysia. The Japanese cut off rubber supplies to Britain, the United States, and other Allied countries. Soon tires, hoses, and all kinds of rubber parts for military vehicles and equipment grew scarce. Scientists quickly set to work to find ways that rubber could be made with chemicals instead of the liquid from rubber trees. Those scientists did find many ways to make synthetic rubber. When the war ended in 1945, shipments of rubber from Malaysia to the Allied countries began again. Natural rubber was soon back in use, but synthetic rubber continued to be used as well. If you look around your classroom, you will probably see many rubber products. We should thank the Lord for giving us such useful materials as natural rubber and for giving man the ability to make other materials like synthetic rubber.

Vietnam

The eastern side of the Indochinese Peninsula is comprised of the countries of

A Vietnamese soldier during the Vietnam War

Vietnam, Laos, and Cambodia (Kampuchea). France gained control of these lands in the late 1800s, and thereafter this area was called French Indochina.

Vietnam won its independence from France in 1954. At that time communism split the country into two parts. South

---

Singapore
Area: 225 sq. mi. Population: 2,512,000

At the southern tip of mainland Malaysia sits the little island country of Singapore. An Englishman, Sir Stamford Raffles, founded a trading post on the island in 1819. Because of its location along a major sea route, Singapore became an important port. Trading ships traveled through the Strait of Malacca (between the Malay Peninsula and the island of Sumatra) to ports all over the Far East. They stopped at Singapore to take on supplies and to load their ships with the products of Southeast Asia.

Singapore grew from a little trading post of two hundred people to a modern city of two and one-half million. Most Singaporeans have a Chinese heritage. Their island is a busy travel and business center. After being a part of Malaysia for two years, Singapore became independent in 1965. Its people are some of the most prosperous in all Southeast Asia.

Countries with the Greatest Population Density

Country	Population per square mile
Singapore	11,167
Malta	2,975
Bangladesh	1,736
Bahrain	1,637
Barbados	1,513
Taiwan	1,510
Maldives	1,462
Mauritius	1,269
South Korea	1,088
Netherlands	911

Vietnam established its own free republic. North Vietnam became a Communist country, but it was not satisfied with control of just half the country. The Communists wanted control of all Vietnam. South Vietnam struggled to keep its freedom, but in 1975 it fell to the Communists.

The story of Vietnam is especially important to Americans. The United States tried to help the South Vietnamese people fight against the Communists. Over three million American soldiers fought in Vietnam. Thousands were killed there as they tried to protect the freedom of South Vietnam. Today, however, the South Vietnamese people are the slaves of communism.

The Land of Vietnam

Before we learn more about what happened to Vietnam, let's take a quick look at the land of the Vietnamese. Vietnam is nearly one thousand miles long, but it is only about three hundred miles wide at its widest part. This long, narrow country lies along the coast of the South China Sea. Look at the map of Vietnam, and you will see that the coastline of the country is in the shape of an *S*.

Rugged countryside and thick tropical forests fill most of Vietnam. The Annamese Cordillera mountain range covers much of the land. Mountains and hills make large areas of the land unsuitable for farming. The lands near the Red River in the north and the Mekong River in the south are the only areas in which an abundance of crops can be produced. In the past farms in the Red and Mekong river valleys have grown large crops of rice and other foods to feed the many people who lived in Vietnam.

Farming has always been the main activity of the Vietnamese people. The majority lived and raised their crops in the fertile river valleys while some tribes

A Vietnamese village

of Vietnamese people raised their crops on the mountainsides. Although they did not live in wealth and splendor, the Vietnamese people were able to live freely in their homeland until recent years.

The French Rule of Vietnam

When the French came to take control of Vietnam in the 1800s, the Vietnamese people's way of life was threatened. French missionaries tried to convert the people to Roman Catholicism. Some did become Roman Catholics, but many continued to follow Buddhism, ancestor worship, and other common religions. The French controlled the Vietnamese government and businesses. While the Vietnamese farmers and workers remained poor, the French prospered by exporting the rice, rubber, coal, and other products of Vietnam. Only the Vietnamese people who could speak French and would work with the French people gained wealth and power. Discontent grew among the Vietnamese.

The Communist Leader of Vietnam

Many of the Vietnamese people believed that their lives would be better if the French would leave and give Vietnam

Only four other countries in the world have more people than Indonesia. Yet, over half of the country's large population lives on one island, Java. While Java is crowded with cities, villages, industries, plantations, small farms, and mountains, most of the other islands have few people.

The Dutch controlled the Indonesian islands for over three hundred years. They supervised the growing of rubber, spices, tea, and other products. In 1945, the Indonesians declared their country's independence from the Netherlands. The new country, however, faced a difficult task in uniting its people.

While the people in crowded Java were concerned with business, housing, and other matters, the farmers, fishermen, and tribesmen of the other islands had other interests. The different languages and customs of many Indonesian groups kept them from cooperating with each other. The Indonesian government has often acted harshly to keep the people united. Though the government still faces difficulties, it has preserved the unity of Indonesia and protected it from the rule of communism as well.

The Philippines

Ferdinand Magellan, the Spanish explorer, discovered the Philippines in 1521. This group of over seven thousand islands between the Pacific Ocean and the South China Sea was named for the Spanish king, Philip II.

Spain controlled the Philippines for over three hundred years. During that time Spanish missionaries brought the Roman Catholic religion to the Filipinos. Today, about three-fourths of the people of the islands are Roman Catholics.

In 1898, the United States defeated Spain in the Spanish-American War. As a result, the Philippines became an American possession. The United States controlled the islands until 1946 when the Philippines gained their independence.

Like Indonesia, the Philippines is a large group of islands. The two largest islands are Luzon and Mindanao. Luzon in the north shelters the capital city,

---

Brunei
Area: 2,226 sq. mi. Population: 135,000

The small country of Brunei (broo NYE) shares the large island of Borneo with parts of Malaysia and Indonesia. For nearly one hundred years, this little spot in the tropics was a part of the British Empire. Finally in December of 1983, Brunei became an independent country.

A rich sultan rules Brunei. He and many of his countrymen live in splendor at the edge of the jungle. Most of the people have good homes, cars, televisions, and many other luxuries. Such comforts are possible because oil has made Brunei rich. Large deposits of petroleum have brought so much wealth to the little country that its people no longer live in poverty like most people of Southeast Asia.

Despite all the money that the oil industry has brought to Brunei, its people still have a great need. Most of them are Moslems who follow the teachings of the Koran. Although they are rich and religious, the people of Brunei are spiritually poor because they do not know Christ as their Saviour.

Manila, capital of the Philippines

Filipinos working in the sugar cane fields

Manila, on the shore of a large bay. Manila is a prosperous, modern city, but on its edges and in the countryside live many poor farmers and other poor workers. Conflicts between the rich and poor people of the Philippines trouble this nation as such conflicts trouble many nations in Southeast Asia and around the world. Both the rich and the poor struggle to gain more wealth, and that brings contention.

The Bible tells us that "godliness with contentment is great gain" (I Timothy 6:6). No matter how rich or how poor a Christian is, he can live peacefully knowing that the Lord has promised to meet all his needs. Those without Christ do not have such assurance. They worry and fight over money and possessions. They need to know first of all about the salvation they can have through Jesus Christ. Then, they need to learn about God's care for all their needs.

> But seek ye first the kingdom of God and his righteousness: and all these things shall be added unto you. (Matthew 6:33)

Tree-covered mountains cover the Philippine islands. Coconuts, bananas, and sugar are welcome products of the forests and the fields. Rice, the Philippines' most important crop, grows throughout the country. In the mountains of northern Luzon, rice paddies sit on the slopes like giant stair steps. For hundreds of years Filipinos have grown their rice in these terraced fields.

The southern island of Mindanao is less populated than Luzon and the Visayan Islands between them. Mindanao still has large areas of rain forests. It also is the home of a large number of Moslem Filipinos.

The islands of the Philippines contain many volcanos. Some of them are active and erupt on occasion, covering nearby areas with lava and ash. Sometimes the volcanic eruptions cause earthquakes and tsunami (giant waves). Such natural disasters have brought death and destruction to many areas of the Philippines. There is a refuge for the Filipinos, but they need to be told. Some missionaries are now preaching the gospel in the Philippines, but more need to go to tell them of the salvation and safety God has provided for them.

> God is our refuge and strength, a very present help in trouble. Therefore will not we fear, though the earth be removed, and though the mountains be carried into the midst of the sea; Though the waters thereof roar and be troubled, though the mountains shake with the swelling thereof.
> (Psalm 46:1-3)

The Philippines need faithful missionaries, and so do many other lands. Will

A Filipino farmer

you be willing to go to such a faraway country if God wants you to?

Section Review

1. What valuable treasure did European explorers find in the East Indies?

2. What island of Indonesia has the largest population?

3. What nation controlled the Indonesian islands for many years?

4. What two countries have controlled the Philippines in the past?

5. What is a person from the Philippines called?

A sugar mill in the Philippines

Terms to Remember

rice
Southeast Asia
monsoon
Irrawaddy River
Mekong River
Red River
paddy
threshing
Indochinese Peninsula
South China Sea

Strait of Malacca
Andaman Sea
pagodas
guerrillas
teak
bamboo
rattan
Malay Peninsula
Ho Chi Minh

Things to Know

1. What food is a main part of the diet of many Southeast Asians?

2. What is the seasonal wind that brings rain to Southeast Asia during the growing season called?

3. What is a water-covered rice field called?

4. What are the two peninsulas of mainland Southeast Asia?

5. What three countries of Southeast Asia are controlled by Communists?

6. The Dutch East Indies are now what country?

7. What Southeast Asian country once belonged to the United States?

Things to Talk About

1. Many Southeast Asian nations and many other countries of the world are plagued by strife among their peoples. Many times hatred and violence occur between the rich and the poor. The rich want to keep their wealth and get richer. The poor want to become rich, sometimes by forcefully taking what belongs to the rich. Read I Timothy 6:6-10 and Hebrews 13:5. What should be a Christian's attitude toward wealth? Is it a sin to be rich? Is it a sin to covet (desire) wealth?

2. What part of the United States would be suited for growing rice? Why?

Things to Do

1. Find out if your family has articles made of teak, bamboo, or rattan. If they do and will permit you to do so, bring the articles to class to show the other students.

2. How many things can you list that are made of rubber (either natural or synthetic)?

3. Bring envelopes of spices (pepper, cloves, ginger, and nutmeg) to class. See if your classmates can identify the spices first by smell, then by taste, and finally by sight.

Geography Skills

Use the maps on pages 214 and 219 to answer the following.

1. What little country lies at 115°E longitude and 5°N latitude?

2. Using the scale of miles, how far is it from Hanoi, Vietnam, to Manila, Philippines?

3. Singapore lies near what important strait?

4. List ten products of the Southeast Asian islands.

5. The city of Mandalay, Burma, lies beside what river?

6. What is the capital of Laos?

7. What country has shores on both the Andaman Sea and the Gulf of Thailand?

8. What kind of fish would many Vietnamese fishermen catch?

CHAPTER 12

CHINA AND MONGOLIA

Land of the Orient

In the past the people of Europe thought of China as a mysterious land of the Far East. Europeans called China and the other areas of Asia the **Orient,** meaning "east."

Today we use the word *Oriental* to describe the countries, the people, the customs, and the products of eastern Asia. Although Westerners (Europeans and Americans) have learned much about the Orient, its lands are still mysterious. Its mountains, deserts, and plains are unlike the landscape of other parts of the world.

The appearance and customs of the Oriental people set them apart from other peoples. These people of the Far East usually have yellowish-brown skin, dark eyes with a fold of skin that makes the eyes appear slanted, and black hair. Their languages, religions, art, and manners are very foreign to people from the West.

For hundreds of years Westerners have admired and sought the marvelous products of the Orient. Some of the countries of Southeast Asia that we studied in the last chapter are a part of the Orient.

Their spices and other products brought European traders to their lands.

China, the largest country of the Orient, has supplied the world with many fascinating and useful items as well. The Chinese people have used the resources of their land to grow or to make things that are still desired all over the world. Three of the most popular products that came from China are **silk, porcelain,** and **tea.**

Silk

A little caterpillar called a silkworm spins a long, strong thread around itself to form a cocoon. The Chinese found that this thread can be woven into a beautiful and costly material called silk. The soft silk cloth was dyed many beautiful colors and made into clothing for the rulers and wealthy people of China.

About the time of Christ, traders from the Middle East and Rome brought silk home with them from the Orient. Soon all the fashionable ladies there wanted silk garments. Traders brought so much silk back from China through Asia that their route became known as the silk road.

China is one of the few places in the world that can produce much silk. Silkworms require two things that China has: a warm climate and mulberry trees. To spin their fine silk thread, silkworms require a diet of mulberry leaves. Chinese workers pick tons of mulberry leaves to feed the hungry little creatures. After nearly a month of eating, the silkworms wrap themselves in their silk cocoons.

If allowed to live in their cocoons, the silkworms would emerge as moths in about two weeks. Their escape, however, breaks the silk threads around them. For this reason, most silkworms are killed by hot air or steam while they are still in the cocoons. Then workers unwind the silk threads from the cocoons. Often each thread is nearly a mile long.

Although the silk threads are strong, they are so thin that it takes the twisting together of thread from ten to twenty cocoons to make the fiber thick enough to weave. Silk may be dyed either before or after it is made into cloth.

Besides making soft and luxurious clothing, silk may be put to many more uses. Flowers made from silk often look as real as if they were just picked in a garden. Silk fiber provides warmth when it is used for insulation in ski jackets and sleeping bags. Until synthetic fibers were developed, silk was the only material

	AREA (Square Miles)	POPULATION	CAPITAL	MAIN LANGUAGES	MAIN RELIGIONS	CURRENCY
COMMUNIST CHINA (People's Republic of China)	3,691,000	1,059,802,000	Peking	Mandarin Chinese	(restricted) Confucianism, Buddhism, Taoism	yuan
TAIWAN (Republic of China)	12,456	18,810,000	Taipei	Mandarin Chinese, Taiwanese	Buddhism, Taoism, Christianity	dollar
MONGOLIA	604,247	1,809,000	Ulan Bator	Khalkha Mongol, Kazakh	(restricted) Buddhism, Shamanism	tugrik

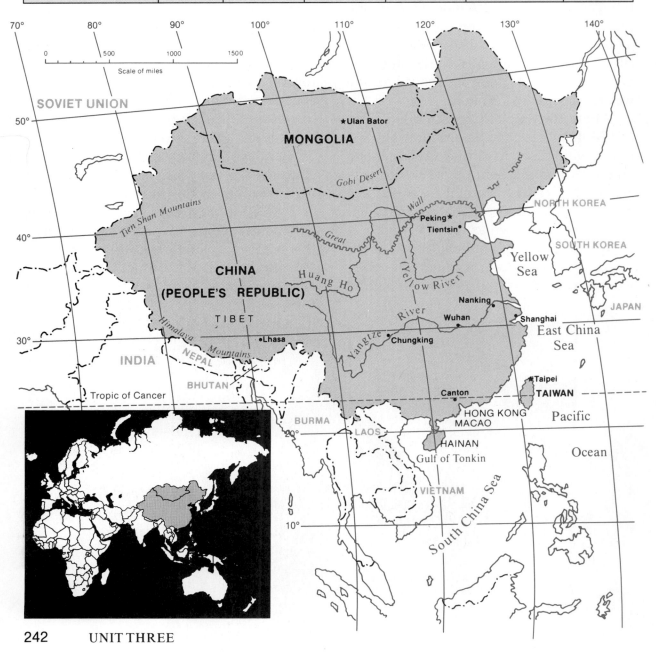

strong and light enough to be used for parachutes. Professional bicycle racers sometimes use tires made of silk. In addition, silk threads and tubes are used for many medical purposes.

Porcelain

The Bible mentions the art of the potter many times. Vessels made of clay were necessary containers for everyday use in Bible times. Museums contain many pieces of ancient pottery molded and decorated many years ago by skillful hands.

A potter is an artist who designs and shapes a lump of clay into a useful vessel. For this reason the Bible compares God to the potter and believers to lumps of clay.

> But now, O Lord, thou art our father; we are the clay, and thou our potter; and we all are the work of thy hand. (Isaiah 64:8)

God uses His Word and the experiences He brings into the lives of His children to mold them into lives that He can use.

Pottery in ancient times was usually made from a reddish or brown clay. When the vessels were baked in ovens, the clay became hard like a brick.

About one thousand years ago, Chinese potters discovered something new. They found a clay mixture that would produce creamy white vessels. They also found that by heating this clay to an extremely high temperature, they made it much harder than other pottery.

This product of the Chinese potters, called porcelain, later became popular in Europe. Europeans delighted in the beauty of Chinese porcelain. Porcelain was so white and thin that they could see light through it. (It was *translucent*.) Chinese paintings on many pieces made the porcelain even more attractive. Because the porcelain came from China, the Europeans began to call it "chinaware" or simply "china."

Although porcelain is now made in many countries around the world, we continue to call it china. We have discovered many ways to make dishes from glass, plastic, and other materials, but china remains the most elegant and beautiful of all dinnerware.

Tea

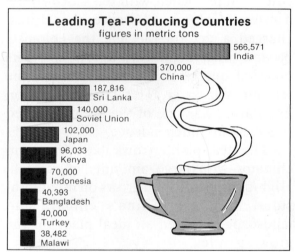

Leading Tea-Producing Countries
figures in metric tons

566,571	India
370,000	China
187,816	Sri Lanka
140,000	Soviet Union
102,000	Japan
96,033	Kenya
70,000	Indonesia
40,393	Bangladesh
40,000	Turkey
38,482	Malawi

Every day millions of people around the world drink tea. In fact, tea is the world's most popular beverage. People drink tea hot or iced. They drink instant and fresh-brewed tea. They drink it with sugar, cream, lemon, mint, and many other additions. Perhaps the British are the most renowned of all tea-drinkers. They drink an average of five cups a day.

Tea was first enjoyed, however, by the Chinese. Sometime before the birth of Christ, the Chinese learned that a pleasant beverage could be brewed from the leaves of the tea plant. The Chinese often used tea in religious ceremonies because they thought that it had special powers. Actually, tea contains caffeine, a chemical found in many beverages that acts as a stimulant to make a person more alert and active.

Tea-drinking soon spread to the other countries of the Orient, but Europeans did not begin to drink tea until about four or five hundred years ago. Merchants brought boatloads of tea back from the Far East, and the new drink became popular in Europe. Before long, the English and the Dutch were growing tea on large estates in their colonies in India and Southeast Asia.

Tea-drinking became popular in colonial America as well. In the 1700s British ships loaded with tea sailed to the Thirteen Colonies. Because the British charged a tax on the tea, the colonists became angry. Finally, a few colonists boarded one of the ships and threw the tea into the water. This famous "Boston Tea Party" was one of the events that led to American independence.

The tea plant grows best in warm climates with large amounts of rainfall. High-quality tea often grows on mountain-sides. Southern China's climate and landscape provided an ideal place for the growing of tea.

A tea plantation

Tea plants may grow up to thirty feet tall, but they must be trimmed down to about four feet. The plants become very bushy, and they produce an abundance of leafy branches. The youngest leaves at the ends of the branches must be picked regularly. After they are picked, the tea leaves are put through rollers and dried. Tea makers can vary certain steps in this process to produce different types of teas.

Section Review

1. What word is often used to refer to the lands of eastern Asia?

2. What three popular products originally came from China?

3. What kind of leaves do silkworms eat?

4. What was new about the porcelain vessels that the Chinese learned to make?

5. What is the most popular beverage in the world?

Geography and History

We have learned about three popular products of China, but there is much more for us to discover about this large and fascinating land of the Orient. First, let's find out more about the geography of this country.

A Large and Varied Land

China is the third largest country in the world. Only the Soviet Union and Canada are larger. While the Soviet Union and Canada have vast areas above or near the Arctic Circle, China lies mainly in the temperate region. A small portion of China lies in the tropics.

Because China is a large country, it has many regions with many different geographical features. Northeastern China, from the area known as Manchuria to the **Yangtze River** (YANG see), is mostly an area of wide plains and hills. Its climate resembles that of our New England and Middle Atlantic states and that of southern Canada. Because the river valleys of this region have provided good farmland, a large portion of the Chinese people have settled in this area.

Southeastern China's climate is mild, but its land is not flat enough for good farming. Many ranges of low mountains cover this region. Although the mountains are not high and rugged like the Rockies or the Himalayas, they are too steep for fields and pastures. The Chinese, however, have built terraces around many of them to provide as much farmland as possible.

Tibet is the name of the large southwestern region of China. Tibet is a high plateau covered with many high mountains. Mount Everest lies in Nepal's Himalayas near the border with Tibet. Because so much of this region lies at a high altitude, only the low-lying areas between the mountains are inhabitable.

Wide, barren deserts cover much of northwestern China. This dry region, which can be very hot in the summer, becomes very cold in the winter. Farming is possible near oases from which water is available, but most of the area is unsuitable to anything but nomadic herding.

Chinese Dynasties

About one billion people or nearly one-fourth of the world's population lives in

Pandas

The panda is native to the bamboo forests of China. There are two kinds: the giant panda and the red panda, sometimes called the lesser panda.

The giant panda is a rare, bearlike animal. Some think it is related to the bear, others to the raccoon. With small, black ears and a white face with black patches around its eyes, the panda is often described as "cute." It is around six feet tall, weighs 300 pounds, and has a stump of a tail.

God created the panda with five clawed fingers on each paw. However, the panda also has an "extra thumb" growing from the wrist. It is actually a bone covered by a fleshy pad. The panda grasps objects between its fingers and the extra thumb.

In 1936 the United States acquired its first live, giant panda. Following President Nixon's visit to China in 1972, the Chinese presented a pair of giant pandas to the United States.

The Chinese Language

The Chinese language is one of the oldest living (still used) languages. Seven hundred million people speak Chinese, and it has been spoken since about 2000 B.C.

It takes many years to become an expert in classical Chinese. To learn the English language, you must know the twenty-six letters of the alphabet. However, to learn Chinese, you must memorize up to 3,500 different characters in order to read ordinary books. Each character represents a word or idea in the Chinese language.

| I | man | eye |

Scholars must know at least 10,000 characters to read classical Chinese literature, but in a large dictionary there are 40,000 to 50,000 characters.

In the 1950s the Chinese Communist government introduced a new Chinese alphabet to make the language easier to write, but it is still one of the world's most difficult languages.

China. For every one American, there are about four Chinese people. All but a few million of the people in China are Han Chinese. This is the largest Chinese national group. Other groups such as the Manchus, Mongols, Tibetans, and Uigurs live along some of China's borders.

The heritage of the Chinese people goes back nearly four thousand years. They first settled by the Yellow River or **Huang Ho** in northeastern China. Through the years the Chinese and their way of life spread over most of the land.

Chinese history is usually divided into several periods. These periods are named for the family that ruled the people during that time. A strong Chinese ruler would pass his authority on to a brother, son, or other family member when he died. Several families controlled China for a while in this way. We call such a group of rulers a **dynasty.** The chart on the next page shows us the main dynasties that ruled over China. The chart also shows some of the great accomplishments that were made by the Chinese people.

The Great Wall of China

While the dynasties ruled China, the Chinese people developed their own way of life. Most of the people were farmers

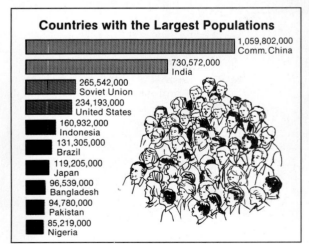

Countries with the Largest Populations

1,059,802,000 Comm. China
730,572,000 India
265,542,000 Soviet Union
234,193,000 United States
160,932,000 Indonesia
131,305,000 Brazil
119,205,000 Japan
96,539,000 Bangladesh
94,780,000 Pakistan
85,219,000 Nigeria

The Main Dynasties of China

Dynasty	Dates	Accomplishments
Shang	about 1500 B.C. to 1000 B.C.	The oldest written records, pottery, and bronze objects found in China were made during this period.
Chou	about 1000 B.C. to 256 B.C.	The famous Chinese teacher Confucius lived during this time.
Ch'in	221 B.C. to 202 B.C.	China gets its name from this dynasty. Thousands of Chinese worked to build the Great Wall of China during this time. This huge wall is over 1,500 miles long, about 25 feet high, and 15 feet wide at the top. The wall was built to protect China from enemies to the north. Portions of this amazing wall still stand on the hills of northern China today. It is the only manmade structure on earth that is visible from the moon.
Han	202 B.C. to A.D. 220	The Chinese invented paper during this time.
T'ang	618 to 907	The Chinese invented printing during this period. Over five hundred years before Gutenberg began to print books in Germany, the Chinese had already learned how to print.
Sung	960 to 1279	Chinese artists painted beautiful scenery, and potters learned to make fine porcelain.
Yuan (Mongol)	1279 to 1368	Powerful Mongols from the north conquered China and ruled over it for nearly one hundred years. The famous explorer Marco Polo came from Venice, Italy, to visit China at this time. The story of his travels and the wonders of China spurred later explorers to find a water route to the Far East.
Ming	1368 to 1644	Chinese rulers regained control of the land. European ships carried on trade with China.
Manchu	1644 to 1912	People from the northeast called Manchus took control of China. All other Chinese men were forced to wear braided pigtails to show their submission to the Manchus.

who owned or rented a small portion of farmland. Floods and droughts often ruined crops and brought starvation to thousands. Rich landlords and powerful rulers often charged the poor farmers with heavy taxes. Life was very hard for the many peasants of China. The government officials, merchants, craftsmen, and others who lived in Chinese cities usually had a more comfortable life.

Whether they lived in country or city, family ties were very important to the Chinese. Often several generations of one family lived together in the same house. All the family members honored and obeyed the oldest man in the house. All the girls and young women had to please not only the men but also the older women of the household.

Besides respecting living family members, the Chinese also honored those who had already died. They thought that the spirits of their dead ancestors could bring them good or evil in their lives. To keep the spirits happy, they practiced **ancestor worship.** They offered food, flowers, and other gifts on the graves of the dead in hopes that the spirits would bring them happiness.

The teachings of **Confucius** encouraged the Chinese people to honor their family. Confucius was a teacher who lived about five hundred years before Christ. He taught that people should obey their rulers, that children should obey their parents, and that everyone should follow rules of good behavior.

Confucius

The Chinese studied the teachings of Confucius. Educated men had to pass examinations about his ideas before they could become government officials. The Chinese also accepted the teachings of other teachers (philosophers), and many

The former Imperial Palace of China

followed Buddhism when it was introduced into China. The Chinese people believed that they had learned wisdom from these men. They did not search any further for truth because they thought they had found all that they needed to know in life. Yet they had not found the One whom they needed to know.

> The fear of the Lord is the beginning of wisdom: and the knowledge of the holy is understanding. (Proverbs 9:10)

When European traders came to China in the 1600s, 1700s, and 1800s, the Chinese tried to keep these foreigners out. The Chinese believed that their own way of life was superior and that the countries of the West had nothing they wanted. Perhaps the Chinese could have lived happily without the products of Europe, but they also rejected the missionaries who brought them the gospel. Only a few missionaries were able to reach the Chinese with the story of salvation.

China's Division

In the early 1900s, China faced several enormous problems. European countries wanting to trade with China had forced their way into the country. The Chinese were angered by the way these foreigners acted in their country. Because they had shunned the ideas of Europe, the Chinese

Ho-I

Ho-I (HEE-ee) of China was an idol-maker by trade, and a very wicked man in character. With his evil friends, he committed all kinds of crimes. Often the Chinese authorities arrested Ho-I and publicly beat him. Still nothing seemed to turn him from his sinful ways.

Ho-I became acquainted with some missionaries led by Jonathan Goforth (1859-1936). At first he would have nothing to do with the gospel. In fact, when Ho-I's brother became a Christian, Ho-I tried to kill the missionary who had witnessed to him.

God worked in Ho-I's heart, however. He became more interested in the message of salvation. Ho-I became a Christian secretly at first, and then proclaimed his salvation publicly. He began to work with Jonathan Goforth and the other missionaries, trying to win other Chinese to Christ. He tried to reach his old, rough friends. They rejected him. Once they hung Ho-I from a tree by his thumbs, then beat him. Ho-I would not give up trying to reach them, however.

In 1900 fighting broke out in China. Gangs of Chinese rioters destroyed anything they could find that was linked to the white foreigners. They murdered many missionaries. They slaughtered thousands of Chinese Christians, calling them traitors to China. Ho-I urged Goforth and the other missionaries to hide. After the missionaries left, Ho-I stayed at the mission compound to guard it. City officials arrested Ho-I, beat him, and dragged him through the angry crowds to the courthouse.

Before the judge in that courthouse, Ho-I gave a testimony of his salvation. His witness of the change Christ brought to his life amazed the official. He released Ho-I, who then returned home and labored for more than thirty years among the Chinese people.

lacked the weapons, machinery, and other developments that could have helped them defend their country.

Not only were the Chinese people angry with foreigners, but they also were unhappy with their own rulers. The Chinese hated the Manchu leaders that controlled the country. The poor peasants were heavily taxed by their landlords and the government. The rich and powerful still lived in luxury while millions of poor Chinese suffered terrible hardships.

In 1911 the Chinese arose in revolt against the Manchu government. Sun Yat-sen led their movement to form a Chinese republic. The Manchu Dynasty was ended, but Sun's hopes for a good Chinese government that would help solve the problems of the country were not fulfilled. Strife and rebellion in China grew.

Top: Chiang Kai-shek **Bottom:** Mao Tse-tung

Chiang Kai-shek (CHANG KYE-SHEK) followed Sun in seeking to establish a stable government in China. While he tried to gain control of the large and unhappy country, Communists began to spread their teachings. Chiang fought against the Communists with little success. The Communists, led by **Mao Tse-tung** (MOU tsuh-TOONG), made friends with the Chinese peasants by promising them a better life under communism. Fighting began between Chinag and the Communists.

Chiang's problems increased when Japan began to attack and conquer portions of China. He tried to fight both the Communists and the Japanese, but neither was stopped. The Chinese people were in turmoil. Finally, Chiang and the

Communists agreed to fight together against the Japanese. When Japan was defeated at the end of World War II (1945), China regained her territory, but the Communists tried to take over the country.

Chiang fought for four more years to stop the Communists. During those years, more of the Chinese became convinced that the Communists would improve the bad conditions in their country. In 1949, Chiang and many of his followers fled to the island of **Taiwan** and set up the government of Free China. Mao and his followers set up their rule over Communist China. Since that time there have been two Chinas.

Modern Chinas

Communist China

The Communists control the large area of China on the Asian continent. The name of their country is the People's Republic of China. You may hear it called not only the People's Republic but also Mainland China, Communist China, or Red China. Mao Tse-tung led its Communist government until his death in 1976.

At first, many of the Chinese people rejoiced when the Communists took over. They believed that prosperity would now come to their land. At the urging of the Communists, the peasants killed or imprisoned the rich landlords and the old government officials that they thought had caused their difficulties. Many of the people eagerly worked to help their new Chinese government.

Soon, however, the Chinese found that their new life under communism was not what they had expected. Gradually, the Communist government took away their freedoms. As in other Communist countries, the people cannot speak or write what they think. They cannot travel to another city without permission. They cannot worship as they choose.

Most of the Chinese people work on farms controlled by the government. Even with millions of farmers, the Chinese have barely enough food to feed themselves. The government has built factories to produce machinery and materials it needs, but the people must live without items that they would like. Houses and apartments are crowded with people. Because of the shortage of food and living space, China's huge population faces great difficulties. Couples may not marry without the government's permission. Married couples

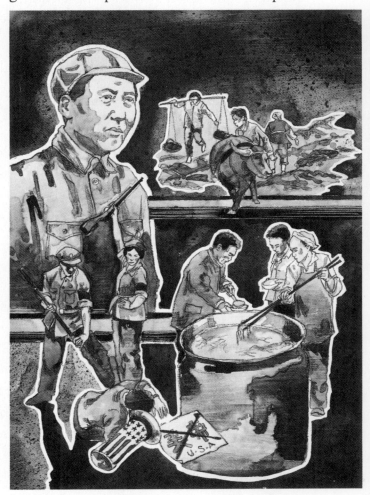

Communist China

are encouraged to have only one child. If a family has more than two children, their wages may be lowered, the third child may be denied an education, or other punishments may be given.

Free China

The other China is the Republic of China. This China, too, goes by several names: Free China, Nationalist China, or Taiwan. Taiwan is the Chinese name for the large island lying just over one hundred miles off the east coast of Mainland China. Portuguese traders discovered the island in 1583 and called it Formosa (Beautiful), a name that was used for many years. It was to this island that Chiang Kai-shek brought his government in 1949.

Free China

On Taiwan the Nationalist government, as it was called, met several difficulties. First, the natives of the island and the Chinese who had been living there for many years were alarmed by the sudden coming of Chiang and over two million Nationalists. They felt as if they were being invaded. Chiang, however, set about to build a good, stable government for all the people in Taiwan. Soon, with some help from the United States, order and prosperity came to the island. The free people on Taiwan began to produce more goods for its people than were produced in all Communist China.

Another difficulty for Taiwan was the threat of Communist China. The Communists said that they were the rightful government of all of China, including Taiwan. On the other hand, Chiang declared that his Nationalist government was the only legitimate government of all China. For a few years the Communists attacked some of the small islands controlled by Taiwan, but the people of Free China stood firm. Though there is no open fighting today, both sides have fortified their beaches and are always ready for an attack. The Taiwanese people still fear that the Communists will come and take away their freedoms.

Like many areas of Mainland China, Taiwan is crowded with people. Nearly twenty million people live on the island that also contains many mountains and forests. Taiwan lies on the Tropic of Cancer, and its climate is mild. Although most of its people live in cities, its farmers use all available farmland to grow large amounts of rice, sweet potatoes, sugar cane, pineapple, and other crops.

Taiwan's cities are busy with activity. The people have worked in their businesses and factories to make their land one of the most industrialized and prosperous countries in Asia. Because there are so

Peking and Taipei

Peking

Peking (also called Beijing) is the capital of Communist China. The city, with a population of nearly eight million, is the sixth largest city in the world. Located on the plain of northeastern China, Peking holds a mixture of ancient Chinese culture, busy city activity, and the strange coldness of Communist domination.

To the outsiders who visit the city, Peking displays the wonders of its palaces and museums. The Imperial City, a park-like area in the center of Peking, contains the Forbidden City (pictured below). Chinese rulers once lived in the splendor of the Forbidden City's palace. Only the emperor and his household could enter the beautiful Forbidden City then, but today the buildings are museums that are open to the Chinese people and to visitors. Just outside the city, a portion of the Great Wall of China winds through the countryside, providing another interesting sight for foreign visitors.

Most of the people of Peking live in crowded conditions. Old houses line the narrow streets of central sections of the city. Drab apartment buildings stand side by side in the suburbs. The Communist party assigns the people to their dwellings as well as to their jobs. Few luxury goods are available, and wages are very low. Only the basic necessities are found in most homes— beds, tables, and shared kitchens and bathrooms. Most people do not own cars, although many have bicycles for transportation in the city. Both men and women usually wear dark pants and shirts. The people are discouraged from practicing their traditional

religions. Many of their temples are now used by the government for other purposes. Even cultural performances, such as plays and operas, are used to promote the ideas of the Communist government. There is little variety in the lives of the Chinese who live under communism.

Taipei

Nationalist China's capital, Taipei, lies on the northern end of the island and is surrounded by mountains. This city of over two million people is a busy industrial center. Offices and factories of all descriptions bustle with activity.

Workers in the city go home at night to their own apartments and houses where they enjoy the many comforts and luxuries they have bought with their money. The people of Taipei dress in the latest fashions. Many have their own cars, and even more own motorcycles. All kinds of entertainment are available in the city, and temples and churches are open to all worshipers.

Taipei's history reaches back less than three hundred years, but the city boasts of its museums that hold many priceless treasures of China's past. It also offers theater, opera, and other classical cultural performances. The chains of communism do not hold this modern city back from enjoying its freedom, prosperity, and its Chinese heritage.

many people, housing conditions in Taiwan are often crowded. The people there have the freedom to speak, worship, and move about as they please. There are also many markets and stores where they may buy goods and foods of all descriptions.

Macao

Area: 6 sq. mi.   Population: 300,000

Macao (muh KOU), a tiny area near Hong Kong on the coast of southern China, is also a colony. Established over four hundred years ago by the Portuguese, Macao is the oldest European colony in Asia. Portugal still controls the six square miles of this port in the Orient.

Like Hong Kong, Macao is a free trade port. Because it is so small, the colony must import food and other supplies from China. Each year many tourists visit Macao, a city that blends the Chinese and Portuguese cultures.

Chinese Culture

Most of the people in Taiwan practice the native Chinese religions. These include a combination of beliefs in Buddhism, Confucianism, and superstitious or magical practices. Families often have shrines in their homes, and there are many temples in the cities and the villages. The gospel is also preached in Taiwan, for missionaries are allowed to come to this free land. The Chinese in Communist

The Portuguese colony of Macao

Hong Kong

Area: 399 sq. mi. Population: 4,900,000

The four hundred square miles of the British colony of Hong Kong lie on the southern coast of Mainland China. The British established a trading center there in 1841 because they were not welcome in other Chinese cities. In 1898 the British and Chinese signed an agreement whereby Britain would govern the colony for 99 years. Hong Kong prospered as a city of commerce, trading with countries around the world. Hong Kong's fine natural harbor and its central position in the South China Sea made it an important crossroads for shipping.

Today, Hong Kong is an important world center of trade. Its many businesses and industries provide work for its people. Since the Communists took over Mainland China, many thousands of Chinese have escaped to find refuge in Hong Kong. Many Vietnamese refugees also live in this little colony.

Most of the people of Hong Kong live in the capital city of Victoria on Hong Kong Island and in a district of the mainland called Kowloon. These areas are also the central business and industrial districts of Hong Kong. Other industries and huge housing areas are in another mainland district called the New Territories. Farmers in the New Territories raise pigs and poultry as well as vegetables and rice. However, the colony cannot support its large and growing population. The rest of Hong Kong's food and much of its water must be imported, mainly from nearby Communist China.

Hong Kong faces a great problem of overcrowding. To cope with this problem, the government has built many high-rise apartment complexes on reclaimed land (parts of the sea along the coastline that are filled in). Many people also live on boats in the harbor areas.

Communist China has insisted that the British give up their colony. Therefore, when the lease expires in 1997, most of the colony will fall under the control of Communist China. Even though the Communists have promised that Hong Kong's businesses can continue to operate, many of Hong Kong's people fear that the future may bring a loss of freedom and prosperity under the rule of communism. Chinese Christians in Hong Kong also realize that under a Communist government they will no longer be able to worship God freely as they have in the past.

China, however, do not allow missionaries there, and they even discourage or prohibit the native Chinese religions.

The Chinese are known for their food and the way they eat. The many Chinese immigrants and their descendants in America have introduced us to foods such as chow mein (fried noodles), egg rolls, and sweet-and-sour pork. Chop suey, which we also think of as a typical Chinese dish, was actually invented in America. There are many other foods eaten in China (both Communist and Nationalist) that we probably would not care to try. The Chinese find such things as preserved duck eggs, snake meat, and snails to be tasty.

Section Review

1. What is the name of the southwestern region of China, which is a high plateau covered with mountains?

2. What is the name of the religion that honors the spirits of dead relatives?

3. The teachings of what Chinese man have guided the lives of many Chinese for over two thousand years?

4. Who was the leader of the Chinese Communists?

5. On what island did the Free Chinese set up their government?

Mongolia

The Mongolian People's Republic sits in the middle of Asia surrounded by two giant neighbors. The Soviet Union on the north and Communist China on the south enclose the dry and mountainous land of Mongolia. This country, twice the size of Texas, lies far from the sea and from centers of trade and industry. Though it has a small population, Mongolia's position between two large Communist countries makes it an area of importance.

Its History

The people of Mongolia, the Mongols, have lived in this central Asian area for several hundred years. About seven hundred years ago, a Mongol leader named Genghis Khan conquered large areas of Asia and Eastern Europe. For about one hundred years the Mongol dynasty (the Yuan) controlled China. Later, China came to rule most of Mongolia.

In 1911, when China overthrew the Manchu Dynasty, the Mongols of northern Mongolia declared their independence from China. The Mongols who lived to the south of the **Gobi Desert** remained under the rule of China. The Chinese call the region of northern China where many Mongols live "Inner Mongolia." Outer Mongolia is the area that lies to the north outside China. Even today the Mongolian People's Republic is sometimes called Outer Mongolia.

When the Mongols fought to win and keep their independence from China in the early 1900s, Russia helped by sending soldiers and supplies. In 1924 the Soviets pushed Mongolia into becoming the second Communist country in the world. Since that time, the Soviet Union has supervised the activities of this weaker Communist neighbor.

Its Way of Life

The Mongol's way of life has changed rapidly in recent years. Once most Mongols were nomadic herders. They lived in round tents with thick felt walls to keep them warm in the cold Mongolian climate. The herders moved from place to place to find pastures for their sheep, goats, horses, cattle, and camels. They owned little besides their herds, tents, and the furs and cloth they used for clothing.

Their diet was poor, and few could read or write.

Today, nearly half of the Mongols live in cities. Only a few continue to roam the countryside with their herds. Many work on government-controlled farms. The Mongols are still a poor people, but most of them have learned to read and write. The Communist government has taken away most of their land and their animals. As in other Communist countries, the people work where the government tells them to work, and they have only what the government provides for them.

Religion in Mongolia

In the past, most Mongols followed their native religion, which used magic and superstition. They also accepted the teachings of Buddhism. Mongol families faithfully gave their oldest sons to become Buddhist monks called lamas. Then, the families gave portions of their own food to the lamas. They believed such good works would bring them eternal happiness. When the Communists took control, they destroyed most of the monasteries where the lamas had lived. Many lamas fled the country. Others were killed. Today, under communism, the Mongols have no freedom to worship as they choose.

Mongolian Food

Mongolia lies just to the south of the cold Siberian region of the Soviet Union. Nearly covered with mountains and hills and far away from oceans and seas, Mongolia's climate is almost as cold as that of Siberia. Few crops grow well in such regions; most of the Mongols' food comes from their animals. Mongolian tea, which is made with Chinese tea, mare's (horse's) milk, butter, salt, and maybe some beaten eggs or mutton fat, is more like a soup than a beverage. This favorite brew, made by the Mongols, is offered to their guests as Americans might offer

coffee to their own visitors. No polite guest could ever refuse the hospitality of a Mongol host who offers him a bowl of hot Mongolian tea.

The Land

Mongolia receives very little rainfall, making farming almost impossible in most regions. The cool Gobi Desert covers a large area of the southeastern portion of the country. Few people live in that bleak and barren area. Most of western Mongolia is very mountainous, and large areas of forested mountains and hills cover the northern regions.

Only small areas of northern and eastern Mongolia are suitable for farming. There, on rolling steppe land (prairie land like that in the eastern part of the Soviet Union), state operated farms produce crops of wheat and oats. Other farms raise sheep, goats, cattle, and other livestock. Sheep's wool is the country's major item of export. The hills and mountains of the country hold many natural resources, but few of them have been put to use in industries.

Compared to the countries of Europe and other continents, Mongolia is not a small country. Yet, Mongolia has only about a million and a half people living in its nearly 1500-mile wide territory. Because its population is so low, Mongolia encourages its people to have many children. Mothers of large families are awarded medals of honor. While this country wants more people to settle its land, Communist China to the south has more people than it knows what to do with.

Mongolia, Communist China, and other countries of the world seek to gain power and greatness. Some, like Mongolia, remain poor while others rise in strength. Regardless of whether a country is large or small, whether it has many people or few, whether it has many natural resources or none, whether it follows Buddhism or any other religion, every nation will one day know that God is ruler over all. How much better it would be if nations would acknowledge Him now. Psalm 33:12 says, "Blessed is the nation whose God is the Lord."

Section Review

1. What two large countries surround Mongolia?

2. What Mongol leader conquered much of Asia?

3. What desert lies in southeastern Mongolia?

4. What is Inner Mongolia?

5. What product does Mongolia export?

Terms to Remember

Orient	dynasty
silk	ancestor worship
porcelain	Confucius
tea	Chiang Kai-shek
Yangtze River	Mao Tse-tung
Tibet	Taiwan
Huang Ho	Gobi Desert

Things to Know

1. What word describes the lands and the people of eastern Asia?

2. Name two important rivers of China.

3. What is the highland region of southwestern China called?

4. What is the rule by members of a single-family line called?

5. What Chinese philosopher taught the Chinese people how they should behave?

6. Who led the Free Chinese to the island of Taiwan?

7. Who ruled the People's Republic of China for many years?

8. What British colony lies on the coast of Mainland China?

9. What country lies between the Soviet Union and Communist China?

10. What cool desert lies in southeastern Mongolia?

Things to Talk About

1. Potters make their vessels by first shaping the clay. They press the wet clay between their fingers until the desired shape is formed. Sometimes they spin the clay on a wheel to make a round vessel, or they press the clay into a mold to form a specific piece. After the clay piece has dried, it is dipped in a liquid that will give it a shiny surface or glaze. Finally, it is baked in a very hot furnace to harden. The finished vessel is a strong and useful piece for the potter to use or sell. How would you compare the making of such a vessel out of clay to the life of a Christian?

2. What is a dynasty?

Things to Do

1. On a separate sheet of paper, match each of the following names with the China to which it belongs. Place an A beside the name if it describes Communist China and a B beside it if it describes Free China.

   a. Mainland China

   b. Nationalist China

   c. People's Republic of China

   d. Red China

   e. Republic of China

   f. Taiwan

2. Have an afternoon tea time in your classroom.

3. Bring examples of porcelain and silk for your classmates to see.

Geography Skills

Use the map on page 242 to complete the following.

1. What three Southeast Asian countries lie on China's southern border?

2. Using the scale of miles, how far is it from Taipei, Taiwan, to Peking?

3. What is the name of the Chinese island that lies to the south of China across the Gulf of Tonkin?

4. What large cities lie along the Yangtze (Chang) River?

5. What seas lie along China's coast?

6. What is the latitude and longitude of Peking?

7. What city lies near 107°E, 30°N?

CHAPTER 13

JAPAN AND KOREA

Tomoko and her friend Yuki talked excitedly of their plans as they walked to their bicycles. In a few weeks their school

year would end, and they would have a few weeks of vacation before they returned to school in April. Yuki's father was planning a week-long business trip to **Tokyo** during that vacation. He was taking his family—Yuki, her little sister, Natsu, and their mother—along with him. He had said that Tomoko could come too, and Tomoko's parents had given their permission. The girls had been so busy thinking about the trip that it was hard for them to keep their minds on their schoolwork.

"While Father works during the day, Mother will take us and Natsu sightseeing

	AREA (Square Miles)	POPULATION	CAPITAL	MAIN LANGUAGES	MAIN RELIGIONS	CURRENCY
JAPAN	143,750	119,205,000	Tokyo	Japanese	Shintoism, Buddhism	yen
SOUTH KOREA	38,025	41,366,000	Seoul	Korean	Confucianism, Christianity, Buddhism	won
NORTH KOREA	46,540	19,185,000	Pyongyang	Korean	(restricted) Buddhism, Confucianism	won

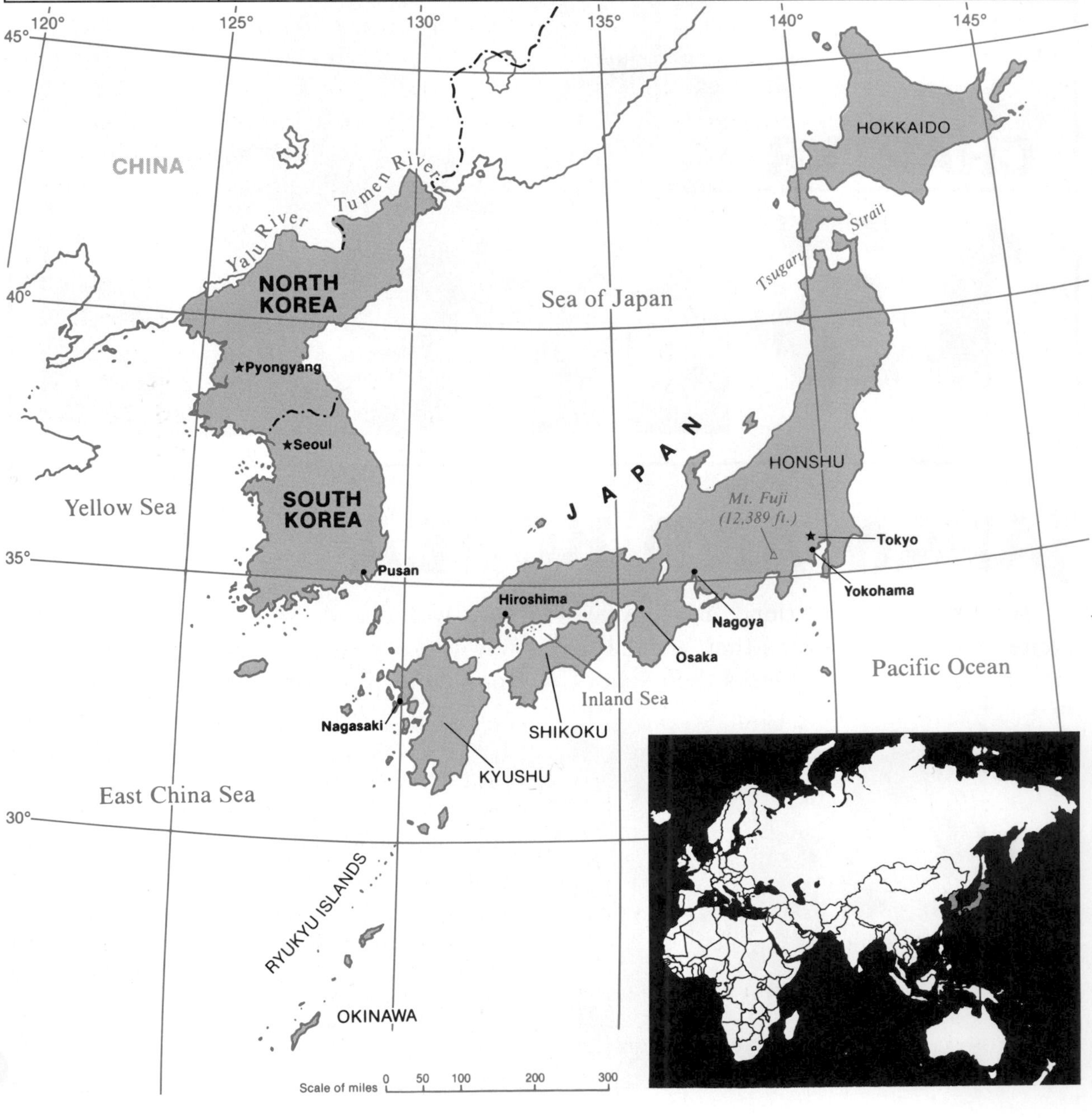
120°
125°
130°
135°
140°
145°
45°
40°
35°
30°
CHINA
Yalu River
Tumen River
NORTH KOREA
Pyongyang
Seoul
SOUTH KOREA
Pusan
Yellow Sea
Sea of Japan
Tsugaru Strait
HOKKAIDO
HONSHU
JAPAN
Mt. Fuji (12,389 ft.)
Tokyo
Yokohama
Nagoya
Osaka
Hiroshima
Inland Sea
SHIKOKU
KYUSHU
Nagasaki
Pacific Ocean
East China Sea
RYUKYU ISLANDS
OKINAWA
Scale of miles
0 50 100 200 300

and shopping," Yuki said. "We should make a list of the things we want to do."

"I'm so glad that school lasts only for half a day on Saturdays," said Tomoko. "We can make our list this afternoon. Can you come to my house?"

"I think so," said Yuki as they reached the bicycle racks, "but I must ask my parents."

Before they could fasten their safety helmets and ride away, a girl about their age walked up to them. Her light brown hair and green eyes made it obvious that she was not Japanese. The girl smiled and stuttered a little as she said, *"Kon nichi wa,"* which means "good day" in Japanese.

The girls smiled and replied, *"Kon nichi wa."* They were curious to find out about this stranger. Although they often saw foreigners in their city of **Osaka,** they rarely met foreign children.

The girl tried to use Japanese words to tell them that her name was Debbie and to ask them their names. When Tomoko and Yuki understood what she was saying, they told her their names. Then they asked her where she was from.

When Debbie said that she was from America, Tomoko spoke a phrase she had learned in English class, "Hello, how are you?"

"I'm fine, thank you," Debbie said happily. "Do you speak English?"

"A little," Tomoko replied. Actually, she had only begun to study English this year. All Japanese students in junior high and high school must take courses in English.

For the next several minutes all three girls asked and answered questions using a mixture of Japanese, English, and hand signals. Finally, Debbie handed each girl a paper printed in Japanese inviting them to a Bible club that afternoon. Tomoko and Yuki were not sure what a Bible club was, but the invitation said that there would be stories and songs. Debbie said that they would make her very happy if they came.

Tomoko and Yuki looked at each other. Yuki said, "If we go, we will still have plenty of time to make our list of things to see in Tokyo."

"And this is our chance to get to know an American girl," added Tomoko. Tomoko wanted to improve her English, and she thought this might be a good way. "Let's see what our parents say."

School in Japan

- School days in Japan are about as long as they are in America, but Japanese students also attend school on Saturday mornings.
- Instead of a long summer vacation, Japanese students have two shorter vacations, one in the spring and one in the fall.
- There are no janitors in Japanese schools—the students pitch in to do the cleaning.
- There are no school busses in Japan. Students either walk, ride their bikes, or ride a city bus to school.
- Junior high and high school students all belong to some kind of a club that they attend after school. Types of clubs include swimming, gymnastics, flower arranging, and English.
- During their last year in junior high (9th grade) and again in their last year of high school, Japanese students take a large set of examinations. The students must do well on these exams in order to be admitted to high school and to college. The students with the best scores are accepted at the best schools.
- Japanese students take class trips to visit places like shrines, museums, and historical sites. Most trips are to places nearby, but older students may take longer trips that last several days.

The girls told Debbie that they would try to come. They said *Sayonara* ("good-bye"), then they quickly rode their bikes to the big apartment house where Yuki lives. They ran up the stairs to the fourth floor, and then they took off their shoes at Yuki's doorway. The Japanese never wear their street shoes inside their homes. In the apartment, Mrs. Suzuki met them and all three bowed in greeting.

"Honorable Mother," Yuki said, almost out of breath, "May I please go to Tomoko's house this afternoon?" Mrs. Suzuki asked about her homework, and Yuki promised to work all evening on it if she could go this afternoon. When her mother agreed, Yuki pulled her invitation out of her pocket. "If Tomoko can go, may I go with her to this meeting? An American girl invited us—we met her at school today. We would like to meet her family."

Mrs. Suzuki read the invitation. "This club meets in the apartment building where your uncle lives. I suppose it will be all right, but make sure to come straight home after the meeting."

Yuki quickly put her schoolbooks on the desk in the next room. The girls bowed and said goodbye to Mrs. Suzuki. They put on their shoes and went back down to their bicycles. They pedaled swiftly to Tomoko's house five blocks away. The streets were crowded with cars, motorcycles, and bicycles. They had to be very careful as they rode through all the traffic.

They parked their bikes outside Tomoko's house and removed their shoes in the entryway. Tomoko's grandmother was making a new flower arrangement. She was wearing a blue **kimono** with a white *obi*. A kimono is a long robe, often made of silk, and it is tied around the waist with a wide sash called an obi. The kimono is the traditional clothing of the Japanese.

Today, however, most people in Japan wear the same kind of clothing worn in America and Europe. Tomoko often thinks that her grandmother is very old-fashioned for wearing kimonos all the time. Now most Japanese wear them only on special occasions.

Tomoko's mother was preparing lunch, and her father was reading the newspaper. The girls bowed to each of the adults, and Tomoko's mother welcomed Yuki. The girls helped Mrs. Kato set the table. For their meals, the Katos still sit on the floor around a low table, although many Japanese homes have Western-style dining tables and chairs.

Japanese Respect
● The Japanese are careful to give honor to their elders. They address them with respect, and it is the custom to bow in greeting and in parting.

Houses in Japan

- Houses and apartments are usually small. Traditional houses have large rooms that may be divided into smaller rooms by wood and paper sliding doors.
- The Japanese traditionally sat on cushions on the floor and had only a few pieces of furniture. Today, however, they often use chairs and many other pieces of furniture.
- The floors of houses in Japan are covered with *tatami,* thick mats made of straw.
- The Japanese traditionally slept on the floor on soft, thick quilts, but now many have beds.
- Japanese houses are not very warm in cool weather because they are heated only with small electric or kerosene heaters.

- Most Japanese homes have televisions, refrigerators, stereos, and many other modern appliances.

When everything was ready, Mrs. Kato called everyone to the table. Tomoko's older brother, Masao, came from his desk where he was studying. Tomoko's father and grandmother came to the table and sat down. (The men crossed their legs Indian-style, and the women sat with their legs tucked underneath them.) Each person had individual bowls and plates for rice, soup, and vegetables. Each also had a small tea cup without a handle and a set of chopsticks.

Mrs. Kato had prepared fish soup and rice. The Japanese often eat rice three times a day just as the people of China and Southeast Asia do. There were also pickled turnips and toasted seaweed with hot green tea to drink.

After everyone had finished eating, Tomoko pulled out her invitation to the Bible club. She handed it to her father and told him about the American girl. She explained that Yuki had permission to go and that they hoped to practice their English with the American girl. When Grandmother heard that it was a Bible club, she sternly said that the girls should not go where they teach Christianity. The girls had already learned about religion from their families.

Food in Japan

- The Japanese traditionally eat rice and fish at every meal. They may eat fish raw, dried, or cooked in one of a number of ways.
- They eat many pickled vegetables.
- They eat many kinds of seafood: squid, octopus, eels, lobster, and shrimp.
- *Sukiyaki,* a well-known Japanese dish, is made with strips of beef, vegetables, bean curd, and noodles.
- Most Japanese today eat many of the same foods Americans eat along with their own Japanese foods.

Mr. Kato thought for a minute and then said that it would be good for the girls to make friends with some Americans. "It will not hurt them to listen to some religious stories. They know our Japanese way of worship, and they can learn about Christianity without accepting any foolish foreign teaching. They can go."

The girls helped clear the table, and then they got a pen and paper to begin their Tokyo list before they left for Bible club. The girls sat near the open sliding doors that overlooked a small garden at the back of the Kato house. Although the air was a bit cool, the afternoon sunshine brightened the room. A few trees, shrubs, and unusually shaped rocks surrounded a tiny pond in the well-groomed little garden. Instead of flower gardens and vegetable gardens, the Japanese prefer this kind of garden for its simple beauty.

Before long it was time to leave for Bible club. They were excited to go and also very curious about this Christianity that upset Grandmother so. They hopped on their bicycles and rode to the apartment building where the club was to meet. It was only a few blocks away.

Debbie met them at the door of her apartment with a big smile. Debbie's mother, Mrs. Hayes, stepped up to greet them, and they all bowed. Debbie happily introduced them as Tomoko and Yuki, the girls she had met earlier that day at the school. Mrs. Hayes spoke Japanese well. Her parents were missionaries, and when she was younger, she had spent several years with them in Japan. Now she and her husband and family had returned as missionaries. She asked the girls to join the group of children seated on the floor at the other side of the room.

About ten children were there sitting in front of an easel holding a large flannel-covered board. One of the children was Debbie's ten-year-old brother, Stephen. The others were Japanese, and the girls recognized a few of the group from school. The girls sat down by Debbie on the floor. Mrs. Hayes stood by the flannel board, and she asked everyone to bow their heads and close their eyes while she prayed.

Tomoko and Yuki bowed their heads like everyone else, but they did not understand the prayer. When it was over, Mrs. Hayes asked one of the children to hold a big card that had the words to a song in Japanese. Tomoko and Yuki had never heard the song before, but most of the boys and girls seemed to know it. They listened as the others sang. There were two more new songs, and then Mrs. Hayes put the words of a Bible verse on the flannel board. "For the Son of man is come to seek and to save that which was lost" (Luke 19:10). In Japanese it looked like this:

人の子がきたのは、
失われたものを尋ね
出して救うためである

Tomoko and Yuki practiced saying the verse over and over with the other children until they knew it by heart. Mrs. Hayes explained that the Son of man was Jesus. "The Bible tells us that Jesus was a man, but He was also the Son of God. He came to earth, lived a perfect life, died on a cross, and rose again. He paid the penalty for everyone's sin. Because we all have sinned, we need Jesus to save us from our sins.

If we do not accept Him, we are lost and we cannot go to heaven."

Tomoko and Yuki had never heard about Jesus before. They did not even know what "sin" and "heaven" were. What Mrs. Hayes was saying sounded strange to them, but they sat quietly and listened. Everyone repeated the verse one more time, and then Mrs. Hayes put the words away and placed some pictures on the flannel board.

Tomoko and Yuki listened carefully as Mrs. Hayes told a story about a short man named Zacchaeus. This small man had cheated many people out of their money, but when Jesus came to his town, Zacchaeus wanted to see Him. In order to see over the crowd of people that surrounded Jesus, Zacchaeus had to climb up in a tree. Jesus looked up at Zacchaeus and told him to come down, and then Jesus went to his house to visit. Zacchaeus realized that he was a sinner. He decided to turn from his sin and repay those he had wronged. Zacchaeus trusted in Jesus, and he was saved.

When the story came to an end, Mrs. Hayes said, "All of us, like Zacchaeus, need to realize that we are sinners. We need to turn from our sin and accept Jesus as our Saviour, too."

Tomoko and Yuki enjoyed watching Mrs. Hayes use the pictures on the flannel board to tell the story. They thought the story was good, but there were many things they did not understand. Perhaps they could ask Debbie or Mrs. Hayes some questions later. Mrs. Hayes then held up the words to a song about Zacchaeus, and everyone learned how to sing it together.

After the song, Mrs. Hayes prayed again. Then she told everyone that if they had any questions they should feel free to ask them before they left. She invited everyone to come back for Bible club next Saturday. "And before you leave," she added, "there are cookies and lemonade on the table for everyone."

While the others hurried over to the table for the refreshments, Debbie looked at Tomoko and Yuki. She used the Japanese words she knew to ask if they had had a good time. Both replied that they had, but Debbie could see that they were a bit troubled. "Let's go get some cookies," she said, pointing to the table, "and then if you have any questions, you can ask Mother."

The three girls got their cookies and lemonade while Mrs. Hayes was talking to the other children. After a while she turned to Tomoko and Yuki and told them how glad she was that they came to Bible club. She asked them if they had ever heard about Jesus before. When they both said that they had not, she said that if they could stay a few more minutes she would be happy to talk with them. They both replied that they could stay just a little while longer.

After she had said goodbye to the other children, Mrs. Hayes invited Tomoko and

Yuki to sit on the couch. She brought a Bible and sat down beside them. Then she began to explain briefly what the Bible is and who Jesus is. The girls asked Mrs. Hayes about sin and heaven, and so she tried to explain those subjects too. The girls listened, but there were so many things that were new and strange to them.

As they were getting up to leave, Mr. Hayes came home. He was a tall man with a pleasant smile. Mrs. Hayes introduced him to Tomoko and Yuki, and they bowed. Debbie asked the girls to come back next week for Bible club, and Mrs. Hayes added that they were welcome to come and visit any time. Tomoko and Yuki thanked them and left.

"I hope they come back," Debbie said to her parents after the girls left.

"Yes, but we must be sure to pray for them," said her mother. "They heard many things today that were very new to them. We must pray that they will want to come back to hear more about Jesus and that their parents will let them return."

Mr. Hayes added, "Japanese children grow up in a land where either **Shintoism** or Buddhism is practiced by nearly everyone. These religions are a part of their heritage. It's hard for them to accept something different."

"Like it's hard for us to accept eating Japanese food?" Stephen asked.

"Maybe a little like that," Mr. Hayes said with a smile.

Section Review

1. In what city do Tomoko and Yuki live?

2. What city are the girls going to visit?

3. What is the name of the long robe worn by the Japanese?

4. What is an obi?

5. What two religions do many Japanese follow?

Japanese Life

Religion in Japan

Shintoism originated in Japan. It probably began as a type of nature worship in which people believed that such things as mountains, trees, and streams contained godlike spirits. Along with this reverence for things in nature, Shintoism also developed into ancestor worship. The Japanese have great respect for their dead ancestors, but they especially worship their emperors.

According to legend, the first emperor of Japan was the great-great-grandson of the Sun Goddess. He was a god, and the whole line of emperors that descended from him were gods as well. After World War II the Japanese officially abolished emperor worship, but until that time, the emperors were revered as gods.

In almost every Japanese home today there is a "god shelf." This is a place in a room where the family goes to reverence their dead ancestors. They believe the spirits of the dead ancestors can help them or give them trouble. A flower arrangement and often pictures of family members who have died sit on the god shelf. Every morning food is placed on the shelf to satisfy the spirits of the dead.

Besides having these family shrines in their homes, the Japanese also visit many shrines located in the cities and countryside. These shrines were often built on or near objects of nature such as waterfalls or mountains that were believed to possess spirits. On special occasions like New Year's, Japanese families go to visit shrines.

Along with the practices of Shintoism, most Japanese also participate in Buddhist activities. They worship at Buddhist temples before large statues of Buddha. Some become Buddhist monks and live

Top: The gateway to a Shinto temple **Bottom:** The Heian Shrine

The Great Buddha of Kamakura, Japan

in monasteries. Many have small statues of Buddha on the god shelves in their homes. Japanese Buddhism allows the worship of dead ancestors, and it also emphasizes the mysteries of death. Although the Japanese often have Shinto weddings, they usually give their dead an elaborate Buddhist funeral ceremony. Yet, neither Buddhism nor Shintoism teach people about heaven and hell. Despite all their rituals, prayers, and traditions, most of the Japanese people are lost in sin. The Japanese are polite, respectful, and hard-working people, but they still need the Saviour.

> But to him that worketh not, but believeth on him that justifieth the ungodly, his faith is counted for righteousness. (Romans 4:5)

Japanese Language

Buddhism came to Japan from the Chinese about fifteen hundred years ago. China also had other influences on Japan. Although their words sound different, the Japanese use Chinese characters for writing. In order to read common books and newspapers, school children must learn about two thousand Chinese characters plus other characters that the Japanese have added. The Japanese also learn to write their language using our Latin alphabet. Although learning their language is very difficult, practically all Japanese people can read and write. Many can understand English as well.

The word *Japan* also comes from China. Japan lies only a few hundred miles off the east coast of China. Because the sun rises in that direction, the Chinese gave these eastern islands the name "Land of the Rising Sun." Japan's flag is a red circle on a white field representing the "rising sun" of the east.

Geography and Resources

Osaka, where Tomoko and Yuki live, lies on the southern part of the island of **Honshu.** Honshu is the largest of the four major islands of Japan. The other three are Shikoku, Kyushu, and Hokkaido. Find these islands on the map of Japan. Scattered among the main islands are several thousand small islands lying in the waters nearby.

From the bay of Osaka, a long area of water stretches between Honshu and Shikoku to Kyushu. This water is called the Inland Sea. Many little islands dot this beautiful and peaceful waterway. The Sea of Japan lies to the west of Japan, and the Pacific Ocean lies to the east.

With about three million people, Osaka is the second largest city of Japan. Tokyo,

Earthquakes

An earthquake is a shaking of the earth's surface. Thousands of earthquakes occur every year, but most of them are so mild or else centered in an area far away from large population centers that they pass without notice. Only the scientific instrument called the seismograph detects the vibrations of those quakes. A few major earthquakes occur every year, and these can be felt by people as well as measured by the seismograph.

Major earthquakes may cause great damage if they occur in an area where many people live. Buildings, roadways, bridges, dams, and pipelines may crumble or break. People are often killed by falling debris and by the fires that spread quickly in the wreckage. Afterwards, people are left without homes, food, and water.

Earthquakes, along with hurricanes, floods, tornados, and other destructive occurrences are often called natural disasters. Man has no control over these forces that can cause death and destruction on the earth. Although the power of earthquakes can be frightening, the Christian knows that God not only created the earth but also controls the forces of nature displayed on earth.

God is our refuge and strength, a very present help in trouble. Therefore will not we fear, though the earth be removed, and though the mountains be carried into the midst of the sea; Though the waters thereof roar and be troubled, though the mountains shake with the swelling thereof. (Psalm 46:1-3)

Several severe earthquakes have occurred in Japan. One that struck near Tokyo in 1923 left over 140,000 people dead. Now the Japanese are careful to build their structures so that they will withstand the shaking of earthquakes. They know that their islands lie in an area where earthquakes are common.

the capital, is about three times larger than Osaka. There are many large cities in Japan, and in all of them the Japanese people are busy building, manufacturing, buying, and selling. Japan has become a modern industrial country. Only a small part of its people live on farms and raise food to make their living.

Japan's geography has influenced the country's development of industry. Japan is smaller than the state of California, and mountains cover most of the islands. Even by using all available lowland and by making terraced fields on the mountainsides, the Japanese still lack enough farmland to supply themselves with food. In the past when most of the Japanese were farmers, their farms were so small that few could prosper from their labor. As we shall learn later, farming has changed since the country has become industrialized.

Besides a lack of farmland, Japan also lacks other resources. Its deposits of coal are of poor quality, and it has only small amounts of iron ore and other minerals. Along with needing more food for its people, the country also requires raw materials and fuels to manufacture needed items.

It would seem that Japan would be a poor country because it has such great needs. Two factors, however, have helped to make Japan a very prosperous country in this modern world. One is Japan's history, and the other is the determination of the Japanese people. Let's first find out what Japan's history had to do with its recent rise in wealth and influence.

Japan's Past

Early History

You remember that Japanese legend says that the first emperor of Japan descended from the Sun Goddess. All the emperors that followed were in the same family line. Although the legend is make-believe, for all of Japan's recorded history (about fifteen hundred years), there has been an emperor of Japan. For a large part of that time, however, the emperors were not the actual rulers of Japan. For many centuries powerful military leaders called shoguns controlled both the emperors and the country.

Europeans first reached Japan in the 1500s. Portuguese traders were followed by the Spanish, Dutch, and British to Japan. Roman Catholic missionaries also went to Japan and converted many to their religion. Before long the Japanese shoguns became suspicious of the Europeans. They thought that the Japanese who had accepted Catholicism would turn against the rule of the shogun. They were also afraid that the European countries would send their armies to take control of Japan.

These fears led the shoguns to cut Japan off from the rest of the world. Beginning in the early 1600s, the Japanese no longer allowed European traders and missionaries in their land. Only a few Dutch merchants were allowed to do business in just one city. Japanese Roman Catholics were persecuted and even killed. Furthermore, the Japanese were prohibited from building boats big enough to sail to other countries. For over two hundred years the Japanese lived in isolation on their islands. They lived mainly as farmers, not knowing about the inventions and discoveries being made in the rest of the world.

Japan Opens Its Doors

Finally Japan's isolation was ended. In 1853 Commodore Matthew Perry of the United States sailed to Japan with four large warships. His mission was not to fight but to make an agreement with the Japanese to begin trade. They made that agreement when he returned in 1854. Perry brought with him several inventions that amazed the Japanese people. One was a telegraph system, which could send messages from one town to another. Another was a miniature train and railroad track. Japanese officials took turns riding around on the small train pulled by its own steam locomotive. The Japanese quickly realized that they had much to learn if they were to catch up with the rest of the world.

The Japanese began to trade not only with the United States but also with other

Joseph Hardy Neesima

Neesima Shimeta (born in 1843) lived in an unusual time in Japanese history. In the 1800s Japan began to adopt Western ways and practices in industry, diet, and dress. Young Shimeta watched these changes with avid interest. He diligently studied Dutch and Chinese and tried to learn all that he could about the world outside of Japan. Two little books in particular interested him. One was a book about the Bible written in Chinese. From it, Shimeta began to believe in the Christian God, although he did not at first understand Christianity. The other book, also in Chinese, was a history of the United States.

Shimeta longed to visit the United States and receive an education there. Japanese law, however, still forbade any native from leaving the country. Therefore, in 1864, Shimeta went to a seaport in northern Japan. There he learned English and persuaded an American captain to smuggle him out of the country. He sailed first to China, then to Boston, Massachusetts. The crew members thought "Shimeta" was too difficult to pronounce, so they called him "Joe."

In Boston the young Japanese received support from Alpheus Hardy, the owner of the ship he had traveled in. Hardy wanted to help this young man learn more about the Bible and become a minister. Neesima's understanding of the gospel increased, and he was converted. He kept his new name, except that he used the more proper form, "Joseph." Mr. Hardy thought this appropriate. He told Neesima that the young Japanese, like the Joseph of the Old Testament, could prove a means of salvation to his people. In appreciation for the ship owner's help, Neesima took the middle name of "Hardy."

Supported by Alpheus Hardy, Neesima received an excellent education. After graduating from seminary, Neesima returned to Japan. He desired to reach his people for Christ. Although he believed in the preaching and printing ministries of the missionaries already there, Neesima wanted to do something more. He wanted to found a Christian university. He hoped to train not only ministers of the gospel but also to train Christian nurses, merchants, tradesmen, and others who would carry the gospel to all walks of Japanese life. Although opposed by many Buddhists and Shintoists in the Japanese government, Neesima opened the *Doshisha* (meaning "one purpose company") school. The difficult labor of building his school into a full-fledged university weakened his frail health. Neesima died in 1890 at the age of forty-seven, having established a means of proclaiming the gospel throughout all Japan.

countries. Soon the Japanese were using the modern ideas and inventions used in Western countries. They built factories of their own to make new products. They sent some of their young men to the United States and Europe to learn more about the new developments of industry. They began to build a large, powerful navy of their own.

In the midst of all this modernization in Japan, the rule of the shogun lost power. In 1868 the emperor, Meiji, became the ruler of the land. He helped Japan accomplish many of the achievements listed above. Japan became so strong that in 1895 it defeated China in a short war. Only ten years later, Japan defeated Russia. Japan had become stronger than these two large enemies because her people had educated themselves and worked to achieve high goals.

Japan and World War II

Such success led Japan to overstep her boundaries. In 1910, Japan took over Korea. To supply more raw materials for their industries and to provide more land for the growing population, the Japanese set out to control all of eastern Asia as well. They believed that the Japanese and their divine emperor should rule that part of the world. In 1931 they conquered the northeastern section of China called Manchuria. During World War II they controlled most of China, Southeast Asia, and many islands in the Pacific Ocean.

To prevent the United States from stopping their conquests, the Japanese bombed the American naval base at Pearl Harbor, Hawaii, in 1941. This attack destroyed or damaged a large part of the United States navy in the Pacific. In response to the attack, America entered the war. But the U.S. had to build quickly a large navy to fight against the Japanese. While America prepared, Japan built up its strength on the conquered islands and lands. After a while the United States began to take back one by one the islands controlled by Japan.

After three and one-half years of fighting and hundreds of thousands of casualties, the United States ended the war by dropping two atomic bombs. One fell on the city of Hiroshima and the other on the city of Nagasaki. Large portions of these Japanese cities were destroyed, and Japan surrendered.

After the War

When the war ended in 1945, the United States supervised the government of Japan. The emperor, Hirohito, lost his power and became a figurehead much like the monarch of Great Britain. A new republican government was established. A constitution called for a parliament elected by the people and a prime minister to lead the country. Cities were rebuilt after the destruction of warfare. Factories began to produce peacetime products again. Trading with other nations was restored.

In 1952 Japan was again able to handle all of its own affairs. Though defeated in the war, the Japanese people once again concentrated on educating themselves and working hard to strengthen their industry and trade.

Japan's Economy

Since World War II, Japan's economy has grown and prospered. This little island country produces everything from giant oil tanker ships to tiny transistor radios and digital watches. Automobiles, television sets, computers, stereo equipment, and cameras are a few more of its successful products. Such articles made in Japan are usually noted for their high quality.

In addition to being well made, Japanese products often cost less than similar items made in America or Europe.

The Japanese attack on Pearl Harbor, Hawaii

The main reason is that Japanese workers usually make less money than Americans or Western Europeans. Since the labor to make Japanese products costs less, the price is lower. This does not mean, however, that Japanese workers are poorer. They also pay less for the goods they make. Most Japanese are able to buy the basic modern conveniences that Americans enjoy. They live in comfortable apartments and houses, and most families have a car.

Because Japan lacks farmland and natural resources, it imports food and raw materials. In return, it exports its manufactured goods to other countries. Although Japan does not have much land for farming, its farmers use modern equipment and efficient methods to make their land produce abundantly. The Japanese farmers own their own land. Along with producing their traditional crops of rice and vegetables, they also grow wheat, fruit, and other foods.

Japan Becomes Westernized

Until about one hundred years ago the Japanese people did not eat meat other than fish. Because they did not keep cattle, they did not eat dairy products such as milk and cheese either. With the coming of outside ideas, the Japanese diet became more varied. Now the Japanese eat beef, pork, chicken, and eggs along with their traditional foods. Japanese farms do not have room to raise enough livestock to satisfy the people; therefore much of the meat must be imported.

As you can see, the Japanese people have adopted many of the ways of the United States and Western Europe. Their country is the most prosperous in Asia, and they continue to look for ways to improve. Although their way of life has been largely "Westernized" (made like that of the United States and Europe), they still cling to ideas and traditions of their own heritage. Missionaries are free to take the gospel to the Japanese, but becoming a true Christian is a hard step for a Japanese person to make. To accept Christ means that he must stop participating in the worship of his native religions. Such a change would displease his family, and it would make him different from his fellow Japanese.

Being a missionary in Japan, as in the United States or in any other country, is not easy. But it is a work that the Lord commands of us, and it is a work that He rewards.

> Go ye into all the world, and preach the gospel to every creature.
> (Mark 16:15)

> He that goeth forth and weepeth, bearing precious seed, shall doubtless come again with rejoicing, bringing his sheaves with him. (Psalm 126:6)

> The fruit of the righteous is a tree of life; and he that winneth souls is wise. (Proverbs 11:30)

Let's consider some of the methods missionaries like those in Japan can use to reach people with the gospel. (See the next page.) How many of these could you or your church use in some way now in witnessing to people where you live?

In case you were wondering what happened to Tomoko and Yuki, after they left the Hayes', they went to their homes, ate supper with their families, worked on their homework, and went to bed. In the next few weeks they went to school as usual, and they also returned to Bible club on Saturdays. They met Debbie at other times to teach her more Japanese, and she helped them with their English.

The girls learned more about what the Bible says. They began to notice the things they did wrong. They knew now that those things were sin. When Tomoko saw her grandmother bow each day before the god shelf and pray to the spirits, she wondered if there really were such spirits. She knew that the Bible states that there is only one God, and He alone must be worshiped.

Shintoism and Buddhism did not seem to have answers for the questions the girls had. Mr. and Mrs. Hayes always found their answers in the Bible. Tomoko and Yuki were troubled.

After school was dismissed for vacation, the time came for the girls to take their trip to Tokyo. The girls put thoughts about the Bible and Jesus Christ aside. Tokyo is one of the largest cities in the world, and they were looking forward to having a good time.

Tomoko rode with Yuki's family on one of the super-express trains that runs from Osaka to Tokyo at speeds of over one hundred miles per hour. They stayed in a big hotel, and they traveled around the city in taxis and busses, and in the subway. They tried not to travel during rush hours because Tokyo has terrible traffic jams. Also the subways become so crowded that some men have the job of pushing people in or out of the packed subway trains so that the doors will close.

Tokyo is the capital of Japan, and one of the first things the girls wanted to see there was the Imperial Palace. This home for the emperor sits in the center of the city, surrounded by a large park-like area. The palace and its inner grounds are closed to visitors during most of the year, but everyone can enjoy the beautiful surroundings at any time.

Near the palace is the National Diet Building. Japan's parliament is called the **Diet,** and it meets in this building to discuss and pass the laws for the country. Tomoko, Yuki, Mrs. Suzuki, and Natsu spent one of their days exploring these sites.

They spent two days in Ueno Park. Besides the statues, pagodas, and ponds, this lovely area contains a zoo, museums, and many old buildings. The girls and Natsu, who was only five years old, liked the zoo better than any of the other attractions.

One night Mr. Suzuki took them all to a baseball game. They ate popcorn and cheered loudly for the Tokyo Giants. The Japanese have made baseball their most popular sport, although they participate in many others.

Another day was spent shopping in the Ginza District. This area of the city is well-known for its multitude of shops that sell practically everything. Although they did not buy much, the girls had a good time seeing all the merchandise and the activity.

There always seemed to be plenty for the girls to do in Tokyo. Each night they returned exhausted to their hotel. On the

final day the girls visited the famous Meiji Shrine dedicated to the emperor Meiji. They saw a Shinto priest there reciting chants. Many people were bowed in prayer to the spirit of the Meiji. Even Mrs. Suzuki and little Natsu joined in the worship. Tomoko looked at Yuki and said, "These people are worshiping the spirit of a man who is dead."

Yuki replied, "The Bible says that we are supposed to worship only the one true God." Pointing to the people around her, she added, "This religion seems so useless."

"When we get back to Osaka," Tomoko said, "I want to learn more about the God of the Bible."

"I do too," said Yuki. "Let's go visit Mrs. Hayes when we get back."

The girls told Mrs. Suzuki and Natsu that they were ready to leave the shrine. Before they took the bus back to their hotel to begin packing, they stopped at a *takoyaki* stand to buy some of the little fried octopus meat balls that the Japanese enjoy eating.

Section Review

1. What is the traditional religion of Japan?

2. What person did the Japanese worship in the past?

3. What does Japan's name mean?

4. Name the four largest Japanese islands.

5. What is Japan's parliament called?

Korea

Lying between Korea and Japan is a body of water commonly called the Sea of Japan. The Koreans, however, call it the East Sea. They prefer not to favor Japan in the name of this sea that touches their land. You see, the Koreans still remember, with some anger, that the Japanese took away their independence in

1910 and ruled their country for thirty-five years.

Today, Korea and Japan trade and cooperate with each other in many ways, but the memory of Korea's captivity under Japan lingers. The Koreans celebrate August 15 as the anniversary of their liberation from Japan. When that day in

Oceania

FOUR

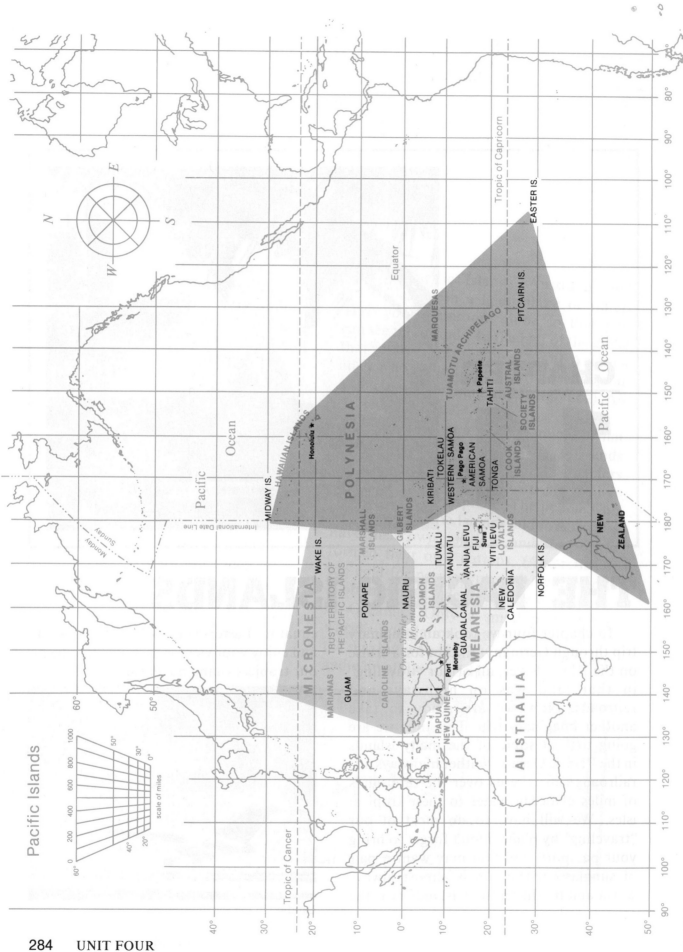

Pacific Islands

scale of miles

0 200 400 600 800 1000

60° 40° 20° 0° 30° 50°

N E
W S

POLYNESIA

MICRONESIA

MELANESIA

AUSTRALIA

NEW ZEALAND

EASTER IS.

PITCAIRN IS.

MARQUESAS

TUAMOTU ARCHIPELAGO

AUSTRAL ISLANDS

SOCIETY ISLANDS

TAHITI

★ Papeete

COOK ISLANDS

TONGA

AMERICAN SAMOA

★ Pago Pago

WESTERN SAMOA

TOKELAU

KIRIBATI

GILBERT ISLANDS

MARSHALL ISLANDS

MIDWAY IS.

HAWAIIAN ISLANDS

Honolulu ★

WAKE IS.

PONAPE

CAROLINE ISLANDS

MARIANAS

GUAM

TRUST TERRITORY OF THE PACIFIC ISLANDS

NAURU

SOLOMON ISLANDS

GUADALCANAL

Owen Stanley Mountains

Port Moresby ★

PAPUA NEW GUINEA

TUVALU

VANUATU

VANUA LEVU

VITI LEVU

FIJI ★ Suva

LOYALTY ISLANDS

NEW CALEDONIA

NORFOLK IS.

Equator

Tropic of Capricorn

Tropic of Cancer

Pacific Ocean

Pacific Ocean

International Date Line

Monday Sunday

Sunday

80° 90° 100° 110° 120° 130° 140° 150° 160° 170° 180° 170° 160° 150° 140° 130° 120° 110° 100° 90°

40° 30° 20° 10° 0° 10° 20° 30° 40° 50°

INDEPENDENT COUNTRIES	ISLAND GROUP	AREA (Square Miles)	POPULATION	CAPITAL	MAIN LANGUAGES
FIJI	Melanesia	7,055	672,000	Suva	English, Hindi, Fijian
KIRIBATI	Micronesia	264	57,000	Tarawa	Gilbertese, English
NAURU	Micronesia	8	7,000	Yaren (district)	Nauruan, English
PAPUA NEW GUINEA	Melanesia	178,259	3,259,000	Port Moresby	Pidgin English, Matu
SOLOMON ISLANDS	Melanesia	11,500	254,000	Honiara	English, Pidgin English
TONGA	Polynesia	270	104,000	Nukualofa	Tongan, English
TUVALU	Polynesia	10	8,000	Fongafale	English, Tuvaluan
VANUATU	Melanesia	5,700	127,000	Vila	Bislama, English, French
WESTERN SAMOA	Polynesia	1,097	160,000	Apia	Samoan, English

TERRITORIES	CONTROLLING COUNTRY	ISLAND GROUP	AREA (Square Miles)	TERRITORIES	CONTROLLING COUNTRY	ISLAND GROUP	AREA (Square Miles)
Cook Islands	New Zealand	Polynesia	199	Norfolk Island	Australia	Polynesia	14
Easter Island	Chile	Polynesia	64	Pitcairn Island	Britain	Polynesia	2
French Polynesia	France	Polynesia	2,500	Eastern Samoa	United States	Polynesia	76
Midway Islands	United States	Polynesia	2	Tokelau Islands	New Zealand	Polynesia	4
New Caledonia	France	Melanesia	7,374	Trust Territory of the Pacific Islands	United States	Micronesia	687
Niué	New Zealand	Polynesia	100	Wake Island	United States	Polynesia	3

Polynesia

Flying to Polynesia

We first make a short stopover in Hawaii. Our fiftieth state is a group of islands nearly twenty-five hundred miles off the coast of California. The Hawaiian Islands are part of a much larger group of islands in the Pacific Ocean called **Polynesia** (PAHL uh NEE zhuh). Melanesia and Micronesia are the two other large groups of islands in the Pacific. Find Polynesia, Melanesia, and Micronesia on the Pacific area map. Our trip will take us to islands in all three of these groups, and we will begin with Polynesia.

The name *Polynesia* comes from Greek words meaning "many islands." These

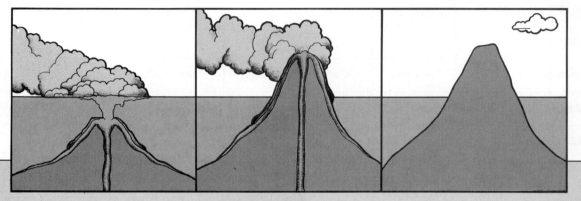

High and Low Islands

How were the islands of the Pacific formed? Scientists believe some islands, like Guam and Hawaii were formed from volcanoes that rose from the ocean floor. This process did not take thousands of years as the evolutionists argue. In 1963 off the southwest coast of Iceland, scientists watched Surtsey Island grow out of the Atlantic Ocean. In a matter of weeks the island was formed from the eruption of a volcano. By the next year Surtsey Island developed sand beaches, white cliffs, and lagoons. Today the island has plants and animals. Likewise in the Pacific Ocean as volcanoes erupted, molten rock pushed up through the ocean floor and formed islands.

Some Pacific Islands are really the peaks of volcanic mountains. For example, the island of Hawaii from the ocean floor to the peak of Mauna Kea is the tallest mountain on earth. Its total height is four thousand feet taller than Mt. Everest. Islands formed from volcanoes are called "high islands" because they usually tower high above the sea.

Another kind of island in the Pacific took shape in a different way. This kind is a coral atoll, and it is called a "low island." Low islands are usually flat islands that do not rise high above the water. How did these islands form?

Over a period of many years tiny sea animals died, and their skeletons built up around the rim of an underwater mountain top. These stony skeletons piled up to form coral reefs. Over a period of time the coral became so thick that it reached the surface of the water. Sand, soil, and later plants and animals collected on the ring-shaped atoll. A protected area of water called a lagoon usually is found in the middle of the low islands made of coral.

many islands lie within a large triangular-shaped area with Hawaii at its northern corner. Easter Island sits by itself at the eastern corner, and the large islands of New Zealand are at the western corner. Within this giant triangle covering thousands of square miles of ocean lie several small groups of islands like tiny specs in a vast sea of blue.

After a short layover in Honolulu, we climb back aboard a different plane for another long flight that will take us to explore our first Polynesian island, Tahiti (tuh HEE tee). Though our plane travels at a speed of over five hundred miles per hour, it takes us about five hours to reach Tahiti in the middle of Polynesia. Finally after flying over the seemingly endless ocean, we descend upon Tahiti. From our plane the island appears to be shaped like a giant figure eight. We land on the island's airstrip, which is perched along the shoreline near Tahiti's largest city, Papeete (PAHP ee ATE ee).

The Island of Tahiti

Two large volcanic mountains form the shape of Tahiti. The Isthmus of Taravao joins the rugged landscape surrounding each of the volcanic domes. Small villages, tiny farms, and tourist hotels are scattered along the shoreline, but thick tropical forests cover much of the mountainous interior of the island. A coral reef surrounds most of the island, giving it a protected lagoon.

We take a bus from the airport to our hotel in Papeete. Along the way we notice Polynesian natives wearing colorful clothing and garlands of beautiful tropical flowers. We also see many tourists enjoying the warm climate and the Polynesian scenery. Stores, restaurants, street names, and signs are often written in French. French and English are the main spoken languages on the island instead of the native Tahitian language.

French is spoken there because Tahiti and many other islands of Polynesia are controlled by France. France controls five groups of islands in this Polynesian area.

Scenes from Tahiti: Cook's Bay *(left)* and a young Tahitian dancer *(above)*

Tahiti is the largest island of the group called the Society Islands. The other four groups are the Tuamotu (TOO uh MOH too) Islands, the Gambier (GAM beer) Islands, the Tubuai (TOO boo EYE) Islands (also called the Austral Islands), and the Marquesas (mahr KAY zuhs) Islands. All of these groups together are called French Polynesia.

After settling into our hotel rooms, we find a restaurant and order a Polynesian supper. When it comes, we enjoy roast pork, sweet potatoes, and *poi,* a polynesian fruit pudding. There are plenty of bananas, coconuts, papayas, and other tropical fruits as well. After eating, we stroll down to the beach to watch a beautiful Tahitian sunset.

A Tour of the Island

We rise early the next morning, eat a quick breakfast at the hotel, and then board a bus for a tour of the island. Though the sun has been up only a few minutes, the streets of Papeete are full of activity. The central marketplace is crowded and noisy with people. Some are buying or selling fish caught by Tahitian fishermen during the night. Others display fruits, vegetables, baked goods, baskets, clothing, and all kinds of goods for sale in their stalls and shops. While the Tahitians make their morning purchases, they exchange the latest news of the island.

Once outside the city of Papeete, we begin our trip around the island. A narrow highway circles the island, following the low land near the shore. As we travel, we pass bicycles, motorcycles, cars, and several crowded old busses. A Tahitian bus is called *le truck,* and each one seems to be crammed full of people traveling to or from Papeete. On top of the bus sit the passengers' belongings. Among the baggage are baskets, bicycles, and even crates of chickens.

Tahitian houses lie along the road in small villages and clearings. The natives no longer live in grass huts as they did in the past, but most of their homes are still small and hastily built. Yet many have electricity and other modern conveniences.

A seventy-five mile trip takes us completely around Tahiti, an island about one-third the size of the state of Rhode Island. As we travel along the shore, we see fishing boats in the water bringing in catches of fish and seafood. Outrigger canoes paddled by Polynesian boys slice through the water toward shore, and people in sailboats and on surfboards enjoy riding the waves. Along the beach tall palm trees sway in the gentle breeze.

At Matavai Bay we make a brief stop to view this place where the famous explorer of the South Pacific, Captain Cook, anchored his ship in 1769. He was one of the first Europeans to see Tahiti and many of the other Pacific Islands. Going on, we complete our tour, returning to Papeete.

On to Moorea

After lunch we gather our things and take a twelve-mile boat ride across the Sea of the Moon to the nearby island of Moorea. The rugged peaks of this island create breathtaking scenery for us as we approach its shore. After checking into our hotel, we take a quick ride to see some of Moorea's sites. We find lush forests, tropical gardens, and coffee and pineapple plantations. For the evening, we make our way back to our hotel where our modern rooms have thatched roofs on the outside to make them appear more Polynesian.

The next day we take a plane ride from Moorea to the northwest over some more of the Society Islands. We fly by Huahiné (wah HEE nee), Raiatea (RAH yah TAY ah), and Tahaa (thu HAH). Then we land on the beautiful island of Bora Bora. Two small volcanic peaks rise above this small island, while sandy beaches and a coral reef with a lagoon surround it. We can take a bike ride around the island in just a few hours. We will explore Bora Bora on our own. Just don't forget to return in time for our flight back to Tahiti this afternoon.

The Samoa Islands

When our time for exploring ends, we fly back to Tahiti and then catch another flight that takes us away from French Polynesia. We fly west for over one thousand miles to Samoa (suh MOH uh), another group of Polynesian islands. The Samoa Islands are divided into two parts. The two largest islands along with some nearby small islands make up the independent country of Western Samoa. Eastern Samoa is usually called American Samoa because it is a territory of the United States.

As the sun sets, our plane lands in American Samoa on the island of Tutuila (TOO too EE lah). We spend this night in American Samoa's capital, Pago Pago (PANG-oh PANG-oh). United States Navy ships used Pago Pago's beautiful harbor as a fueling station for many years. In 1929, Eastern Samoa officially became a United States territory. Only about thirty thousand people live on the small islands of American Samoa. Their total land area of seventy-six square miles lies over five thousand miles away from California's coast.

Bora Bora

Because Pago Pago was an important Pacific port for America, the United States built a large naval base there. Many American sailors visited or worked at this harbor in the early 1900s. The Samoans who lived on this island became very familiar with American ways, and many forgot much of their traditional Polynesian way of life. The American navy base closed in 1951, but American Samoa, especially the island of Tutuila, continues to be very "American." Native costumes and customs are displayed mainly for the tourists. Cruise ships still anchor in Pago Pago's harbor, and many of the town's citizens are busy working in the fishing or canning industry.

After a good night's rest, we drive through Pago Pago for a quick tour of the city. Then we head for the waterfront where we board a small schooner called the *Mauna Tele.* This old sailing vessel is headed for Western Samoa where it will pick up a load of **copra,** dried coconut meat. The copra is brought back to a processing plant in Pago Pago. Coconuts are an important resource in the Pacific Islands, and for some of the islands, copra is the only product they have to trade.

You probably do not eat a great deal of coconut. Except as an ingredient in cookies, pies, and cakes, we do not think of coconut as an important food. To the Pacific Islanders, however, the coconut palm tree provides not only food, but also building materials, ingredients for medicines and oils, and materials for articles of clothing, ropes, mats, and many kinds of useful products. Islanders sell copra, which is used to make margarine, soap, and cosmetics. The illustration below shows us why the coconut palm tree is such an important resource in the Pacific Islands.

The coconut tree provides many useful products.

As we sail out of Pago Pago's harbor, the smell of the salty sea air mingles with the unpleasant odor of sour copra lingering in the empty hold of the schooner. We sail west to the island of Upolu and head for port in the capital city of Apia on the north shore. Dark clouds, which we saw far in the west as we left Pago Pago, are now rapidly rolling toward us. The wind picks up, and the waves begin to toss our little ship. Although our Polynesian captain is experienced, we are thankful to reach the harbor safely before the storm breaks. We hurry to our hotel as the rain begins to fall.

Western Samoa

Tropical storms often occur in Samoa during the rainy season from December to April. Hurricanes sometimes hit these and other Pacific Islands. We eat a late lunch at our hotel while the rain falls fiercely outside. After a couple of hours, however, the storm passes over, and the sky begins to clear. How grateful we are that this was just a small storm and not a violent hurricane.

When the raindrops stop falling, we rush out for a walk through Apia. In Pago Pago it seemed as if half the people were from the United States or Europe, but here in Western Samoa, nearly all the people we see are native Polynesians. Other than in the modern business district by Apia's harbor, most of the Western Samoans live in a more simple, traditional style. Although some men wear Western clothing, we see some wearing the *lava-lava*, a cloth skirt. Near the edge of the city we find a few *fales*, houses with thatched roofs and open sides. The Samoans who still live in these homes lower blinds made of coconut palm leaves for protection against wind and rain. But most of the time, the open construction of these houses allows the gentle breezes to keep the Samoans cool even if it does not give them much privacy.

On our walk, we pass many churches. During the 1800s, many Protestant and Roman Catholic missionaries came to Samoa and the other islands of the Pacific to convert the islanders to their religions. Some of the missionaries truly preached the gospel, and some of the nationals were saved. Other islanders, however, simply accepted the ways of Christianity in order to obtain the new tools, medicines, and other things the missionaries brought with them. Others conformed to Christianity because native chiefs forced it on them.

Missionaries came to Samoa in the 19th century.

The native Samoan chiefs, called *matais*, ruled large family groups. Today, *matais* are still influential in Western Samoa's representative government. Local customs are also carried on by these chiefs. For example, in one traditional ceremony, the chief's daughter serves honored visitors a beverage made from water and the pounded root of a special tree. The drink is served in a large wooden bowl, and a little is spilled on the ground for the gods. Although most Samoans and many other Pacific Islanders claim to be "Christians," belief in spirits and other native superstitions continue.

We walk back to our hotel noticing that the sky is now clear. As darkness approaches, the stars God made begin to appear and twinkle brightly in the tropical sky. Our trip to the Pacific Islands is reminding us of all the wonders God has created and given to us to enjoy. We are seeing some of the beauty and variety of our earth, and when by salvation through Jesus Christ we know the God Who created all, we have great reason to rejoice.

> Sing unto the Lord a new song, and his praise from the end of the earth, ye that go down to the sea, and all that is therein; the isles, and the inhabitants thereof. (Isaiah 42:10)

The next morning after breakfast, we take a half-hour bus ride to the airport on the eastern end of the island. On the way we pass several more *fales* along with many more traditional houses and buildings. Beside some of the houses and buildings, coconuts lie cracked and spread over the ground or on tables to dry in

the sun. Some Samoans use the copra harvest from a few trees to provide a small income for their family. Others own many coconut palm trees, and for them, copra production is a big business. Another important crop that we find in Samoa is cacao, and our road to the airport passes a cacao plantation. We also notice several truck loads of bananas headed for market in Apia.

Crossing the International Date Line

At the airport we board a plane that will take us to Nauru (nah OO roo), a tiny island country in Micronesia. Our flight takes us not only from Western Samoa to Nauru, but it also takes us from today to tomorrow. As we fly, we cross

what is known as the **International Date Line.** This imaginary line marks the boundary between one day and the next. To understand why such a line is necessary, let's use our classroom globe and a flashlight.

Let the flashlight represent the sun, and shine its light on the Pacific Ocean area of the globe. We will say that it is early Friday morning in Nauru (or use New Zealand if you cannot find Nauru on your globe). Now, holding the flashlight in the same position, slowly begin to spin the globe to the right. The light now reaches Australia and then Asia. When the sun rises this Friday morning in China, it is already afternoon in Nauru.

Keep turning the globe slowly so that the light reaches Europe. While it is Friday morning in Europe, it is Friday evening in Nauru, where the sun has already set. Continue to spin the globe until the light shines on North and South America. Now it is Friday on these continents, and the sun is just rising on this same Friday morning in Hawaii. Shortly after the sun rises in Hawaii, it rises in Nauru. Since Friday has already passed in Nauru, its new day is Saturday. Now, while it is Friday morning in Hawaii (and Samoa), it is Saturday morning in Nauru.

Actually, the International Date Line could have been drawn from north to south anywhere on the earth. All that was needed was a place where each new day could begin. The middle of the Pacific Ocean along or near the 180° line of longitude was accepted as that place. Look at the map on page 284, and you will notice that the Date Line has been bent in a few places to keep groups of islands together in the same day.

Because we cross the International Date Line from east to west on our long flight from Samoa to Nauru, we leave at 10:00 A.M. today (Friday), and we will arrive about 2:30 P.M. tomorrow (Saturday). The flight does not last twenty-eight and one half hours. We are in the air only about six hours, but we lose a day as we fly across the Date Line and move into another time zone.

If we had begun our flight on the western side of the Date Line on a Friday and flown east across it, we would have landed in Samoa or Tahiti on Thursday, the day before we left!

In case you are confused about what day it is, just remember that when you cross the Date Line from east to west, you move your time one whole day (twenty-four hours) ahead. In doing this you "lose" a day. And if you cross from west to east, you subtract one whole day from your time. You "gain" a day.

Section Review

1. To which Pacific Island group does Hawaii belong?

2. What country controls Tahiti?

3. What Polynesian islands are a United States territory?

4. What is dried coconut meat called?

5. Would you gain a day or lose a day if you flew west across the International Date Line?

Micronesia

Our flight to Nauru takes us out of Polynesia and into Micronesia, a large area of islands lying north of the Equator in the western Pacific. **Micronesia** (MY kroh NEE zhuh) means "small islands," and the people of these islands are slightly different from the Polynesians. The Micronesians are usually a little smaller and thinner than the people we saw on the Polynesian islands. Also the skin and features of the Micronesians bear some resemblance to those of the people of Southeast Asia and China. We must realize, however, that especially in recent years, some of the Pacific Islanders have moved to other islands. We may find some Polynesians (or Melanesians) in Micronesia, and we may see some Micronesians in those other islands.

Nauru

One lonely little island, Nauru, is one of the smallest independent countries in the world. Its nearest neighbor island lies nearly two hundred miles away. Nauru's soil will not produce the tropical fruits and vegetables found in abundance on other Pacific Islands. Its only water supply is rainwater, which is caught and held in barrels and tanks. Our view of the island as we land convinces us that most of Nauru is barren and useless.

Nauru does have one very important resource. Deposits of phosphate, an ingredient used in fertilizer, nearly cover the island. Since 1906 Nauru's mines have produced millions of tons of high-quality phosphate. Most of it has been sold to Australia and New Zealand. Nauru's

One of the children of Micronesia

people have grown wealthy from the sale of phosphate, but their wealth may not last. Very soon Nauru's supply of phosphate will run out. Unless the people are prepared for the future, they will be left on a little barren island without any business to support themselves. They will use up all their money to buy the food and supplies they need, and then they will be poor and helpless.

The Nauruans can prepare for their future by finding other businesses that may prosper on their island. They may also bring in shiploads of soil to fill in the old mine areas. Food products grown in the new soil could help feed the people in the future.

Nauru's situation reminds us that we need to prepare for our future as well. We need to get a good education and develop our skills to prepare us for making a living when we are older. More important than that, we need to prepare for eternity. Only by salvation in Jesus Christ can we be assured of a home in heaven.

> Labour not for the meat which perisheth, but for that meat which endureth unto everlasting life, which the Son of man shall give unto you: for him hath God the Father sealed. (John 6:27)

The United States Trust Territories

Our stay on Nauru is very brief. We must continue flying northwest to the island of Ponape (POH nuh PAY). We have written to some missionaries on that island, and they will be waiting for us. Ponape lies in a group of islands called the Carolines (KAR uh LINEZ). The Carolines, along with the Marianas (MARE ee AN uhz) and the Marshall Islands, are controlled by the United States. These island groups cover a large area of Micronesia, and together they are called the **Trust Territory of the Pacific Islands.**

Making Friends on Ponape

After a couple more hours of flying, we land on Ponape. The missionary and a large number of islanders are there to meet us at the airport. They give us a friendly welcome. Two pick-up trucks wait nearby to take us, our baggage, and all our new friends to the missionary's house by the church. Everyone is crowded for the bumpy ride, but no one seems to mind.

When we arrive, we see a crowd of islanders waiting for us. A huge table covered with food sits under the trees. There are bowls and plates full of fish, rice, yams, coconut, taro, bananas, and breadfruit. A few youngsters are waving palm leaves over the table to keep insects away.

The missionary and his wife speak English, but only a few of the islanders know our language. They all speak a Ponapean language. Even though we cannot understand much of what they are saying, we know that these Christians on Ponape are very glad to welcome us to their island. After a prayer of thanks to God for our safe trip and for the food prepared for us, the feast begins. In Ponape the men are always served first, and so we follow their custom. The ladies wait while the men get their food first. Everyone eats heartily even though our group is getting a little tired of tropical food. We have never eaten so many fish, coconuts, and bananas in all our lives as we have in the past few days. Even so we are grateful for the hospitality of our new Ponapean friends.

After the meal everyone gathers around a bonfire for a time of singing and testimonies. The missionary interprets into English what the islanders sing and say so that we will understand. He also interprets our words for the islanders. A few of the men have guitars, and they accompany the singing. The islanders sing

Guam

Area: 209 sq. mi.   Population: 89,996

On March 6, 1521, Magellan discovered Guam (GWAHM) during his voyage around the world. Guam, the largest of the Mariana islands, lies in the western Pacific. Magellan's discovery, however, was not a pleasant one. Natives boarded his ship, robbed Magellan's men, and even took one of their small boats. The next morning Magellan got revenge. His party went ashore, killed several natives, burned their huts, and took some food. Magellan called the Marianas "Islands of Thieves" because of his experiences there. About a month later natives in the Philippines killed Magellan, and only a few of his men were able to return to Spain.

Foreigners have been interested in Guam ever since Magellan's discovery. In 1565 Spain took over the island, and a hundred years later Spanish missionaries brought Roman Catholicism to the island. In 1898 during the Spanish-American War, the United States captured the island without any bloodshed. After the war America purchased Guam from Spain along with the Philippines and Puerto Rico for $20 million. During World War II several thousand Japanese troops occupied the island. But in 1944 after a bloody battle, the United States recaptured it.

Today Guam is a United States territory. Though only thirty miles long and a few miles wide, Guam is an important American military base and a stopover for ships and airplanes traveling between the United States and Asia.

The original inhabitants of Guam were the Chamorros, a tall people with brown skin and long black hair. Today the Chamorros, also called Guamanians, make up half of the population of the island. The rest are Hawaiians, Filipinos, and Americans. The people of Guam are American citizens, but they cannot vote in United States elections. The president appoints a governor of the island, but the residents elect members of their own legislature. Agana is their capital. Many of the people are farmers, and copra is the main export item.

many hymns and psalms. We recognize some of the tunes, but the words are Ponapean. The voices of the island people ring out beautifully in the stillness of the tropical night. We could listen to them sing praises to the Saviour all night, but tomorrow is a busy day, and we must get some rest.

Sunday in Ponape

It seems as if we hardly had time to close our eyes before morning arrived. The girls stayed in the missionary's house, while the boys slept in the church building. We must hurry and get ready for Sunday school and church. We have a big day ahead of us.

The islanders who live nearby walk or ride bicycles to church, while the pick-up

Going to church on Ponape

trucks round up those who live farther away. The simple little church building is filled when the services begin. The Ponapeans joyfully sing a cappella (that is, without any instruments to accompany them). In the church service the missionary invites our group to sing a hymn in English for the people.

After church and a quick dinner, we divide into groups to go witnessing with the Ponapeans. Although we cannot speak their language, they seem pleased to have us go with them. Some go to visit patients in a hospital. Others go to hold a service in the local jail. The rest of us give tracts to the islanders we find on the streets. The Ponapean Christians are faithfully trying to spread the gospel to their island neighbors. Their enthusiasm to serve the Lord makes us ashamed that we do not work harder to tell others about Jesus Christ in our land.

We meet back at the church for a Bible class and then the evening service. Afterwards some of the islanders stay to eat and fellowship with us. We have quickly grown to love these people who have been so kind to us. It makes us sad to think that we must leave their island in the morning.

Early in the morning we are on our way to the airport. Loaded in the pickup trucks with us are several of the Ponapeans who are going to bid us farewell. They have given us many beautiful handmade gifts to take with us. We slowly climb aboard our plane as we wave back to our Ponapean friends. As our plane takes off, we look out the windows to see them still waving at us.

Section Review

1. What does Micronesia mean?

2. What important resource does Nauru have?

3. What three island groups are found in the Trust Territory of the Pacific Islands?

4. To what country does the Trust Territory of the Pacific Islands belong?

5. What are some common foods on the Pacific Islands?

Melanesia

Papua New Guinea

With a few stops on other islands, we fly over one thousand miles to the southwest to the big island of **New Guinea.** You remember that the western half of this island is a part of the country of Indonesia (see Chapter 11). The eastern half, however, is the independent country of Papua New Guinea (PAP-yoo-uh NOO GIN-ee). Before its independence in 1975, Papua New Guinea had been controlled by Germany and Britain, and later by Australia. Now the young country is learning to handle its own affairs.

Papua New Guinea lies in the area called **Melanesia** (MEL uh NEE zhuh). *Melanesia* means "black islands," and it probably received that name because the people of these islands usually have very dark skin.

We are going to Port Moresby, the capital of Papua New Guinea, on the southern shore. On our way, we cross over the Owen Stanley Mountain Range, which extends along the eastern peninsula of the island. New Guinea has many mountains nearly as high as those in the Rocky Mountains of North America. The forest-covered mountains divide the inland areas into many isolated valleys. Along the coast, swamps and jungles swarm with mosquitos.

Papua New Guinea sells four major products to other countries. Copper mining on Bougainville, one of Papua New Guinea's many smaller islands, is the country's leading industry. Coffee grown in the mountainous areas, and cacao and copra grown in the coastal areas and on the smaller islands make up the rest of the country's "four *C's.*"

A Land of Contrasts

In Port Moresby, we see tall, modern buildings and all the activities of a busy little city. We soon learn, however, that Papua New Guinea is a land of strange contrasts. Although the official language of the country is English, the people speak more than seven hundred different languages. Communication between groups that speak different languages would be nearly impossible if it were not for the fact that a large number of the people can speak pidgin (PIJ un). Pidgin is a combination of English words with native words and some words from other languages. All are mixed together in such a way that they are not understandable to most of us who speak English. In pidgin, a table fork is an "engine belong kau-kau," milk is "susu," and "kisim" means "to give him." "Mipela laikim motaka," could be translated, "We like the car."

When Papua New Guinea became an independent country in 1975, it established its own representative government with a parliament and a prime minister. While the government leaders in Port Moresby deal with matters of industry, education, and commerce, a few of the backward tribes in the highlands occasionally go to war with one another using spears, bows, and arrows. In the cities the people wear business suits, fashionable dresses, and other Western clothing. The tribal people in the highlands still often wear skirts made of leaves and feathers, feathered head-dresses, and for decoration, necklaces of

The colorfully garbed natives of New Guinea

shells or pig's teeth and feather quills in their noses.

Some of the Papua New Guineans have received a good education in other countries, and now many more are being trained in their own land. Still, over half the people of Papua New Guinea cannot read or write. The cities have modern houses and apartments. Most of the people in the countryside continue to live in small, crowded houses made with woven mat walls and thatched roofs. Few roads have been built through the rugged landscape. Therefore, few cars and trucks are used for transportation. Yet, many landing strips for airplanes have been built all over the country. Air transportation provides the fastest, most efficient way for people and supplies to reach the mountainous inland areas of Papua New Guinea. Early missionaries brought Christianity to the island, and now most of the people claim to be Christians. Most continue, however, to believe in spirits and to practice sorcery.

Around Papua New Guinea

On Tuesday morning we take an airplane tour of some of the sites of Papua New Guinea. We visit a coffee plantation in the central highlands. Coffee trees with their shiny leaves and ripe red berries cover many of the mountainsides. Coffee grows well in warm, moist climates like that of Papua New Guinea. Workers pick the berries by hand when they are ripe. The berries contain two small green beans, which are processed and dried at the coffee plantation. Later, these coffee beans will be blended with other varieties, roasted, and ground for use in coffee pots around the world.

We make another stop at an animal farm that keeps many of the rare animals found in New Guinea. One of the unusual animals we see is a green tree python snake. Another is a cus-cus, a furry mammal about the size of a cat but with a pouch for its young like a kangaroo. Many beautiful birds of paradise also live at this farm.

Our last stop before we return to Port Moresby for the night is in the Sepik River Valley. There we see a *haus tambaran,* a spirit house with a tall, pointed thatched roof. Only men are allowed inside, and so the girls in our group will have to wait for the boys to describe it for them. Men use the spirit house as a gathering place to smoke, talk, and play their hand-carved flutes and drums. Ugly masks and carved figures hang from the walls and ceiling. Also in the spirit house, ceremonies are held to proclaim that a boy has achieved

manhood. During the ceremony, the boy's back is cut to leave many scars. On hearing this information, the boys in our group are ready to leave.

The Trip to Fiji

After the night back in Port Moresby, we leave Wednesday morning to fly to our last stop in the Pacific before we return home. While we take this two-thousand-mile flight to the islands of Fiji (FEE jee), we find plenty to talk about. A little to the north of our course lie the Solomon Islands. These islands received their independence from Great Britain in 1978. One of the islands, Guadalcanal, was the scene of heavy fighting between Japanese and United States forces during World War II.

The Japanese captured many of the Pacific Islands, including the Solomon Islands, during the early years of World War II. One of the first American campaigns in the Pacific to free these islands and defeat Japan began on Guadalcanal. United States Marines landed on the island in August of 1942, but it took nearly six months of bitter fighting to secure Guadalcanal. Marine, army, and navy losses were heavy.

Guadalcanal is only one of many places in the Pacific made famous to Americans by the battles of World War II. We should be very grateful for the many Americans who gave their lives during World War II to protect and defend our own country as well as these islands in the Pacific. We should also be thankful for those who now serve our country in the armed services. If you know someone in the Army, Navy, Air Force, Marines, Coast Guard, or National Guard, remember him in prayer today.

On our flight to Fiji, we fly over the islands of Vanuatu (VAN noo AH too). Before their independence in 1980, these islands were controlled by both the British and the French. The island group was known as the New Hebrides.

One of the islands of Vanuatu, Pentecost, is known for its land divers. If you are a good swimmer, perhaps you are courageous enough to go off the high dive at a swimming pool. The land divers of Pentecost dive head-first off a platform up to eighty feet high. Beneath them is no swimming pool—only solid ground.

To break their fall and prevent their death, the divers tie vines, which are attached to the platform, to their ankles. The vines stretch and stop the diver's fall precisely as his head touches the ground. If the vines are too long, the fall could be fatal, but if the vines are too short, the diver will swing into the platform and maybe suffer great injury. Only on special occasions do these daring divers fall through the air. The practice probably began as a test that proved a boy's manhood, but today the land divers seem to enjoy it as a dangerous sport.

An Island with Two Sides

Our plane lands at the airport at Nadi on the western side of Fiji's largest island, Viti Levu. As we drive to our hotel in Nadi, we wonder if our plane took a wrong turn somewhere and brought us to India instead of Fiji. Most of the people we see in the town are dressed like the people of India. The women are wearing saris and a lot of jewelry. Signs on stores have Indian names, and we pass a Hindu temple.

We soon learn that we really are in Fiji, but that about half the people in this island country are Indians. Many people from India came to Fiji about one hundred years ago to work in the British sugar plantations. The descendents of those workers continue to labor in the sugar industry. Others operate businesses, and some have become doctors and lawyers.

After a night in Nadi, we drive to the other end of the island. We take the coast road along the southern shore of Viti Levu. During the first part of our journey we pass sugar plantations where fields of sugar cane are growing in the tropical sun. Here along the coastal plain are small workers' houses and some bamboo and thatch huts. Before long we see mountains rising in the distance to the north. The mountainsides and the plains on this side of the island appear dry and brown. After a couple of hours of driving and almost before we realize it, we enter an area of thick tropical forests that stretch from the coast up to the mountainsides. Instead of being dry and brown, the scenery changes to green. We cross several swift-flowing rivers and streams, and waterfalls trickle over rocks beside the road.

We learn that the mountains are responsible for the different climate and vegetation we now see. Most of the warm ocean winds that blow over Fiji come from the east. As they blow over the eastern half of the island and up into the central mountains, the air loses its moisture. Heavy rains often fall, filling streams and rivers. As the winds blow on over the mountains to the western side of the island, however, they become dry. This explains the differences we saw on our drive.

We see fewer Indians in Suva. Most of the people here seem to be Fijians or Europeans. Most of the Fijians are Melanesians with dark skin and curly black hair, but we also see some that appear more Polynesian with lighter skin and straighter hair. Occasionally we overhear some conversations in Fijian or an Indian language, but most of the people speak English. Although most of the Fijians dress in the kinds of clothing we wear, the traffic officers, guards, and some other officials dress in an interesting manner. Their shirts are red, blue, or black with shiny buttons and badges like those of a soldier or a police officer. Instead of slacks, they wear white *sulus* (wrapped, knee-length skirts with notched edges). A pair of sandals and often a pair of white gloves completes their uniform.

A Cannibal King Becomes a Christian

Only 150 years ago, many tribes of fierce warriors lived on the islands of Fiji. Often the menus of their feasts included *bokolo,* another name for roasted enemies. One cannibal chief, Cakobau, who was born in 1817, gained power on the islands. He led his people to war against enemy tribes, murdered those who displeased him, and gave cannibal feasts. During his reign, however, Christian missionaries came to Fiji to preach the gospel.

In 1854 Cakobau decided to accept Jesus Christ as his Saviour. He changed his ways, ended cannibalism on his island, and publicly told his people that he was a Christian.

Cakobau's power grew, even though he was no longer a fierce cannibal warrior. In 1867 he became king of Fiji, and his people lived in peace on the islands. Today most Fijians claim to be Christians. Many, however, have accepted only the form of religion instead of truly accepting Jesus Christ as their Saviour. Like others around the world, these people need to be shown the way of salvation. They may no longer be cannibal warriors, but they still need to find Jesus as their Lord and Saviour just as King Cakobau did.

In Suva near the Government House where the Fijian parliament meets, hundreds of tropical flowers bloom in a botanical garden. In a nearby park we see Fijians playing Rugby, soccer, and cricket, games popular in Fiji as well as in Britain. At the docks of Suva's harbor, cargo and cruise ships load and unload.

Tonight we attend a Fijian feast and watch some of the men perform a ceremonial war dance. The performers dress in traditional warrior costumes, carry spears, and paint their faces to make themselves appear very ferocious. Musicians chant, beat drums made from hollow logs, and thump the ground with bamboo sticks. The feast is an exciting end for our last night in the Pacific Islands.

Underwater Adventure

Friday morning we rise to eat breakfast and then hurry down to the shore. At one of the docks we board a boat for a morning tour. This tour is a bit unusual for us. We are going to explore the area near the island that lies underwater. Our boat has a glass bottom, and we sit around the edge looking down at the sights on the ocean floor. After our glass-bottomed boat leaves the harbor, it cruises along the shore. The guide points out the many different kinds of fish and sea creatures that live below us. Many kinds of colorful coral, shellfish, and sea plants come into view. We see lobsters, sea turtles, and even a shark. We think of the fact that we have been traveling for days on or near the ocean, but we never really stopped to realize that God created such a beautiful and interesting world under the seas.

O Lord, how manifold are thy works! in wisdom hast thou made them all: the earth is full of thy riches. So is this great and wide sea, wherein are things creeping innumerable, both small and great beasts. (Psalm 104:24-25)

When our cruise ends, we go to a Fijian restaurant to eat one last tropical meal before we journey home. We eat our fill of fish, yams, papaya, coconut, pineapple, and bananas, and then we go to our hotel to pack. Within an hour we are on a plane that will swiftly take us back across the island to the international airport at Nadi. Before long, we are in a big jet airplane headed back to the United States.

Our Journey's End

Shortly after we leave Fiji, we cross the International Date Line, and Friday afternoon becomes Thursday afternoon. We gain the day that we lost nearly a week ago when we crossed from the eastern side of the Date Line to the western side. It is dark when we reach Hawaii. We change planes and take a night flight from Honolulu back to the mainland.

As we settle in for our last long flight, we remember all the Pacific Islands we visited. Although we saw many places and many people of different cultures, we visited only a tiny number of the islands scattered in this huge ocean. There are thousands of people living on those islands who need to hear the gospel, and there are few missionaries working in those far-away places to tell them about Jesus. Perhaps the souvenirs and the memories we take home will remind us to pray faithfully for the missionaries and the Christians of the Pacific Islands. We can write to them, and we can send them packages or offerings to help them. Perhaps when we finish our schooling, some of us can return to the Pacific Islands as missionaries ourselves.

Section Review

1. To what large island group does Papua New Guinea belong?

2. On what island does Papua New Guinea lie?

3. Which of the Solomon Islands saw heavy fighting during World War II?

4. What are the New Hebrides Islands now called?

5. Many of Fiji's people are from what Asian country?

Terms to Remember
Polynesia
copra
International Date Line
Micronesia
Trust Territory of the Pacific Islands
New Guinea
Melanesia

Things to Know
1. What are the three major island groups in the Pacific Ocean?

2. To what country does Eastern Samoa belong?

3. What line is used to establish where each day begins?

4. What are the islands of Micronesia that belong to the United States called?

5. What country lies on the eastern half of New Guinea?

Things to Talk About

1. The islands of the Pacific usually do not have large industries. Why do you suppose this is true?

2. Read Psalms 89:9 and 107:23-31. What do these verses teach us about the control of the sea?

3. Why must there be an International Date Line?

4. What lessons can we learn from the Christians on Ponape?

Things to Do

1. Find or draw a large map of the Pacific Islands. Trace the route of our trip in this chapter on the map.

2. Read about the war in the Pacific during World War II. Locate the islands on which major battles occurred.

3. Prepare a feast like that you might enjoy on a tropical island. Include as many fresh tropical fruits as possible.

Geography Skills

Use the map of the Pacific Islands on page 284 to answer the following questions.

1. What island lies at 10° South latitude, 160° East longitude?

2. Fiji lies on one side of the International Date Line, and Tahiti lies on the other. If it is Monday afternoon in Fiji, what day is it in Tahiti?

3. Using the scale of miles, calculate the distance from Port Moresby, Papua New Guinea, to Pago Pago, American Samoa? (Use the scale of miles for a latitude of 0°.)

4. Which of the French-controlled Loyalty Islands (south of Vanuatu) is the largest?

5. About 2,500 miles west of the big island of Hawaii lies a little island controlled by the United States. What is it? (Use the scale of miles for a latitude near 20°.)

6. What mountain range is found in Papua New Guinea?

7. Using the direction of the compass below and the compass rose on the map, what direction would you sail from Pago Pago to reach each of the following places? (Using a protractor to measure the angle and comparing that angle to the compass will help you determine the direction accurately.)

a. Suva, Fiji

b. Papeete, Tahiti

c. Nauru

d. Honolulu, Hawaii

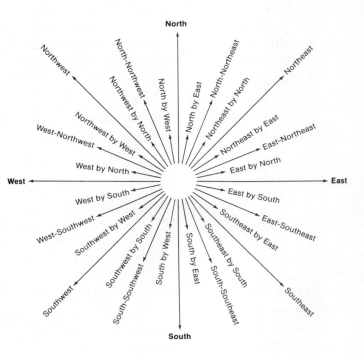

CHAPTER 15

AUSTRALIA, NEW ZEALAND, AND ANTARCTICA

Australia

"Something is missing," thought the scientists of a few hundred years ago. They knew about Europe and the vast expanse of Asia. From explorers they learned of Africa and the Americas. These were large continents with great areas of land, but most of these lands lay in the Northern Hemisphere. They knew that the earth is a sphere and that it turns on its axis. Surely, they thought, there must be a large continent in the Southern Hemisphere to help balance the earth.

Early explorers like Magellan had sailed across the wide Pacific Ocean and found only a few small islands. Other explorers began to search the Pacific for a great southern continent. Although no great continent was found, mapmakers drew maps showing a huge mass of land they believed to be in the Southern Hemisphere. They called this land *Terra Australis Incognita,* a Latin phrase meaning "the Unknown Southern Land."

Finally, in 1606 a Dutchman named Willem Jansz sighted land. He and his crew sailed along a small area, but he found the land dry and barren and the dark-skinned natives hostile. His findings gave

Europeans little hope that the new land held wealth and promise. Over the next 150 years, other Dutch sailors explored parts of the northern, western, and southern coasts of Australia. They found that it was a large land, but not nearly as large as they had imagined. Instead of finding gold and spices, they found treacherous reefs, swamps, deserts, and unfriendly natives. This new southern land seemed useless.

Captain James Cook

Then in 1770 the great English explorer **Captain James Cook** sailed along the eastern shore of Australia. He found this side of the continent more pleasant than the other explored areas. The east coast had woodlands, streams, and abundant animal life. Safe harbors and sandy beaches lined the shore. Cook claimed the east coast for England, and Europe soon heard of his findings.

Despite Cook's report, England was not interested in settling such a faraway, mysterious land. Besides, British colonies in North America provided plenty of room for English settlers. The thirteen American colonies, however, soon broke away from Britain in their War for Independence.

America's independence, in an unusual way, prompted Britain to begin the settlement of Australia. For a number of years before the War for Independence, Britain had sent some of her convicts to the American colony of Georgia. (These were not hardened criminals but debtors and those who had committed relatively minor crimes.) Transporting lawbreakers to a distant place kept the prisoners away from British society, relieved the crowded prisons in England, and served as punishment for the convicts. Because of the war, Britain could no longer send convicts to Georgia, and soon English prisons became overcrowded again. A place had to be found for the extra prisoners. Then someone thought that perhaps Australia would make a good prison.

In January of 1788, the first settlers of Australia arrived. Eleven British ships carrying over one thousand people landed at Botany Bay, just to the south of the present city of Sydney. About 800 passengers on this First Fleet were convicts. The ships brought food, seeds, farm animals, tools, and other provisions so that its passengers could build a permanent settlement in this land far away from England.

Finding Botany Bay unsuitable, the whole group sailed on to the large harbor of Port Jackson. There they built the first settlement at Sydney Cove. Although this location provided a pleasant setting for these new Australians, difficulties soon arose. The beautiful eucalyptus trees, whose grey-green leaves shaded the area, were so hard to cut that they quickly dulled axes and saws. (The settlers called the eucalyptus trees "gum" trees because of the sticky substance that seeped from the wood.) Because timber was hard to cut and there was no mortar for building with stone, constructing shelters for all the people was a difficult task. Another hindrance was that there were not enough

	AREA (Square Miles)	POPULATION	CAPITAL	MAIN LANGUAGES	MAIN RELIGIONS	CURRENCY
AUSTRALIA	2,967,909	15,265,000	Canberra	English	Protestant, Roman Catholic	dollar
NEW ZEALAND	103,736	3,142,000	Wellington	English, Maori	Protestant, Roman Catholic	dollar

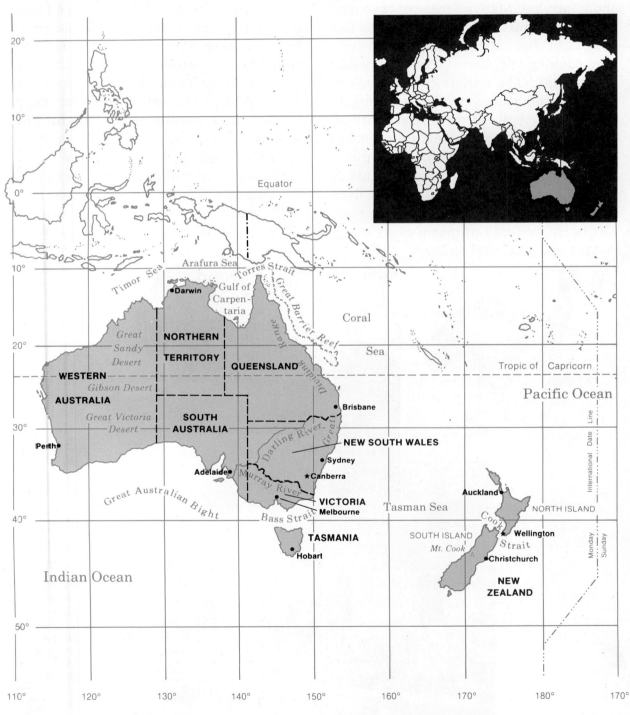

soldiers and officers to supervise all the convicts. Captain Arthur Phillip, who commanded the Fleet, managed to build the settlement and keep the convicts in order in spite of all the difficulties.

Providing food for the settlers was another difficult task. The people found some areas of good farmland nearby, but only a few of the settlers knew anything about farming. Many of the seeds brought from England did not grow in the Australian soil. Before long, provisions were running low, and starvation became a possibility. The settlers collected many kinds of wild plants and hunted animals for food. They ate fern roots, cockatoos, crows, and many other plants and animals. One type of bird, the emu, provided much of the settlers' meat. The emu, a flightless bird almost as large as an ostrich, lives only in Australia. The settlers of the First Fleet were the first Europeans to see many of Australia's unusual animals.

After the settlers had experienced a year of low food supplies, sickness, and other hardships, ships with provisions and more convicts arrived. The little colony, called New South Wales, endured many difficulties through the following years. The town of Sydney grew as new settlers arrived and businesses and industries developed. Farmers learned to raise crops in the Australian soil, and they found that livestock could thrive in this new land. Cattle raising was profitable, but sheep could bring even more wealth to their Australian owners. Wool shipped to England earned money for the sheep herders, and mutton was food for the settlers.

Today **Sydney,** Australia's largest city with over three million people, surrounds the area in which the first settlement was built about two hundred years ago. The colony of New South Wales is one of six states that have united to form the

Far left: Emus
Top right: Harbor Bridge, Sydney, Australia
Bottom center: Sydney, Australia

Commonwealth of Australia. This country of Australia, originally founded as a place for Britain's convicts, has become a modern nation of free people. Its unusual history, geography, plant and animal life, and the culture of its people make this land a fascinating place for us to study.

The Land Down Under

Because Australia lies in the Southern Hemisphere on the opposite side of the earth from Europe and North America, people often call it "The Land Down Under." One big difference between those lands of the Northern Hemisphere and Australia is that Australia's seasons are opposite those in the north. When it is summer in the United States and Europe, it is winter in Australia. Summer heat bakes Australia while Americans wear their winter coats.

Australia contains nearly three million square miles. The whole continent is about the size of the United States not including Alaska. Australia is smaller than any of the other six continents of the world. But unlike the other inhabited continents, the whole continent of Australia makes up only one country. The country of Australia is the sixth largest country in the world.

The Eastern Highlands and the Northern Tropics

Australia is a flat continent. Unlike those of the other continents, Australia's hills and mountains do not reach to great heights. Mt. Kosciusko, its highest mountain, stands only 7,316 feet tall. All the other continents, including Antarctica, have mountains over twice that height.

The location of Australia's mountains helps explain why the area along the eastern coast receives more rainfall than many other areas of the land. The highest lands of Australia extend from the northeast corner to the southeast corner

The eastern highlands of Australia

of the continent. This highland area along the eastern coast is called the **Great Dividing Range.** As air moves across Australia from the east and rises to pass over the mountains, it drops much of its moisture. Most of the rain falling in these highlands flows down in streams and rivers to the ocean on the east coast. Some of the water flows west into the Murray River system. The **Murray River** and its tributaries, Australia's only large river system, flow on the western side of the Great Dividing Range to the south coast.

The northern third of Australia lies in the tropics. Much of the northern coast receives a large amount of precipitation during the rainy season. Its dry season occurs during the winter and spring (June to November in Australia). Tropical forests grow along much of the northern coast, and in many areas swampland lies near the ocean. The northern coast, the eastern coast, and a small area at the southwestern corner of the continent receive adequate amounts of rainfall. The remainder of Australia, however, receives little precipitation throughout the year.

The Outback

The vast, dry interior and western regions of Australia are known as the **outback.** The early settlements of Australia, like Sydney, were built along the coasts. There ships could reach them, and there they found water and vegetation to meet their needs. Only in the late 1800s

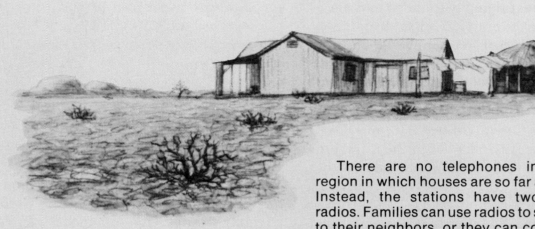

Living in the Outback

Living in the outback means living hundreds of miles from the nearest city. It means living where the climate is hot and dry almost all year long. It means a way of life that would seem quite unusual to most of us.

Families on the cattle or sheep stations of the outback often live a hundred miles away from their neighbors. Only occasionally do they see those neighbors and other people besides the workers on their station. Many station owners have their own small airplanes. They use them not only to check on their livestock, which may be pastured far away from the station house, but also to take trips to the nearest town.

There are no telephones in this region in which houses are so far apart. Instead, the stations have two-way radios. Families can use radios to speak to their neighbors, or they can contact a "flying doctor" if they need medical help. The Royal Flying Doctor Service provides medical information over the radio, and a doctor will fly to the stations to treat people who are seriously ill or injured.

The two-way radio meets another need of station families: the children go to school by means of the radio. They have their books and papers at their homes, and there they sit by the radio and listen as a teacher explains their lessons and assignments. If one of these students has a question, he asks the teacher over the radio. The teacher can teach and hear all of the many children scattered over hundreds of miles of the outback. Parents make sure that the students complete their lessons, and then the schoolwork is mailed to the teacher for grading.

did men begin to cross the large desert regions of the outback. Even then, the traveling was difficult, and many of the explorers lost their lives, dying of thirst in the desert.

Today the outback remains a barren land with only a few roads. Travelers are warned to take plenty of water, food, and provisions with them if they journey into the outback. Houses and gas stations are hundreds of miles apart. The hot sun shines on the sandy plains, often raising temperatures to 110°F or higher. If a car has a mechanical failure in the outback and its passengers set out on foot, they may be overcome by the scorching heat before they reach safety. It is better for them to stay with their car and wait for another vehicle to come along and rescue them than to walk in the desert heat.

Those who take trips in the outback must prepare for their journey. They need water so that they will not die of thirst. They need food and protection from the sun and heat. Our lives are often compared to journeys, and sometimes the difficulties and suffering that we face seem like the difficulties of desert travel. It is good for us to remember that if we know the Lord Jesus as our Saviour, we can trust Him to walk with us and help us through the troubles of our lives.

> They shall not hunger nor thirst; neither shall the heat nor sun smite them: for he that hath mercy on them shall lead them, even by the springs of water shall he guide them. (Isaiah 49:10)

Not all of the outback is useless desert. Huge sheep ranches (called sheep stations in Australia) cover some areas. One station may contain hundreds of square miles so that its sheep have room to find enough food as they graze on the sparse vegetation. Occasionally a sudden rainfall will turn a portion of the outback into a garden.

Plants that have been small and brown for months or years burst forth into colorful new life. But soon the blazing sun dries up the land, and the desert life turns brown once more.

Section Review

1. What English explorer gave a good report about the land of Australia?

2. Who were the first European settlers of Australia?

3. What city grew from the first Australian settlement?

4. What is the highland region of eastern Australia called?

5. What is the dry western region of Australia called?

The People of Australia

About fifteen million people live in Australia. That means that about the same number of people who live in the New York City area live in the whole continent of Australia. Nearly all those fifteen million Australians live in the large coastal cities. The nearby inland areas and the huge outback have only a few inhabitants.

The Aborigines

The first "settlers" of Australia entered the land hundreds of years before the British convicts and their keepers came. These dark-skinned native people, called **aborigines** (AB uh RIJ uh neez), were hunters and gatherers of food. They used spears and a throwing stick called a boomerang to kill animals for food. Some of the aborigines tried to fight against the Europeans who came to take their hunting grounds and sacred areas. Their spears were no match for guns, however. Many soon died, either from wounds inflicted

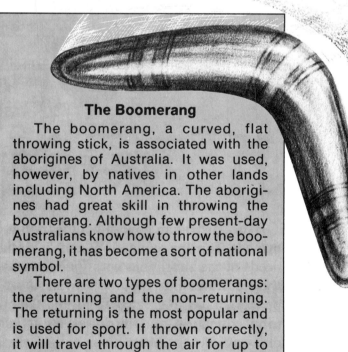

The Boomerang

The boomerang, a curved, flat throwing stick, is associated with the aborigines of Australia. It was used, however, by natives in other lands including North America. The aborigines had great skill in throwing the boomerang. Although few present-day Australians know how to throw the boomerang, it has become a sort of national symbol.

There are two types of boomerangs: the returning and the non-returning. The returning is the most popular and is used for sport. If thrown correctly, it will travel through the air for up to 100 yards before it curves around to return to the thrower. The non-returning boomerang was once used as a weapon for hunting small game.

Africa

FIVE

INTRODUCTION

Africa

What do you think of when someone mentions the continent of Africa? Is it thick jungles, lions, and crocodiles? Is it hot temperatures and black-skinned, cannibalistic natives? Is it grass huts, witch doctors, and spears? These things are commonly associated with Africa, but they are not really so common there.

There are jungles in Africa, but deserts and grasslands cover four times the area that jungles do. Africa, the second-largest continent, holds a wealth of wildlife, but hunting and other perils have greatly decreased the animal population. Laws in many African countries protect lions and other endangered animals from extinction. While some areas of Africa are very hot, others, even near the equator, have comfortable temperatures year-round.

Most of the people of Africa have dark skin, but there are millions, especially in northern Africa and South Africa, that have light skin. Cannibalism is very rare in Africa. And, while witch doctors are still to be found, the African governments are discouraging their practice. Many rural Africans still live in houses made of grass, mud, and sticks, but thousands in cities and towns have modern houses or apartments. While some Africans still hunt with spears, others work with computers and scientific instruments.

Africa is a unique mixture of the old and the new. It is an old world where many continue to carry on the traditions and superstitions of the past. It is also a new world where many are trying to learn skills and reach high goals in a fast-moving modern world. African nations face many difficulties as they try to modernize their lands without abandoning their heritage.

Most Africans face a greater problem than modernization, however. Without Christ as their Saviour, many will suffer eternally for their sins. Missionaries have told many Africans that they can know the salvation of Jesus Christ. Many more need to turn from their religious works and superstitions to trust Jesus as their Saviour. It is through Him that we all can be made "new creatures," free from the sin that condemns us.

> Therefore if any man be in Christ, he is a new creature: old things are passed away; behold, all things are become new. (II Corinthians 5:17)

The three chapters of this unit will tell us more about this amazing land of Africa. Perhaps you will find it to be a continent full of surprises.

CHAPTER 16

NORTH AFRICA

The Sahara

Imagine a place almost as large as the United States (including Alaska). Imagine that in that place there are less than one hundred villages and no cities. Imagine that between those villages lie hundreds of miles of sand and rock. Only an occasional scrubby tree or bush stands on the barren landscape.

Imagine temperatures climbing above 100°F in the day and then falling to near freezing at night. While the sun blazes down on this land, hardly a creature stirs. But in the coolness of the night and early morning, snakes, lizards, insects, and even some gazelles emerge from their cover to seek food. Years may pass in parts of this land before a drop of rain falls. When rain does come to this parched place, the water rolls quickly over the sand and rock. Soon, however, the scorching heat licks up the moisture, and the land is hot and dry once more.

Imagine a place that few Europeans or Americans had explored until about one hundred years ago. Before then, the few who dared to enter this land were usually killed either by thirst or by the attacks of fierce Berber tribesmen or Arabs who

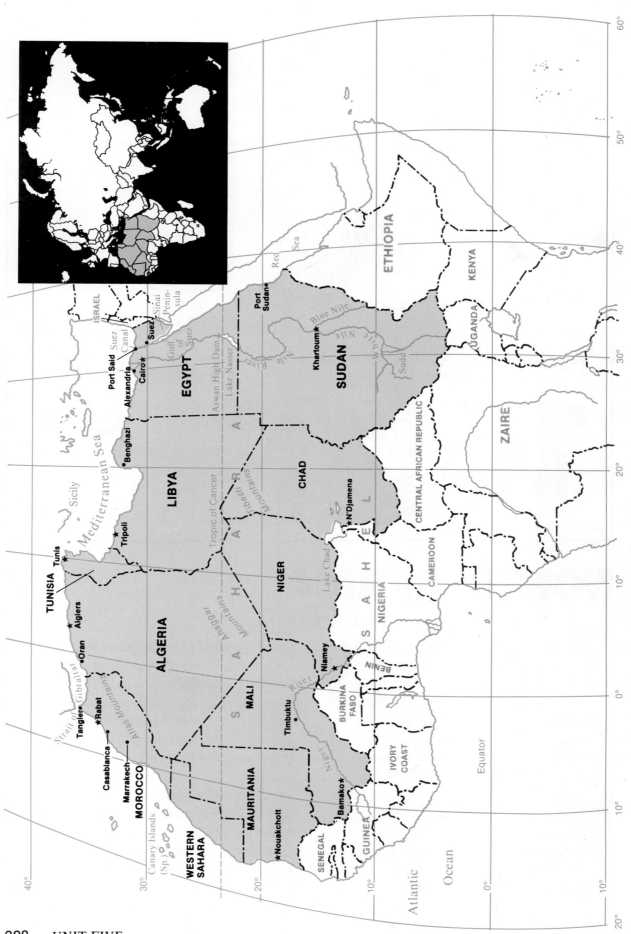

ISRAEL
Port Said
Suez Canal
Suez ★
Cairo ★
Alexandria
EGYPT
Sinai Peninsula
Gulf of Suez
Aswan High Dam
Lake Nasser
Red Sea
Port Sudan ★
Blue Nile
Khartoum ★
SUDAN
White Nile
Nile River
Sudd
ETHIOPIA
UGANDA
KENYA
CENTRAL AFRICAN REPUBLIC
ZAIRE

Benghazi ●

Mediterranean Sea
Sicily

LIBYA
Tropic of Cancer
Tibesti Mountains
CHAD
N'Djamena ★
SAHARA
CAMEROON

Tunis
TUNISIA
Tripoli ★

Algiers ★
Oran ●
ALGERIA
Ahaggar Mountains
NIGER
Lake Chad
NIGERIA
S A H E L

Strait of Gibraltar
Tangier ●
Rabat ★
Casablanca ●
Marrakech ●
MOROCCO
Atlas Mountains
MALI
Timbuktu ●
Niger River
Niamey ★
BURKINA FASO
BENIN
IVORY COAST
Equator

Canary Islands (Sp.)
WESTERN SAHARA
MAURITANIA
Nouakchott ★
Bamako ★
SENEGAL
GUINEA

Atlantic Ocean

60°
50°
40°
30°
20°
10°
0°
10°
20°

40°
30°
20°
10°
0°
10°
20°

	AREA (Square Miles)	POPULATION	CAPITAL	MAIN LANGUAGES	COLONIZED BY	DATE OF INDEPEND-ENCE
EGYPT	386,660	45,851,000	Cairo	Arabic	Britain	1922
LIBYA	679,359	3,498,000	Tripoli	Arabic, Italian, English	Italy	1951
TUNISIA	63,170	7,020,000	Tunis	Arabic, French	France	1956
ALGERIA	919,591	20,695,000	Algiers	Arabic, Berber, French	France	1962
MOROCCO	172,413	22,889,000	Rabat	Arabic, Berber, French, Spanish	France and Spain	1956
MAURITANIA	397,954	1,591,000	Nouakchott	Arabic, French, tribal languages	France	1960
MALI	478,764	7,393,000	Bamako	French, tribal languages	France	1960
NIGER	489,189	6,083,000	Niamey	French, tribal languages	France	1960
CHAD	495,753	4,990,000	N'Djamena	French, Arabic, tribal languages	France	1960
SUDAN	967,494	20,539,000	Khartoum	Arabic, Nubian, English	Britain	1955

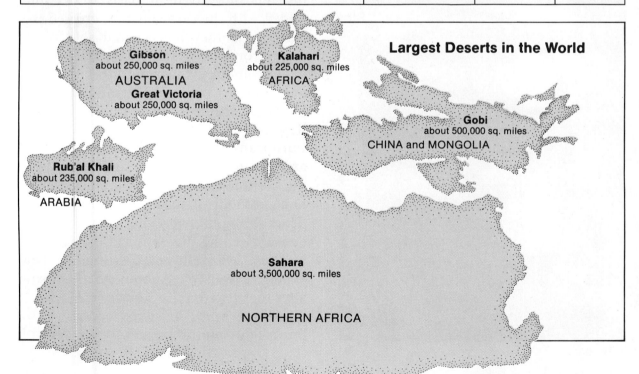

Largest Deserts in the World

Gibson about 250,000 sq. miles
AUSTRALIA
Great Victoria about 250,000 sq. miles

Kalahari about 225,000 sq. miles
AFRICA

Gobi about 500,000 sq. miles
CHINA and MONGOLIA

Rub'al Khali about 235,000 sq. miles
ARABIA

Sahara about 3,500,000 sq. miles

NORTHERN AFRICA

did not trust outsiders. Even today, travelers in this land may meet their death if they run out of water, but the tribesmen living in the region are more friendly than in the past.

The place you have just imagined is the largest desert in the world, the **Sahara.** The Sahara stretches for three thousand miles across northern Africa from the Atlantic Ocean to the Red Sea. It reaches southward from the Mediterranean coast or nearby mountains for over one thousand miles.

The Sahara's Past

When Christ was on earth, the Romans ruled most of the northern Sahara near the Mediterranean. They built port cities along the sea and trading cities at places further inland. They dug wells to provide their water supply. They irrigated fields that produced abundant crops. Grain from northern Africa helped feed the people across the sea in Rome. The Romans used the few resources of northern Africa to reap the benefits of farming and trade.

A Berber

Roman soldiers went on patrols into the desert. They protected the Roman settlers from the **Berber** tribesmen who lived there. The Berber tribes often fought among themselves and attacked villages and trading caravans. The Berbers were the light-skinned people of northern Africa. They lived in the desert in tents or in oasis villages. They raised livestock and led camel caravans through the desert to trade salt, crafts, and precious metals with peoples at the edge of the Sahara.

When Roman power declined, the Roman settlers deserted the farms and cities of northern Africa. The Roman soldiers left, and the land was left to the control of Berbers and invading peoples. The Roman cities fell into ruins. The farmland that had been carefully irrigated and cultivated by the Romans returned to barren desert.

After the Romans left, Arabs invaded northern Africa from the east. They brought their Islamic religion from Arabia, and soon many of the Berbers became Moslems. The Arab invaders did not build farms and cities as the Romans had. Instead, they lived in oasis towns and traded with the caravans that crossed the desert, and they bought and sold black slaves from areas south of the Sahara.

For about a thousand years the Arab and Berber tribesmen continued their herding, trading, and raiding in the Sahara. A few hundred years ago Europeans began to sail along the coastal areas of northern Africa and to trade in the coastal towns. But, the vast Sahara remained out of reach to explorers. The fierce Moslem tribesmen guarded their desert dwelling places from any advance by those who followed Christianity. Few explorers lived to tell about what they saw after they entered the Sahara.

About one hundred years ago, European countries began to win control

Oases

An oasis is a spot in the desert where plants can easily grow. Underground water lies near the surface in an oasis to provide the moisture needed by the vegetation. Natural springs sometimes offer water to animals and humans. If not, wells dug in an oasis bring clear water to the surface.

Oases vary in size from a patch of green around two or three palm trees to many square miles. Thousands of people live in the larger oases, but no one or only one or two families can make their living on the small oases. Oasis farmers usually grow crops of fruit and vegetables. Date palms are the most important resource for oasis dwellers. These trees provide both food and shade from the hot sun.

over the tribesmen of northern Africa. They conquered the coastal cities and began patroling the Sahara. European settlers came to farm the watered lands near the coast, while the Arabs and Berbers continued their village and desert life more peacefully. Eventually, the Europeans brought the slave trade to an end, and most of the camel caravans ceased to make their journeys through the desert.

The Sahara Today

Today, the Sahara has been explored by truck and by plane, but it still offers hardships to those who live there and to those who travel there. **Oases** (oh AY SEEZ), springs, and wells are widely scattered. The Arab and Berber people who live in the desert villages grow dates and other fruits and work with native arts and crafts. Since most of the tribesmen have stopped their desert wandering, the villages have become crowded and water supplies have run low.

Travel from place to place is most comfortable by plane. Many of the desert villages lie only two or three hours of flying time away from the coastal cities. Very few paved roads and almost no railroads reach into the desert, however. Only people equipped with desert vehicles dare to travel the desert paths that connect villages hundreds of miles apart.

Travelers must carry plenty of spare parts for their vehicles and water and food for themselves. Rocky terrain with steep wadis makes driving across the desert like riding a bucking bronco. Winds may blow dust and sand into a swirling blizzard. Hot, sharp rocks may puncture tires, and loose, soft sand may swallow wheels until a vehicle can go no further. Along with these hazards is the uncomfortable heat of desert days. If it is so difficult to travel the Sahara in a motor vehicle, imagine what it would be like to walk or ride a camel!

The Sahara is by no means a level desert region. In some areas sand dunes may grow to heights of six or seven hundred feet. In other places rocky hills, plateaus, or mountains emerge from the sand and gravel. Two mountain ranges lie in the central Sahara, and the highest mountain, Emi Koussi (AY-meh KOO-seh) in Chad, has an elevation of over 11,000 feet. Snow sometimes falls in these mountainous regions, and herders often find spots of pasture for their sheep and goats in these highlands.

The Sahara covers over three million square miles of northern Africa, and it is growing. Needing firewood, the people living on the edges of the desert cut down the few trees that grow there. They allow their herds and flocks to eat all the plants that grow. When the plants and trees are gone, the ground becomes dry and barren. The spreading of desert land in this way is called *desiccation* (DES uh KAY shun). Desiccation threatens many regions around the Sahara.

The People of the Sahara

Sahara is the Arabic word for desert. Many of the people of northern Africa speak the Arabic language and have customs similar to those of the Arabians. Most of the two million people that live in the Sahara also bow five times a day toward Mecca to say their prayers to Allah.

These people live in a vast desert with few plants and animals. They live in poverty and are often sick because they do not have enough clean water and good food. Deposits of oil and other resources lie below the desert in some areas. However, these riches do not help most of the poor people of the Sahara because they are not skilled to work in industries. They live in crowded oasis villages with few comforts and little education. Earthly riches lie beyond their reach, and the riches of Christ are unknown to most of them.

> In whom we have redemption through his blood, the forgiveness of sins, according to the riches of his grace. (Ephesians 1:7)

The Countries of the Sahara

The Sahara covers large areas of eleven countries in northern Africa. These nations share not only the dry climate and the rough terrain of the desert but also people who live in ways far different from the way we live. Let's take a closer look at the lands of northern Africa.

Section Review

1. What is the largest desert in the world?

2. What people once ruled northern Africa, built cities, and grew crops there?

3. Who are the native tribesmen of northern Africa?

4. What is a watered spot where plants grow in the desert called?

5. What religion do most people of the Sahara follow?

Egypt

Aside from the Sahara desert, the most outstanding feature of northern Africa is the **Nile River.** This great river is about four thousand miles long. As it flows northward through eastern Africa, its waters bring life to a narrow area of the desert. For this reason, it has often been said that the land of Egypt is the "gift of the Nile."

Egypt is more than ten times the size of the state of Indiana, but desert covers about 95 per cent of the country. The only fertile land is that of a few scattered oases and the Nile Valley. A green strip of life from two miles to fifteen miles wide follows the Nile for 750 miles along its course from the Sudan border in the south to the city of Cairo. North of Cairo the river fans out to form the fertile delta that empties into the Mediterranean Sea. On either side of this long oasis of the Nile, the brown desert stretches far into the distance.

Egypt is not one of the larger countries of northern Africa, yet its population is at least twice as large as that of any other country in the region. Well over forty million people live in Egypt, and nearly all of them live along the Nile. The population map on p. xii clearly shows us that this is true. Although river valleys are often important areas of settlement, rarely are rivers as vital to life as the Nile is to Egypt. Without the Nile's water for drinking and for irrigating their crops, millions of Egyptians could not live. For thousands of years the Nile has provided water for the people of this land, and God has used this mighty river to help shape their heritage.

An irrigation canal in Egypt's Nile delta

Ancient Egypt

Beginning over twenty-five hundred years before the birth of Christ, Egyptian **Pharaohs** ruled this land along the Nile.

Pyramids

They built great monuments to their power. The gigantic pyramids and temples of these early Egyptians are breathtaking reminders of their accomplishments. We have learned much about their lives from the remains of their civilization. Sculptures and wall paintings show Egyptians performing their daily tasks. Egyptian picture writing, called hieroglyphics (HY er uh GLIF iks), has helped us find out even more about life in ancient Egypt.

In the Bible we read about Abraham's visit to Egypt (Genesis 12:10-13:1), about Joseph's slavery and then his leadership in Egypt (Genesis 37-50), about the bondage of the Hebrews in Egypt (Exodus 1), and about Moses and his leading of the Hebrews out of Egypt (Exodus 2-12). We also read that the Christ child found refuge in Egypt from Herod's slaying of the children (Matthew 2:13-21). Egypt served at times as a place of safety for God's people, but it also was a place of temptation and sin.

Athanasius

Athanasius was born around the year 300 in Alexandria, Egypt. Egypt was part of the Roman Empire then, and Athanasius lived during a time of great trouble. Persecution of Christians by the empire stopped while Athanasius was still a teenager, but with peace came other problems. Another man from Egypt named Arius began teaching that Jesus Christ is not God as the Bible says. This belief, called "Arianism," became very popular. Most of the emperors during Athanasius's lifetime were Arians.

Athanasius was a true Christian and opposed Arianism. He strongly defended the doctrine that Jesus is God. When one emperor called a council at Nicea in 325 to discuss the matter, the young Athanasius was there urging the council to defend Christ's deity. The Council of Nicea wrote a creed that declared that Jesus Christ is "begotten of the Father, Light of Light, very God of very God, begotten not made." Athanasius heartily agreed.

The Council of Nicea did not stop Arianism, however. Arian teachers tried to change the creed, or even get rid of it completely. Athanasius became bishop of Alexandria and fought against Arianism in his preaching and writing. The Arians hated him. Opposition became so fierce that a saying went around the empire, "Athanasius

against the world, and the world against Athanasius." Five times Arian emperors exiled Athanasius from Alexandria. Often he had to hide out in the desert from the Roman soldiers who sought to kill him. Once after he left Alexandria, he learned that Roman officials planned to follow his boat up the Nile and kill him. Athanasius ordered that his boat be turned around. When the officials' boat passed that of Athanasius going the opposite direction, one official asked, "Where is Athanasius?"

"Not very far off," replied Athanasius, and continued on his way.

Finally the Arians were defeated, and Athanasius was able to return to Alexandria to stay. He spent his last years preaching to his beloved congregation and died in 373.

By faith Moses, when he was come to years, refused to be called the son of Pharaoh's daughter; choosing rather to suffer affliction with the people of God, than to enjoy the pleasures of sin for a season; esteeming the reproach of Christ greater riches than the treasures in Egypt: for he had respect unto the recompence of the reward.
(Hebrews 11:24-26)

In ancient Egypt the Pharaohs lived in great wealth and luxury. They had servants to wait on them, fine food to eat, and gold and jewels to wear. They said that they were gods, and they made the Egyptian people worship them. Slaves labored to build the pyramids as tombs for the Pharaohs. Treasures, furniture, and food to please the Pharaohs in the afterlife were placed in the pyramids with the bodies of the rulers. The splendor of Egypt was theirs while they lived, and they thought that they could take that splendor with them when they died.

Moses could have continued to live in Pharaoh's household, enjoying the wealth and power. But he realized that the Egyptians did not worship the true God, and he knew he should do right. Although Moses' decision meant that he must give up the riches of Egypt, he eventually gained eternal rewards.

Over a thousand years before the birth of Christ, the Egyptians began to lose their strength and prosperity. Enemy armies weakened Egypt until it fell to the control of the Persians, and then the Greeks, followed by the Romans. About fourteen hundred years ago Moslem Arabs conquered Egypt, and since then other outsiders have ruled this once mighty land. Only since 1952 have the Egyptians been able to rule their country themselves without foreign interference.

Modern Egyptian Accomplishments

Two large building projects have had a great influence on Egypt's geography and on its economy. The first project, the **Suez Canal,** was completed in 1869.

The narrow Isthmus of Suez joined the **Sinai Peninsula** (part of Asia) to the continent of Africa. It also separated the Mediterranean Sea from the Red Sea, forcing ships to sail all the way around Africa if they wished to sail to or from the Far East. A canal across the Isthmus of Suez would make travel between Europe and the East much quicker and easier. The French helped the Egyptians build such a canal, and that 105-mile-long passageway now saves many ships from traveling thousands of extra miles.

Despite the Suez Canal's success as a transportation route, Egypt has not always benefited from the waterway. Shortly after its construction, the government of Egypt fell so far in debt that it sold its share of the canal to Britain. Not only did the French and the British take over the canal, but the British also strongly influenced the Egyptian government. The Egyptians received little or nothing from all the tolls charged to ships using the canal. Egypt took complete control of the canal in 1956 and collected the tolls for its operation. However, from 1967 until 1975 the canal was closed, filled with debris, and heavily guarded following the Arab-Israeli War.

The Sinai Peninsula

The Sinai Peninsula, a small extension of the Asian continent, dangles between the Gulf of Suez and the Gulf of Aqaba. The Mediterranean Sea lies to the north and the country of Israel to the east. The Suez Canal separates the peninsula from the rest of Egypt.

Moses and the children of Israel traveled across the Sinai Peninsula as they left Egypt. One of the many mountains on the peninsula is probably the Mount Sinai where God gave the Ten Commandments to Moses.

In recent years the Israelis have desired to control this important land between the Mediterranean and the Red Seas. Following the 1967 war, Israel occupied the peninsula, but it withdrew its forces from the area in 1982. Now the land is once again under the control of Egypt.

The Suez Canal

Since its reopening, its business has increased and its profits help the country of Egypt. About sixty ships travel through the Suez Canal every day.

The second important building project was the Aswan High Dam. In the past the Nile River would flood in the late spring. The abundant water came just at the right time to help Egyptian farmers. The flooding river brought not only water for their crops, but it also carried rich mud. When the waters went down, the new layer of mud made the soil very fertile. While the Nile was very helpful in these ways, it was not always predictable. Sometimes the flood waters that came from the highlands far to the south of Egypt did not come at the best time. Sometimes there was not enough water, and sometimes there was too much.

If the Nile's flood waters could be controlled, Egypt would receive the right amount of water at the right time. The Egyptians tried to build dams that would control the rise and fall of the river. They built a large dam at Aswan that was finished in 1902, but it could not completely control the river's flow.

In the 1960s a new dam was built about four miles upstream from the old Aswan Dam. This new dam, the Aswan High Dam, is over twice as tall as the old, and the two work together with other river projects to tame the Nile. The new dam has formed a very large manmade lake, Lake Nasser. Water from the lake provides Egyptian farmers with the right amount

The Nile at Aswan

for irrigating their crops. As the water flows through the dams, huge generators use its power to produce electricity for most of Egypt. The Nile's flood plain no longer receives rich new soil every year. Instead the farmers must use fertilizers. But a much larger area of land near the river can now produce crops because of the reliable irrigation the Aswan High Dam has made possible.

Life in Modern Egypt

The majority of the people of Egypt are poor farmers. These peasants, called *fellahin* (FEL uh HEEN), raise crops on small farms along the Nile Valley. The Aswan High Dam has protected them from the Nile's irregular flooding. The fellahin still, however, have the ancient problem of raising the Nile's waters to their fields, which lie above the level of the river and the many irrigation canals. Although a few have bought diesel-powered pumps to perform this task, most continue to use the same devices that have been used in Egypt for thousands of years.

The fellahin live in mud-brick houses that they build themselves, and they wear loose, long shirts called galabias with knee-length trousers. Women often still wear melayas, long black robes, and they cover their faces with veils when in public. They have little furniture, and they eat mostly rice, beans, and flat, round loaves of bread. Hot mint tea and strong coffee are their favorite beverages. They grow crops of cotton, wheat, rice, and fruit. The farmers use buffalo to pull carts, plow fields, and power water wheels. Because this work animal is so important, it sometimes sleeps indoors with the fellahin family.

Diseases often strike the poor fellahin, leaving them blind or weak, or sometimes killing them. Working in the muddy river water and living without proper sanitation causes many diseases to spread quickly. It is hard for these people to realize that if they would keep their homes and their bodies clean, they would have better health. Egyptian farmers have always lived as they do.

Far more tragic than the threat of disease to these people is the fact that they are dying in sin. They could accept God's cleansing through the blood of Jesus Christ, but most of them are Moslems. Their people have followed the teachings of Mohammed for generations. They will continue to believe as they have unless the gospel reaches them and they accept it.

We need to remember that we should keep not only our bodies and our homes clean, but also our hearts. When we accept Jesus Christ as our Saviour, He washes away our sin and saves us. But, after our salvation we need to go before God in prayer to cleanse our lives of sins that would defeat us.

> If we confess our sins, he is faithful and just to forgive us our sins, and to cleanse us from all unrighteousness.
> (I John 1:9)

Egyptians working on a rail line

Cairo

Egypt's capital city was founded only a thousand years ago. While that makes it far older than any city in America, Cairo is young compared to the five thousand years of Egypt's recorded history.

About six million people live in Cairo, and four million more live nearby in the suburbs. This makes Cairo the largest city in all of Africa. The government, business, and transportation of Egypt center in this important city of the North African and Middle Eastern regions.

The minarets of Cairo's many mosques tower over the city. The pyramids and the sphinx lie nearby at Giza, and an old medieval fort called the Citadel is another landmark of the city. Al-Azhar, a university over a thousand years old, is still a center of learning for the Moslem, Arabic world. Thousands of tourists visit Cairo, not only to see these sights, but also to begin their tours of the wondrous and ancient land of Egypt.

While the fellahin live mainly in small villages along the Nile and in oases, some Egyptians are Bedouins that continue to wander with their sheep, goats, and camels. They live in tents and search the deserts and oases for food for their animals.

Cairo (KYE roh) and Alexandria are the two largest cities of Egypt. Cairo, the capital, sits beside the Nile River about one hundred miles south of the Mediterranean Sea. The second largest city and a major port, Alexandria, lies on the Mediterranean coast at the western end of the Nile Delta. Both cities are busy with Egypt's businesses and industries, and both have museums full of the treasures of ancient Egypt. In these cities one can see a mixture of modern ways and age-old traditions. New apartment buildings stand near the shabby homes of the poor. Fashionable stores line wide avenues in some parts of the cities, while bazaars selling the timeless merchandise of the Middle East are crowded along narrow streets in other sections.

Section Review

1. What river flows through Egypt?

2. What were the ancient rulers of Egypt called?

3. What two large building projects have helped Egypt?

4. The Isthmus of Suez joins what piece of land to the rest of Egypt?

5. What lake did the Aswan High Dam create?

Coastal Countries

Along with Egypt, the countries of Libya, Tunisia, Algeria, and Morocco also touch the Mediterranean Sea. In addition, Morocco, Western Sahara, and Mauritania border on the Atlantic Ocean. Although these lands have had many contacts with Europeans in the past, they still display a culture similar in many ways to that of the Middle East.

The vast majority of peoples in these lands follow the religion of Islam, and they speak the Arabic language. Outside the cities, most of these North Africans live by herding, farming, or trading. Their lands are mostly dry and barren, but in recent years they have revealed a wealth of petroleum lying under the surface. Because of such similarities, these lands along with Egypt are sometimes included as the "western arm" of the Middle East.

Libya

To the west of Egypt lies the desert-covered country of Libya. Unlike Egypt, Libya lacks a great river like the Nile to make at least a portion of its land green and productive. Libya has no permanent streams, only wadis that fill with water during the unusual event of a good rainstorm. Most of the time they remain as dry valleys. Without water resources, nearly all the country is rocky or sandy desert.

Only the oases and a narrow area along the coast are useful for raising crops and pasturing livestock. When the Roman Empire controlled the coastal regions, several cities grew beside the Mediterranean. From one of them came Simon, the man who carried Christ's cross (Matthew 27:32).

After the Romans left, the Arabs ruled the land and introduced their way of life. The nomadic herding of the Arab tribesmen ruined much of the farmland that had been cultivated by the Romans. The Turks controlled Libya during most of the 1800s, and the Italians took over in the early 1900s. Little of the influence of these two foreign powers remains, however.

In 1951, Libya became an independent nation ruled by a king. It began as a large but poor country. Over four times the size of California, Libya had a population of less than 1.5 million. The city of San Diego holds more people than the entire nation of Libya. Its people were uneducated and poor. With few resources, Libya struggled to maintain itself. Then, oil was discovered. In the early 1960s, Libya's oil exports began to earn millions of dollars for the country.

Some of Libya's oil money paid for building roads, schools, and housing for the many who flocked to the coastal cities from the rural areas. Despite the improvements brought by the oil industry boom, most Libyans remained poor and unskilled.

In 1969, a military group led by Colonel Muammar al-Qaddafi (kuh DAH fee) took over the government. Qaddafi

Colonel Muammar al-Qaddafi

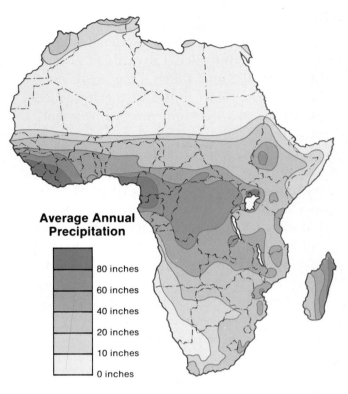

Average Annual Precipitation

80 inches
60 inches
40 inches
20 inches
10 inches
0 inches

pirates, sailing from their North African ports, captured foreign ships and held sailors for ransom. When the European nations and the United States had had enough of this kind of treatment, they began to fight against the Barbary pirates. By 1830, ships could safely sail the Mediterranean, and the French controlled Algeria. France later gained Tunisia and Morocco.

Today these three lands are independent countries. Along the Mediterranean coast of all three of these lands stretch the **Atlas Mountains.** Between the mountains and the sea lies a narrow coastal plain. Nearly all the people of these countries live in this fertile coastal area. South of the Atlas Mountains, the Sahara Desert reaches far beyond the borders of these lands.

Many of the people of these lands remain poor and uneducated. A few work in mineral or petroleum industries. Most are farmers or herders, or they make and sell handicrafts. Merchants in the markets of the cities sell rugs, leather, metal and wooden articles, and many other items made by the local people. Fishing is a common occupation along the coasts of these lands.

established strong ties with the Soviet Union, and he used Libya's oil income to increase Libya's military power. He sought to gain influence throughout the Middle East, and he financed rebel activities in neighboring North African countries. His actions have made him a menace to the free world and a threat to the safety of North Africa. Harsh leaders like Qaddafi bring added strife and hardship to the people of poor countries like Libya and its neighbors.

Tunisia, Algeria, and Morocco

The Arabs called the region of these three lands—Tunisia, Algeria, and Morocco—the *Maghreb,* meaning "the West." It was the western part of their world. In the early 1800s, these lands, along with a portion of Libya, were known as the Barbary States. Their land along the Mediterranean was the Barbary Coast. The waters near the Barbary Coast were a fearful place for European and American sailors in those days. Vicious Barbary

Tunisia

Islamic Customs

Those who follow the religion of Islam often have customs that are very strange to us. Here are a few examples of how the ways of Moslems in North Africa and the Middle East differ from our way of life and our beliefs.

- Moslems are supposed to wash their face, hands, and feet before they pray. (Their usual position for prayer is kneeling with their forehead to the ground. They do not wear shoes when they pray.)
- Friday is the Moslem holy day.
- Moslems number their calendar from the year Mohammed fled from Mecca to Medina. What to us was the year 1900, to the Moslems was the year 1287.
- According to the Koran, a Moslem man may have up to four wives. (Most, however, have just one.)
- Moslems do not eat pork.

- In the past, Moslem women were required to wear veils in public. Only their families were allowed to see their faces. Most women rarely ventured outside their homes. Today, most Moslem women who live in cities do not wear a veil, but few hold jobs in businesses or socialize outside of their homes. In rural areas, many Moslem women still wear the veil.

Tunisia is the smallest of these three countries, but the Sahara does not cover as large a percentage of this land as it does most of the other countries of North Africa. Tunisians use their coastal land to grow wheat, barley, grapes, olives, dates, and other food crops.

Algeria, the second largest country in Africa, has large petroleum resources. The French colonized Algeria in the 1800s, giving up their control of this vast land in 1962. At that time, Algeria became an independent country. As in Libya, income from oil in Algeria has not widely benefited the people of the country. Most are still poor and uneducated. Many do not have jobs. Their way of life remains the same. They live in small stone or mud-brick houses, eating the same spicy foods and chanting the same Islamic prayers that their forefathers have said for centuries.

One of the favorite foods of the northern Africa region is a dish called *couscous*. To make *couscous,* the people cook cracked wheat into a porridge. Sometimes they add chicken, lamb, or goat meat to the porridge.

Morocco has a coastline along both the Atlantic Ocean and the Mediterranean Sea. The Atlas Mountains cover most of the country. At the Strait of Gibraltar, Morocco lies only nine miles away from Spain. A king still rules Morocco, making it one of two remaining monarchies in Africa. The country lacks petroleum resources, but its mines produce phosphate, iron ore, and other minerals. Casablanca, on the Atlantic coast, is the country's largest city and major port. Although this city is the center for much of Morocco's industrial activity and wealth, it also displays the poverty that remains in this North African land.

South of Morocco along the Atlantic coast lies a land called the Western Sahara. Until 1975 this area was a colony of Spain known as the Spanish Sahara. Since that time it has been a disputed territory claimed by its neighbors. Morocco holds the strongest claim to the Western Sahara.

The Southern Saharan Countries

The southern half of the Sahara Desert covers the five countries of Mauritania, Mali, Niger, Chad, and Sudan. Of these five, all but Mauritania and Sudan are landlocked. The remoteness of their desert lands has kept their people even more isolated and backward than those along the north coast of Africa. Even today these countries receive few foreign travelers and businessmen.

Along the southern borders of these countries at the edge of the Sahara, a dry, rolling steep land stretches across the continent. This region is called the **Sahel,** which means "border" in Arabic. Enough rain falls in this region to support the growth of grasses, some crops, and a few trees. However, droughts often strike in this area, leaving the land dusty and the inhabitants thirsty. Overgrazing of the land by livestock results in the desiccation of areas of the Sahel.

While the northern desert regions of these countries are settled by the light-skinned Berbers and the tanned Arabs, mostly dark-skinned peoples live in the Sahel. In the desert, most of the people speak Arabic or French, but many of the people of the Sahel speak their own tribal languages. Islam dominates lives in the northern areas of these countries, and it is common in the southern areas. The people of the Sahel also follow pagan religions or, where missionaries have been, some forms of Christianity.

Mauritania

The Sahara Desert reaches to the shores of the Atlantic in northern Mauritania. Only in the southern third of the country do the occasional rains of the Sahel and the water of the Senegal River add greenery to the landscape.

France made Mauritania one of its colonies in the 1800s. Later, Mali, Niger, and Chad also came under the control of France. All four of these lands became independent countries in 1960, but some of their people continue to speak French and to display French culture. This is true especially in the cities and larger villages of the Sahel region.

Mauritania is over twice as large as the state of California, but its population is also less than that of the city of San Diego. A few camel caravans and desert herdsmen still roam the desert. Farmers in the Sahel raise grain and livestock. But the main industry of the country is mining. Iron ore and some other minerals are plentiful in the land.

Scenes from life in Mauritania

Mali

East of Mauritania lies the larger country of Mali. The **Niger River** flows through the southern part of this country, and thick forests grow in the well-watered area south of the river. The desert supports only a few nomads, and Sahel farmers grow peanuts, cotton, and grain. Although Mali has mineral resources, industries and mining projects have not developed in the country. As a result, Malians produce little more than the food they eat, and they remain a poor people.

Malians learning to read

Mali's largest city is its capital, Bamako, on the Niger River, but its most famous city is Timbuktu. Over five hundred years ago, Timbuktu was a flourishing center of Islamic culture. Arab traders from the north crossed the Sahara in camel caravans to trade salt and other items for gold and slaves. Timbuktu's prosperity did not last, but its name remains legendary. Today it is just a large village beside the Niger River.

Niger and Chad

Niger and Chad are both slightly larger than Mali. Only a small portion of their populations live in the desert areas of the north. Cattle and sheep graze in the Sahel before their owners drive them southward to markets in Nigeria and southern Chad. Southern Chad beyond the Sahel is a savanna region (see p. 359) where cotton grows as a major crop. Nigerians grow peanuts as a major crop near the Niger River in the west and along the southern border. Fishing is an important industry at Lake Chad on the border between the two countries.

The gospel has been barred from many areas of northern Africa because of Islam's control of the people and its influence on governments. Some missionaries have ministered in the southern regions of Niger and Chad for many years. There they have met many hardships and persecutions as they have told these peoples about the Saviour. We should pray for their safety as well as their witness in those lands of drought, famine, and political strife.

Sudan

Africa's largest country, Sudan, lies at the southeast edge of the Sahara. The central area of the country is grass-covered with a few trees, while trees grow more commonly in the south. The Blue Nile flowing from Ethiopia and the White Nile flowing from lands to the south meet at Khartoum in Sudan. From that capital city, the great river Nile flows northward through Egypt to the Mediterranean. The White Nile is navigable for most of its length in Sudan, making it an important transportation link in the land.

In the southern region of Sudan the waters of the White Nile break up into many shallow streams. This area just south of the desert is a swampy land called the Sudd. The papyrus plants that grow along the Nile in Egypt and northern Sudan fill this large swamp.

Most of Sudan's people are farmers who raise the crops they need to feed them-

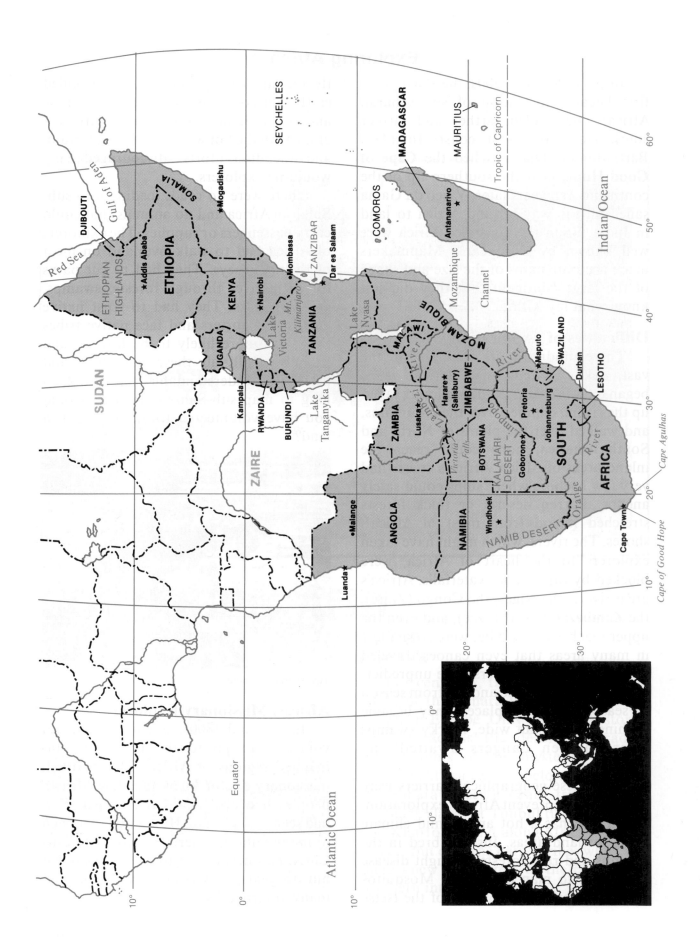

Red Sea

DJIBOUTI

Gulf of Aden

SOMALIA

★Mogadishu

★Addis Ababa

ETHIOPIA

ETHIOPIAN HIGHLANDS

SUDAN

UGANDA

Kampala★

KENYA

★Nairobi

Mombassa

ZANZIBAR

Dar es Salaam★

TANZANIA

Lake Victoria

Kilimanjaro Mt.

Lake Nyasa

RWANDA

BURUNDI

Lake Tanganyika

ZAIRE

MALAWI

MOZAMBIQUE

Mozambique Channel

SEYCHELLES

COMOROS

MADAGASCAR

Antananarivo ★

MAURITIUS

Tropic of Capricorn

Indian Ocean

ZAMBIA

Lusaka★

Harare★ (Salisbury)

ZIMBABWE

Zambezi River

Victoria Falls

Maputo

★SWAZILAND

Durban

LESOTHO

Pretoria★

Johannesburg

SOUTH

AFRICA

Limpopo River

BOTSWANA

Goborone★

KALAHARI DESERT

Orange River

Cape Agulhas

ANGOLA

●Malange

Luanda★

NAMIBIA

Windhoek★

NAMIB DESERT

Cape Town★

Cape of Good Hope

Atlantic Ocean

Equator

60°

50°

40°

30°

20°

10°

0°

10°

20°

30°

10°

0°

10°

	AREA (Square Miles)	POPULATION	CAPITAL	MAIN LANGUAGES	COLONIZED BY	DATE OF INDEPEND-ENCE
SOUTH AFRICA	471,443	30,938,000	Pretoria and Cape Town	English, Afrikaans, tribal languages	Britain	1910
ANGOLA	481,351	7,567,000	Luanda	Portuguese, tribal languages	Portugal	1975
MOZAMBIQUE	309,494	13,047,000	Maputo	Portuguese, tribal languages	Portugal	1975
MADAGASCAR	226,400	9,389,000	Antananarivo	Malagasy, French	France	1960
ZIMBABWE	150,803	8,376,000	Harare (Salisbury)	English, tribal languages	Britain	1980
ZAMBIA	290,584	6,346,000	Lusaka	English, Afrikaans, tribal languages	Britain	1964
MALAWI	45,747	6,612,000	Lilongwe	English, tribal languages	Britain	1964
TANZANIA	364,898	20,524,000	Dar es Salaam	Swahili, English	Britain	1961—Tanganyika 1963—Zanzibar
KENYA	224,960	18,580,000	Nairobi	Swahili, English	Britain	1963
UGANDA	91,134	13,819,000	Kampala	English, Luganda, Swahili	Britain	1962
RWANDA	10,169	5,644,000	Kigali	Kinyarwanda, French	Belgium	1962
BURUNDI	10,747	4,204,000	Bujumbura	Kirundi, French	Belgium	1962
ETHIOPIA	471,776	31,305,000	Addis Ababa	Amharic, English	———	———
SOMALIA	246,200	6,248,000	Mogadishu	Somali, Arabic, Italian	Italy, Britain	1960
DJIBOUTI	8,494	276,000	Djibouti	French, Somali, Afar	France	1977

David
Livingstone

From 1841 to 1873, Dr. David Livingstone roamed the inland areas of southern Africa. He mapped its rivers and lakes, befriended native peoples, and wrote of its plants and animals. This determined Scottish missionary faced all the hardships and perils of African exploration to open the way for the gospel to be spread.

Modern Africa

Africa has changed since Livingstone's travels. Europeans have come and gone. Independent African countries now cover the territory that Livingstone knew only as hostile wilderness. Black leaders rule several of the countries from modern city offices. People travel from place to place by plane, car, and some trains.

But although changes have come, there is still much in Africa that Livingstone would recognize. Its rivers and lakes remain unchanged except where cities have grown on their banks. Its wildlife still fascinates anyone from another land. Though some of the Africans live in modern cities and work in factories, mines, and other businesses, many still live in native villages, hunting and farming for their living. African tribal groups continue to bicker and fight among themselves. And many of the African people, though no longer captured and taken as slaves, are still in bondage to sin. The gospel has reached many areas, but millions more still need to be saved.

Let's take a look at the land and people David Livingstone saw. Let's also find out more about these African nations of today.

South Africa

In 1841, after a three-month voyage from Britain, Livingstone arrived at **Cape Town,** a port city by the Cape of Good Hope. Cape Town, one of a few European ports in southern Africa, had been founded by the Dutch in 1652. Ships on their way to or from India and the Far East stopped at Cape Town to take on fruit, vegetables, and other supplies. Dutch settlers went to Cape Town and the lands nearby to be farmers and merchants.

In the early 1800s, Britain gained control of Cape Town and the surrounding area of southern Africa. Some British settlers began to move to this land. When the British came, many Dutch farmers moved eastward and northward to find new farmlands and to escape British domination. They disliked the British and did not want them to control their land.

Only a few natives lived near the Cape, mostly Hottentots and Bushmen. Many of these had been slaves to the Dutch. Farther east and north, Bantu tribesmen moved in after the Dutch and built their villages and hunted in the bush. Fighting often took place between the Dutch settlers, called **Boers,** and the dark-skinned natives.

That was the condition of the people in the land that is today called South Africa when David Livingstone arrived. He found prosperous Boer and British settlements. Farmers raised cattle, sheep, fruit, vegetables, and grain. There were African natives living in villages and people of mixed blood who often worked for the white settlers. Lions, elephants, and other wild animals roamed the countryside, especially in the northern areas. And he found South Africa to be a beautiful land with mountains, plains, and rivers.

South African Landscape

Most of the inland area of the country lies on a high plateau that stretches far away into the highlands of Ethiopia three thousand miles to the north. Along the southern and eastern edges of South Africa's plateau regions lies a strip of highlands. The Drakensberg Mountains form a large part of this wall that separates the inland plateau from the coastal areas.

South African farmers have found the coastal areas and the eastern half of the plateau to be the best areas for raising their crops. These areas receive more rain and have milder temperatures than the dry plains of the western plateau. Citrus fruits, grapes, wheat, and other crops grow well in these fertile regions, while cattle and sheep graze in the drier grasslands of the west.

Two rivers—the Orange and the Limpopo—form much of the northern boundaries of South Africa. Those rivers and their tributaries water much of the eastern part of the country. The edges of two deserts, the Namib and the Kalahari, reach inside the borders of South Africa along the west coast and in the north central area.

South Africa is about three times the size of California, and its climate is similar to that state's. The coastal regions have mild temperatures all year long with a Mediterranean-type climate near Cape Town. The interior plateau has cooler winters with the mountainous areas receiving snow during June, July, and August. Remember that this land lies in the Southern Hemisphere; its seasons are opposite to ours in the United States.

The productive fruit farms of the Hex River Valley in South Africa

South African Resources

South Africa is a beautiful and varied country, but it is also a land rich in mineral resources. It has produced more gold than any other country in the world. A gold rush in the late 1800s brought miners to the northeastern region of the country. Boer and British settlers flocked to the mining camps to seek their fortunes. One of the camps grew from a small settlement into a large center of mining and other industries. Today, that city of Johannesburg is the home of over two million people.

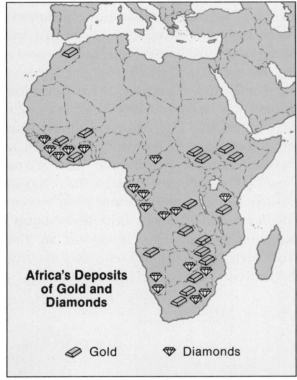

Africa's Deposits of Gold and Diamonds

◇ Gold   ♦ Diamonds

Just a few years before the beginning of the gold rush, the first diamond of South Africa was discovered. That find brought many adventurers to the central part of the country. Diamond mining in South Africa has produced some of the largest, most valuable gems in the world. Over half of the world's gem diamonds continue to come from this African country.

Besides such precious resources as gold and diamonds, South Africa also boasts

Two views of South Africa

large deposits of coal, copper, iron ore, platinum, uranium, and other minerals. These resources have helped to make South Africa the wealthiest and strongest industrial country in all of Africa.

South African Strife

Background

Despite this land's material wealth, it suffers from discord among its peoples. In the past, fighting took place not only between the white settlers and the black natives, but also between the Dutch and the English settlers. The gold and diamond rushes of the late 1800s brought many British settlers to the area where the Boers had moved. With the British settlers came British control, but the Boers rebelled and fought against Britain. The British defeated the Boers in 1902. At that time there were four states in South Africa, two British (the Cape Colony and Natal) and two Boer (the Orange Free State and Transvaal). Britain, shortly after that, allowed these states to govern themselves. Then, in 1910, the four states united to form the Union of South Africa, which became a fully independent republic in 1961. (Since then it has come to be known as the Republic of South Africa.)

Though most of the strife between the South Africans of Dutch and British backgrounds has ceased, other conflicts remain. The white South Africans make up only about one-sixth of the total number of people in the country. Nearly four times as many blacks live there. Besides these groups, a large number of Indians and other Asians, whose ancestors came to work in South Africa, live in some areas. And, many people of mixed blood, called *coloureds,* also are South Africans. The population, then, is divided into four groups, namely whites, blacks, Asians, and coloureds.

Apartheid

The whites of South Africa control the government of the country. They have set aside some areas of South Africa as "homelands" for the blacks. On these homelands, the blacks are supposed to rule themselves independently. Over half of the blacks, however, live outside the homelands in the cities and on the farms of South Africa where they may find jobs. There they must live under the South African government's policy of *apartheid* (uh PART HITE), an Afrikaans (the language spoken by the Boers) word meaning "apartness" or "separateness."

The policy of *apartheid* separates the four races of South Africa. Whites have separate, and usually better, schools, hotels, post offices, and other public facilities. Sections of cities are set aside for each racial group, and jobs and salaries that members of each group may have are regulated. Blacks must carry identification cards at all times, and they are not allowed to move about freely within the country. In addition, until recently, only the whites could vote in national elections. Now Asians and coloureds may vote, but blacks are permitted to vote only in their "homelands."

Many nations have criticized the policies of the white-ruled South African government. Many think that the blacks, Asians, and coloureds are treated unfairly. Racial tensions have led to rioting and violence in recent years. The blacks, especially those that live in the cities, want the freedom to move about as they please. They want a voice in making the policies and laws that rule them. To assert their claims to more power in South Africa, some blacks have used violence. Not only have they fought against the whites, but also against the Asians, coloureds, and among themselves. The blacks are divided into many groups with different leaders and loyalties.

While much is said against the strict rule of South Africa by the whites, we must not forget to examine their point of view. The white settlers have lived in the land for over three hundred years, longer than many of the black tribes have lived in that region. The whites consider themselves to be Africans just as those of us who live in the United States consider ourselves Americans no matter where our ancestors emigrated from. The Dutch, British, and other Europeans have built most of the industries that now thrive in South Africa. They have also built the prosperous cities and farms of the country. They have watched as other African countries have been lost in confusion and poverty when governments changed. (We will learn about some of these countries later in this chapter.) They wish to protect their accomplishments and their country from being destroyed by swift and careless changes. While they are looking for ways to improve the political situation, the whites of South Africa do not want to lose the things they have worked for.

Most of the blacks in South Africa do have better housing, better paying jobs, better education, and better health care than their neighbors in other African countries. But because they see themselves as oppressed, more strife will probably develop. Increasing racial tension and international pressure may force South Africa to abandon *apartheid.* Sudden change, however, may bring chaos to the country. For now, South Africa's peoples live in a divided nation. They need the wisdom to treat each other kindly and fairly. Otherwise, the discord that divides them may eventually destroy their country.

South Africa's Greatest Need

More important than the future of the country of South Africa, however, is the eternal future of the people of that land. Over half follow some form of Christian religion, but few truly know Christ as their Saviour. Most Dutch South Africans, who now call themselves Afrikaners, are members of the Dutch Reformed Church. (The Afrikaners speak their own Afrikaans language.) The English-speaking South Africans are mostly Roman Catholics and Anglicans. The blacks belong to these groups and others of their own design. Some of the blacks in the rural areas continue to follow their traditional religion of spirit worship.

Andrew Murray

Andrew Murray (1828-1917) was born in South Africa. His parents had moved there from Scotland to minister to the Dutch settlers. When Andrew was only ten, his father sent him to Scotland to study. There Murray decided to follow his father's footsteps and enter the ministry. After graduating from Aberdeen University, Murray went to Holland to study. Up to that time, he had often been troubled with doubts about his spiritual condition. But in Holland he received assurance of his salvation. He used his time there for more than just studying theology. He also practiced his Dutch so that he could reach both British and Dutch settlers in South Africa.

In 1848 Andrew returned to his homeland. Over the years he pastored several churches, and became a leader in the Dutch Reformed Church. However, some Dutch Reformed pastors were not preaching the truth. They denied such important doctrines as the deity of Christ and His atonement for our sins through His blood. These men were called liberals. Andrew Murray firmly opposed liberalism. He and the other Bible-believing pastors did everything they could to stop the growth of liberalism in South Africa. Murray followed the Bible's command to "earnestly contend for the faith which was once delivered unto the saints" (Jude 3).

Andrew Murray reached out to the lost through his preaching, evangelistic ministries, and writing. He toured South Africa, preaching in churches all over the country. He saw revivals in several of the churches that he pastored. Murray also helped start a seminary and a school for missionaries. In addition he organized missions to other parts of Africa.

Andrew Murray became most famous for his writing. He wrote over 250 books, in both Dutch and English. His most famous work is *Abide in Christ,* a powerful devotional book.

Namibia

Northwest of South Africa lies Namibia (nuh MIB ee uh). This area, in the past known as Southwest Africa, was once a German colony. After World War I, South Africa took control of the land. In recent years, many nations around the world have opposed South Africa's rule over its neighbor, but South Africa has maintained its authority.

Namibia, a region larger than Texas, contains large areas of dry land. The sandy Namib Desert, over fifty miles wide and a thousand miles long, stretches along the land's Atlantic coast. The dry but grassy region of the Kalahari Desert covers much of eastern Namibia. Often, the Kalahari is alive with animals feeding on the bushes and plants that grow there. But at other times, severe drought makes the land barren. Because rain rarely falls in the Kalahari and the soil is poor and sandy, farming is almost impossible, and few people live there.

Namibia's resources may not include much good agricultural land, but they do include great mineral resources. Diamonds, copper, zinc, lead, uranium, and other minerals lie below the surface of this

Botswana, Swaziland, and Lesotho

These three lands of southern Africa, along with South Africa, were once under British control. However, European settlers never developed industries and authority in these lands as they did in South Africa. The black tribal powers remained in the leadership of each of these nations as they became independent countries in the late 1960s. Since then, they have continued to form their own governments, and they have the freedom to follow their own policies.

Although these lands are independent nations, they are not very prosperous. All three are landlocked. None has great mineral resources or developed industries. Their people raise cattle and grain, but their herds and crops suffer during frequent droughts. Then these countries must rely on food from South Africa. Some of their men also leave to work in the cities of South Africa where they can find jobs to support their families back home. These countries will remain poor and weak unless they can develop their own industries and provide for their own people.

The daily work routine in Africa has not changed greatly in years.

arid land. German settlers and Afrikaner businessmen from South Africa have built large mining industries there. They have also established fishing industries along the coast.

Only about one million people live in Namibia, and little more than one-tenth are Europeans. The remainder are tribesmen, mostly farmers and herders who live in villages. Some of the natives, however, work in the mines and industries of Namibia's few cities.

The South African government divided Namibia into homelands for the native tribes and areas for the whites, as they did in South Africa. They also have applied their policy of *apartheid* to Namibia. This South African system has brought the same problems and arguments to Namibia as to South Africa.

Section Review

1. What are the lands of Africa south of the Sahara Desert called?

2. What missionary explored much of southern Africa?

3. What peoples settled South Africa?

4. What controversial racial policy has been followed in South Africa?

5. What country controls the land of Namibia?

Angola and Mozambique

Livingstone's Travels

David Livingstone's first missionary work in Africa was in the northern area of what is today South Africa. The deserts, forests, diseases, unfriendly natives, and other dangers that lay to the north had kept missionaries from going to the central regions of southern Africa. Livingstone was determined to find areas where missionaries could safely settle so that Africa could be reached with the gospel. This goal led him over thousands of miles of rough African terrain.

Livingstone began his great accomplishments as a missionary explorer by crossing the Kalahari Desert. He was the first white man to cross the Kalahari and discover the shallow and often dry Lake Ngami (ung GAH mee) in Botswana. On a later journey, he traveled north and then east to the Atlantic coast. This trip took him through the interior regions of what is today the country of Angola. Two years later, after another long journey, he reached the coast of what is now

Mozambique on the Indian Ocean. These explorations made him the first white man to travel from coast to coast across southern Africa.

In Livingstone's time, Angola and Mozambique were both Portuguese colonies. The slave trade continued in these

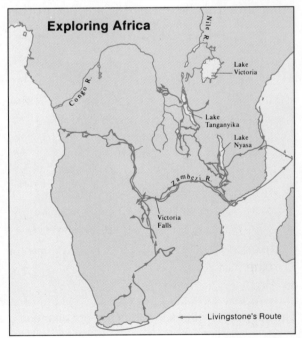

Exploring Africa

Nile R.
Congo R.
Lake Victoria
Lake Tanganyika
Lake Nyasa
Zambezi R.
Victoria Falls

← Livingstone's Route

Madagascar, Comoros, Mauritius, and the Seychelles

Three hundred miles east of Mozambique, the large and mountainous island country of Madagascar (MAD uh GAS kur) sits in the Indian Ocean. Although Madagascar is usually considered an African country, this island, twice the size of Arizona, has little in common with the countries on the continent.

Most of Madagascar's people are not black. They are a tan-skinned people that probably came to the island from the far away islands of Indonesia. Their language, Malagasy (MAL uh GAS ee), and culture are similar to those of Southeast Asia and the Pacific islands.

Clockwise from top left: ring-tailed lemur, aye-aye, and fossa

Living with these people on the island are Arabs, who have traded there for many years, and Frenchmen, who controlled the island as one of France's African colonies. Some Chinese and Indians also live in Madagascar. Madagascar's people are mainly farmers who raise rice, coffee, sugar, and other crops.

Not only are Madagascar's people different from most Africans, the land also differs from the continental lands. The island has a tropical climate, with a hot, rainy season and a cooler dry season. Thick forests grow in many areas, and several unusual animals live in the wild. Among them are lemurs, fossas, and aye-ayes.

Three other small island nations lie in the Indian Ocean east of Africa. France controlled Mauritius (maw RISH us) and Comoros (KOM uh ROZE), and Britain ruled the Seychelles (say SHELZ) until their independence. All three are tiny and weak countries. They rely on tourism, fishing, and tropical crops for their livelihood.

	Area (sq. mi.)	Population
Madagascar	226,658	7,655,000
Mauritius	790	811,000
Comoros	838	267,000
Seychelles	110	54,000

lands well into the late 1800s. Portuguese and Arab slave traders captured slaves or bought them from tribal chiefs. Livingstone's descriptions of this trade helped bring it to an end.

Independence Without Prosperity

Angola, almost twice the size of Texas, and Mozambique, about twice the size of California, both became independent of Portugal in 1975. At that time, thousands of Portuguese settlers left the coastal cities and farms, fearing that they would be overtaken by the nationals. The new,

black-ruled governments did take over the businesses and farms of these countries. They sought aid from the Soviet Union and other Communist countries to help keep their governments in power. Guerrilla soldiers who oppose these governments continue to fight against them. This internal strife adds to other problems of these two new countries.

The Portuguese fled Angola and Mozambique when those colonies received their independence. The departure of the Europeans left these lands without many

African zebras

experienced businessmen and farmers. Most of the nationals have little education. They live in villages and raise just enough food to keep their families fed. Before their independence, these countries traded mainly with Portugal. But now they must look elsewhere for markets where they may trade their few products for the goods they need.

Angola's main products in the past were coffee and sugar. Fishing has been an important activity along the coast. Now, however, oil from the Cabinda region north of the Zaire (Congo) River has become its most important export.

Mozambique lacks petroleum resources, but its warm climate is good for growing cotton, tea, and nuts. The main farming areas of Mozambique lie along the coastal plains, while most of Angola's crops are grown in the highlands.

Zimbabwe, Zambia, and Malawi

As Livingstone made his way eastward to the Mozambique coast, he explored the banks of the Zambezi River. In 1855, he discovered the spectacular **Victoria Falls.** The natives called this waterfall, over a mile wide and 350 feet high, *mosi-oa-tunya,* which means "the smoke that thunders." Victoria Falls lies on the boundary (formed by the Zambezi River) between the present countries of Zimbabwe and Zambia. A large dam built downstream from the falls has created Kariba Lake, the largest manmade body of water in the world. The hydroelectric plant at that dam provides much of the electricity used by both countries.

Zimbabwe and Zambia both lie on the high plateau that stretches along the eastern side of Africa. Only the low-lying river valleys suffer from tropical heat and the disease-carrying insects of Africa. Bands of tree-studded grasslands called

Victoria Falls, Zimbabwe

Savanna

Large portions of the African continent are covered by grass and scattered trees. These grasslands are called savannas. Look at the map on page 360 and find the areas that are savannas.

Savanna regions are usually found in or near the tropics. These regions usually have a rainy season and a dry season with frequent times of drought. Umbrella-like acacia trees and stubby baobab trees often tower above the grass of Africa's savannas.

savannas are found in the higher land, where the climate is pleasant despite the land's nearness to the equator. The rainy season lasts from October through April, and the remainder of the year is dry and cooler. Frost may appear during the winter nights in July and August.

Over twenty years after Livingstone explored these regions, a British businessman named Cecil Rhodes opened them to settlement and development. The lands were named for him—Southern Rhodesia and Northern Rhodesia—and British settlers joined the black peoples living in these lands.

Zambia

As has been common in Africa in recent years, the black majority in these countries has taken control of the government from the white settlers. Northern Rhodesia became independent from Britain in 1964 and has been ruled by blacks since that time. They changed the name of the country to Zambia. The government is strict, and it controls Zambia's businesses and farms. The country has not prospered, however, and tribal conflicts and political fights continue. The black government in power allows only members of its own political party to hold office. Zambians with differing views cannot freely speak out against the government.

The northern section of Zambia is especially important to the nation's economy. The country's major natural resource is large deposits of copper found in that area. Since tsetse flies do not bother the cattle raised on the high plateau, dairy products are also important to the region. Zambian farms, however, are not very productive, and the country must import some of its food.

A poor Zambian village

Missionaries have worked in the land for about a hundred years. Although many of the nationals claim to be Christians, most of them have never truly received Jesus Christ as their Saviour. They may have heard about Him, and some even worship Christ as one of the many gods in their religion, but most of the natives continue to live in their sins without God's gift of eternal life.

Vegetation of Africa

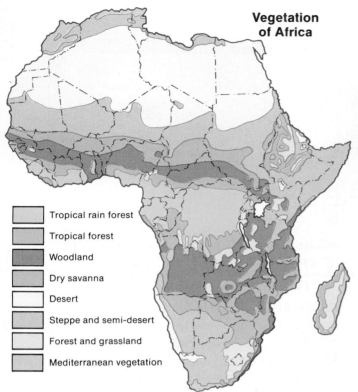

- ☐ Tropical rain forest
- ☐ Tropical forest
- ☐ Woodland
- ☐ Dry savanna
- ☐ Desert
- ☐ Steppe and semi-desert
- ☐ Forest and grassland
- ☐ Mediterranean vegetation

Zambians building new cinder block houses

Zimbabwe

Southern Rhodesia has been a bitter battlefield of racial and political tension in recent years. After more than ten years of rebelling against the British colonial government, this land finally gained its independence from Britain in 1980. Blacks now rule the country that has been renamed Zimbabwe (zim BAH bway). Tribal customs and conflicts, however, continue to divide Zimbabwe's people, and violence has often resulted. The government has been strict, and the whites still living in the land have complained of being treated unfairly.

Zimbabwe's farmers raise tobacco and coffee for sale, and the country contains important chrome resources. Most of the people, however, are poor farmers and workers, continuing to live in much the same way as their ancestors lived for hundreds of years.

The country of Zimbabwe is about the size of Montana, and Zambia is twice its size. Both countries are landlocked as is Malawi, a smaller country to the east of Zambia.

Malawi

Malawi (muh LAH wee), only as large as Indiana, stretches along the western shore of Lake Malawi (discovered by Livingstone in 1859). Malawi contains hills and mountains on its high plateau, and like its neighbors, enjoys a comfortable climate, except in the hot southern lowlands.

Malawi was a British colony until 1964. Until that time, the land had been called Nyasaland. Black leaders took control of the government after the nation's independence. Unlike the case in Zambia and Zimbabwe, the black government of Malawi has not brought great changes to the country. Businesses and farms owned

An agricultural school teaches the Malawians efficient farming methods.

by the whites were allowed to continue with little interference. The living conditions of the black nationals have gradually improved. Malawi raises the food it needs, and it grows tea, tobacco, and cotton for export. Malawi lacks mineral resources; therefore it must depend on its agriculture to provide its needs. Malawi's people have worked together more patiently than most African peoples, and perhaps this quality will help their country prosper in the future.

Section Review

1. What two countries in southern Africa were once Portuguese colonies?

2. What large waterfall did David Livingstone discover?

3. What are the grasslands of Africa called?

4. What were the former names of Zambia and Zimbabwe?

5. What country of southern Africa remained fairly stable when the blacks took over the government?

Tanzania, Kenya, Uganda, Rwanda, and Burundi

During the last few years of his life, David Livingstone explored regions farther north around Lake Tanganyika. This exploration led him through a portion of the country now called Tanzania.

Tanzania and Kenya

Tanzania (TAN zuh NEE uh) is larger than the states of California, Nevada, and Utah combined. The country took its name in 1964 when the large country of Tanganyika (mainland Tanzania) united with the little island country of Zanzibar. To the northeast of Tanzania lies Kenya. Both of these countries have a coastline along the Indian Ocean, and they share many other geographical features.

A low coastal plain reaches along the shores of Tanzania and Kenya, but most of both countries lies high on the east African plateau. Even though the equator cuts through Kenya, the temperatures on the plateau are mild and pleasant. A mountain range extends from north to south through these countries. **Mount Kilimanjaro** (KIL uh mun JAR oh) rises to a height of 19,340 feet in Tanzania near the Kenyan border. This mountain is the highest in all Africa. Two hundred miles to the north sits Africa's second-highest peak, Mount Kenya. These mountains, though very near the equator, are topped by ice and snow all year round.

Through the western portion of Kenya and the center of Tanzania runs a very deep and wide valley. This is part of the **Great Rift Valley** that stretches from north of the Dead Sea in Palestine through the Red Sea and East Africa to Lake Malawi. In Tanzania, a branch of this gigantic valley reaches northward from Lake Tanganyika along the borders of Burundi, Rwanda, and Uganda. Lakes Malawi and Tanganyika, because they lie in such a deep valley, are two of the deepest lakes in the world. Lake Victoria, the largest lake in Africa, lies between the two valleys where the borders of Kenya, Tanzania, and Uganda meet.

The modern Kenyan city of Kisumu

Nairobi

Although less than a hundred years old, Nairobi (nye ROH bee), Kenya, has grown to a population of nearly a million. In the early days, it was a small railroad town. Now it is a center of commerce and activity for much of eastern Africa. As capital of Kenya, it is center of the government for the country. As a transportation center, it is the starting point for thousands of safaris into the African bush.

Like most modern cities, Nairobi boasts many hotels, restaurants, museums, libraries, and schools. Modern department stores line its busy avenues, and bustling traffic fills its streets. But Nairobi still retains its African flavor. Many streetside markets sell handmade cloth, jewelry, paintings, and carvings. Just outside the city lies Nairobi National Park. Many tourists drive through the park and take pictures of lions, zebras, monkeys, and many other animals.

The tourists enjoy not only the wildlife but also the African people and their traditional way of life. Tribal displays and festivities are still common in the rural areas. These are presented for the pleasure of nationals and foreigners alike. Amid the conveniences of modern city life, Nairobi shows its visitors at least a part of its African heritage.

The Animals

Both Tanzania and Kenya have set aside large areas of land for national parks and game reserves. On these lands as well as in many areas of these countries, many kinds of African wildlife roam. Tourists come to make photographic safaris, and they hope to take home spectacular pictures of elephants, lions, giraffes, ostriches, and antelope. Crocodiles lurk by the lakes and streams where buffaloes and hippopotamuses bathe. Rhinoceros, zebra, monkeys, leopards, and hyena are more of the many fascinating animals one might see on an African safari. Some hunting safaris are allowed to kill the wildlife, but these hunts are restricted. If too many of these animals are needlessly killed, we may not be able to enjoy seeing these creatures in years to come.

Animals of Africa: an elephant *(left)*, a Cape buffalo *(center)*, and an ostrich *(right)*

The People

Tanzania and Kenya, like all the countries of sub-Saharan Africa, are the homes of many peoples. There are descendants of white settlers that have lived in those lands for over a hundred years. There are businessmen and merchants from Europe, America, and all parts of the world who make their living in these lands. And, of course, there are the black nationals. In every country of sub-Saharan Africa except South Africa (and Namibia, which it controls), the black nationals have gained control of the government and are the ruling people.

Though the blacks far outnumber other groups, they are themselves divided into many different tribal groups. Distrust and ill feeling between tribal groups have caused much violence in African nations. Even today, when these groups should be working together to build their young countries into prosperous, peaceful nations, they often find excuses to fight each other.

A textile factory in Kenya

The boundaries of African countries have made these problems even worse. When the European countries divided Africa into colonial territories, they drew boundaries that were convenient to them. Most of those boundaries cut through the middle of tribal lands. While part of a tribe may live in one country under its government, relatives in the same tribe may live across the border in another land. Boundaries have not changed since African countries have become independent nations. Tribes trying to unite their people and their lands have brought fierce fighting to many border areas.

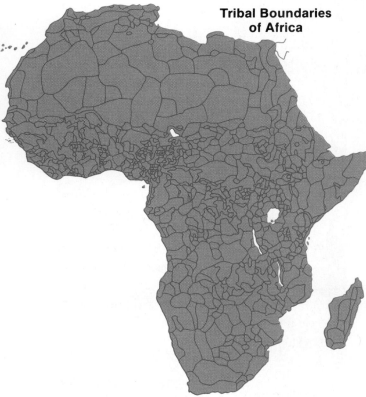

Tribal Boundaries of Africa

Some of the tribes that live in Tanzania and Kenya are the Sukuma, Chagga, Kikuyu, Masai, Kamba, Meru, Nandi, and Luo. Usually the members of a tribe speak their own tribal language. Many East Africans, however, also speak **Swahili** and sometimes English in addition. Swahili is a mixture of African and Arab languages that was spread through the area during several hundred years of Arab trade. It is the official language of both Tanzania and Kenya.

Child tending cattle in Kenya

Tribal Life

Each African tribe has its own customs and beliefs. Although the Africans that live in the cities often dress and live much like we do in the United States, many others wear their native clothing and jewelry and follow their traditional customs. Some tribes are known for their colorful costumes, their hairstyles, the dances and rites of their ceremonies, and even their food. Members of one tribe drink a mixture of the milk and blood of their cattle.

While most of the people who have come to Africa from other continents have brought their own religions with them, most of the nationals practice their native religions. **Animism** is the belief that objects in nature (trees, mountains, animals, rivers, etc.) have spirits that can bring good or harm to people. Many Africans continue to believe that they must keep these spirits happy. They also think that they should worship the spirits of their dead ancestors. The people make or buy idols that represent the spirits, wear charms to keep evil away, and offer sacrifices of animals and food.

> For great is the Lord, and greatly to be praised: he also is to be feared above all gods. For all the gods of the people are idols: but the Lord made the heavens. (I Chronicles 16:25-26)

Missionaries have worked in these lands to tell the people about Jesus Christ, but many more need to learn about our Lord and accept Him as their Saviour.

Tanzania and Kenya have much fertile soil in their valleys and on the high plateaus. Farmers raise crops of coffee, tea, and cotton. In some areas, they herd

Kenyan tea fields

cattle or goats. A kind of mush made from ground grain and similar to hominy grits is one of their basic foods.

Uganda, Rwanda, and Burundi

Uganda, the smaller neighbor of Tanzania and Kenya, has many of the features of its larger neighbors. Its land lies on a high plateau spotted by lakes and streams. Most of its people live by farming. In recent years, Uganda has suffered from harsh rulers and bitterness among its peoples. Conflicts between the tribal peoples of this country may lead to continued strife in this country's future.

South of Uganda lie the two countries of Rwanda and Burundi. Both are about the size of the state of Maryland. These two small countries have large populations, mainly of the Tutsi (Watusi) and Hutu tribes. While the Tutsi people are tall and slender (usually over six feet tall), a few Pygmies of the Twa tribe still live in this area of Africa. Adult Pygmies are usually less than five feet tall. The Hutus are of average size.

Fighting between the Tutsi and Hutu tribes led to the death of thousands of tribesmen in the 1960s and 1970s. Although both countries are more peaceful now, tensions remain. Most of the people are poor farmers without any education. They continue to keep the customs and hatreds of their forefathers.

Ethiopia, Somalia, and Djibouti

Lands and Peoples

The land of Ethiopia stretches from Kenya's northern border to the Red Sea. The country is nearly twice as large as Texas, and a large part of it lies on eastern Africa's high plateau. The coastal area near Djibouti and the large eastern region of Ogaden, however, are dry, desertlike lowlands. While the mountainous plateau regions have a mild climate with some rainfall, the temperatures in the lowlands often climb over 100°F.

The highland areas of the country have fertile soil that sustains crops of wheat, barley, vegetables, and coffee. A grain called teff is also an important food crop.

The dry lowlands serve as pastureland for herds of cattle, sheep, goats, and camels. These animals are raised for meat and milk, as well as for their hides. In many areas of eastern Africa, a person's wealth is often measured by the number of livestock, especially the cattle, he owns.

The people live in small houses made of stone, twigs, mud, or thatch. Only a small portion of the Ethiopian peoples live in cities where the housing and other living conditions are more modern. Some Ethiopians in the cities wear clothing like we wear. Others wear the loose, wrapped clothing common to people in many parts of northern Africa and the Middle East.

Religion

Christianity came to Ethiopia about three hundred years after Christ's death and resurrection. (The Bible mentions Ethiopia in several places, including Acts 8:26-39, which recounts the meeting of Philip and the Ethiopian eunuch. The Biblical land of Ethiopia, however, was probably north of modern Ethiopia in what is now the country of Sudan.) Though many Ethiopians accepted Christianity, they soon turned their worship into a religion of rituals. They professed a knowledge of Christ, but they did not teach and preach the true gospel. Arabs brought the Islamic religion to Ethiopia, converting some of the people. Others still worship spirits.

Today, about a third of the people belong to the Ethiopian Orthodox Church. This form of Christianity uses much music with drums and dancing in its worship. The people follow the many practices taught by the church, and they trust in their religious works for salvation. Other Ethiopians are Moslems, following the teachings of Mohammed, or animists, practicing their tribal religions.

The country has many religious people, all following the way they think will bring them salvation. Few, however, know that Jesus Christ alone is "the way, the truth, and the life" and that nobody stands redeemed before God except by the blood of Christ.

Problems

Drought, famine, and political discontent have plagued Ethiopia in recent years. Tribesmen in the northern region of Eritrea (ER ih TREE uh) and in the eastern region of Ogaden have rebelled against the government's authority. These conflicts have brought border wars with Ethiopia's neighboring countries.

The Soviet Union has tried to influence the government of this land and other struggling African countries. By providing weapons for governments or rebels, the Soviets can promote and force their communistic ideas on parts of the world that are too poor and weak to refuse. The Soviets, however, do not provide the food and medical help that the people really need, and the communism they promote denies the people the freedom to seek the only safe refuge from the troubles they face—salvation through the Lord Jesus Christ. We must not forget that no matter what troubles may come into our lives, the Lord is our refuge.

A street scene in Agaro, Ethiopia

The Lord also will be a refuge for the oppressed, a refuge in times of trouble. And they that know thy name will put their trust in thee: for thou, Lord, hast not forsaken them that seek thee. (Psalm 9:9-10)

Eastern Ethiopia and the country of Somalia form the region that is called the "Horn of Africa." This triangle-shaped piece of African land is bounded by the Gulf of Aden on the North and the Arabian Sea on the east. Somalia covers 270,000 square miles of this dry region. The climate of this land is very hot. Bananas and spices grow in Somalia's tropical climate, and livestock find some pasture growing in the red-colored dust of the landscape. Like Ethiopia beside it, Somalia is a poor country, torn by border war and the discontent of its people.

On the coast between Ethiopia and Somalia lies the little country of Djibouti (jee BOO tee). Though small—only about the size of Massachusetts—Djibouti is important because it sits at the entrance to the Red Sea. Many of the ships passing through the Red Sea and the Suez Canal stop at Djibouti's port. A railroad from the city of Addis Ababa brings much of Ethiopia's trade through the port as well. Though Djibouti's land is hot and lacks resources, its position brings it a prosperous trade.

Section Review

1. What is the highest mountain in Africa?

2. What deep valley stretches from the Middle East into eastern Africa?

3. What language is spoken by many of the people in eastern Africa?

4. What is the belief that objects of nature contain good and evil spirits called?

5. What three problems have made life hard for the Ethiopians in recent years?

Terms to Remember

Cape of Good Hope   savanna
Zambezi River   Mount Kilimanjaro
Cape Town   Great Rift Valley
Boers   Swahili
apartheid   animism
Victoria Falls

Things to Know

1. Who was the missionary explorer of southern Africa?

2. The policy of *apartheid* is followed in what African country?

3. What African country controls Namibia?

4. What are the grass and brush-covered areas of Africa's eastern plateau called?

Things to Talk About

1. What hardships and dangers blocked the exploration of Africa's interior?

2. What is meant by *apartheid?*

3. What happened to Portugal's colonies in southern Africa when they became independent?

4. Why are Mount Kilimanjaro and Mount Kenya topped with ice and snow when they lie so near the equator?

5. How do tribal loyalties sometimes bring about strife in African countries?

Things to Do

1. Collect newspaper and magazine articles for a bulletin board showing current events in Africa. Try to find articles for as many different African countries as possible.

2. Read about one of these explorers of Africa, and then give a report to your class.
   Bartholomew Díaz
   David Livingstone
   Henry Stanley
   Mungo Park
   John Speke

3. In what African country would you find each of the sights listed below? You will need a large atlas or an encylopedia to help you find them.

   a. the mouth of the Zambezi River

   b. the ruins of the civilization of Zimbabwe

   c. the strait of Gibraltar

   d. Stanley Falls

   e. the city of Abidjan

   f. Cape Agulhas

   g. the Qattara Depression

   h. Cape Verde

   i. Lake Volta

   j. Mount Kilimanjaro

Geography Skills

Use the maps on pages 348 and 352 to answer these questions.

1. What African countries have diamond deposits?

2. What African countries have gold deposits?

3. What African countries lie along the shores of Lake Nyasa?

4. What is the name of the area of water that lies between Madagascar and the African mainland?

5. The country of Lesotho is surrounded by what other country?

6. The equator passes through what large African lake?

7. What country's capital is Mogadishu?

8. What large South African city is the farthest west?

CHAPTER 18

WESTERN AND CENTRAL AFRICA

Sade walked proudly along the forest path behind his father, and his two younger sisters followed close behind. Sade carried his new large knife, called a **machete** (muh SHET ee), at his side. For the first time he was going to use his very own machete to help his family prepare the fields. Always before he had borrowed one from a neighbor, but now he clutched his own. His father had bought

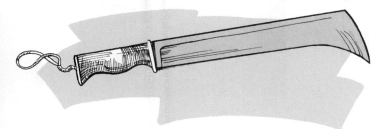

it at the market last week in Bahn. Sade had spent hours sharpening the blade, and he was sure that it would easily cut through the toughest weeds and bushes.

After walking about fifteen minutes through the woods, Sade and the others reached an area covered with grass, bushes, vines, and a few small trees. In a few months, this ground would be covered instead with okra, eggplant, rice, corn, and other food crops. But, in the meantime, Sade and his family had much work to do.

At the edge of their farmland sat a small house made of clay with a thatched roof.

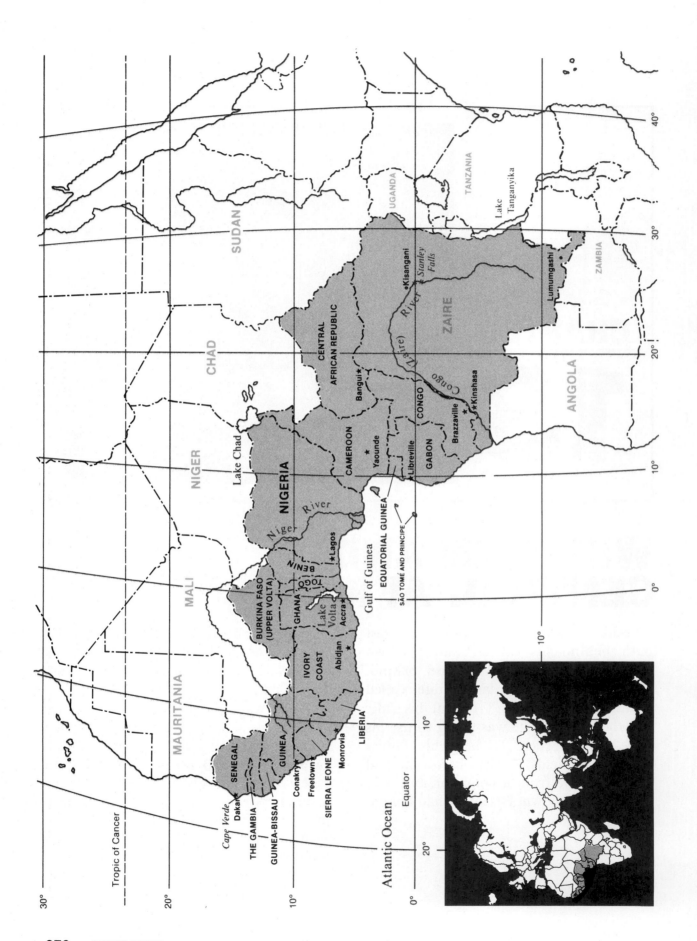

SUDAN

UGANDA

TANZANIA

Lake Tanganyika

CHAD

CENTRAL AFRICAN REPUBLIC

Kisangani
Stanley Falls

(Zaire) River

Congo

ZAIRE

ZAMBIA

Lumumgashi

ANGOLA

Bangui ★

CAMEROON

Yaounde ★

CONGO

Kinshasa ★

GABON

Brazzaville ★

Libreville ★

Lake Chad

NIGER

NIGERIA

Niger River

River

MALI

Gulf of Guinea

EQUATORIAL GUINEA

SÃO TOMÉ AND PRINCIPE

★ Lagos

BENIN

TOGO

BURKINA FASO (UPPER VOLTA)

GHANA

Lake Volta

Accra ★

IVORY COAST

Abidjan ★

MAURITANIA

LIBERIA

SENEGAL

Cape Verde
Dakar ★

GUINEA

Conakry ★
Freetown

SIERRA LEONE

Monrovia ★

THE GAMBIA

GUINEA-BISSAU

Atlantic Ocean

Equator

Tropic of Cancer

30°

20°

10°

0°

30°

20°

10°

0°

40°

30°

20°

10°

0°

10°

20°

	AREA (Square Miles)	POPULATION	CAPITAL	MAIN LANGUAGES	COLONIZED BY	DATE OF INDEPEND-ENCE
SENEGAL	75,750	6,335,000	Dakar	French, tribal languages	France	1960
THE GAMBIA	4,361	638,000	Banjul	English, Mandingo	Britain	1965
GUINEA	94,964	5,430,000	Conakry	French, tribal languages	France	1958
GUINEA-BISSAU	13,948	827,000	Bissau	Crioulo, Portuguese	Portugal	1974
SIERRA LEONE	27,699	3,705,000	Freetown	English, tribal languages	Britain	1961
LIBERIA	43,000	2,091,000	Monrovia	English, tribal languages	———	———
IVORY COAST	124,503	8,890,000	Abidjan	French, tribal languages	France	1960
GHANA	92,099	13,367,000	Accra	English, tribal languages	Britain	1957
BURKINA FASO (Upper Volta)	105,869	6,596,000	Ouagadougou	French, tribal languages	France	1960
TOGO	21,622	2,823,000	Lomé	French, tribal languages	France	1960
BENIN (formerly Dahomey)	43,483	3,792,000	Porto-Novo	French, tribal languages	France	1960
NIGERIA	356,667	85,219,000	Lagos	English, Hausa, Yoruba, Ibo	Britain	1960
CAMEROON	183,568	9,251,000	Yaoundé	French, English, tribal languages	Britain, France	1960
EQUATORIAL GUINEA	10,830	268,000	Malabo	Spanish, Fang, Pidgin English	Spain	1968
CENTRAL AFRICAN REPUBLIC	240,534	2,512,000	Bangui	French, Sango	France	1960
GABON	103,346	921,000	Libreville	French, tribal languages	France	1960
CONGO	132,046	1,694,000	Brazzaville	French, Lingala, Kituba	France	1960
ZAIRE	905,563	31,250,000	Kinshasa	French, Lingala, tribal languages	Belgium	1960

There, Sade's mother was preparing a meal before the family began their afternoon's work. Sade's sister, Yeye, was carrying their little brother, Mwaka, on her back. When she saw Sade, she teased him about his new machete. She asked, "Have you cut yourself on your knife yet? You have sharpened it so much, will there be any blade left to cut the grass and brush?"

Sade ignored her teasing and sat down to eat. Sade ate with the younger children, sharing their bowls of rice, fish, and okra. They used only a spoon or their fingers to eat their food. At the same time, Yeye ate with Mother, and Father ate by himself nearby. In their land it is the custom for men, women, and younger children to eat in their own separate groups. When they had finished eating, Father got up and started cutting the nearby grass and brush with his machete. Likewise, Sade began to slice through the underbrush with his sharp blade. As soon as the others had finished clearing away the bowls and pans, they began to help as well.

All afternoon the family worked together to clear their farmland. Sade was pleased that his new machete slashed through the brush with great ease. But, even with his new knife, he could not keep up with his father. Sade's arms were not as long or as strong as his father's. While Sade finished cutting the brush, his father took an ax and chopped down the small trees in the clearing. He pried up some roots of bushes and trees with a hoe. When the task was completed, they joined the rest of the family in the farmhouse for an evening meal.

The farmhouse provides a cool place for them to escape the heat of the African sun. It also provides shelter from the rainstorms that often come while they are tending their crops. After eating a small meal, they all made their way back along the forest path to their village. The brush that they had cut on their farm will dry for several days. Then they will return and burn it. The ashes will help to make the soil rich. They will plant their crops before the beginning of the rainy season. This kind of agriculture is called "slash and burn," and it is a common method of farming in Africa and in some other parts of the world.

Sade's house is on the edge of a village called Taylay. It was nearly dark when the family arrived. Yeye lit the kerosene lantern so that they could see. The children gathered around their father as he told a story for them before they went to bed. It was a story about life in their tribe long ago. Even Sade sat wide-eyed as Father told of a hunt for a wild elephant. Sade had never seen an elephant. Although they were once common in West Africa, now they are very rare. Over the years, most of the elephants in that area were killed for their ivory tusks or for their meat, or because they trampled over the fields and ruined the crops.

The story ended when a brave tribesman sneaked up beside the huge animal and stabbed it in the belly with a spear. Everyone wanted to hear more, but it was time for bed. Sade went to the little room where he slept with his brother on a straw mattress. He fell asleep thinking of elephants, brave deeds, and his new machete, which lay on the floor beside him.

Sade's family, as well as most of the people in Taylay, are of the Gio tribe. The Gios are one of many peoples who live in the country of Liberia. They live in the interior area of the country, far away from the coastal cities. Taylay has over one hundred houses scattered along or near the dirt road that leads through the woods to the larger town to Bahn. Most of the houses are small and rectangular in shape, with thick mud plaster walls and metal roofs.

The next morning Sade awoke to the sounds of his mother preparing the morning meal. She sent Yeye to a clear stream flowing from the nearby hills. Yeye got the family's drinking water for the morning and brought it back in a pan carried on her head. Sade's mother boiled **plantain,** a fruit similar to bananas, for breakfast. The boiled fruit becomes mushy and is eaten like mashed potatoes.

After Sade ate his breakfast, he and his two younger sisters walked through the village to the school. Like their house, the school building is built of mud plaster and has a metal roof. Inside are three rooms—one for the younger students, one for the third and fourth graders, and one for the older students. Sade is in the sixth grade, the highest grade in the village school. Sade's sister, Yeye, finished the sixth grade last year. Now she stays at home and helps Mother during the day. She will continue to learn from her mother how to prepare food, raise vegetables, make medicine, and master other household skills until the time comes for her to be married.

Sade, however, is going to continue his schooling. In a few months, he will begin to go to the school in Bahn. A larger town than Taylay, Bahn lies about ten miles away. Sade will have to walk for two hours to get there every morning and then walk two more hours each afternoon to return home. There are no school busses that carry children down the dirt road from Taylay to Bahn. Those who continue their education must either walk or else go to a boarding school in a larger city.

At school in Taylay, Sade learns to speak English. He speaks the Gio language with his family at home, but all the school lessons are given in English. In fact, at school Sade has an English name, Jacob. He learns to read and write in English, and learns math and history, too. But when school dismisses in the early afternoon, Sade goes home to help his family.

After school Sade ate a meal of rice and vegetables. Then he picked up a banana to eat as he started off with his mother and little sisters to walk to Bahn. They were going to the market there. Twice a week the people of Taylay hold a little market in one area of the village, but usually there are only some fruits and vegetables for sale. The market in Bahn, however, is full of people buying and selling food and many other things, such as cloth, pots and pans, and baskets. Besides the market area, Bahn also has several stores that sell groceries, clothing, and other items. Usually, some of Sade's family walk to Bahn every week or two to buy the things they need. Sade enjoys seeing the activity in Bahn. He is looking forward to when he will begin school there.

Unlike Sade's village of Taylay, Bahn has electricity, and some of its houses have running water. There are usually several cars and trucks in the streets of Bahn, but rarely does one ever come down the road to Taylay. Several of Bahn's buildings are painted, including a small missionary station. There are no churches or even any missionaries in Taylay. Sade and his family know only the superstitious spirit worship of their tribe.

Every year, Sade sees people offer the first portion of their crops to the "spirit tree," a large tree in Taylay. At some

celebrations he watches as men play drums and dance to ward off evil spirits. Some men wear large wooden masks to represent the spirits as they dance.

Millions of young people like Sade live in Africa. Their customs and surroundings seem unusual to us. Opportunities for getting an education, better health care, and other advantages are increasing in many parts of Africa. Modern conveniences like electricity and cars are becoming more common. But no matter how well off the people of Africa become, their gains will not help them if they do not accept the Saviour. They need to hear that Jesus died to save them from their sin. What can you do to help spread the message of salvation in Africa?

- Pray—II Thessalonians 3:1
- Give—II Corinthians 9:7
- Go—Matthew 28:19-20

Senegal to Benin

Several smaller countries in western Africa stretch along Africa's Atlantic coast from Senegal, just south of Mauritania, to Benin by the **Gulf of Guinea.** The coastal areas of these countries have a warm, wet climate. Streams and rivers flow from the hilly inland regions through the coastal lowlands. **Mangrove** swamps lie along the shores in many areas. (Mangroves are tropical trees and shrubs that grow with their long roots standing like stilts in the water.)

Although the dry Sahara lies only a few hundred miles to the north, most parts of these West African countries receive from 30 to 150 inches of rain each year.

Most of that rain falls during one or two rainy seasons that may come between April and November. In December and January a dry wind called the *harmattan* brings the dust of the Sahara from the north.

Unlike the other areas of Africa that we have studied, thick forests cover much of this part of Africa. Heavy precipitation and warm temperatures allow the growth of rain forests. Mahogany, ebony, satin wood, and other beautiful woods come from these forests. Rubber trees, kola and cacao trees, oil palms, and many kinds of tropical fruit trees offer their products for these countries to use or export.

West African farmers grow crops of millet, corn, rice (usually grown on dry land instead of in paddies), maize, yams, cassava, peanuts, and cotton. West Africans also raise some stock for meat. Because the tsetse fly is often found in the warm, wet lowland areas of these countries, cattle are raised mainly in the northern areas near the Sahel. Sheep and goat herding takes place in the interior regions as well. Pigs are common near the villages of the southern areas, and chickens roost near many West African houses.

Wild animals still roam through the forests and along the rivers of West Africa. Hyenas, jackals, leopards, monkeys, and chimpanzees live in some areas. Hippopotamuses and crocodiles swim in some of the waters. Many snakes also crawl through the brush and rest in the limbs of trees. Among them are African pythons, which may grow up to thirty feet long. Pythons are not poisonous. Instead of biting their victims they strangle them and swallow them whole. Another snake, the green mamba, lives in trees and carries a deadly venom.

Senegal and The Gambia

Senegal, Africa's westernmost nation, lies at the edge of the Sahara. Dry grasslands cover much of the northern area of this country, which is the size of Nebraska. The southern area, however, contains some of the junglelike forests that stretch through the coastal countries to the south and east.

Senegal is a land of transition. The terrain changes from near desert to rain forest. The climate changes from dry to rainy. And, the culture holds a mixture of North African and sub-Saharan traits. Though nearly all the people are dark-skinned, most of them follow the Islamic religion as North Africans do.

Because France once controlled the area, many Senegalese speak French, but more speak their own native languages. Some keep cattle, sheep, and goats. Many raise peanuts for export, and fishing is an important industry along the coast and the rivers. Many of the people live in houses made of sun-dried mud brick. The men often wear long robes and brimless hats. The women wear long wrapped skirts with blouses. Often they wrap colorful scarves around their heads.

Rice production in Senegal

Nearly cutting Senegal in two, the narrow country of The Gambia lies along the banks of the Gambia River. Though the land reaches along the river for over two hundred miles, it is only about twenty miles wide. The country's capital and largest city, Banjul, lies at the mouth of the river.

Slave traders took many slaves from the area of the Gambia River as well as from ports all along the coast of West Africa. African, Dutch, British, French, Portuguese, and American traders participated in the slave trade during the 1500s to the 1700s. In the late 1700s, the British gained control of The Gambia and it became their colony. The land remained under British rule until 1965 when it received its independence.

The countries of Senegal and The Gambia are considering a union. If they can work out agreements, they may join to form one country in the near future.

Guinea and Guinea-Bissau

Along Senegal's southern border lie the two countries of Guinea (GIN ee) and Guinea-Bissau (GIN-ee bi-SOU). Guinea-Bissau, the smaller land, was known as Portuguese Guinea until its independence

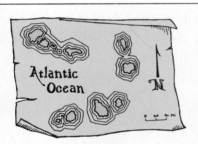

Cape Verde
Area: 1,560 sq. mi. Population: 272,017

The Cape Verde Islands lie in the Atlantic Ocean about four hundred miles off the coast of Africa. They take their name from the cape that reaches toward them from the coast of Senegal. The Portuguese discovered the islands in 1460 and settled them in the following years. Portugal controlled the islands until their independence in 1975.

Drought and famine have plagued Cape Verde since its independence. Most Europeans have left the islands, and many of the Africans have tried to find work in other lands.

in 1974. The country includes the land of several islands that lie just off the coast. Much of the mainland area is swampy lowland.

The people belong to many different tribal groups, and most of them practice their traditional animistic religions and speak their tribal languages. Some, however, speak Portuguese. Most of the people are uneducated and poor. They raise peanuts, coconuts, palm oil, rice, and livestock to make their living.

Guinea is over six times the size of Guinea-Bissau, or about the size of Oregon. France ruled it as a colony from 1894 until 1958, and Guinea still uses French as its official language. Its tribal peoples are mainly poor farmers who grow the crops they need to feed their own families. Some plantations do raise products for export, however. Among these products are bananas, peanuts, coffee, and pineapples. Guinea also mines its rich deposits of bauxite.

Guinea's capital city, Conakry, like all of the capitals in West Africa (except Upper Volta's) lies by the coast and is an important port city. Conakry and the large towns of Guinea display many more modern conveniences than rural villages do. But even in the city, the clothing, the foods, and the people themselves still display their African heritage.

Sierra Leone and Liberia

Sierra Leone (see-ER-uh lee-ONE) and Liberia lie beside each other on the West African coast, and these two countries share a similar background. Both of these lands became homes to freed slaves.

The British founded a colony on the coast of Sierra Leone in 1787. Some of the settlers that came to the colony were slaves who had been freed in America and in England. Others were found and released from illegal slave trading ships in

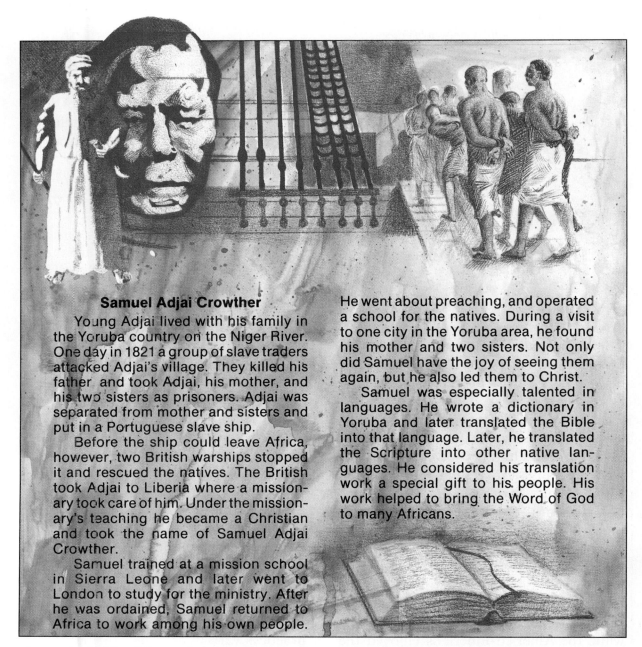

Samuel Adjai Crowther

Young Adjai lived with his family in the Yoruba country on the Niger River. One day in 1821 a group of slave traders attacked Adjai's village. They killed his father and took Adjai, his mother, and his two sisters as prisoners. Adjai was separated from mother and sisters and put in a Portuguese slave ship.

Before the ship could leave Africa, however, two British warships stopped it and rescued the natives. The British took Adjai to Liberia where a missionary took care of him. Under the missionary's teaching he became a Christian and took the name of Samuel Adjai Crowther.

Samuel trained at a mission school in Sierra Leone and later went to London to study for the ministry. After he was ordained, Samuel returned to Africa to work among his own people.

He went about preaching, and operated a school for the natives. During a visit to one city in the Yoruba area, he found his mother and two sisters. Not only did Samuel have the joy of seeing them again, but he also led them to Christ.

Samuel was especially talented in languages. He wrote a dictionary in Yoruba and later translated the Bible into that language. Later, he translated the Scripture into other native languages. He considered his translation work a special gift to his people. His work helped to bring the Word of God to many Africans.

the early 1800s. Most of the settlers lived in the coastal area of Sierra Leone, many in Freetown, the capital. The freed slaves patterned their lives after the cultures they had learned in America and England.

Today, the descendents of those settlers speak English, wear Western-style clothes, and live in houses similar to our houses. These people are known as Creoles, and they generally live apart from the tribal peoples of the country.

Some of the native peoples of Sierra Leone also live in the cities and have gained a good education. Most of them, however, continue to live in the rural areas. They live in houses built with a wooden frame and plastered with mud. The women wear wrapped skirts called lappas with colorful blouses. The men usually wear plain, loose-fitting trousers and shirts. They grow their own food and make most of their own provisions. Polygamy, the practice of a man having more than one wife, is common here as elsewhere in Africa. Additional wives help clear the fields and tend the crops.

A woman of Upper Volta collecting firewood

Liberia, also settled by freed slaves, lies just a few degrees north of the equator. The American Colonization Society helped freed slaves from America find a new home on their home continent. The first settlers arrived in 1821, and in 1847 they declared their land of Liberia to be an independent country.

Liberia is about the size of Pennsylvania. As in Sierra Leone, most of the tribal peoples live in the interior regions of the country while the descendents of the freed slaves live in Monrovia and the other coastal cities. About three-fourths of the Liberians are tribal peoples, but for many years the Americo-Liberians controlled the country. Most of the rural peoples remained poor and uneducated while the Americo-Liberians enjoyed the benefits of schools and businesses.

Through the years tensions between the tribal peoples and the settlers continued. In 1980 a military officer representing the tribal peoples forcefully took over the government. Strife has continued, and the country has become weak and unstable. Political disruptions are common to many countries in West Africa and throughout the continent. Military takeovers, harsh rulers, tribal tensions, financial problems, and other difficulties cause many of these lands to fall deeper and deeper into debt and despair. The peace and prosperity that many Africans hope for may never come, but the Lord offers them His perfect peace. The people of Africa need to accept Jesus Christ so that they might have peace in their hearts though they live in troubled lands.

Ivory Coast, Ghana, and Upper Volta

A Land of Some Prosperity

The Ivory Coast is a square-shaped country a little larger than the state of New Mexico. Dense forests cover much of this country, which once provided the ivory of many elephant tusks for European traders. The Ivory Coast was a French colony for 120 years. Since 1960 the independent country has remained one of the few reasonably stable and prosperous countries in Africa.

Over sixty different tribes live in the Ivory Coast. Each has its own distinct features. The material or style of a tribe's clothing may differ at least slightly from those of its neighbors. It makes its own designs of jewelry, sculpture, and crafts. Each tribe has its own folklore and performs its own traditional dances. Special songs and homemade instruments accompany the dancing during celebrations. Also, the religious traditions and practices vary from tribe to tribe, though all are involved in spirit worship. Tribal differences exist not only in the Ivory Coast, but throughout sub-Saharan Africa.

The tribal peoples have succeeded in working together with their leadership better than those in most African countries. Education, growth of industry, road building, and other improvements have progressed slowly but steadily through the years. The country benefits from its sale of cacao, coffee, and hardwoods. Businesses have grown, especially

Scenes from the Ivory Coast: the processing of cotton fibers *(left)*, children at school *(center)*, and husking coconuts *(right)*

in the modern capital city, Abidjan. With patience, diligence, and continued effort, perhaps the Ivory Coast's prosperity will continue.

A Land of Strife

Political problems have plagued Ghana, the Ivory Coast's neighbor, since its independence from Britain in 1957. Kwame Nkrumah (eng KROO muh), the country's first president, tried to make Ghana a Communist land. He ruled as a dictator, treating his people harshly and spending money unwisely. Ghana's problems multiplied until the army overthrew Nkrumah's government. Strife and corruption did not stop, however. The governments that followed could not bring Ghana's problems under control.

Though the land contains rich forests, very fertile soil, and many other resources, the country of Ghana still remains a poor, unproductive land. It has lacked the stable and wise leadership known across the

border in the Ivory Coast. Realizing that other countries suffer under bad or weak governments, we should be thankful for the government that has kept our country strong and prosperous for so many years. We should pray for our government leaders today. We should remember to ask the Lord to give wisdom to those that govern us.

> I exhort therefore, that, first of all, supplications, prayers, intercessions, and giving of thanks, be made for all men; for kings, and for all that are in authority; that we may lead a quiet and peaceable life in all godliness and honesty. (I Timothy 2:1-2)

A Land of Poverty

One of the poorest countries of Africa lies to the north of Ghana and the Ivory Coast. Upper Volta, now called Burkina Faso, has suffered from political turmoil and the poverty and famine brought by drought. Savanna grasslands cover nearly all of the country, which is larger than the state of Colorado. Burkina Faso does not have the thick forests or the seacoasts enjoyed by the other countries of western Africa. Rain usually falls in the land from May to October. But the hot dry months that follow turn the grass and crops brown. If the dry season is severe and long, the country's seven million people undergo great hardships.

A village in Upper Volta

Burkina Faso's farmers grow millet, sorghum, maize, and peanuts. Herders keep cattle, sheep, goats, and in the drier areas, some camels. Since many of the people cannot make a living in their own land, they migrate to the Ivory Coast and other lands where jobs on plantations and in forests are available.

Upper Volta was a colony of France, and it received its independence in 1960. Its governments have not been able to bring stability to the poor land. Hoping for a brighter future, in 1984 a military president changed the country's name to Burkina Faso, meaning "ancestral home of those who are dignified."

Togo and Benin

The long and narrow countries of Togo and Benin sit side by side with short coastlines on the Gulf of Guinea. Both countries were French colonies until 1960. Many of their people speak French as well as their tribal languages.

Christian missionaries have been active in these countries, but most of the people hold to their animistic beliefs. In recent years, Benin's government has discouraged missionary activity, but Togo remains an open and fruitful mission field. Though most of the Togolese practice spirit worship, some are Moslems. From its stronghold in the northern part of the continent, the Islamic religion has penetrated into many areas of West Africa. Africans, whether they trust in animism, Islam, or even a false Christianity, need to know the Lord Jesus Christ, "In whom we have redemption through his blood, the forgiveness of sins, according to the riches of his grace" (Ephesians 1:7).

Missionary working among nationals in Togo

Section Review

1. What kind of tree often grows near the coasts of West African countries?

2. What country nearly surrounds The Gambia?

3. Who founded the colony of Sierra Leone and the country of Liberia?

4. What West African country had stable leadership and some prosperity after its independence?

5. What religions are commonly followed in West Africa?

Central West Africa

Nigeria

With a population of about ninety million, Nigeria is Africa's most populous country. The country is larger than Texas, but it holds six times as many people as that state. Not only does Nigeria have a large number of people but it also has a wide variety of people. Over two hundred tribal groups live in Nigeria, and each has its distinctive customs, traditions, language, and way of life. Some are Moslem, some are "Christian," and some are animists. Some are rich; many are poor. Some are highly educated; many are illiterate.

Nigeria became independent from Britain in 1960. Despite its varied population, it survived as a fairly prosperous and stable country for a few years. Then troubles between its peoples mounted. Four large tribal groups—the Ibo, the Yoruba, the Hausa, and the Fulani—distrusted one another. Government leaders from one tribe could not hold the allegiance of the other tribes. During an uprising in 1966, the Hausa cruelly killed as many as thirty thousand Ibo.

In 1967, the Ibo declared the eastern part of Nigeria to be their own independent country of Biafra. The Nigerian government fought against the Ibo to stop this rebellion. For three years, the Nigerian Civil War (or Biafran War) raged. The ravages of war worsened a great famine in Biafra. Thousands of children died of starvation. Finally the Ibo surrendered and Nigeria was united once again.

Though it has remained a single country, Nigeria has suffered from poverty and discontent since the war. Its efforts to establish a good government have failed. Hatred among its peoples, dishonesty, greed, and corruption among its leaders, and widespread lawlessness have

A small Nigerian girl

prevailed. Even the advantages of petroleum resources and good farm land have not brought Nigeria peace and prosperity. Many continue to live in fear and die in misery.

Cameroon and Equatorial Guinea

Southeast of Nigeria lies the country of Cameroon, a land larger than California. The western part of the country was once a British colony, and the eastern part belonged to France. Today, French and English are spoken in that land along with the languages of 140 different tribes. Imagine what it would be like if California had that many different groups of people with their own cultures and languages.

Cameroon contains a varied landscape of tropical forests, volcanic mountains, and grassy plains. One of its villages, Debundscha, receives nearly 400 inches of rain each year, making it one of the wettest spots in the world. Gorillas, giraffes,

Wildlife of Kenya: a giraffe *(top)* and a lioness *(bottom)*

elephants, and other wildlife roam its countryside.

Cameroon has enjoyed a stable government since gaining its independence. Although most of its people are still poor and uneducated, the country has made slow and steady progress through the years. It takes time for a land of poor people without many industries or schools to become a modern, productive country. Good results often require much work and patience. Cameroon's people are working patiently to attempt to make their country prosperous.

Cameroon's people grow coffee, tea, pineapple, and other crops in the rich volcanic soil of their highland areas. They also grow cacao, cotton, and rubber for sale. Most of the people, however, grow only the crops they need to feed their families. Because Cameroon has been one of the more stable countries in Africa, foreign investors have brought businesses to the country. These good conditions may bring more progress to this tropical land.

The island of Bioko and a small region south of Cameroon form the little African country of Equatorial Guinea. (This is the third country on the continent with the name of Guinea—Guinea and Guinea-Bissau are the other two.) A Spanish colony until 1968, Equatorial Guinea is a very poor and backward country. Perhaps the most outstanding residents of the country are the giant frogs that live by the jungle streams. They grow to three feet long and weigh over five pounds!

Central African Republic

East of Cameroon in the middle of Africa, the Central African Republic covers a large plateau area. The grass and scattered trees of the savanna extend over most of the country. A small area of rain forest stands in the southwestern region. A rainy season comes to the land from June to October, but the grasslands often turn yellow and brown during the hot, dry months that follow.

Many of the people of the rural areas live in mud huts with thatched roofs. One of their main foods is a thick porridge made of manioc roots. The large, long roots of this tropical shrub are poisonous if they are eaten raw. The women must soak the roots in water, dry them in the sun, pound them into flour, and then cook the flour into a paste. Vegetables and bits of fish or meat are added to make a typical

---

São Tomé and Principe
Area: 372 sq. mi.   Population: 73,800

The two islands of São Tomé and Principe (SOUN too-MEH and PREEN-see-puh) lie about one hundred twenty-five miles away from the African continent in the Gulf of Guinea. Portugal ruled São Tomé and Principe for five hundred years before they became an independent country in 1975. A few Portuguese remain, but most of the islanders are Africans. Fishing and farming are the major occupations of the people, and cocoa, copra, and coffee bring the islands most of their income.

meal. Tropical fruits such as mangoes, papayas, and guavas add more flavor to the diet.

Political turmoil and poverty have afflicted the people of the Central African Republic. The lack of wise and steady leadership threatens the future of this African land in addition to the many others we have seen. For now, most of the people continue to meet their physical needs by raising their own food and by hunting and fishing.

Section Review

1. What is Africa's most populous country?

2. In what country did the Biafran War take place?

3. What African country was controlled by both France and England and has enjoyed slow progress since independence?

4. The island of Bioko is a part of what African country?

5. The root of what plant is poisonous if eaten raw?

Equatorial Lands

Gabon and the Congo

Gabon (gah BAWN), a country the size of Colorado, straddles the equator on the Atlantic coast of Africa. Hot and humid jungles cover most of the land. The sounds of tropical birds fill the trees, and gorillas and leopards lurk in the shadows.

Most of the people live in cities and towns along the coasts. The jungles remain the homes of the animals and a few Pygmies who continue to live in their traditional ways. The oil industry has brought modest prosperity to Gabon. Along with petroleum resources, the land also holds deposits of manganese, uranium, and gold. A wealth of useful wood also grows in Gabon's forests. The land has the potential to become a modern, industrial country.

Gabon's larger neighbor to the east, the Congo, lies along the mighty **Congo River.** The Congo has a wide, treeless coastal plain bounded by thick jungles that reach far into the interior. Mountain areas and swamps lie within the jungles. Temperatures in the Congo are usually between 80° and 90° F all year long. Rains fall often, and the air stays hot and humid.

Most of the people live in the cities and in villages in the plains areas and along

Lumber is becoming a key product in Gabon.

the rivers. Education has become widespread in the country. The people use the French language as well as their tribal tongues. They grow coffee, cacao, and tobacco for sale as well as raising their own food. Oil resources and timber help bring foreign trade to the land.

The Congo River

The second longest African river, the Congo, flows over twenty-seven hundred miles through central Africa to the Atlantic Ocean. The Congo carries so much water that in places the river swells to a width of six miles. Only the Amazon River in South America carries a greater volume of water.

The basin of the Congo lies on both sides of the equator. Because rainy and dry seasons in the tropical zone on one side of the equator are usually opposite to those on the other side, half of the river's basin is nearly always receiving rainfall. These waters keep the Congo growing as it flows to the ocean. The Congo's waters enter the Atlantic so swiftly that sediment does not have time to collect, and so the Congo has no river delta.

In 1482 a Portuguese explorer first visited the mouth of the Congo. The Portuguese gave it the name *Zaire* (ZYE eer) from an African word for "river." Others who visited the region called it *Congo* after an earlier African kingdom.

However, not until Henry M. Stanley explored it from 1874 to 1877 did Europeans know much about the Congo. With three white men and over three hundred Africans, Stanley made a dangerous trip down the Congo from its source to its mouth. In 1877 Stanley reached the Atlantic. All of his white companions and half of the Africans died during the trip.

In 1971 when the Democratic Republic of the Congo (the Belgian Congo) changed its name to Zaire, it also changed the name of the Congo River to Zaire.

Zaire

The land of Zaire covers most of the Congo (Zaire) River's drainage area. The largest country in sub-Saharan Africa, Zaire is about the size of the part of the United States east of the Mississippi River. A narrow strip of land connects this large central African country with a short coast on the Atlantic Ocean. The rest of the land, lying deep inside the continent, contains a wealth of resources and a wide variety of landscape.

Zaire's forests, savannas, rivers, and mountains are the homes of many kinds of wildlife. In its cities and villages live thirty million people. Though most of the animals and people of Zaire appear similar to those of other African countries, we find that some are quite unusual.

The Small People

Most of Africa's **Pygmies** live in the forests of northeastern Zaire. The lives of these little people have hardly changed although modern ways have come to many other areas of the country. About forty thousand Pygmies live by hunting and gathering food. They use bows and arrows, spears, and nets to obtain meat. They find fruit, nuts, and berries growing wild.

The Pygmies live in little houses made from a frame of sticks covered with leaves. Ten or twenty families build a little village of these huts. After living in one place for a few months, they move to a new area and build new homes. In their villages, they celebrate special events with their own songs and dances, and they worship forest spirits.

Not only are the Pygmies smaller, but also their skin is lighter than that of the other African tribal peoples. Yellowish or light brown in appearance, their short figures blend in with the shaded growth of the forests. They wear clothes made from plants and animal skins. They usually stay strong and healthy in their forests, but they often suffer from disease and even sunstroke when they leave their shadowy homes for the villages and cities.

Wild Animals

An usual animal that lives in the forest is the okapi. This relative of the giraffe grows to a height of six feet. It has dark brown fur with white on its face and white stripes on its legs. It lives only in Africa near the Congo River, where it eats grass, leaves, fruit, and small plants. Its slender tongue reaches far out of its mouth to grab its food.

The peaceful okapi remained hidden in its forest home until the early 1900s, when news of its existence reached the rest of the world. Now about fifty of the creatures live in zoos.

Another unusual animal of Zaire is the electric catfish. Like several other species of fish, the electric catfish generates its own electricity. It can give up to a 350-volt shock to its food or foes. The shock stuns small animals that the fish eats, and it scares away enemies. Fishermen who catch the electric catfish in their nets often receive a jolt when they try to haul in their catch. The electric catfish swims in the muddy waters of the Congo and in many other rivers and lakes of tropical Africa.

Zaire's People and Products

Along with the extraordinary Pygmies of Zaire, over two hundred tribal groups live in the country. Like the other peoples of sub-Saharan Africa, they live in villages, towns, and cities. Some continue in their traditional ways, but many are learning how to read and write. They are also learning skills that help them make their lives more comfortable and their country more prosperous.

Zaire contains a wealth of mineral resources including copper, uranium, cobalt, tin, zinc, and some diamonds. Its fertile soils encourage the growth of coffee, cotton, rubber, palm oil, and many other agricultural products. Valuable timber grows in its forests, and many kinds of wildlife enrich every area of the country. The Congo and its tributaries provide a large supply of water teeming with fish and useful for transportation and hydroelectric power.

Despite Afrca's advances in technology and education, many people still live in poverty.

Problems and Prospects

Although Zaire is rich in natural resources, like so many African countries, its people lack unity. Known as the Belgian Congo, the land was a colony of Belgium for over fifty years. Its people rejoiced when they gained independence in 1960. Immediately, strife erupted in the land: the army rebelled; areas of the country tried to break away to form their own nations; leaders quarreled.

In 1965 Joseph Mobutu, an army general, took over the Congo. He established a strong government under his control. He brought strict changes to the country, and the people were forced to support his plans. He changed the name of the Congo to Zaire in 1975. He changed the name of the Congo River to the Zaire, although it is still generally called the Congo. He even changed his own name to Mobutu Sese Seko. He desired to drive foreign influence out of Zaire and to run the country his own way. However, Zaire did not prosper under such leadership.

Businesses have faltered, and the people have remained discontent. Corruption, greed, and dishonesty plague the government. Hatred and violence threaten Zaire's future, as they do so many other African nations. The only hope of Zaire's people lies in the message of the gospel. The truth that we find in God's Word is the answer for Zaire's needs and for the needs of a world that is lost in sin. Let's be faithful to do our part in spreading the news of the Saviour to an unsaved world. Let's be thankful for all that the Lord has done for us.

> O praise the Lord, all ye nations: praise him, all ye people. For his merciful kindness is great toward us: and the truth of the Lord endureth for ever. Praise ye the Lord. (Psalm 117)

Section Review

1. In what country would you be if you were on the west coast of Africa and your latitude were 0°?

2. What are the small native people of central Africa called?

3. What forest animal of Zaire was not discovered until the early 1900s?

4. To what European country did Zaire once belong?

5. Who changed the name of the Congo to Zaire?

Terms to Remember

machete   mangrove
plantain   Congo River
Gulf of Guinea   Pygmies

Things to Know

1. Many of West Africa's countries lie along the shore of what large gulf?

2. What two countries were settled by freed slaves?

3. What African country has the most people?

4. Who are the small forest people of central Africa?

5. What was the former name of Zaire?

6. What important river flows through Zaire and empties into the Atlantic Ocean?

Things to Talk About

1. What can you do to help reach Africans with the message of salvation through Jesus Christ?

2. How do the coastal regions of many West African countries differ from the inland regions?

3. What condition brought about the Biafran War?

4. Describe the weather in the land near the Congo River.

Things to Do

1. Write your own ending to the story about Sade in the beginning of this chapter. What happened when Sade went to the market in Bahn? Did he get to go to school in Bahn? Did he meet any missionaries?

2. Make a bar graph that shows the five largest African countries by size and another graph that shows the five largest by population.

Geography Skills

Use the maps on pages xi and 370 to do the following exercises.

1. In what African country would you have been if you were at each of these locations?

   a. 15°N, 30°E   f. 20°N, 15°W

   b. 30°S, 20°E   g. 8°N, 5°W

   c. 10°N, 10°E   h. 20°S, 30°E

   d. 30°N, 0°   i. 10°N, 50°E

   e. 0°, 40°E   j. 23°S, 45°E

2. From each of the following lists of cities, choose (1) the one that lies the farthest north and (2) the one that lies the farthest west.

   a. Accra, Ghana; Lagos, Nigeria; Addis Ababa, Ethiopia

   b. Nairobi, Kenya; Maputo, Mozambique; Dar es Salaam, Tanzania

   c. Libreville, Gabon; Luanda, Angola; Kinshasa, Zaire

   d. Tripoli, Libya; Cairo, Egypt; Bangui, Central African Republic

   e. Bamako, Mali; Monrovia, Liberia; Khartoum, Sudan

EPILOGUE

Thou, even thou, art Lord alone; thou hast made heaven, the heaven of heavens, with all their host, the earth, and all things that are therein, the seas, and all that is therein, and thou preservest them all; and the host of heaven worshippeth thee. (Nehemiah 9:6)

God did not make this world around us and then step back and forget about it. His care for every part of His creation continues day after day. His mighty power controls the winds, waves, and every other force on earth. He watches the plants and animals that He has made. He also knows the ways of man on this earth.

Our study of the Eastern Hemisphere has introduced us to the people of many nations and their ways of life. Millions of these people are lost in sin. Some may have gathered riches in this world or achieved great honors. Others may have established powerful governments. Many are very religious. Even so, without salvation through the Lord Jesus Christ, they all face eternal judgment.

Though millions strive to earn their own salvation through religious works or trying to live a good life, their works are in vain. Not only the people of the Eastern Hemisphere, but each one of us needs the forgiveness of sins offered through Christ alone. Have you accepted Him as your personal Saviour? Will you willingly and gratefully worship Him when He returns as King of Kings and Lord of Lords?

And there was given him dominion, and glory, and a kingdom, that all people, nations, and languages, should serve him: his dominion is an everlasting dominion, which shall not pass away, and his kingdom that which shall not be destroyed. (Daniel 7:14)

GLOSSARY

A

absolute monarchy Rule by a monarch who has complete power over the government.

altitude Height above sea level.

atheism The belief that there is no God.

B

bauxite Aluminum ore.

bay Section of a body of water that is partly surrounded by land.

bazaar A street market, especially in the Middle East.

Bedouin Nomadic herdsman, especially in the Middle East.

C

canal A manmade body of water used for irrigation or transportation.

cape A point of land sticking out into an ocean or another body of water.

climate The kind of weather a region has over a long period of time.

coke A fuel made from coal.

compass rose A map symbol that indicates directions on a map.

constitutional monarchy Rule by a monarch who is subject to the laws of a national constitution.

continent One of the seven large landmasses on the earth.

current Flow of water.

czar Russian ruler before the Communist revolution.

D

delta A triangular area of land formed by deposits of sediment at the mouth of a river.

democracy Government ruled directly by the people.

dictator A person who takes complete control of a country and commands what is to be done by the people.

dike A strong wall used to keep water out of an area of land.

E

Eurasia The combined landmass of Europe and Asia.

exports Goods taken out of a country.

F

fjord A long narrow inlet of the sea with steep sides made by a glacier.

G

geyser A bursting fountain of hot water.

glacier A large mass of ice moving slowly over land.

gulf Section of an ocean or sea that is partly surrounded by land and is usually larger than a bay.

H

harbor A sheltered area of water on a seacoast where ships may dock safely.

hemisphere One half of the earth.

highland Land with hills, mountains, or plateaus that is higher than surrounding land.

Huguenots French Protestants.

hurricane Violent storms that develop in tropical regions of the Atlantic and Pacific Oceans.

hydroelectricity Electricity produced by water power.

I

icon Picture used for worship in the Eastern Orthodox religion.

immigrants People who move from one country to settle in another.

imports Goods brought into a country.

Iron Curtain An expression used to indicate the boundary between the free countries of Western Europe and the Communist countries of Eastern Europe.

island A landmass entirely surrounded by water.

isthmus A narrow strip of land that connects two larger landmasses.

L

lake An inland body of fresh or salt water.

landlocked Lacking a sea coast.

lowland Land that is lower than surrounding land and that is usually level.

M

monarch A king or queen who rules.

mountain High, steep land that rises above the surrounding land.

mouth The end of a river that empties into a larger body of water.

myth Story about the gods and goddesses of ancient Greece or Rome.

N

nationality A group of people with a common language and heritage.

natural resources Materials and sources of energy that are useful to man.

O

ocean The large body of salt water that covers about two-thirds of the earth's surface and has four main parts.

ocean current A stream of water moving in a pattern through the ocean that moves warm or cold water to different places.

P

passport A government document that shows the identity and citizenship of a foreign traveler.

peasant Poor farmer.

peninsula A body of land surrounded by water on three sides.

permafrost Ground that is permanently frozen.

plain Broad, level land that is usually treeless.

plateau Flat land, higher than surrounding land.

polder Land below sea level that has been drained of water.

pope Leader of the Roman Catholic church.

prairie Treeless grassland.

precipitation Moisture that falls to earth (usually rain or snow).

prime meridian The first meridian or line of longitude (0°) from which all other lines of longitude are measured.

projection A method of drawing the earth's surface on a flat map.

R

raw materials Materials either excavated or grown to be used in manufacturing.

reef A ridge of coral-formed rock or sand at or near the surface of water.

republic Government by elected leaders.

river A large stream of water that flows into a larger body of water.

S

saints Persons officially recognized by the Roman Catholic church as deserving of great reverence as well as having the ability to intercede for the prayers of those on earth.

sea A large body of water partly or completely enclosed by land.

seacoast Land next to an ocean or a sea.

shrine A religious site considered holy because of experiences or objects considered sacred there.

sound A body of water between one or more islands and the mainland, or a wide inlet of the ocean.

source The beginning of a river, usually in a highland area.

steppe Prairie lands of eastern Europe.

strait A narrow passage of water that connects two larger bodies of water.

T

textile Fabric or cloth.

tundra Land in cold regions where few plants live.

V

valley Low land between mountains or hills.

volcano A mountain formed of rock, ash, or dust thrown up through an opening in the earth.

INDEX

Hillary, Sir Edmund 210
Himalaya Mountains 195, 210
Hindi 196
Hinduism 197-200, 207, 211
Hindu Kush 208
Hitler, Adolf 77, 82, 134, 151, 153, 173
Ho Chi Minh 230
hogs 147
Hong Kong 254
Huguenots 87
Hungary 81-82, 156
Huss, John 155
hydroelectricity 115

I

Iberian Peninsula 93
Iceland 120-21
icons 102
India 96, 193-204, 207, 227, 299
Indian Ocean 198
Indonesia 220, 234-36, 296
Indus River 204
Industrial Revolution 22-23, 52
Inland Sea 268
Inquisition (Spanish) 94
International Date Line 292, 301
Iran 188-90
Iraq 186-88
Ireland 20, 38-41
Iron Curtain 74, 143, 149
iron ore 25, 148
Irrawaddy River 215, 221
Islam 175, 180-83, 185-86, 197, 205, 207, 330, 341
Israel 170-76, 335
Istanbul, Turkey 185
Italy 97, 99-101
Ivory Coast 378-79

J

Japan 227, 249-50, 259-75
Jerusalem 172, 175-77, 179
Jews 77, 172-76
Jordan 179

Jordan River 171-72, 179
Judaism 173-74
Jura Mountains 85, 87
jute 202, 206
Jutland Peninsula 117

K

Kalahari Desert 351, 355-56
Kampuchea 233-34
Kemal Ataturk 185
Kenya 361-65
Khyber Pass 207
Kilimanjaro, Mount 361
kimono 262
Knox, John 38
Koran 181
Korea, North and South 275-78
Korean War 276-77
Ko Tha Byu 223
Kremlin 138
Kuwait 183

L

Lang, John Dunmore 311
Laos 233
Lapp 109, 111-12, 115
latitude 10, 34
Lebanon 176-77
Lenin, Nicholai 126, 128, 132, 134-35, 138
Lesotho 355
Liberia 373-74, 376, 378
Libya 339-40
Liechtenstein 85
Lipizzaner horses 82
Lisbon, Portugal 96-97
Livingstone, David 350-51, 356-61
Loire River 47
London, England 24, 29, 31-32
longitude 10, 34, 292
Lutheranism 78, 114
Luther, Katherine von Bora 78
Luther, Martin 77-78
Luxembourg 56-57

M

Macau 253
machete 369, 372-73
Madagascar 357
Madrid, Spain 94
Malacca, Strait of 221, 228
Malawi 360-61
Malay Peninsula 226
Malaysia 226-28
Maldives 208
Mali 342-43
Malta 106
mangrove 374
Maoris 315-16, 319
Mao Tse-tung 249-50
map key 13
map projections 10-11
maps 10-13, 34
map scale 12
Marx, Karl 132, 135
Mauritania 339, 342
Mauritius 357
Mecca 180-82, 341
Mediterranean climate 91, 171
Mediterranean Sea 46-47, 89, 91
Mekong River 215, 229-30, 233
Melanesia 286, 296, 299, 319
Melbourne, Australia 312
Mesopotamia 186-87
Micronesia 286, 292-94
Middle East 167-90
Midnight Sun 111-12
Mohammed 180-82, 341
Monaco 56
monarch 29-30
Mongolia 255-57
monsoon 198, 215-16, 218
Moorea 289
moors 28
Moravia 153
Moscow, Soviet Union 130, 138-40
Moslems See Islam
Mozambique 356-58
Munich, West Germany 79
Murray, Andrew 354

PHOTO CREDITS